Sioux Massacre
at Spirit Lake

Sioux Massacre at Spirit Lake

Two Accounts of the Santee Sioux Attack on the Iowa Settlements in 1857

The Spirit Lake Massacre
Thomas Teakle

A History of Dickinson County, Iowa
(Extract)
R. A. Smith

Sioux Massacre at Spirit Lake
Two Accounts of the Santee Sioux Attack on the Iowa Settlements in 1857
The Spirit Lake Massacre
by Thomas Teakle
and
A History of Dickinson County, Iowa
(Extract)
by R. A. Smith

First published under the titles
The Spirit Lake Massacre
and
A History of Dickinson County, Iowa

FIRST EDITION

Leonaur is an imprint
of Oakpast Ltd

Copyright in this form © 2013 Oakpast Ltd

ISBN: 978-1-78282-199-1 (hardcover)
ISBN: 978-1-78282-200-4 (softcover)

http://www.leonaur.com

Publisher's Notes
The views expressed in this book are not necessarily
those of the publisher.

Contents

The Spirit Lake Massacre   7
A History of Dickinson County, Iowa (Extract)   209

The Spirit Lake Massacre

Contents

(Original) Editor's Introduction	11
Author's Preface	13
The Advancing Frontier	15
Indian Wrongs and Discontent	21
The Unprotected Frontier	26
The Grindstone War and the Death of Sidominadota	34
The Frontier and the Winter of 1856–1857	43
Okoboji and Springfield in March 1857	48
The Journey East for Supplies	59
The Inkpaduta Band	62
Inkpaduta Seeks Revenge	69
The Smithland Incident	73
From Smithland to Okoboji	77
The First Day of the Massacre	84
The Second Day of the Massacre	93
From Okoboji to Heron Lake	97
News of the Massacre Reaches Springfield and Fort Ridgely	104
Relief Sent from Fort Ridgely	108

Preparations for Defence at Springfield	111
Inkpaduta Attacks Springfield	116
The Settlers Flee from Springfield	122
Relief Arrives from Fort Ridgely	126
Organisation of Relief at Fort Dodge and Webster City	130
The March from Fort Dodge to Medium Lake	137
From Medium Lake to Granger's Point	145
The Burial Detail	152
Return of the Relief Expedition	162
The Death of Mrs. Thatcher	168
The Ransom of Mrs. Marble	174
The Death of Mrs. Noble and the Ransom of Abbie Gardner	179
Pursuit and Punishment of Inkpaduta	188
The Memorial Tributes of Iowa	198
Changes of Sixty Years	205

(Original) Editor's Introduction

The massacre of the white settlers in the region of Lake Okoboji and Spirit Lake in 1857 by a band of Indians under the leadership of Inkpaduta has come to be known as "The Spirit Lake Massacre", although the tragedy was for the most part enacted on the borders of Lake Okoboji. There seems, however, to be no substantial reason for renaming the episode in the interest of geographical accuracy; and so in this volume the familiar designation of "The Spirit Lake Massacre" has been retained.

Benj. F. Shambaugh
Office of the Superintendent and Editor
The State Historical Society of Iowa
Iowa City Iowa

Author's Preface

It is probable that no event in the history of northwestern Iowa has aroused more popular interest than that of the Spirit Lake Massacre of March, 1857. Not alone in northwestern Iowa but also in the adjacent sections of Minnesota and South Dakota is the story of its events and associated incidents well known.

The Spirit Lake Massacre came as the culminating episode in a long series of incidents intimately connected with the settlement of northern and western Iowa. For years previous to 1857 the Indians of the Siouan tribes had obstinately resisted white settlement and had succeeded in a marked degree in retarding the movement. It may be said with a reasonable degree of certainty that if the events of March, 1857, had not occurred the settlement of this region would have been postponed for some years: the massacre not only aroused the authorities of the State of Iowa to the necessity of exerting the force of military pressure upon the Indians to discourage or end their forays, but it also enlisted the efforts of the Federal authorities in the same direction. This joint interest and protection could have only one result—the retirement of the Sioux to the region of the Missouri and the rapid influx of white settlers. The massacre definitely settled the Indian question for Iowa: henceforth the red man ceased to play any important part in the history of this Commonwealth.

While the following pages are, as far as practicable, based upon primary materials, the writer acknowledges his obligation to many other sources in the notes and references which follow the text. Since no adequate history of the Spirit Lake Massacre can be written wholly from primary materials, considerable reliance upon secondary sources has been found necessary in this work. Furthermore, the writer is well aware that he has taken a number of new positions concerning causes and incidents of the massacre; but in this he feels well sustained by the preponderance of authority.

Without the unflagging interest and the tireless enthusiasm and encouragement of Dr. Benj. F. Shambaugh the more than four years of research involved in this work would never have been undertaken or carried through to its close. To many others the author also feels himself obligated for invaluable assistance. Among these may be noted Curator E. R. Harlan, Librarian Alice Marple, Assistant Editor Ida M. Huntington, and Superintendent of Archives C. C. Stiles, all of the Historical Department of Iowa. Dr. Dan E. Clark, Associate Editor in The State Historical Society of Iowa, assisted in editing and verifying the manuscript; and to him the author is indebted for the index.

Thomas Teakle
The North High School

Des Moines Iowa

CHAPTER 1

The Advancing Frontier

Clothed in myth and legend and held in sacred awe by the Siouan Indian, Lake Okoboji and Spirit Lake had rested in seclusion for ages at the headwaters of the Little Sioux. To the red men these lakes had been a sort of Mecca, second only to the red pipestone quarry to the northwest, for the silent adoration and worship of the Spirit.[1] Although the region had been little disturbed by the whites the Sioux were becoming uneasy as the frontier continued its westward advance. By the middle of the nineteenth century the meeting and clashing of the two races became more frequent.

This rivalry of the races was engendered by the white man's disregard of what the Indian held as sacred: it was embittered by the unstable policies of the government. Finally, in the early days of March, 1857, came one of those tragic events in the long series of misguided attempts to deal with the Indian and solve the problem of the frontier. In this terrible tragedy in the pioneer history of northwestern Iowa, the lives of more than forty white people were sacrificed. The Spirit Lake Massacre was the result of an Indian policy which has been characterized as "vacillating, full of inconsistencies incongruities, of experiments and failures."[2] For the Sioux this policy had been the cause of frequent humiliation.

It must be frankly admitted that in dealing with the Indian the whites too often lost sight of the fact that the red man was really a human being, seeking to have his person as well as his rights respected. To compel the respect which his proud spirit demanded, he frequently resorted to massacre. In fact, an Indian was open to insults and abuse

---

1. See Richman's *John Brown Among the Quakers, and Other Sketches.*
2. *Senate Documents*, 1st Session, 32nd Congress, Vol. III, Doc. No. 1..

from his fellow tribesmen until he had killed a foe.[3]

To some extent the Indian appreciated his own inferiority, and he was expectantly on the alert to prevent being over-reached and deceived by the whites. Suspicious by nature, he became doubly so when his activities brought him into relation with another race. Unhappily he was not always wrong in his suspicions of the white man's deception, and many unpleasant border difficulties sprang from his attempts to match deception with deception. Physically superb, he too often had recourse to those physical means of redress that have marked the history of the frontier with tales of tragic revenge.[4]

Accustomed to the matching of intellects, the whites frequently resorted to the stilted verbiage of treaties in their efforts to push the Indian farther toward the setting sun. In these treaties the red man found much cause for complaint—not so much in the strict wording of the documents themselves as in the management of affairs they induced. This too often exasperated and provoked the Indian.[5] To him the Iowa country was a paradise. Not only was it his home and hunting ground, but here centred much of the traditional lore of his tribe and race. Thus Iowa was doubly dear to him and worth his most determined effort to hold. As the wave of settlements advanced, the Indian was induced to sell—sometimes under circumstances provoking a strong suspicion of compulsion rather than voluntary agreement in the transfer. He felt instinctively that he had to retire, but in his racial pride he resented the necessity. He knew well the later traditions of his race, in the light of which he could foresee that in a very brief time force, which "comprises the elements of all Indian treaties",[6] would be used to drive him from his domain.

As tract after tract was ceded, lands that the Indian did not want were given to him in exchange—lands devoid of good camping places and wanting in such game as was essential to his very existence. Moreover, the very lands the Indians prized most were the most sought

---

3. Flandrau's *State-Building in the West* in the *Collections of the Minnesota Historical Society*, Vol. VIII.
4. Judge Charles E. Flandrau's *State-Building in the West* in the *Collections of the Minnesota Historical Society*, Vol. VIII.
5. Rev. Moses N. Adams's *The Sioux Outbreak in the Year 1862* in the *Collections of the Minnesota Historical Society*, Vol. IX.
6. "The inferior power knows perfectly well that, if it does not accept the terms, it will ultimately be forced out of its domains, and it accepts. This comprises the elements of all Indian treaties."—Flandrau's *State-Building in the West* in the *Collections of the Minnesota Historical Society*, Vol. VIII..

for by the whites. The qualities causing them to be prized by the one made them desirable for the other. Thus the Indian's subsistence became so precarious that often he was on the verge of starvation. Coupled with this deprivation of favourite pleasure and hunting grounds was the white man's idealistic dream of civilizing the Indian by making him work at tilling the soil or at the various trades. This seemed to the haughty red man a real degradation. He could die fighting, if need be; but work he would not. His steadfast refusal to work or become civilized could only end in banishment from the lands he valued so highly. In view of this policy of forcing him into an involuntary exile, one ceases to wonder that he grew discontented and rebelled rather than submit.[7] He could not have done otherwise and retain his pride of race.

Forcible dispossession of his ancestral hunting ranges, however, would not have provoked in him an overweening hatred for the white man if it had not been so often coupled with a show of military force. The sole purpose of such military campaigns seems to have been to frighten the Indian in order that he might learn to be peaceful and pliant through fear of punishment.

These campaigns—of which the one by General Harney against the Sioux ending in the affair of Ash Hollow on September 3, 1855, is the most cruel example—sometimes ended not in pacification but in massacre in which the ferocity of the white man vied with that of the Indian. Harney had been recalled from Europe and sent into the West against the Indians for no other purpose than that of terrifying them.[8]

7. Flandrau's *State-Building in the West* in the *Collections of the Minnesota Historical Society*, Vol. VIII.
8. The massacre at Ash Hollow, often mentioned as a cause of the massacre at Okoboji, was the culmination of a campaign of terror planned by Gen. Harney against the Oglala and Brulé Sioux. The line of march was Fort Leavenworth, Fort Kearney, Fort Laramie, and Fort Pierre. At Ash Hollow near the Blue River and about four miles from the left bank of the North Platte he found Little Thunder's band of the Brulé Sioux. When his cavalry had surrounded the Indians, he planned an advance with his infantry. Little Thunder desired a council. Gen. Harney refused, saying that he had come to fight. As Harney advanced, he motioned the Indians to run. They did so and ran directly into Harney's cavalry. Finding themselves trapped, they fought savagely to the end. "The battle of Ash Hollow was little more than a massacre of the Brulés. Though hailed as a great victory the Battle of Ash Hollow was a disgrace to the officer who planned and executed it. The Indians were trapped and knew it and the massacre which ensued was as needless and as barbarous as any which the Dakotas have at any time visited upon the white people."—Robinson's *History of the Dakota or Sioux Indians* in the *South Dakota Historical Collections*, Vol. II. See also *General Harney* in the *South* (continued next page),

Such affairs as this were most unworthy of the American soldier. Nor did the Indian soon forget these atrocities: thereafter he seldom let an opportunity pass which offered revenge.

The military expeditions referred to were frequently followed by the making of treaties providing for land cessions and the consequent westward recession of the Indians. Moreover, these treaties, the making of which was stoutly resisted, were usually acknowledged only by a tribal remnant; and so they were not deemed as binding by the widely scattered major portion of the tribe. Their provisions were not always observed, and often blood had to flow to secure a temporary obedience. Thus the story of the government's relations with the Sioux became an alternation of treaties and Indian and white retaliatory measures. A treaty was only too often accepted by the Indians as a challenge for some shrewdly devised scheme of vengeful retaliation.

Through a series of treaties extending from 1825 to 1851 the Indian occupants of Iowa soil were slowly but surely dispossessed. They felt the westward push of white migration, and were fearful of being unable to stem it. Unluckily for themselves they fell to intertribal quarrelling, and for the moment, being off their guard, they accepted white mediation. Thus, the two treaties of Prairie du Chien had attempted to settle the differences between the Sioux and their traditional enemies, the confederated Sacs and Foxes.[9]

But they did not succeed, since the line established in the first of these two treaties was so indefinite that neither white man nor Indian could locate it to his own satisfaction. To the Sioux their claim to northern and western Iowa seemed assured, and they proceeded confidently to its occupation. The Sacs and Foxes believed the same concerning their rights in southeastern Iowa and jealously sought to exclude all others from it.

By the second treaty of Prairie du Chien there was established the Neutral Ground, which only aggravated the difficulties already existing.[10] Then, by the treaty of September 15, 1832, the eastern portion of the Neutral Ground was designated as a reservation for the Winnebagoes.[11] The Wahpekuta Sioux never forgot this action, which

---

Dakota Historical Collections, Vol. I, pp. 107, 108; Beam's *Reminiscences of Early Days in Nebraska* in the *Transactions and Reports of the Nebraska State Historical Society*, Vol. III; *House Executive Documents*, 1st Session, 34th Congress, Vol. I, Pt. II, Doc. No. 1.

9. Royce's *Indian Land Cessions in the United States* in the *Eighteenth Annual Report of the Bureau of American Ethnology*, Part II; Kappler's *Indian Affairs: Laws and Treaties*, Vol. II.

10. See references in note 9 above.

11. Royce's *Indian Land Cessions*; Kappler's *Indian Affairs: Laws and Treaties*, Vol. II.

they regarded as a violation of their proprietary rights in the district; and from that time on they became increasingly more difficult to deal with and more restive of restraint. Later the Winnebagoes by two successive treaties made an absolute cession of this land.[12] It was then opened to settlement, and the Sioux sulkily retired westward.

In 1832 Black Hawk, the able Sac and Fox leader, burning with revenge for past wrongs and fearful of his waning power as a tribal leader as well as of the steady advance of the westward moving frontier, declared war. The conflict was brief, resulting in the defeat of Black Hawk. By four successive treaties covering the period from 1832 to 1842 he or his people were compelled to accede to agreements which had for their purpose the removal of the Indians to lands west of the Missouri wholly unsuited to their needs.[13]

Likewise the Iowas were required to surrender all claims which the United States had recognised in former treaties as entitling them to occupy Iowa soil.[14] With the surrender of all right or interest which they held in the Iowa country they were in turn removed to a reservation beyond the Missouri. Southern Iowa had not as yet been cleared of its aboriginal inhabitants, for remnants of the Pottawattamies, Chippewas, and Ottawas yet remained. By the treaty of June 5 and 17, 1846, however, these Indians agreed to withdraw to other reserves further west and south.[15]

The withdrawal of these tribes left only the Sioux who were striving to maintain a precarious foothold in northwestern Iowa. The steadily advancing frontier was menacing their peace of mind, as it now became increasingly evident that they in turn would be ejected. Two conditions, the urgent demands of alarmed and annoyed border settlers and the troublesome character of the Sioux themselves, determined the Indian authorities at Washington to remove the members of these tribes. When informed of the government's intention to remove them, the Sioux begged to retain their lands. Notwithstanding Indian importunities representatives of the Sissetons and Wahpetons were cited to appear at Traverse des Sioux, Minnesota, to consider withdrawal. Here they gloomily gathered at the time appointed. Though outwardly ready to treat for withdrawal they did not conceal their displeasure. On July 23, 1851, however, the treaty of Traverse

---

12. Royce's *Indian Land Cessions*.
13. *Ibid*; Kappler's *Indian Affairs: Laws and Treaties*, Vol. II.
14. Royce's *Indian Land Cessions*; Kappler's *Indian Affairs: Laws and Treaties*, Vol. II.
15. *Ibid*.

des Sioux was witnessed, by the terms of which these Indians were to definitely withdraw from northwestern Iowa to lands on the Minnesota River.[16]

At the close of the conference all seemed settled. But within a brief time the Sioux, who had not been parties to the treaty, positively refused to abide by its provisions. Later, at Mendota, Minnesota, on August 5, 1851, the Mdewakanton and Wahpekuta tribes, in part, acceded to the Sisseton and Wahpeton cessions.[17] These cessions had not been accomplished without considerable opposition: strong tribal parties refused their consent outright and threatened trouble.[18] For the period of nearly a decade the frontier settlements of the northwest were not free from the alarms created by these discontented bands.

---

16. In exchange for all lands claimed by the Sioux in northwestern Iowa and southwestern Minnesota they were granted a reservation as follows: "all that tract of country on either side of the Minnesota River, from the western boundary of the lands herein ceded, east, to the Tchay-tam-bay River on the north, and to Yellow Medicine River on the south side, to extend, on each side, a distance of not less than 10 miles from the general course of said river; the boundaries of said tract to be marked out by as straight lines as practicable".—Kappler's *Indian Affairs: Laws and Treaties*, Vol. II, p. 590; Hughes's *The Treaty of Traverse des Sioux in 1851* in the Collections of the Minnesota Historical Society, Vol. X, Pt. I. Royce's *Indian Land Cessions*; Kappler's *Indian Affairs: Laws and Treaties*, Vol. II. 18. "It was with great reluctance that the Sioux Indians consented to surrender this favorite hunting and camping ground to the whites, as they did by the treaty of 1851."—Gue's *History of Iowa*, Vol. I.

CHAPTER 2

Indian Wrongs and Discontent

Unhappily the relinquishment of the Iowa country had not been free from a strong suspicion of wrongs done the Indians. The Indians had obstinately contested the giving up of these lands, and at no time was a treaty of relinquishment signed that may be said to have expressed the tribal will. These treaties of cession had instanced bad faith toward the natives, unwarranted interference on the part of the trader element, compulsion which at times approached intimidation in the securing of signatures, allotment of lands to the Indians as reserves that appeared worthless from the Indian viewpoint, undue urgency of prospective settlers anxious to "squat" upon the vacated lands, and the forceful effect of the presence of the military. All of these factors had operated to secure cessions at the doubtful price of irritating the Indian and arousing his resentment.

Officers in administrative charge of Indian affairs, far removed from actual contact with the Indians, too often failed to realise that Indian treaties should be regarded with some deference to their observance. Promises were made concerning the payment of annuities which were long delayed in their fulfilment or never kept: to the Indian these promises seemed to be made only to be broken—as happened in the treaty of Traverse des Sioux. According to second chieftain Cloudman, the Indians for five years following the making of this treaty remained quietly upon their reserve. At the expiration of that time, not having heard of or received any of the money promised, they began raiding the adjacent frontiers in an effort to produce action.[1]

---

1. The Indian Chief Jagmani said of this treaty: "The Indians sold their lands at Traverse des Sioux. I say what we were told. For fifty years they were to be paid $50,000 *per annum*. We were also promised $300,000 that we have not seen."—Bryant and Murch's *A History of the Great Massacre by the Sioux Indians, in Minnesota*. See *House Executive Documents*, 1st Session, 35th Congress, Vol. II, Pt. I.

Lack of good faith in treaty matters often precipitated long periods of bad feeling, and occasionally blood was shed before the Indians could be convinced that faith was being kept or that agreements entered into were in turn to be kept by them. If treaties had been honestly and faithfully carried out in every instance it is not unlikely that the Sioux and other Indians might have been far readier to refrain from wrongdoing than was often the case. Altogether the conditions on the frontier tended to create disaffection among the Indians and a loss of respect for government promises.

Not infrequently, as has been noted, the Indians were allotted lands that were wholly inadequate to supply their needs. The Sioux had outlived "the means of subsistence of the hunter state": they were unable longer to eke out an existence exclusively through the spoils of the chase.[2] The buffalo and larger game were rapidly disappearing. But what was still worse, the Sioux often found upon going to the specified reserves that their coming had been anticipated by other hunters and the game was gone, if indeed any had ever been there. In the presence of such conditions it was useless to appeal to the garrison commanders—to whom such complaints seemed absurd. On the other hand, the killing of intruders was nearly always resorted to as a warning against marauders.[3] To live it was necessary to resist the encroachment of others not of their kind, for barbarism demands a wide range of untrammeled activity. Thus the Indians came to think that "if they would have game to kill, they must kill men too."[4]

A great deal of Indian discontent is traceable in the final analysis to another cause: the presence upon the Indian reserve, as well as on the white frontier, of a large number of undesirables, both red and white. As forerunners of white settlement, many adventurous characters found their way to the frontier posts and systematically preyed upon the Indian. Undesirable as elements of civilization, they were equally troublesome on the frontier. In civilized communities it was possible to restrain them, but along the borderland this power was either lacking or not organised. Oftentimes when these adventurers pushed matters to an extremity, the outraged feelings of the Indian would demand a settlement or make one. Unhappily, post commanders were often only too willing to take up the needless quarrels of these frontier disturbers and exact a severe and not always just settlement in their behalf. Later when

---

2. *Senate Documents*, 1st Session, 32nd Congress, Vol. III, Doc. No. 1.
3 & 4. Pond's *The Dakotas or Sioux in Minnesota as They Were in 1834* in the *Collections of the Minnesota Historical Society*, Vol. XII.

the more peaceably disposed settlers—the real pioneers—began to arrive the Indian refused to make any distinction between them and their more turbulent predecessors.

Again, the National government when settling the Indians upon their reserves took no account of the fact that there were both good and bad Indians—that there were Indian criminals as well as Indians willing to abide by the rules of tribal law. Both good and bad were settled indiscriminately upon the same reserve. The seditiously disposed were constantly creating trouble, and the Indian people as a whole incurred the blame and displeasure arising from the misdeeds of a few. These matters irritated those Indians who were well disposed and created an ever-ready excuse for an attack.

Such, in the main, had been the attitude of the government toward the Sioux as the last of the Indian races inhabiting the Iowa country. It had not been an altogether enlightened policy; nor had it been one that was calculated to secure their good will. Instead, it had stirred the Indians to wreak vengeance at every convenient opportunity. However mistaken this policy toward the Indians had been, the attitude toward the frontier and its white inhabitants had been no wiser and at times scarcely as wise. Much Indian trouble and no few massacres resulted from the loose administration of frontier affairs—more specifically from the lack of control exercised over various commercial interests whose chief justification for existence seemed to have been that they might prey upon the nearby red inhabitants. The government failed to appreciate the need for an adequate defence of the frontier.

Venders of whiskey and other intoxicants frequented the frontiers and Indian villages—unmolested, oftentimes, in pushing their sales.[5] It is true that laws had been enacted by Congress with a view to putting an end to the liquor nuisance among the Indians; but the effective enforcement of these measures had scarcely been attempted. If a more than usually zealous Indian agent forbade dealers to carry on their nefarious business within reserved grounds, they would erect their cabins upon the ceded lands immediately adjoining the reserves—places to which the Indians were at all times free to go. To make matters yet worse the agent was in some cases powerless to act even though he desired to do

---

5. "At Crow-wing (Minnesota) there are no less than five whiskey shops, and (they) are only five miles from this agency. Five whiskey shops and not half a dozen habitations beside!"—*Senate Documents*, 1st Session, 35th Congress, Vol. II, Pt. I. See the *Letter of Governor Grimes to President Pierce* in the *Roster and Record of Iowa Soldiers*, Vol. VI; *Annals of Iowa* (Third Series), Vol. III.

so. The Chippewa agent, for example, complained that the treaty of 1855 deprived him of assistants or force through which to punish or apprehend violators of departmental rules and regulations.[6]

Thus was produced that state of affairs where the Indian was being robbed and debauched, while innocent settlers were threatened by Indian violence during the periods of his drunken orgies. Not infrequently the massacre of isolated settlers completed the tale of an Indian visitation to a nearby liquor dealer's establishment. Fortunate it was that the Sioux, "the Iroquois of the West", were slow to take up and make their own the vices of their white neighbours.[7]

To the activities of another type of frontiersman, the trader, Indian wars were sometimes due. In many instances the trader was an individual who was unable to earn an honest living among his white neighbours further east: necessity had made of him an exile from civilization. These traders secured the confidence and good esteem of the Indians in various and devious ways, and the latter soon became indebted to them. In fact their deliberate aim in most cases was to secure upon the Indian a leverage of such a character as to render necessary the surrender of most of the Indian's profits from the chase or treaties. Because of the Indian's profligacy it was necessary that he should buy on credit if he bought at all. When government payments became due, traders were always on hand, and their books invariably showed Indian indebtedness enough to absorb a considerable portion if not all of the payment. The Indians kept no books as a matter of course; and not understanding those of the traders, they could not deny the debt. As a matter of fact, the Indians were always willing to anticipate the next payment in order to get credit. In the face of this situation "the poverty and misery of the Indian were continually growing". Again, the Indian could not sue in the courts if he had so desired. Out of such conditions trouble or bad feeling inevitably arose.[8]

Owing to their long residence in the Indian country and their keen knowledge of Indian character, the traders had become "the power behind the throne". This was especially true in treaty-making. The Indian commissioners grew to realise the power of the traders in the securing

---

6. This treaty "did away with all the *employés* ... whereas, before, the agent had a force to assist him in finding, destroying, and preventing the introduction of whiskey; now, he is entirely alone."—*Senate Documents*, 1st Session, 35th Congress, Vol. II, Pt. I.

7. *Senate Documents*, 1st Session, 35th Congress, Vol. II, Pt. I.

8. Hughes's *The Treaty of Traverse des Sioux in 1851* in the *Collections of the Minnesota Historical Society*, Vol. X, Pt. I.

of treaties and were not slow to request their services. It was to the financial interest of the traders that treaties should be made, for thus there was insured a steady supply of money with which the Indians could pay their debts. "The commissioners did not do much more than feed the Indians and indicate what they wanted; the traders did the rest."[9] Due to their influence, the government habitually incorporated in treaties a clause providing for the compulsory payment of the Indian debts to the traders. These debts, in some cases, were in the aggregate equivalent to small fortunes. To prevent abuses, the traders were to be paid out of the first cash annuities.[10] It was not an uncommon thing to have these debts absorb even more than these first annuities. Hence, the Indian had to wait long for his first money. Concerning this plan the Indians were not always consulted, but the traders expressed their satisfaction.

In time matters grew so bad and the Indians became so rebellious that Congress, in March, 1843, stipulated by law that no payment of Indian debts to traders should henceforth be provided for in treaties. But the traders were ingenious and evaded the law.[11] Matters came to a crisis in 1853 when the Indians rebelled, claiming that by misrepresentation in the treaties of Traverse des Sioux and Mendota in 1851 they had signed away their annuities to the traders to the amount of two hundred thousand dollars. Investigation proved nothing.[12] As Superintendent Cullen remarked upon this act of fraud, "it is equally important to protect the Indians from the whites as the whites from the Indians." It is safe to say that if the traders had been curbed in their operations many a frontier horror might have been averted. It is no wonder that the Indian's "untutored mind was, now and then, driven to the distraction of savage vengeance".[13]

---

9. Murray's *Recollections of Early Territorial Days and Legislation* in the *Collections of the Minnesota Historical Society*, Vol. XII.
10. Hughes's *The Treaty of Traverse des Sioux in 1851* in the *Collections of the Minnesota Historical Society*, Vol. X, Pt. I.
11. Robinson's *History of the Dakota or Sioux Indians* in the *South Dakota Historical Collections*, Vol. II.
12. Thomas Hughes, in his article on *The Treaty of Traverse des Sioux in 1851*, says concerning this: "The Indians, however, repudiated this agreement, and asserted that it was a base fraud, that, as they were told and believed at the time, the paper they signed was represented to be only another copy of the treaty, and that they did not discover its real import, and the trick played upon them, until long afterward."— *Collections of the Minnesota Historical Society*, Vol. X, Pt. I.
13. Address of Greenleaf Clark on *The Life and Influence of Judge Flandrau* in the *Collections of the Minnesota Historical Society*, Vol, X, Pt. II; Daniels's *Reminiscences of Little Crow* in the *Collections of the Minnesota Historical Society*, Vol. XII.

CHAPTER 3

The Unprotected Frontier

While failing to protect the Indians against the traders, the government also failed to protect the frontier in an adequate manner against the vengeance of the Indians who had a desire to even matters. Apparently the government failed to realise that as the frontier expanded to the west and northwest in Iowa there was also a growing need for protection. Many unfortunate incidents had occurred along the border before a government surveyor by the name of Marsh, from Dubuque, was attacked near the Des Moines River in 1849.[1] Upon the filing of Marsh's complaint, soldiers, dispatched from Fort Snelling in Minnesota, established Fort Clarke (later renamed Fort Dodge) on August 23, 1850.[2] The inadequate garrison of this post, numbering two officers and sixty-six men, was at this time practically the only defence on the northwestern Iowa frontier.[3] Following the establishment of this fort the predatory Sioux bands generally retired westward ten or twenty miles.[4]

By 1851 the last remaining Sioux lands within the limits of Iowa had been ceded and opened to settlement. Trouble for a time seemed at an end. Until that time the only protection against the Indians

---

1. C. C. Carpenter's *Major William Williams* in *Annals of Iowa* (Third Series), Vol. II; *Senate Executive Documents*, 1st Session, 31st Congress, Vol. II.
2. This fort was established by Brevet Major Samuel Woods, Sixth Infantry, with Company E of the same, from Ft. Snelling, Minnesota. It was established by General Orders No. 19, War Department, Adjutant General's Office, of May 31, 1850. Major Woods and men were detailed by Orders No. 22, 6th Military District, St. Louis, Missouri, July 14, 1850. Major Woods and men arrived on the site August 23, 1850. See *Fort Dodge, Iowa*, in the *Annals of Iowa* (Third Series), Vol. IV; Jacob Van der Zee's *Forts in the Iowa Country* in *The Iowa Journal of History and Politics*, Vol. XII.
3. *Fort Dodge, Iowa*, in the *Annals of Iowa* (Third Series), Vol. IV.
4. Flickinger's *Pioneer History of Pocahontas County, Iowa*; Fulton's *Red Men of Iowa*.

was the "watchfulness, courage and trusty arms" of the settlers themselves, with the nearest troops probably one hundred fifty miles away at Fort Randall on the Missouri and Fort Snelling in Minnesota near the mouth of the Minnesota River. Occasional rumours of Sioux activity still came from the outlying settlements. The most definite of these came from the valley of the Boyer more than fifty miles to the southwest of Fort Dodge. Here a family was attacked and some of its members carried away as prisoners. This was in October, 1852. A detachment was sent from Fort Dodge which took and held as hostages the Indian leaders, Inkpaduta and Umpashota. Upon the return of the prisoners, the Indians were liberated. Other Indian incursions reported from the north usually dissipated into mere rumors.[5]

The apparent quietness of the Indians in this section induced General Clarke, commanding the Sixth Military Division, to direct the abandonment of Fort Dodge. This order, which was issued on March 30, 1853, directed the removal of the garrison to Fort Ridgely.[6] With the abandonment of the post by Major Woods, there were left at Fort Dodge only Major Williams, his son James B. Williams, and two discharged soldiers. A more ill-advised order could scarcely have been issued; for following the actual abandonment of the post on June 2, 1853, the Indians "inaugurated a reign of terror among the settlers as far east as the Cedar river."[7]

Many settlers in alarm began the abandonment of their homes; but many others, having staked all in the development of their claims, decided to remain and appeal to both the State and National governments for protection. Appeal to the latter availed nothing. The Indian authorities at Washington were entirely out of touch with the situation: they were firm in the belief that the treaties of Traverse des Sioux and Mendota had definitely settled the question of Indian occupation in this section and that the Indians had withdrawn or had ceased be-

---

5. Samuel J. Albright's *First Organised Government of Dakota* in the *Collections of the Minnesota Historical Society*, Vol. VIII; Fulton's *Red Men of Iowa*.
6. Fort Clarke, by General Orders No. 34, Army Headquarters, on June 25, 1851, had been changed in name to Fort Dodge. By Order No. 9, Sixth Military Department Headquarters, St. Louis, Missouri, on March 30, 1853, the abandonment of Fort Dodge was ordered. By the same order, Major Woods was directed to establish the new post.—See *Fort Dodge, Iowa*, in the *Annals of Iowa* (Third Series), Vol. IV; Carpenter's *Major William Williams* in the *Annals of Iowa* (Third Series), Vol. II, pp. 148, 149; Van der Zee's *Forts in the Iowa Country* in *The Iowa Journal of History and Politics*, Vol. XII.
7. Flickinger's *Pioneer History of Pocahontas County, Iowa*.

ing troublesome.

Parties of Indians frequently returned to their former hunting grounds, and nearly as frequently committed depredations more or less terrorising to the widely scattered settlers along the Des Moines.[8] Weary of making unheeded appeals to National authorities, while the Indian depredations became more alarming, the settlers appealed to the State officials. Major William Williams,[9] who had accompanied the troops at the time of the founding of Fort Dodge and who had remained after its abandonment, was authorized by Governor Hempstead to organise a force, if necessary, to protect the frontier.[10] Little, however, could be done in the way of organising an adequate force on account of the widely scattered character of the settlements.

In a letter to Governor Grimes in 1855 Major Williams again expressed his great anxiety for the safety of the frontier as the Indians had become increasingly bolder. His former commission was renewed and he was granted full power to act upon any sign of hostility. Not only did Governor Grimes receive urgent letters from Major Williams, but from others as well: he was beset with petitions for protection. The governor appears to have been wholly at a loss as to what course to pursue, since he believed he had no power to act. He appealed, therefore, to the Commissioner of Indian Affairs at Washington—although he believed that his only reward would be an acknowledgment of his letters with promise of action. Failing here, he appealed to the President, but received no response.

Finally, in apparent despair, he wrote to Secretary of State George W. McCleary that he knew not "how much credit to give to any of" the letters he had received and in fact he had about made up his mind to disbelieve them all.[11] As a last appeal for action, the governor addressed a letter to the Iowa delegation in Congress on January 3, 1855,

---

8. Carpenter's *Major William Williams* in the *Annals of Iowa* (Third Series), Vol. II.
9. While Major Woods' detail was on its way from Fort Snelling *en route* to the future site of Fort Dodge it was joined on the Iowa River by Major Williams who became later the post sutler and was destined to play a large part in the history of northwestern Iowa. This was in 1850.—Carpenter's *Major William Williams* in the *Annals of Iowa* (Third Series), Vol. II.
10. Carpenter's *Major William Williams* in the *Annals of Iowa* (Third Series), Vol. II; letter from William Williams to Governor Hempstead, September 1, 1854, in the Public Archives, Des Moines, Iowa.
11. Letters from Governor Grimes to Secretary of State, George W. McCleary, February 14, November 5, and December 1, 1855, and to Congressman S. R. Curtis, February 28, 1855, in the Public Archives, Des Moines, Iowa.

in which he expressed the hope that they would co-operate with him in pressing the matter upon the attention of the proper Federal officials and in urging badly needed relief.[12]

Not only were the settlers near Fort Dodge alarmed, but those in Woodbury, Monona, and Harrison counties were even more disturbed, owing to the hostile attitude of large bands of Omahas and Otoes in that section. Near Sergeant Bluff large bands of Sioux had gathered and expressed their determination to remain, while nearly five hundred Sioux were encamped in the vicinity of Fort Dodge. These Indians amused themselves by stealing hogs, cattle, and other property of the settlers. Fears for the safety of the settlers were increased, in view of the fact that the National government was now preparing to chastise the Sioux near Fort Laramie for their manifold crimes committed along the California and Oregon trail in Nebraska and Wyoming. It was thought this action would cause the Sioux to seek refuge east of the Missouri and, as a matter of revenge, carry death and destruction with them as they fled toward the Mississippi Valley frontier.[13]

Because the Indians were becoming more threatening, appearing in larger numbers than heretofore, and extending their depredations over an increasingly wider territory, in the early winter of 1855 Governor Grimes was asked to call out the militia; but he declined since he believed he was "authorized to call out a military force only in case of an actual insurrection or hostile invasion."[14] Nearly everyone now anticipated bloodshed. White men, illy disposed, were reaping large profits from the sale of whiskey; while the Indians were "becoming devils". Hence, Governor Grimes on December 3, 1855, addressed a letter to President Pierce urging that the Indians be removed to their treaty reserves.

The governor pointedly stated that the government owed protection to these settlers in the homes it had encouraged them to occupy. He further stated that a post in this section would curb the Indians and give quiet to northwestern Iowa.[15] To be sure these troubles had

---

12. Letter from Governor Grimes to the Iowa Congressional Delegation, January 3, 1855, in the *Annals of Iowa* (Third Series), Vol. II.
13. Letter from Governor Grimes to the Iowa Congressional Delegation, January 3, 1855, in the *Annals of Iowa* (Third Series), Vol. II.
14. Letter of Governor Grimes to Congressman S. R. Curtis, February 28, 1855, in the Public Archives, Des Moines, Iowa.
15. Letter of Governor Grimes to President Pierce, December 3, 1855, in the *Annals of Iowa* (Third Series), Vol. III; *Roster and Record of Iowa Soldiers*, Vol. VI.

not reached any great magnitude, "yet there was a continuous succession of annoying and suspicious occurrences which kept the frontier settlements in a state of perpetual dread and apprehension, and made life a burden".[16] Even in the presence of this distressing condition of affairs the military authorities of the National government did nothing to relieve matters. No troops were sent to protect the settlers, nor were the letters of Governor Grimes even granted consideration. Thus there developed slowly but surely a situation where the Indians grew sufficiently emboldened to make a general attack.[17]

Such a policy, characterized by a disregard not only for Indian welfare but also for the well-being of the white frontiersmen, could only bring unhappy consequences. It became more and more apparent that the Indians were bent upon concerted action of some sort. Annoyances now occurred along the whole frontier, no part of which was free from alarm. War parties were in evidence in nearly every section, and the attitude of the Indians became one of defiance. Not only in Woodbury, Monona, and Harrison counties, but in Buena Vista and what are now Humboldt, Webster, Kossuth, Palo Alto, and Sac counties the settlers were feeling the effects of Indian enmity.[18]

The resentment of the Indians at this time arose partly from a feeling of jealousy toward the whites, partly from the fact that they were retrograding, and partly from the undue influence of the American Fur Company.

---

16. Smith's *The Iowa Frontier During the War of the Rebellion* in the *Proceedings of the Pioneer Lawmakers' Association of Iowa* for 1898.

17. "He (Secretary of State in Iowa, Geo. W. McCleary) also writes me that these Indians are manifestly making preparations for war, and have been and are now making great efforts to induce all the Mississippi River Sioux to unite with them in hostilities upon the whites. I hear from various sources that several runners have been sent by the Sioux west of the Missouri river, to those in this State, and in Minnesota, with war belts, urging the latter to make common cause with them. The result of all this is a great state of alarm along the whole frontier."—Letter of Governor Grimes to President Pierce, December 3, 1855, in the *Annals of Iowa* (Third Series), Vol. III. Charles Aldrich in an editorial in the *Annals of Iowa* (Third Series), Vol. III, remarked that "Had the earnest appeals of Gov. Grimes been heeded, the Spirit Lake Massacre would not have occurred."

18. The notable depredations charged to Indian outlawry at this time were in Buena Vista County where whole settlements were routed; at Dakota City in Humboldt County; near Algona and Bancroft in Kossuth County. In fact both the spring and summer of 1855 and 1856 were never free from depredations somewhere. For further information consult *The Spirit Lake Massacre and Relief Expedition* in the *Roster and Record of Iowa Soldiers*, Vol. VI; Ingham's *Ink-pa-du-tah's Revenge* in the *Midland Monthly*, Vol. IV.

From the start the Indians, particularly the Sioux, had been jealous and suspicious of the whites. As time passed and the Indian observed indications of a general and permanent occupation by the whites of the territory which he had known as home, his jealous fears increased. The land of his fathers, the home of his traditions, was about to pass into the hands of another people, to the intense sorrow of the Indian. It "was a trying ordeal" and "naturally awakened in his breast feelings of bitter regret and jealousy."[19] His "distrust grew into open protest as claims were staked off, cabins built, and the ground prepared for cultivation." It seemed that the Indians had resolved not to submit "until they had entered an armed protest against the justice of the claim which civilization makes to all the earth."[20]

In addition to this feeling of jealousy and distrust of the whites, the Indians were gradually retrograding by taking unto themselves many of the vices of the white race. This was the inevitable result of a loose administration of the frontier which permitted it to be invaded in many places by refugees from civilization. Although this statement may seem to be somewhat sweeping, it is a well-known fact that among the first to appear on the frontier there were always some men of the reckless, rough-and-ready type whose contempt for the finer things of civilized life made a longer residence amid such surroundings undesirable and frequently impossible.

Foremost among the causes of the red man's retrogression may be cited whiskey.[21] But there were other causes, such as the treaty of 1855

---

19. Hughes's *The Treaty of Traverse des Sioux in 1851* in the Collections of the Minnesota Historical Society, Vol. X, Pt. I.
20. Albright's *The First Organized Government of Dakota* in the Collections of the Minnesota Historical Society, Vol. VIII.
21. "It is a matter of history that whiskey is, and has been since the advent of white men in this country, the 'bane of the Indians,' and that there is scarcely a tribe or an individual Indian but that would at times give all his possessions for whiskey. When under its influence he knows not what he does. All of the depredations committed by them upon the whites; all murders among themselves; or personal injuries inflicted by them upon each other, are perpetrated while under the influence of that destructive bane, or to revenge acts done while labouring under intoxication ... men will wonder why the agent will let whiskey go into the Indian country, as has been heretofore reported,'*without let or hindrance*.' The same men, being in the Indian country ostensibly, solely for the good of the 'poor Indian,' will pass an Indian with a five or ten gallon keg on his back, and not attempt to destroy it; knowing at the same time that he has an equal authority for so doing as the agent, and just as much money furnished for expenses of prosecutions."—*Report of D. B. Herriman, Chippewa Agent*, September 15, 1857, in *Senate Documents*, 1st Session, 35th Congress, Vol. II, Pt. I.

with the Chippewas, which rendered the agent powerless to control the Indian or his seducers if he had so desired.[22] Then there were the errors committed by people who were brought to the frontier by the government as helpers in advancing the Indian's welfare, but who had, through mistaken methods, produced opposite results.

Again, the Indian had been mistakenly led downward "by many years of luxurious idleness and riotous living. . . . In this state of demoralization they were gathered up and thrown together on their little reserve, where all the worst characters could act in concert, and where they found bloody work for their idle hands to do."[23] The government had liberally supplied them with tobacco, and they had never lacked money with which to buy whiskey. Their wants had been looked after so paternally that they had little else to do but spend their time in idleness. Craving entertainment they soon learned to find it in a wrong way. They no longer cared to hunt for food, since they did not need to do so. Soon their expeditions became mere raids upon their protectors, accompanied by unrestrained destruction committed to gratify their craving for some form of entertainment. Thus, while the forces of retrogression were at work the Indian was daily becoming more of a menace to the well-disposed border settlers who viewed his changing attitude in helpless terror.

But most insidious of all in keeping the Indian inimical to his white neighbours was the influence of the fur traders—especially those of the American Fur Company. The admitted purpose of this organisation was to keep the Indian a savage hunter and at the same time to frighten the white settlers away from the frontier in order that the annual crop of cheaply obtained but valuable furs might not suffer diminution. To keep the Indian in such a condition it was necessary to prevent him from assuming too friendly an attitude toward the whites—in order that he might the better beat back or discourage their westward advance. There were strong suspicions that more than one attack upon border settlers by Indians occurred because the presence of these settlers threatened the fur-gathering preserves of the American Fur Company.

It would be wrong, however, to create the impression that the fur traders operated in secret. Practically everyone knew their purpose

---

22. See note 11 last chapter, and *Senate Documents*, 1st Session, 35th Congress, Vol. II, Pt. I.
23. Pond's *The Dakotas or Sioux in Minnesota as They Were in 1834* in the *Collections of the Minnesota Historical Society*, Vol. XII.

and methods: their purposes they openly admitted, and their methods consisted largely in dispensing "fire water" and in selling to the Indian on credit. The latter practice was useful, for it obligated the Indian to serve the company in realising its ends. Perhaps the most notable example of the company's interference with plans of Indian amelioration is to be found in the case of the Winnebagoes. Their agent, Joseph M. Street, one of the most enlightened Indian agents the Iowa country ever knew, had for some years been striving to improve the condition of the Winnebagoes, but without success. He had failed, not because his plan was impracticable, but because he came into direct conflict with the purposes and methods of the American Fur Company.[24]

---

24. Ida M. Street's *A Chapter of Indian History* in the *Annals of Iowa* (Third Series), Vol. III.

CHAPTER 4

The Grindstone War and the Death of Sidominadota

The strained relations between the whites and the Indians resulted in unfortunate incidents which served to intensify the bad feeling already engendered. Of these, two may be noted as especially significant in the frontier history of northwestern Iowa. Thus, in 1854 and 1855, the so-called "Grindstone War" caused the whites to abandon the frontier for a time and spread alarm far and near. This incident might properly be said to have had its origin in intertribal hatred.

For some time a group of Winnebago families had been accustomed to camp near Clear Lake. In this they had been encouraged by an old Indian trader by the name of Hewett. At the same time there also encamped among these Winnebagoes some Sac and Fox Indians who for years, in the Iowa country, had been the greatest enemies of the Sioux. When the latter became aware of the presence of these Sacs and Foxes among the Winnebagoes they swooped down upon them and by mistake scalped a Winnebago. Greatly alarmed, Hewett and his Indian friends fled down the valley, telling their story, which appears to have suffered somewhat from repetition as they proceeded. Within a brief time about one hundred armed settlers collected at Masonic Grove. According to some reports, about four hundred Sioux warriors fortified themselves some twelve miles distant.[1] Thus matters remained during 1854 with no action from either party.

As time passed the Sioux became bolder, until matters reached a climax in an incident which occurred near Lime Creek. A settler,

---

1. Petition of R. B. Clark, *et al,* to Governor Hempstead, July 6, 1854, in the Public Archives, Des Moines, Iowa; Report of Major William Williams to Governor Hempstead, September 1, 1854, in the Public Archives, Des Moines, Iowa.

James Dickerson by name, possessed an unusually fine rooster which was craved by a begging band of Indians. In chasing the rooster, a young brave upset and demolished a grindstone, and then made off with the largest piece in continued pursuit of the fowl. Dickerson pursued the Indian and, seizing a piece of the grindstone, knocked him to the ground, where he lay for a time insensible. The Indians, enraged at Dickerson's act, demanded a settlement for the injury to the brave, making it plain that only Dickerson's best horse or one hundred dollars in money would satisfy them. After no little parleying, in which Mrs. Dickerson acted as mediator, the Indians were pacified when Mrs. Dickerson had given them about six dollars in money, a number of quilts, and many other articles of household use.

This "grindstone incident" caused the settlers to become greatly alarmed: men from Clear Lake, the Mason City settlement, and vicinity organised and undertook to drive the Indians out of the country. After a chase of some miles, the band of over twenty-five white men came in sight of the rapidly fleeing Indians, who, realising that they would soon be surrounded and punished, signified a desire to settle matters. Following an interchange of protests, the peace pipe was smoked, after which the Indians resumed their way westward. This understanding, however, did not allay the fears of the settlers who fled panic-stricken to Nora Springs, abandoning for a time their claims in the vicinity of Lime Creek and Clear Lake.[2]

However ready the Indians may have seemed to make peace, the settlers feared for the future; and so along the line of settlements they spread the alarm that the Indians were on the warpath. Many appeals were made to Governor Hempstead for aid. But when he sent Major William Williams from Fort Dodge to investigate the charges, the Major reported that no danger from further attacks seemed to exist. Unable to secure State protection, the settlers armed themselves. Doubtless the "grindstone incident" soon ceased to impress the settlers with any permanent sense of impending danger, for it was not long before they began to return to their deserted claims.

But not far from the scene of this near tragedy there occurred another incident which displays the temper not alone of the Indian but also of the white borderer of the more troublesome type. It appears that this tragic event grew to undue proportions mainly through the

---

2. Mrs. Abbie Gardner-Sharp's *History of the Spirit Lake Massacre* ((Republished by Leonaur as *History of the Spirit Lake Massacre and Captivity of Miss Abbie Gardner* by Abbie Gardner Sharp). Flickinger's *Pioneer History of Pocahontas County, Iowa*.

vengeful hate of a frontiersman by the name of Lott. The incident, somewhat trivial in itself, has been given so much prominence as a reputed chief cause of the massacre at Okoboji that it is deemed worthy of somewhat extended notice in this place.[3] Its connection with later events may well be a matter of conjecture, owing to the character of the Indians concerned.

******

For nearly a decade after the whites had begun to settle in northwestern Iowa the inhabitants of that region had been obliged to endure constant molestation from a roving band of Sisseton Sioux Indians.[4] Though at first composed of only about five lodges—mainly, it is said, of desperadoes and murderers—the band had grown by the gathering of like characters, fleeing from their avenging fellow-tribesmen, until it numbered at times nearly five hundred.[5] The band as a whole only assembled from time to time for the purpose of united warfare against others—particularly against isolated bands of the Sac and Fox Indians.[6] It was known and feared from the Des Moines westward to the Vermillion and northward to the Minnesota River on account of its peculiarly ferocious and quarrelsome character. It was, in short, a band of Indian outlaws. As such, it was hated and feared by red men and white men alike. In its forays it spared neither friend nor foe, but preyed upon both without discrimination. It claimed no home, but

---

3. Fulton's *Red Men of Iowa*; Gue's *History of Iowa*, Vol. I; Ingham's *Ink-pa-du-tah's Revenge* in the *Midland Monthly*, Vol. IV; Hughes's *Causes and Results of the Inkpaduta Massacre* in the *Collections of the Minnesota Historical Society*, Vol. XI.
4. Fulton's *Red Men of Iowa*.
5. Fulton's *Red Men of Iowa*; N. H. Winchell's *Aborigines of Minnesota*.
6. Other Indian chieftains who were leaders of the consolidated bands and who were to play a prominent part in later Indian history were Titonka, Ishtahabah or Young Sleepy Eyes, Umpashotah, Wahkonsa, and Kasominee. The great battles of Iowa's inter-tribal Indian history were fought during the period of the supremacy of these leaders. These battles were mostly fought along the Des Moines, Skunk, Iowa, and Cedar rivers. The most notable were: Mud Lake, southeast of the present site of Webster City, against the Musquakies; a terrific contest with the Sac and Fox near Adel; a second contest quite as sanguinary with the same Indians about six miles north of the present city of Algona in 1852; a second battle with the Musquakies in April, 1852, near Clear Lake; and one on the banks of the Lizard, in which the Sioux, victorious, ended their long contest with the Sac and Fox. It was in the Algona battle that the "lingering remnants of two great nations who had for more than two hundred years waged unrelenting warfare against each other had their last and final struggle."—Smith's *History of Dickinson County, Iowa*, (*vide* the second part of this Leonaur double edition). Also Fulton's *Red Men of Iowa*; Gue's *History of Iowa*, Vol. I.

roamed at will wherever its fancy might lead.

Leadership of this band had been early acquired by one Sidominadota or "Two Fingers". He had succeeded to the leadership of this loosely consolidated band upon the death of Wamdisapa, an Indian of somewhat milder disposition than his successor. Sidominadota well maintained the savage character of the band and may be credited with the inspiration of many vengeful and frightful deeds committed during his brief leadership.[7] He was only nominally the head of the united group, while really the leader of a small band seldom numbering more than fifteen and frequently less. By all who had to deal with him, red or white, he was looked upon with distrust. His fellow leaders associated with him only in time of dire necessity, for they well knew that Sidominadota would go any lengths to accomplish an end. While he continued to make his refuge and headquarters along the Vermillion, as did his predecessors, his favourite haunts were the headwaters of the Des Moines and Little Sioux Rivers and the region of the Iowa lakes.[8]

About 1847 Sidominadota began to frequent that portion of the Des Moines Valley where Fort Dodge now stands. It was his band that in 1849 attacked a party of surveyors in charge of a man by the name of Marsh about three miles from the present site of Fort Dodge. Marsh and his party had been sent from Dubuque to run a correction line across the State. After crossing to the west side of the Des Moines River, they were notified by Sidominadota not to proceed with their work as this territory was Indian land. With the departure of the Indians, the surveyors continued to run their line. In a short time the Indians returned, destroyed the instruments and landmarks of the surveyors, stole their horses, and drove the men back across the Des Moines.[9] About a year later some settlers, more adventurous than their fellows, located near the mouth of the Boone River. Sidominadota, becoming aware of the arrival of these settlers, paid them a visit and ended by destroying their cabins and driving the people out of the country. This sort of behaviour was continued toward every white man who ventured into that territory until the founding of Fort Dodge in 1850.

---

7. Smith's *History of Dickinson County, Iowa*; Hoover's *Tragedy of Okoboji* in the *Annals of Iowa* (Third Series), Vol. V; Richman's *The Tragedy at Minnewaukon* in *John Brown among the Quakers*.
8. Smith's *History of Dickinson County, Iowa*.
9. See note 1, chapter 3.

"Among others who had received indignities from this band was one Henry Lott. . .who in 1846 settled near the mouth of Boone River in Webster County."[10] Lott's past had been a varied one and much of it was obscure. He boasted of New England origin, while his wife claimed to be a daughter of an early Governor of Ohio or Pennsylvania. If, however, we are to accept the judgment of their contemporaries the family had degenerated.[11] Lott is almost always described as being notoriously lawless, a horse thief, a vender of bad whiskey, a criminal, half-civilized, a *desperado*, an outlaw, and a murderer.[12] Up to the time he appeared in the valley of the Des Moines his whole life had been one of adventure.

His first appearance in Iowa, so far as known, was at Red Rock, Marion County, in 1845, where he essayed the role of Indian trader while dealing out bad whiskey to the Indians and surreptitiously stealing their ponies. It is said that his Red Rock neighbours in 1846 requested him to leave the neighbourhood—which he did by moving on to Pea's Point. Here his stay seems to have been brief, for during the same year he is found located on the Des Moines River near the mouth of the Boone, where he erected a cabin and resumed his whiskey-selling and horse-stealing.[13]

Lott's horse-stealing activities caused the Indians to grow suspicious; and finally they traced the loss of five ponies directly to him and his fellow marauders. This led to an Indian council which decided that Lott should be driven out of the country. Accordingly he was waited upon by Sidominadota and warned "that he was an intruder; that he had settled on the Sioux hunting grounds"; and that he was expected to get off at once. Lott contended that he was not an intruder and refused to go. The Indians then began the destruction of his property: his horses and cattle were shot, his beehives rifled, and his family threatened. Lott seems to have been something of a coward, for when the Indians began taking summary action he fled. While

---

10. Smith's *History of Dickinson County, Iowa*. The date of settlement here is frequently stated as 1847.
11. Hughes's *Causes and Results of the Inkpaduta Massacre* in the Collections of the Minnesota Historical Society, Vol. XII.
12. For statements concerning the character of Henry Lott see Hubbard and Holcombe's *Minnesota in Three Centuries*, Vol. III; Lucas's *The Milton Lott Tragedy*; Hughes's *Causes and Results of the Inkpaduta Massacre* in the *Collections of the Minnesota Historical Society*, Vol. XII; *The Spirit Lake Massacre and Relief Expedition* in the *Roster and Record of Iowa Soldiers*, Vol. VI, p. 890; Gue's *History of Iowa*, Vol. I.
13. Flickinger's *Pioneer History of Pocahontas County, Iowa*.

the Indians were destroying or stealing his property and abusing the helpless members of his family he, according to his own story, crossed the river and secreted himself in the brush. Later he and his stepson, leaving his wife and young children to the mercy of the Indians, fled down the Des Moines River to Pea's Point, a short distance south of the present site of Boone.

Here Lott related his story to John Pea and others of the settlement. Aroused by his tale, the settlers organised a relief party to return to his cabin and if possible to punish the Indians. An appeal for more help was sent to Elk Rapids, sixteen miles away. At this point lived Chemeuse or "Johnny Green", a half-breed Pottawattamie and Musquakie chief, with many of his people who traditionally hated the Sioux. The chief with twenty-six of his men and seven settlers from Pea's Point went to Lott's assistance. It was past the middle of December, and the weather was intensely cold. After Lott's flight from his cabin, his twelve-year-old son, Milton, had started in search of his father, but when about twenty miles from his home and three miles from Boonesboro had frozen to death.[14]

The relief party, on December 18, 1846, found the dead body of the boy a short distance below the village of Centerville. After burying the body on the spot where it was found, the party continued on its way to Lott's cabin. When they arrived they found that the Indians had gone. The family was safe, though suffering and destitute as they had been robbed of everything. The wife, however, had been so mistreated and had suffered so extremely from exposure that she died a short time thereafter.[15]

Vowing vengeance, Lott moved south to the settlements and built a second cabin.[16] Here and at other points in the vicinity he remained a few years, according to all accounts, and bided his time in true frontier style. In the autumn of 1853 he and his stepson passed through Fort Dodge on their way to settle at a new location. In early November he selected a site for his cabin about thirty miles north of Fort Dodge, in Humboldt County, at a point where a small creek joins the Des Moines River. This creek has since been named Lott's Creek in

---

14. The Madrid (Iowa) Historical Society, on December 18, 1905, the fifty-ninth anniversary of the boy's death, placed an iron marker upon his grave which had but lately been identified.—Lucas's *The Milton Lott Tragedy.*
15. The death of Mrs. Lott is said to have been the first white death in what is now Webster County.—Fulton's *Red Men of Iowa.*
16. This cabin was in Dallas County, about five miles southwest of Madrid. Here Lott lived until the autumn of 1847.—Lucas's *The Milton Lott Traged.*

honour of the first white settler in that vicinity.[17] With three barrels of bad whiskey, he re-opened trade with the Indians. And the trade was good; for at this time there was only one cabin, other than his own, north of Fort Dodge—the cabin of William Miller which was located six miles from Fort Dodge.

In January following Lott's new settling, Sidominadota and his family—which was composed of his squaw, mother, four children, and two orphan children—came up the Des Moines and encamped on "Bloody Run", a short distance below the mouth of Lott's Creek. Aware of the coming of the old chief, Lott plotted his destruction. Going to the lodge of Sidominadota, where he perceived that he was not recognised, Lott reported the presence of a large drove of elk feeding on the Des Moines bottom at a point since known as the "Big Bend".[18] The chief's family being in sore need of food, the Indian was easily trapped by the ruse. Sidominadota, having been liberally treated to whiskey, mounted his pony and set out for the hunt; while Lott and his stepson followed. When a safe distance away from the Indian camp and beyond earshot, Lott and his stepson fired upon the Indian, killing him outright. Secreting themselves during the day, the murderers, at the coming of darkness, disguised themselves as Indians, returned to the lodge of the murdered Indian, raised a terrific war cry for purposes of deception, and then surprised and killed all the members of the family except a boy of twelve and a girl of ten years who escaped under cover of darkness.[19]

Completing the work of destruction, Lott returned to his own

---

17. To be definite, the cabin of Lott was in Section 16, Township 93, Range 28 West, very near the west line of the section.—Fulton's *Red Men of Iowa*.

18. Stories as to the ruse used differ, but all now quite generally accept the elk incident. At the same time the assertion has been made that the incident never happened, but that Lott found at the lodge of Sidominadota silverware stolen from him in 1847, and committed murder forthwith.

19. Some writers concerning this incident aver that both the girl and boy escaped unharmed while others more romantically mention the boy as left for dead, while the girl escaping unharmed in the darkness later returned to the rescue of her brother. The boy, whose name was Joshpaduta, was later taken charge of by a white family named Carter who gave him a home. The boy would often leave and be gone for many days when he would again return. He is said, just before the Spirit Lake Massacre, to have warned these people of the impending trouble and then to have disappeared. He never returned, and the presumption is that he became a member of that band or was killed by them for telling.—Flickinger's *Pioneer History of Pocahontas County, Iowa*; Gue's *History of Iowa*, Vol. I; Smith's *History of Dickinson County, Iowa*.

cabin, burned it to make the whole affair appear the work of Indians, and in the company of his stepson fled down the Des Moines Valley. Some years later a report came back to Iowa that he had made his way to California and had there been lynched by a vigilance committee.[20]

Something more than a week after the murder of Sidominadota and his family a band of Indians from a camp on the Lizard Creek, while hunting in the vicinity of the mouth of "Bloody Run", discovered what had taken place. They reported the fact not only to Fort Ridgely but also to Major Williams at Fort Dodge, demanding an investigation and the righting of the wrong as far as possible. Major Williams at once raised a company of whites and Indians and set out in an attempt to locate the murderers, but to no avail. The Indians were firm in their conviction that Lott had committed the deed. A coroner's jury under the direction of Coroner John Johns met at Homer, the county seat of Webster County, and placed the guilt upon Lott and his stepson. But no very great effort was or could be made by the authorities to secure the offenders, owing to the start of ten days which they had secured. Later they were indicted by a grand jury sitting in Des Moines, which ended the attempt to find and punish them.[21] The Indians were highly incensed not only at the murder itself, but at the apparent inaction of the authorities in apprehending and punishing the murderers.

Many reports became current as to the final disposition of the dead chief's body after it had been taken to Homer for the inquest. These reports only added to the embitterment of the Indians, who had expected much from the inquest, having been told that this would settle matters. That the inquest took somewhat the form of a farce was due to the attitude of the prosecuting attorney of Hamilton County, Granville Berkley, who humorously conducted the affair.

Fearing later unpleasant results, the whites attempted to pacify the Indians with many promises. But the Indians grew sullen and suspicious and behaved in such a manner as to create the impression that they might retaliate. It soon became evident that the authorities had no intention of keeping their promises. The Indians after some threat-

---

20. See Fulton's *Red Men of Iowa*; Flickinger's *Pioneer History of Pocahontas County, Iowa*; Ingham's *Ink-pa-du-tah's Revenge* in the *Midland Monthly*, Vol. IV; Smith's *History of Dickinson County, Iowa*; Gue's *History of Iowa*, Vol. I.
21. Fulton's *Red Men of Iowa*; Flickinger's *Pioneer History of Pocahontas County, Iowa*; Lucas's *The Milton Lott Tragedy*; Hughes's *Causes and Results of the Inkpaduta Massacre* in the *Collections of the Minnesota Historical Society*, Vol. XII.

ening seem to have disappeared.[22] One can understand how such incidents, coupled with past grievances, "real or only imaginary", might in the end lead to desperate deeds.

---

22. Another report declared that the prosecuting attorney of Hamilton County had nailed the head above the entrance to his home in Homer. Note what is said in Flickinger's *Pioneer History of Pocahontas County, Iowa*; Ingham's *Ink-pa-du-tah's Revenge* in the *Midland Monthly*, Vol. IV; Hughes's *Causes and Results of the Inkpaduta Massacre* in the *Collections of the Minnesota Historical Society*, Vol. XII.

CHAPTER 5

The Frontier and the Winter of 1856-1857

With the Indians in a most unhappy and vengeful state of mind the Traverse des Sioux Treaty lands were thrown open for settlement in 1853. For several years people had settled along the border of this territory patiently awaiting the opening. Assurances were given the settlers that the Sioux were all established upon their reserve seventy miles north of Iowa's northern boundary. With these assurances of safety, the settlers rapidly pushed to the westward of the Des Moines River which hitherto had been the farthest limit of their movement.

The line of frontier settlements by 1857 extended in a semi-circle from Sioux City to Fort Dodge as a centre and thence to or near Springfield (now Jackson) in Minnesota.[1] Only a brief time served to destroy this line as the settlers moved westward in search of the choicest claims. Before discussing the events which were soon to transpire it will be well to note the outward movement of this frontier to the northwest. The effect upon the Indians of the sudden outward bulging of the line was little short of maddening, as they felt themselves being swept onward by a tide they could not stem. All of their illy concealed hatred of the whites now bade fair to be loosed, while all past wrongs seemed about to be avenged.

Times were now "flush" and the tide of emigration "swept across the state with an impetus that carried everything before it."[2] During the summer of 1855 "land-hunters, claim seekers and explorers"

---

1. Smith's *The Iowa Frontier During the War of the Rebellion* in the *Proceedings of the Pioneer Lawmakers' Association of Iowa for 1898.*

2. Smith's *The Iowa Frontier During the War of the Rebellion* in the *Proceedings of the Pioneer Lawmakers' Association of Iowa for 1898.*

43

steadily flowed into northwestern Iowa. At this time little more was done by many of the settlers than to make temporary improvements, after which they returned eastward planning to take up permanent possession in the following summer.[3]

The main arteries for this westward movement were the Little Sioux and the Des Moines. From Fort Dodge the wave spread out in fan-shape to the furthermost limits of the frontier. The lines of the movement were in the main determined by two facts: Fort Dodge had been established as a United States land office for the territory west and north, and Lizard Creek made that region readily accessible to settlers. Up the Des Moines, settlers had pushed to the point where Jackson, Minnesota, now stands. Many had stopped at occasional points along the Des Moines and made permanent settlements. Near the present site of Algona, in 1854, two brothers, Asa C. Call and Ambrose A. Call, made "the first settlement on either branch of the Des Moines above the forks."[4] To the west of Algona at Medium Lake was the "Irish Colony"—a group of five or six families of Irish extraction from Kane County, Illinois. This settlement has become the Emmetsburg of today.[5] George Granger had staked out and settled upon a claim in Emmet County just south of the State line, and beyond this was Springfield, Minnesota, with six families. Thus a line of isolated settlements extended up the Des Moines Valley from Fort Dodge to Springfield.

To the northwest of Fort Dodge the incoming settlers moved up the course of Lizard Creek, which they followed to its beginning. Thence they crossed to the Little Sioux and settled near Sioux Rapids and Peterson. Near the latter place in the midwinter of 1855-1856 had come J. A. Kirchner and Jacob Kirchner, in company with Ambrose S. Mead. They did nothing at this time but select claims and return to Cedar Falls, from whence they returned in the early spring. After putting in his crops J. A. Kirchner had returned to New York. About the time of his departure, James Bicknell with his family and two men by the name of Wilcox also arrived at the little settlement in Clay County. Up the Little Sioux to the north were about six families at what became known as Gillett's Grove.[6] In the early spring of 1856

3. Carpenter's *Major William Williams* in the *Annals of Iowa* (Third Series), Vol. II.
4. Ingham's *Ink-pa-du-tah's Revenge* in the *Midland Monthly*, Vol. IV.
5. The *Spirit Lake Massacre and Relief Expedition* in the *Roster and Record of Iowa Soldiers*, Vol. VI.
6. Gue's *History of Iowa*, Vol. I; Fulton's *Red Men of Iowa*; *The Spirit Lake Massacre and Relief Expedition* in the *Roster and Record of Iowa Soldiers*, Vol. VI; Gillespie and Steele's *History of Clay County, Iowa*.

the Hon. William Freeborn of Red Wing, Minnesota, and others projected a settlement at Spirit Lake. Their first attempt had not met with much success, and they now awaited the coming of the spring of 1857 to renew the attempt.[7] In the late summer of 1856 about forty people had settled along the shores of Lake Okoboji and Spirit Lake.

Following the original movement up Lizard Creek and the Des Moines River, settlers had begun pushing up the course of the Little Sioux from the Missouri River to a later junction with those coming by way of Lizard Creek to Sioux Rapids and beyond. This movement was marked by an initial settlement at the present site of Smithland, Woodbury County, in about 1851 by a group of three apostate Mormons from Kanesville.[8] In the spring of 1856 the Milford, Massachusetts, Emigration Company had founded a colony of about twelve families near Pilot Rock in Cherokee County.[9] The site chosen was a little north of the present city of Cherokee. Nearly ten miles above this point was a second settlement. To the northeast of these, in Buena Vista County, was the Weaver family at Barnes's Grove. Above this in O'Brien County was H. H. Waterman, at Waterman, who could boast of being the only white man within the confines of that county. Further up the Little Sioux, in the southwestern corner of Clay County, were the families of Mead, Kirchner, and Taylor.[10]

This stretch of settlements outlined the extreme limits of the frontier. To the west there were no settlers; while to the north and northeast the nearest settlements were those on the Minnesota and Watonwan Rivers.[11] Although on ceded ground, all of these settlements were in the heart of the Indian country, where the passing of Indian bands was not uncommon. All were separated from each other by vast stretches of prairie, and frequently the settlers of one place were wholly unaware of the presence of any other white people in the region. Their complete isolation from each other and consequent helplessness in case of Indian attacks were probably best known by the Indians who not infrequently visited them. This isolation appears the more complete when it is recalled that the nearest railroad station in

7. See note previous and also Mrs. Sharp's *History of the Spirit Lake Massacre*; *House Executive Documents*, 1st Session, 35th Congress, Vol. II, Pt. I.
8. A. Warner and Company's *History of the Counties of Woodbury and Plymouth, Iowa*.
9. W. S. Dunbar and Company's *Biographical History of Cherokee County, Iowa*.
10. Wegerslev and Walpole's *Past and Present of Buena Vista County, Iowa*; Perkins's *History of O'Brien County, Iowa*.
11. Flandrau's *The Ink-pa-du-ta Massacre of 1857* in the *Collections of the Minnesota Historical Society*, Vol. III.

Iowa at that time was Iowa City—over two hundred miles away.

By 1857, therefore, the northwestern frontier may be described as "commencing at Sioux City and extending irregularly in a northeasterly direction, by way of Correctionville, Cherokee, Waterman, Peterson, Sioux Rapids, Gillett's Grove and Okoboji, to Spirit Lake; thence turning abruptly to the east by way of Estherville and Emmet to the headwaters of the Des Moines and Blue Earth Rivers, where it extended into Minnesota, terminating at Mankato."[12]

Thus was the meeting-ground of the Indians and the white settlers rather roughly demarked when the winter of 1856-1857 began. Although the fertility of its soil had not been doubted and its great natural beauty and attractiveness as a region of boundless prairies had never been disputed, the northwest had acquired a reputation of climatic extremes—of hot summers and cold winters. This partly accounted for the fact that many settlers delayed their permanent coming to the region until they were amply prepared for the vicissitudes of climate which they must endure in their new homes. Glowing reports had brought the region into general notice, and by the fall of 1856 many people to the east were preparing to migrate to this wonderful country in the not distant future.

"The winter of 1856-7 set in with a fury, steadiness and severity, which make it a landmark in the experience of every person"[13] who passed through it. The storms came early in November, and for weeks northwestern Iowa witnessed nothing but a succession of terrific blizzards, accompanied by the most intense cold. By December 1, 1856, the snow was three feet deep on the level and from fifteen to twenty in the ravines and other low places. Communication of settlement with settlement was well-nigh impossible. The scattered settlers were illy prepared for such a winter: their cabins were unfinished and generally without floors, as all lumber had to be hauled a distance of more than one hundred miles. Most of the settlers had planted no crops during the preceding growing season; hence provisions were scarce and could only be obtained by the use of snowshoes and hand sleds. Wild game was nowhere to be had, for it had either migrated before the oncoming storms or perished in the snow.

As the season progressed the intensity of the cold also increased; while heavy wind-driven snows continued to fall at frequent intervals.

---

12. Smith's *The Iowa Frontier During the War of the Rebellion* in the *Proceedings of the Pioneer Lawmakers' Association of Iowa for 1898.*

13. Carpenter's *Major William Williams* in the *Annals of Iowa* (Third Series), Vol. II.

The prairies became bleak and barren snow-covered wastes, lashed by terrific winds and untenanted by man or beast. The closing of February and the opening of March witnessed no abatement in the severity of the winter. The snow which had been falling the whole winter long yet remained on the ground. Indeed, the season was so prolonged that it is said spring came only in late April, while May and June were cold. In July great banks of snow were yet to be seen in some of the sheltered places.[14]

Although the white settlers suffered considerably from self-imposed denial of food and from unsuitable houses in which to shelter themselves, their privations could not compare with those of the Indians. In Dakota, which was their winter home, they suffered terribly. Their game was gone—where they did not know. Nor were they able to follow it if they had known. As the winds swept over the prairies of Dakota and sharply penetrated the thickets wherein they lodged, their desperation grew apace. At last, in the closing days of February, the intense suffering from cold and famine could be endured no longer and they sallied forth. The course of their march spread out to the east, the north, and the south, and took them to the white settlements along the Iowa and Minnesota frontiers where they sought and took both food and shelter.[15]

---

14. Hughes's *Causes and Results of the Inkpaduta Massacre* in the *Collections of the Minnesota Historical Society*, Vol. XII.

15. For further reading concerning the character of the winter of 1856-1857 see Hubbard and Holcombe's *Minnesota in Three Centuries*, Vol. III; Richman's *The Tragedy at Minnewaukon* in *John Brown among the Quakers*; J. F. Duncombe's *The Spirit Lake Relief Expedition of 1857* in the *Proceedings of the Pioneer Lawmakers' Association of Iowa for 1898*; *The Spirit Lake Massacre and Relief Expedition* in the *Roster and Record of Iowa Soldiers*, Vol. VI; Carpenter's *Major William Williams* in the *Annals of Iowa* (Third Series), Vol. II, p. 152; Hughes's *Causes and Results of the Inkpaduta Massacre* in the *Collections of the Minnesota Historical Society*, Vol. XII; Carpenter's *The Spirit Lake Massacre* in the *Midland Monthly*, Vol. IV.

CHAPTER 6

Okoboji and Springfield in March 1857

Of the settlements made or projected in northwestern Iowa previous to 1857, those having preeminent interest in this connection were along the shores of Lake Okoboji and Spirit Lake in Dickinson County. Although this lake region had been visited many times in the spring and summer of 1855, no settlements had been made at that time. The visitors had simply planned to return as soon as arrangements for permanent occupancy could be perfected. They had been attracted thither by the tales told by Indians and traders concerning the great natural beauty of the region.

For some time the lake region had been well-known to the traders and voyageurs of the upper Mississippi Valley, and their tales concerning it were all favourable. The French interpreter of the Lewis and Clark expedition wrote so clearly of the region as to leave no doubt as to his having been there. He it was who first wrote of the *Lac D'Esprit*, mentioning it for its great natural beauty of location and as being the chief seat of one of the Dakotan tribes. Hunters, traders, trappers, and adventurers visited the region frequently thereafter, but left only oral accounts as to its character and worth. The same region was visited in the summer of 1838 by Nicollet and John C. Fremont, who made observations as to elevation, latitude, and longitude. It was following this official visit that white frontiersmen began to frequent the locality.

All reports of the region indicated it was the favoured home of the Wahpekuta Yankton Sioux. Spirit Lake especially was believed by this tribe to be the scene of various myths and legends intimately connected with the origin and life of the tribe. It was reputed to be always under the watchful care of the Great Spirit whose presence therein was clearly evidenced by the lake's turbulent waters which were never at rest. It was this suggestion of the supernatural—a sort of mystic veil surrounding the region—that led many people to visit it. Some came only to view the lake and, having done so, departed to add perhaps one more legendary tale to the volume of its romance. Practically every visitor enlarged upon the great charms of the groves of natural timber bordering its shores.

But in nearly all of the accounts and tales of the region there was persistent confusion with regard to the several bodies of water. The Indians had always plainly distinguished at least three lakes; while reports by white men as persistently spoke of only one. The Indians knew of Okoboji, "the place of rest", of Minnetonka, "the great water", and of Minnewaukon, "the lake of demons or spirits" or *Lac d'Esprit* or Spirit Lake as it is known today. It is the first of these, Lake Okoboji, with which this narrative is primarily concerned. Upon its borders the first permanent white settlers built their cabins and staked their claims; and here was perpetrated the awful tragedy which has come to be known as the Spirit Lake Massacre.

The lakes, lying closely together as a group, occupy a large portion of the townships of Spirit Lake, Centre Grove, and Lakeville. The northernmost and somewhat the largest of the group is Spirit Lake, which is about ten square miles in area. The northern shore of this lake touches upon or extends into Minnesota along practically the whole of its course. To the south, not connected at this time, and extending in a narrowed, almost tortuous course, stretches East Okoboji for a distance of over six miles. At no point is East Okoboji much over three-quarters of a mile in width. West Okoboji lies to the west of its companion and is connected with it by a narrow strait a few yards in width. The west lake stretches to the west and north, circling in a segment of a circle nearly halfway back to the north and east to Spirit Lake. In length it is about the same as the east lake, although its width is over four times as great at one point. Issuing from the southernmost bay of East Okoboji is the outlet stream, which at a distance of six miles from its source effects a junction with the main stream of the Little Sioux.

The shores of the Okoboji lakes are in the main well wooded, while those of Spirit Lake have only occasional clumps of trees. Along the shores of the latter prairie and water usually meet without interruption by bands of timber. In some respects the Okobojis present a reasonably good reproduction of the smaller lakes of southern New

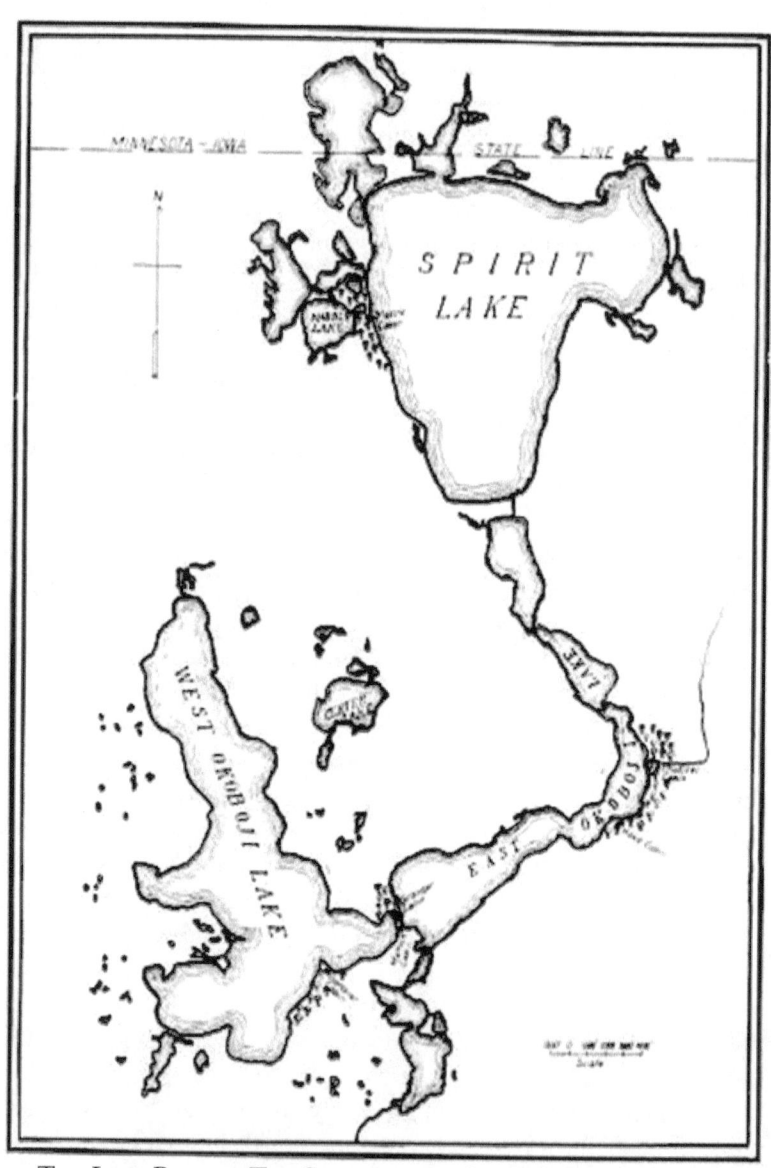

The Lake Region: The Scene of the Spirit Lake Massacre

York and New England. Thus easterners felt that here could be reproduced the familiar scenes of "back home". Although the attractiveness of the place was widely known, no one had settled in the region before the middle of the century. The vanguard of the permanent settlers came on July 16, 1856, with the arrival of Rowland Gardner and his family.

Rowland Gardner was a native of Connecticut, having been born in New Haven in 1815. Here he spent his boyhood years and learned the trade of comb-maker. Growing tired of life in New Haven he migrated to Seneca, New York, where he resumed his trade. At the occupation of comb-maker he had been able to accumulate some three thousand dollars, which, for the time, was considered rather a comfortable little fortune.[1] On March 22, 1836, he married Frances M. Smith, and four children, Mary, Eliza, Abigail, and Rowland, were born while the family lived at Seneca. Abigail, the youngest daughter who is to figure so largely in the story of the Spirit Lake Massacre, was born in 1843. Later the father abandoned the trade of comb-maker and turned to that of sawyer. This change in occupation did not come, however, until the family had again moved—this time to Greenwood, New York. Again, in 1850, they removed to the near-by town of Rexville.

But Gardner had a love for roaming that could not be satisfied by short moves; and so it was not long before he left Rexville for Ohio. His first stop in that State was at Edyington, where he opened a boarding house. His next resolve was to go to the then Far West. Thus, in the spring of 1854 he made his way with his family to Shell Rock, Iowa.[2] Here the family spent their first winter in the West and suffered much from the change of climate. Shell Rock, however, was only a temporary stopping place, for Gardner had no thought of settling short of the farthest bounds of the frontier.

In the early spring of 1855 Gardner, in company with his son-in-law, Harvey Luce, made a rather extensive prospecting tour to the west and north. He seems to have decided to settle, for a time at least, at Clear Lake; for a little later we find him and Luce with their united families moving up the Shell Rock Valley to Nora Springs and thence across the prairie to Clear Lake. This journey consumed the greater portion of April and early May. Settling too late to plant crops that season, the families could not look forward to a very comfortable year.

---

1 & 2. Mrs. Sharp's *History of the Spirit Lake Massacre*; Lee's *History of the Spirit Lake Massacre*.

Gardner and Luce decided upon Clear Lake for the same reason that later led them to settle at Lake Okoboji. To a New Englander accustomed to the lakes and streams of his native parts, Clear Lake with its waters and groves made a strong appeal—one that could not readily be resisted. Open prairies seemed to be "the abomination of desolation" itself. The Mason City settlement on Lime Creek was thought of, but the natural advantages of Clear Lake outweighed any inclination in that direction. At this time Mason City was little more than a station on the westward trail: it consisted of only three or four houses on the open, wind-swept prairie.

It was while the Gardner family was living at Clear Lake that there occurred the so-called "Grindstone War", in which indeed they were active participants. After the scare had spent its force, Gardner again grew uneasy; and, having heard of the attractiveness of the lake region farther to the west along the frontier, he became anxious to settle there. Thus, scarcely had they harvested a first crop when the Gardners were once more *en route* to the westward. The small returns from the sale of the claim at Clear Lake were invested in some oxen, cows, and young cattle.[3]

To the homeseeker the lake region was regarded as a "promised land". This was largely due to its natural beauties as well as to the very great abundance of fish in the lake waters and the plenitude of wild game in the groves along its shores. Many claim seekers had visited the region previous to July, 1856, but no claims had been staked out. The Gardners found no settlers at the time of their arrival.[4] In fact no settlers had been seen by them since leaving the claim of the Call brothers near the present site of Algona.

The journey from Clear Lake had been an arduous one, having been made with ox teams hitched to heavy, cumbrous carts into which had been loaded not only the family but the household goods and the farming implements as well as the food supply. Thus burdened the oxen could make only slow progress even under the most favourable conditions. Furthermore, it seems that the Iowa plains had suffered from an over-abundance of rain that summer: numberless quagmires were encountered; while many streams could hardly be forded on account of their swollen condition. Added to these conditions was the uncertainty of the route—due to lack of knowledge of the country.

---

3. Mrs. Sharp's *History of the Spirit Lake Massacre*.
4. Lee's *History of the Spirit Lake Massacre*; Carpenter's *The Spirit Lake Massacre* in the *Midland Monthly*, Vol. IV; Mrs. Sharp's *History of the Spirit Lake Massacre*.

Many a time it was necessary to unload and carry articles of freight over difficult places. Enduring these trials with the fortitude of well-tried pioneers they steadily pushed on. Upon July 16th they came to the southeastern shores of West Okoboji; and here they rested, for they were at their journey's end.

Since leaving New York the Gardner family had been augmented by a union with the family of Harvey Luce. The latter had planned from the first to unite his fortunes with those of the Gardners, but had been unable to do so at the time of their leaving New York. Luce had married Mary, the eldest of the Gardner girls; and at the time of their arrival at Lake Okoboji, the family numbered two children, Albert aged four and Amanda aged one.[5] The Gardner-Luce party was thus composed of nine persons at the time of its arrival.

Luce and Gardner did not settle at once: while the families tented, the men spent several days in a careful survey of the lake shores and the surrounding prairie region, the better to determine a suitable site. Since the lake region was to be the place of their permanent settlement they desired to make a careful selection of lands.

In the end it was decided to build cabins upon the southeastern shore of the west lake. The location selected was several rods southeast of what is now Pillsbury's Point upon the high, oak-wooded ridge which terminated in that point of land. The site was ideal. To the north and northwest the outlook presented a sweeping view of the lake; while to the south there was as fair a prospect of prairie land as any country could afford. No better selection for a home could have been made. The erection of a log cabin for the Gardners was begun at once. Fronting south, this cabin was for its time rather pretentious, since it was one and one-half stories high.

The season being far too advanced for the planting of crops little could be done besides preparing the land for the next year. This was accomplished by breaking some of the prairie sod. In addition hay was made as feed for the oxen and other cattle during the long winter season. The making of the hay was largely carried through by Mrs. Gardner and her children, including Mrs. Luce; while Gardner and Luce pushed ahead with the building of the cabins in order to afford protection for all as soon as possible. Shelter was also provided for the cattle. By the time this had been done, the season was so far advanced that, though the Luce cabin had been begun, its completion had to be postponed until the return of favourable weather in the coming

---

5. Mrs. Sharp's *History of the Spirit Lake Massacre.*

year. Thus it came about that the Luces took up their abode with the Gardners for the winter which was now upon them.[6]

While out prospecting for claim sites in the two or three days following their arrival, Luce and Gardner heard a report of fire-arms and upon tracing it to its source found that other settlers had just arrived in the vicinity. The camp of the new arrivals was in process of being pitched on the shore of the west lake near the strait connecting the two Okobojis. The party was composed of Carl and William Granger, Bertell E. Snyder, and Dr. Isaac H. Harriott. They had come to the lake region for the purpose of examining the country with a view to future settlement.[7] Having completed their reconnaissance, the members of the party were preparing to spend some time in the neighbourhood hunting and fishing.

These newcomers came to be so well pleased with the advantages of the region that they finally resolved to spend the winter here and possibly make a permanent settlement. After reaching this conclusion they constructed a cabin on Smith's Point north of the strait. These men, moreover, were members of a town site company which had been founded in May, 1856, at Red Wing, Minnesota. As promoters it was their purpose to start a town on the border of some one of the lakes in this region. The Grangers as leading stockholders in the concern laid claim to the point upon which the cabin was built, as well as to all the land lying along the northern shore of the east lake. After resolving upon permanent settlement all but William Granger decided to remain during the coming fall and winter and engage in preparing the town-site for prospective settlers. William Granger was the only married man of the group, and his purpose in returning to Red Wing was two-fold—that of advertising the town-site which had been selected and of bringing back his family in the spring of 1857.[8]

Although the Gardner and Luce families were the first to arrive at the lakes, they had not long to wait before other groups began to arrive, all of whom hurried preparations for the winter that was now not far removed. The sound of the saw and hammer was soon heard

---

6. Mrs. Sharp's *History of the Spirit Lake Massacre*; *The Spirit Lake Massacre and Relief Expedition* in the *Roster and Record of Iowa Soldiers*, Vol. VI.
7. Mrs. Sharp's *History of the Spirit Lake Massacre*
8. Hughes's *Causes and Results of the Inkpaduta Massacre* in the *Collections of the Minnesota Historical Society*, Vol. XII; Mrs. Sharp's *History of the Spirit Lake Massacre*; Carpenter's *The Spirit Lake Massacre* in the *Midland Monthly*, Vol. IV; *The Spirit Lake Massacre and Relief Expedition* in the *Roster and Record of Iowa Soldiers*, Vol. VI.

in a number of places along the lake shores, while signs of still greater activity in the future grew apace. All of the newcomers located within a radius of six miles of the Gardner cabin.[9] The nearest settlement was that at Springfield, Minnesota, about eighteen miles to the northeast; while to the south the nearest was at Gillett's Grove, more than forty miles away.[10] Neither of these settlements had made any provision for its protection against a hostile party of any kind. So far as anyone knew no reason existed for their apparent feeling of assurance against danger.

So rapidly had emigration set in that by November 1, 1856, there were six separate groups of people prepared to spend the winter in this vicinity. The first family to arrive after the Gardners was that of James H. Mattock, who came with his wife and five children directly from Delaware County, Iowa. They settled south of the strait, nearly opposite the site chosen by the party from Red Wing, and the place of their settlement has since become locally known as Mattock's Grove. The site was about one mile from the Gardner-Luce cabin. With the Mattock family had also come a Robert Madison, who was about eighteen years of age. Robert Madison had preceded the other members of his family, who were still in Delaware County but were planning to move to the lake region when suitable accommodations had been provided for them by the son.[11]

From Hampton, Franklin County, Iowa, there came in the late fall the families of Joel Howe, Alvin Noble, and Joseph M. Thatcher. These people had been neighbours at Hampton and had come west as a group. They settled along the east shore of East Okoboji, some two or three miles from the Mattock cabin. The Howe family was large, consisting of Mr. and Mrs. Howe and six children. Jonathan, the eldest of the children and a young man of twenty-three, remained in Hampton, since it was planned that he should come out in the following spring or as soon as he could procure the supplies which would be needed by the three families in their work of pioneering. Alvin Noble, Howe's son-in-law, brought with him his wife and one child—a two year old

---

9. Mrs. Sharp's *History of the Spirit Lake Massacre*; *The Spirit Lake Massacre and Relief Expedition* in the *Roster and Record of Iowa Soldiers*, Vol. VI.

10. Neill's *The History of Minnesota*; Mrs. Abigail Gardner Sharp in the *Midland Monthly*, Vol. IV.

11. Mrs. Sharp's *History of the Spirit Lake Massacre*; Carpenter's *The Spirit Lake Massacre* in the *Midland Monthly*, Vol. IV; *The Spirit Lake Massacre and Relief Expedition* in the *Roster and Record of Iowa Soldiers*, Vol. VI; Hughes's *Causes and Results of the Inkpaduta Massacre* in the *Collections of the Minnesota Historical Society*, Vol. XII.

son. The Thatcher family was also small, consisting of Mr. and Mrs. Thatcher and a child about seven months of age.

The Howe cabin was the first to be erected and was also the nearest to those on West Okoboji. When it had been completed, all hands joined in the erection of a cabin about a mile beyond or northeast of Howe's place which was to be jointly occupied by the Noble and Thatcher families until further arrangements could be made. Boarding with the latter families was Morris Markham—a sort of frontiersman from Hampton, Iowa.[12]

Late in September came Mr. and Mrs. William Marble from Linn County, Iowa. Having stopped temporarily on the Okoboji lakes, the Marbles after some prospecting decided to locate on the southwest shore of Spirit Lake—distant, in an air line, about six miles from the Gardners and perhaps a mile less from the Howes. Their cabin was the most isolated of all—which made it easily possible for events to transpire upon the shores of the Okobojis without the knowledge of the Marbles for days or even weeks.[13]

Such was the chain of settlements of those pioneers who were to pass the frightful winter of 1856-1857 on this isolated frontier. As winter closed in upon them they felt reasonably secure, since Indians had only very rarely been seen. With little or no experience of frontier life on an American prairie, they believed their supply of provisions to be ample for the closed season. No one anticipated an unusual winter. During February a trapper named Joseph Harshman came to the cabin of the Red Wing people. Being a man of genial disposition he was encouraged to spend the remaining portion of the winter with them. Whence he came no one knew; nor did anyone inquire concerning his antecedents, since on the frontier such questions were regarded as discourteous to the stranger.

About eighteen miles to the northeast, on the Des Moines River in Minnesota, was the newly formed settlement of Springfield. Here were to be found by the winter of 1856-1857 about six or seven families. The town had been platted in the summer of 1856 by three brothers—William, George, and Charles Wood of Mankato, Minnesota. For many years these brothers had been widely known in Minne-

---

12. Lee's *History of the Spirit Lake Massacre,* Carpenter's *The Spirit Lake Massacre* in the *Midland Monthly,* Vol. IV; *The Spirit Lake Massacre and Relief Expedition* in the *Roster and Record of Iowa Soldiers,* Vol. VI; Mrs. Sharp's *History of the Spirit Lake Massacre.*

13. Mrs. Sharp's *History of the Spirit Lake Massacre.*

sota and the northwest as Indian traders. By the winter of 1856-1857 they had concentrated their trading interests in a store in Springfield, which made the little village the meeting and trading place of the Indians and whites for many miles around. Indeed, Springfield was the only settlement of note within a radius of fifty miles.[14]

Most of the settlers comprising the Springfield, or as it was sometimes called the "Des Moines City" settlement, had come from northeastern Iowa. The vanguard had appeared in August, 1856, and had located on the east side of the Des Moines River. The Wood brothers had come somewhat earlier and had established their post on the west side of the river, where they laid out the town which they planned to promote. As in the region of the lakes, the cabins were widely scattered up and down the river for seven or eight miles.[15] By the opening of winter the settlement had about seventeen able-bodied men and twelve adult women; but by March, 1857, the number had somewhat increased so that the settlement had about forty-seven people in all, living in seven or eight family groups.

In general the cabins were centred about the home of J. B. Thomas, who had built in the edge of the timber near the river about one and a half miles from the Wood brothers' store. In this family were Mr. and Mrs. Thomas and five children, the eldest of whom was a boy, Willie, of twelve or thirteen years. About two miles from the Thomas cabin upon the open prairie lived Joshua Stewart with his wife and three children; while the Wheeler cabin was about three-fourths of a mile and the John Bradshaw home nearly one and a half miles away. The Adam P. Shiegley cabin, where he and one son lived, was the most isolated, being far removed from all of the others. In addition, there were the homes of Strong, Skinner, Smith, Church, and Harshman.

In the family of Dr. E. B. N. Strong, the community surgeon, were Dr. and Mrs. Strong, two children, and Miss Eliza Gardner, the daughter of Rowland Gardner of the Okoboji settlement.[16] The Strongs had made the acquaintance of the Gardners after the latter had come to the lakes. As Mrs. Strong was not in good health Eliza Gardner had been prevailed upon to accompany the Strongs to their new

14. Mrs. Sharp's *History of the Spirit Lake Massacre*.
15. Jareb Palmer's *Incidents of the Late Indian Outrages* in the *Hamilton Freeman*, July 23, 1857; Hughes's *Causes and Results of the Inkpaduta Massacre* in the *Collections of the Minnesota Historical Society*, Vol. XII.
16. Dr. Strong had gone from Fort Dodge to Okoboji with the thought of locating there, but had finally decided upon Springfield. Eliza Gardner had been induced to spend the winter with the Strong family at Springfield.

home at Springfield. In the Church home were Mr. and Mrs. William L. Church, two children, and Miss Drusilla Swanger, a sister of Mrs. Church. The family of J. B. Skinner comprised, beside himself, his wife and two children; while in the Harshman home there were also two children. Mr. and Mrs. William Nelson had one child; while Mr. and Mrs. Robert Smith and a second Harshman and wife were without children.[17] The unmarried men of the community were Joseph Cheffins, Henry Tretts, Jareb Palmer, David N. Carver, Nathaniel Frost, John Henderson, and John Bradshaw. As the result of being badly frozen during the winter of 1856-1857, it had been necessary for Dr. Strong to amputate both of Henderson's legs and one of Smith's. These operations had been performed shortly before the visit of the Indians in March, 1857.[18]

---

17. Jareb Palmer's *Incidents of the Late Indian Outrages* in the *Hamilton Freeman* (Webster City), July 23, 1857; Hoover's *Tragedy of Okoboji* in the *Annals of Iowa* (Third Series), Vol. V.

18. Jareb Palmer's *Incidents of the Late Indian Outrages* in the *Hamilton Freeman* (Webster City), July 23, 1857.

CHAPTER 7

The Journey East for Supplies

By February the unusual severity of the winter was occasioning some alarm at the lake settlements—particularly as the stock of provisions laid by for the winter was nearing exhaustion. In view of the deep snow and the intense cold it seemed more than foolish to think of attempting to make one's way even to the nearest depot of supplies—which was Fort Dodge. The banks of snow were fifteen and often twenty feet high and offered an almost impassable obstruction to the use of teams. Add to this the intensity of the cold, and one can well imagine what courage or dire necessity it must have required to induce the traveller to set out for the purpose of making his way over an untrodden and in many respects an unknown waste of snow. But the food situation was such that it became increasingly evident that some effort must soon be made to relieve a condition which might become intolerable. Moreover, no one had had any experience in this section which would serve as an index to indicate how long the winter season might continue.

Finally, it was decided that Luce and Thatcher were to return to their former homes in the eastern section of the State in quest of the needed food. With a sled and an ox team they set out in the early days of February. The journey proved to be one of almost incredible hardships: the cold was nearly unendurable, while the banks of snow so impeded their progress that not infrequently little advance was made as the result of a whole day's effort. In the end, however, they made their way safely to Hampton, but only to suffer the disappointment of learning that the settlers here could do little or nothing for them. Compelled to go still farther, they pushed on to Shell Rock, Cedar Falls, and Waterloo before they were able to obtain sufficient supplies for all the people at the lakes.

Securing at last the needed supplies, they remained at Cedar Falls for a brief time to permit the recuperation of both their oxen and themselves. Finally, they began preparations for the return journey which would probably prove more trying than the one east, for now they would be compelled to face the cutting winds and hard driven snows of the open prairies. Although warning of the possible hardships of such a journey was given by Luce and Thatcher, the prospects did not deter four young men from accompanying the two settlers upon their return to the lakes. These men were Robert Clark, a young friend of Luce from Waterloo; Jonathan Howe, the son of Joel Howe already settled at Okoboji; Enoch Ryan from Hampton, a son-in-law of Joel Howe; and Asa Burtch, a brother of Mrs. Joseph M. Thatcher.

In spite of the difficulties encountered, all went well on the return until the party reached a point known as Shippey's near the mouth of Cylinder Creek in Palo Alto County, about ten miles south of the "Irish Colony". Here the overloaded and exhausted oxen were unable to proceed any further. After some deliberation it was decided that Burtch and Thatcher should remain at Shippey's and care for the oxen until they had regained their strength sufficiently to allow them to proceed upon the journey. Meanwhile, Luce, Clark, Howe, and Ryan were to hasten onward to the lakes with the good word that succor was near at hand. They made the trip on foot and in two days, reaching the settlements on the evening of March 6th. Here they found all well with the settlers who rejoiced at the prospect of relief in the near future.[1]

By a careful husbanding of resources and a system of mutual exchange the settlers had been able to prevent much suffering which a lack of care might have entailed. But the time had not elapsed without the occasional appearance of Indians. Apparently a number of red men were wintering in the groves near by, as it seemed unlikely that they could have come from any great distance. They were always friendly in their attitude toward the whites, who from time to time took occasion to relieve their too evident suffering from cold and hunger. They had not only been invited within the cabins to share the comfortable

---

1. Some authors give only three, Robert Clark, Enoch Ryan, and Jonathan Howe, as accompanying them upon their return. There seems good evidence to support the claim that Asa Burtch also made the return trip. See *The Spirit Lake Massacre and Relief Expedition* in the *Roster and Record of Iowa Soldiers*, Vol. VI; Mrs. Sharp's *History of the Spirit Lake Massacre*; Smith's *A History of Dickinson County, Iowa*; Carpenter's *The Spirit Lake Massacre* in the *Midland Monthly*, Vol. IV.

firesides, but were also encouraged to share in the settlers' humble meals if they happened to arrive at mealtime. They never left a settler's cabin empty-handed at any time.

But as the time for the opening of spring neared it had been noted that the Indians grew more restless and less sociable: they seemed to avoid contact with the whites as much as possible. At the same time, the settlers, untrained in Indian ways, saw nothing singular in their later attitude and felt no occasion for alarm. Future developments, however, were to show that there had been more than one occasion for alarm. More than once the Indians had been observed to stalk each cabin and in other ways manifest an undue interest in the settlers. This, however, was accounted for at the time as untutored curiosity in things new and strange.

CHAPTER 8

The Inkpaduta Band

For a number of years preceding the killing of Sidominadota another Indian band, similar in character to that led by the murdered leader, had roamed the country and terrorized the people between the Des Moines and the Big Sioux Rivers. Under the leadership of Inkpaduta or "Scarlet Point", this band had frequented in particular the headwaters of the Des Moines: they resorted to the Big Sioux and beyond only when fleeing from punishment.[1] Their refuge beyond the Big Sioux was with the Yanktons, whose camps along the James or Dakota River were always an asylum for outlawed and disorderly Sioux bands.

Here Inkpaduta was free to go at any time for shelter and defence. But with no other group was Inkpaduta able to maintain even the semblance of friendly relations.[2] The Inkpaduta band of Indians had become well-known either by the name of its leader or as the "Red Top" band, from the fact that it frequently carried pennons of red

---

1. In spite of their villainous character the Sioux pitied the apparent misfortunes of the Inkpaduta band and explained their unhappy lot as follows: "Long ago some chiefs and principal men of the Iowas returned from Canada to Prairie du Chien in the winter, and attempted to pass through the Dakota territory to their own country. They were kindly received and hospitably entertained by the Wabashaw band, who sent messengers to the Wahpekutas, then encamped at Dry Wood, requesting them to receive the Iowas in a friendly manner and to aid them in their journey. The Wahpekutas returned a favorable answer and prepared a feast for the Iowas, but killed them all while they were eating it." Thereafter, these Wahpekutas were very unfortunate, many were killed, and the band nearly perished. Their wickedness on this particular occasion was held to account for all their calamities of the future. In this connection read Pond's *The Dakotas or Sioux in Minnesota as They Were in 1834* in the *Collections of the Minnesota Historical Society*, Vol. XII.
2. Lee's *History of the Spirit Lake Massacre.*

cloth attached to lance ends.[3]

Inkpaduta, the leader of the band, was a Wahpekuta Sioux of a villainous and unsavoury reputation even among his own tribesmen, who feared or hated him. Due to his misdeeds he had been expelled from membership in his own *gens* division of the Wahpekuta Sioux.[4] But this did not serve as a lesson in proper conduct; instead it seemed only to enrage him to the point of committing other and worse deeds—if such were possible. Owing to his lawless disposition a serious quarrel arose among the Wahpekutas. Originally this division seems to have arisen out of a very marked difference in opinion as to the proper attitude to assume toward their hereditary enemies, the Sac and Fox Indians. One section advised a cessation of hostilities which seemed to have resulted in the accomplishment of no purpose. Moreover, in several of the encounters the Wahpekutas had suffered severe losses which they had not been able to successfully recoup.

A second division of the tribe led by Wamdisapa, or "Black Eagle", was so quarrelsome and revengeful that it stoutly opposed any consideration looking toward peace. Black Eagle is characterized as "a reckless, lawless fellow, always at war" with other tribes. After the treaties of Prairie du Chien in 1825 and 1830, he was "one of the first" of the Sioux to violate their provisions by making war upon the neighbouring tribes. His conduct in this respect grew especially bad after the treaty of 1830, when his attitude won for him the "ill will of all his people", who claimed that his conduct provoked their enemies to make many reprisals upon them. Refusing to alter his conduct, Wamdisapa and a small group of kindred spirits were virtually driven away from the tribe and no longer considered as its members.[5]

Striking out boldly across the prairies of Minnesota, the outlaws took a course which led them south and west: they were evidently headed for the lower James, the place of their future rendezvous. Their

---

3. Hughes's *Causes and Results of the Inkpaduta Massacre* in the *Collections of the Minnesota Historical Society*, Vol. XII.
4. The term *gens*, as here used, implies descent in the male line. It is also well in this connection to recall the fact that the Sioux were in no sense a nation but acted as bands, each band being entirely separate, distinct, and independent from any other.—See Dorsey's *Siouan Sociology* in the *Fifteenth Annual Report of the Bureau of American Ethnology*.
5. Richman's *The Tragedy at Minnewaukon* in *John Brown among the Quakers*, pp. 207, 208; Hodge's *Handbook of the American Indians*, Pt. II; Robinson's *A History of the Dakota or Sioux Indians* in the *South Dakota Historical Collections*, Vol. II; *House Executive Documents*, 1st Session, 35th Congress, Vol. II, Pt. I.

course led them to the present site of Algona, where they tarried for some time. Resuming their flight, they travelled westward, crossing the Big Sioux. Finally, they established themselves on the Jacques or James River in the vicinity of Spirit Lake, South Dakota.[6] After removing to this region they were not infrequently known as the "Santies" of the James. They seemed to have lost their identity with the Wahpekutas.

As this party of defection grew in numbers, differences of opinion arose among them. After suffering disruption the band reorganised under two leaders or chieftans—Wamdisapa and Tasagi ("His Cane"). Under this dual leadership, they seemed for a time to prosper as never before. But their misdeeds became so numerous that the neighbouring Sioux requested them to leave the country.[7] The dual chieftanship was not continued beyond the lives of the original holders, since internal jealousies and ambitions rendered it not only undesirable but impossible. The quarrels were largely due to temperamental differences in the leaders. Tasagi was of a mild disposition; while Wamdisapa was noted for his quarrelsome, ferocious, and revengeful nature.

After signing the treaty of 1836, Wamdisapa shifted his band to the Blue Earth region. From here he conducted raids into the Iowa country against the Sacs and Foxes, who, in retaliating, made no distinction between the Indians of Wamdisapa and those of Tasagi on the Cannon River. This caused much suffering among the Cannon River people; but Wamdisapa could not be prevailed upon to discontinue his raids. In the meantime Wamdisapa's son, Inkpaduta, had grown to manhood and leadership. He seems to have inherited to the full the relentless cruelty of his father. More ambitious for leadership than his father, he planned to unite as speedily as possible the leadership which his father had been content to share with Tasagi.

When the consolidation of the leadership did not progress as rapidly as Inkpaduta wished, it is said that he hastened the event by securing the murder of Tasagi. This occurred probably in 1839.[8] As Inkpaduta had planned so it came to pass that upon Wamdisapa's early death the two divisions accepted in the main Inkpaduta's leadership. At the same time a strong faction refused his leadership. Becoming alarmed for his safety Inkpaduta fled further into the Blue Earth country, hoping

---

6. *House Executive Documents*, 1st Session, 35th Congress, Vol. II, Pt. I; *The Spirit Lake Massacre and Relief Expedition* in the *Roster and Record of Iowa Soldiers*, Vol. VI.

7. Robinson's *History of the Dakota or Sioux Indians* in the *South Dakota Historical Collections*, Vol. II.

8. *Executive Documents*, 1st Session, 35th Congress, Vol. II, Pt. I; Hubbard and Holcombe's *Minnesota in Three Centuries*, Vol. II.

thereby to gain time for the firmer union of his loyal followers.[9] Even so he could not tarry long since the Cannon River Wahpekutas were on his trail. With a still smaller number of followers he again fled—this time to northern Iowa—preferring to brave the hatred of the Sacs and Foxes to that of his fellow Wahpekutas.

It is thought that the incident of Tasagi's murder and the later flights nearly broke up the band of Wamdisapa, so that it could scarcely be said to exist. In a few years, however, through a prolonged series of intertribal quarrels conditions had become such that Inkpaduta was recognised as the undisputed master of the greater and more turbulent sections of both of the original bands. By the time of the successful realisation of his plans—about 1848—Inkpaduta had made a reputation for relentless savagery that had spread throughout northwestern Iowa, Dakota, and Minnesota. Upon him rests the stigma of having planned the murder not only of Tasagi but also of his own father.[10] His band seemed to thrive upon its evil reputation: thus it is said that "from time to time some villainous Sioux committed a murder, or other gross crime upon some other member of the tribe, and fled for fear of vengeance to the outlawed band of Wahpakootas for protection."[11]

The Inkpaduta band of Indians became, as it were, accursed. It could call no place its home—excepting perhaps the temporary winter rendezvous with the Spirit Lake Yanktons. Thus the members of this band became as "Ishmaelites whose hands were against all other

---

9. Following the murder of Tasagi, Inkpaduta either through choice or fear became an exile from the band of Tasagi. His flight to the band of his father had automatically made him one. Doane Robinson in his *Sioux Indian Courts* in the *South Dakota Historical Collections*, Vol. V, pp. 404, 405, thus describes how a Wahpekuta became an exile: "If the offense was peculiarly repellent to the better sentiment of the camp the court might insist upon the summary infliction of the sentence imposed. This might be the death penalty, exile or whipping; or it might be the destruction of the *tepee* and other property of the convict.... For some offenses a convict was exiled from the camp, given an old tepee and a blanket, but no arms, and was allowed to make a living if he could. Sometimes he would go off and join some other band, but such conduct was not considered good form and he usually set up his establishment on some small hill near the home camp and made the best of the situation. If he conducted himself properly he was usually soon forgiven and restored to his rights in the community. If he went off to another people he lost all standing among the Sioux and was thereafter treated as an outlaw and a renegade. The entire band of Inkpaduta, once the terror of the Dakota frontier, was composed of these outlaws." It was Inkpaduta's flight to his father's band at this time that lost, for him, all standing with the followers of Tasagi. See also Robinson's *A History of the Dakota or Sioux Indians* in the *South Dakota Historical Collections*, Vol. II.

10 & 11. Hubbard and Holcombe's *Minnesota in Three Centuries*, Vol. III.

men".¹² The character of its members was that of its leader, who acted as a magnet to draw to him the worst types from the surrounding tribes. Even according to the Indian moral code they would be classed as toughs and criminals. Inkpaduta was universally reputed as the most blood-thirsty Indian leader in the Northwest. Whites and Indians upon whom his displeasure might fall feared him as death itself. The members of his band became widely known as the renegades and outlaws of the frontier. Spending their lives as wanderers and marauders, they never remained long in any locality. "They went as far west as the Missouri, as far north as the Cheyenne, as far south and east as the Upper Des Moines, in Iowa."¹³ Their life of necessity was but an outgrowth of their villainous disposition. It has been said that their actions grew so unbearably bad that even Sidominadota—by many regarded as an arch fiend—left the band and went far down the course of the Des Moines the better to escape the wrath of its leader.¹⁴ It was soon after this act that Sidominadota and Lott crossed paths with the result that the Indian's life paid the forfeit.

Many of the unpleasant incidents in frontier life from 1836 to 1857 in Minnesota and Iowa were directly chargeable to these Bedouins of the prairies who tarried at a "trading house but a few minutes and in seeming fear and dread hurried away." The first exploit officially credited to the band was the massacre of Wamundiyakapi, a Wahpekuta chief, along with seventeen warriors on the headwaters of the Des Moines in Murray County, Minnesota, in 1849. Prior to 1850 they had broken up, plundered, and driven away two parties of United States surveyors. The cabins of numerous settlers in the upper Des Moines country had also been wantonly destroyed and they had been driven from the country—in face of the fact that it was well known what band was at work and where its usual rendezvous was located.¹⁵ Settlers along the Boyer River had also suffered outrages at its hands as late as 1852. Major William Williams stated it as his opinion that a general attack upon the frontier was planned to occur about 1855; but the plans failed for some unknown reason. Inkpaduta seems to have been much displeased thereat and attempted to take upon himself the execution of the original plan.¹⁶

The unusually strenuous life which had been led by the band was

---

12/13/14 Hubbard and Holcombe's *Minnesota in Three Centuries*, Vol. III.
15. Hubbard and Holcombe's *Minnesota in Three Centuries*, Vol. III; Robinson's *A History of the Dakota or Sioux Indians* in the *South Dakota Historical Collections*, Vol. II.
16. Ingham's *Ink-pa-du-tah's Revenge* in the *Midland Monthly*, Vol. IV.

having a telling effect upon its membership: by 1852 there were evidences of a near dispersion. It seems that even to a criminal Indian compulsory exile from his race was distasteful, and one by one the followers of Inkpaduta were slipping away. To stimulate an interest in his band, Inkpaduta appears to have settled upon a plan of making concerted attacks upon the northwestern frontier of settlements; and he was successful in creating in the minds of some the belief that he had general control of no less than five or six hundred warriors operating along the frontier in isolated bands of fifteen or twenty Indians each. It is now positively known that such was not the case and that at the time of its greatest prosperity the Inkpaduta band did not number more than fifty or sixty souls. By the autumn of 1856 the group had become so diminished in numbers that it was upon the eve of dispersion.

This rapid disintegration of the band could be accounted for by the character of its leader. His arrogance was rapidly rendering followers impossible. Inkpaduta, in 1856, was evidently between fifty and sixty years of age. He was born, probably in 1800, on the Watonwan River in Minnesota. For a Wahpekuta Sioux he was large, being probably more than six feet tall and very strongly built. He was not a person of pleasing appearance; for, coupled with the immoral character of his life, smallpox had badly marked him. Indeed, he presented an unusually repulsive appearance. His features were coarse; his countenance was of brutal cast; and he was very near-sighted. His near-sightedness became total blindness in old age, so that at the time of the battle of the Little Big Horn he was carefully piloted about by his small grandsons who, managing to save him from the general slaughter, succeeded in having him safely carried into Canada in the party of Sitting Bull.[17]

Although his band as a whole was of bad repute, Inkpaduta stood out above his followers on account of his hatred for the whites, his revengeful disposition, and his nearly matchless success in war.[18] Mrs. Sharp speaks of him as "a savage monster in human shape, fitted only for the darkest corner in Hades."[19] "Of all the base characters among

---

17. Hubbard and Holcombe's *Minnesota in Three Centuries*, Vol. III; *South Dakota Historical Collections*, Vol. VI.
18. Mrs. Sharp's *History of the Spirit Lake Massacre*.
19. *Ibid.* It is to be regretted that much of Mrs. Sharp's characterization of the Sioux evidences an animus and a tendency to emphasize the bad rather than the good traits. The following from her book is evidently unfair: "No other tribe of aborigines has ever exhibited more savage ferocity or so appalled and sickened the soul of humanity by wholesale slaughtering of the white race as has the Sioux".

his fellow outlaws, his nature seems to have been the vilest, and his heart the blackest."[20] "It was only as a war chief that he won a place in the admiration of the Indians. In civil life they would have none of him. Except where bloodshedding was the business in hand, they knew by sore experience he was not to be trusted.... It is scarcely probable from all of his conduct that he was other than he seemed, a terrible monster."[21]

His unusual disposition was coupled with an ambition to see his people and tribe restored once again to their wide and extensive hunting ranges. As he witnessed the frontier expanding westward he saw his great ambition vanish, and he was irritated beyond control. Unspeakably immoral himself, he nevertheless hated the vices of the whites that were slowly taking hold upon the members of his band and race.

He yearned to be a party to the treaties of the Wahpekutas as a chief and to share in the annuities which resulted therefrom. The annuities, with the exception of those of 1854 and 1856, he was permitted to enjoy. Upon the death of Wamdisapa it appears that Inkpaduta was definitely dropped from membership in the Wahpekutas; and so he was not consulted regarding the disposal of the Minnesota and northwestern Iowa lands. It was thought that he had forfeited his council rights; but when the first payment was made he was on hand and demanded his share—which was denied him by the agent. He then turned his attention to the treaty-making Indians and compelled them to pay him the share which he claimed in the annuities. Thereafter he appeared annually, and only twice was he definitely refused. This denial was an affront extremely hard for him to bear, for it was to him a denial of his rights in the name and birthright of the Wahpekuta Sioux.[22] Claiming the Yankton and Santee tribal rights he appears to have gained an acknowledgment of them by the year 1865.

---

20. Hubbard and Holcombe's *Minnesota in Three Centuries*, Vol. III.
21. Robinson's *History of the Dakota or Sioux Indians* in the *South Dakota Historical Collections*, Vol. II.
22. Hodge's *Hand Book of the American Indians*, Pt. II; *South Dakota Historical Collections*, Vol. I; *House Executive Documents*, 1st Session, 35th Congress, Vol. II, Pt. I; Mrs. Sharp's *Spirit Lake Massacre*.

CHAPTER 9

Inkpaduta Seeks Revenge

Burning with hatred for Indians and white men alike, Inkpaduta and his band left the Fort Ridgely Agency of the Lower Sioux in the autumn of 1856. They appear to have gone westward to the Big Sioux, where they spent some time in hunting and fishing. Their next and final move, before entering camp for the winter, was to the Yankton camp near Spirit Lake, South Dakota. There Inkpaduta planned to spend the winter of 1856-1857 with his well-tried friends and protectors. Doubtless during the fearful ordeal of that unusual season when they suffered from cold and hunger they recalled past wrongs, which they now credited with causing their present condition, and planned revenge upon their persecutors.[1]

The question has frequently been raised as to where the Inkpaduta band of Indians really passed the winter season of 1856-1857. Some writers have held that they remained at Loon Lake, in Minnesota; while others have insisted that they camped among the Yanktons in Dakota. The latter seems the more probable. Indeed, it is highly improbable that any Indians, after having suffered, as all agree this band had suffered during the winter in the valleys of the Des Moines and Little Sioux, would go down the valley of the one, as they are reputed to have done, and finding no food on the way down, as all taking this view agree was the case, until they arrived at Smithland, would then have doubled back upon a trail known to be barren. It is far more probable that the band wintered in Dakota, and with the approach of spring returned to their favourite hunting grounds. When they had been denied food at Smithland, they at once started up the Little Sioux and hastened to the hunting grounds of presumed plenty.

---

1. Hubbard and Holcombe's *Minnesota in Three Centuries*, Vol. III.

One thing is certain: at the first breaking of winter they were on the move.[2]

It so happened that in February, 1857, there came a promise of spring, and with this promise Inkpaduta and his band of Indians left their winter camp. Verging upon starvation, they hastened on foot or on horseback toward the white settlements along the Iowa frontier; and it can truly be said of Inkpaduta that "wherever he appeared, murder and theft marked his trail".[3] Reaching the Big Sioux, he and his followers passed down its course and across its waters to the beginning of the white settlements upon the Little Sioux in eastern Woodbury County.

At the time of arrival at these settlements the band was not large—having, presumably, been sadly depleted by desertion or by the severity of the winter. Apparently there were only about ten lodges in all, comprising men, women, and children. So far as known the warriors in February, 1857, included the following: Inkpaduta, the leader; Roaring Cloud and Fire Cloud, the twin sons of Inkpaduta; Sacred Plume; Old Man; Putting on Walking; Rattling, son-in-law of Inkpaduta; Big Face; His Great Gun; Red Leg; Shifting Wind; and Tahtay-Shkope Kah-gah, whose name does not appear to be translatable. Nothing further need be said of the band's personnel than that they had been well trained by Inkpaduta for the work in hand.[4]

As the settlements were neared it doubtless seemed to the Indians that they were approaching a land of plenty, for game which had hitherto been seen nowhere now began to make an occasional appearance. It must have seemed to their primitive minds that this region, their land of plenty, had been usurped by the whites. They were eager for revenge and prepared to carry arson, murder, and pillage the full

---

2. *Roster and Record of Iowa Soldiers*, Vol. VI; Fulton's *Red Men of Iowa*; Smith's *History of Dickinson County, Iowa*; Hubbard and Holcombe's *Minnesota in Three Centuries*, Vol. III.

3. Robinson's *History of the Dakota or Sioux Indians* in the *South Dakota Historical Collections*, Vol. II.

4. The strength of the band was not great. Originally it is said to have numbered one hundred fifty lodges, but this estimate appears to be too high. At the time it started up the Little Sioux from Smithland it probably numbered not more than fifteen lodges at the highest estimate. Its depletion was due to dissatisfaction in the band and to the fact that the band did not draw annuities which caused many to drop out and return to the Agency in order to secure them. See Mrs. Sharp's *Spirit Lake Massacre*; Hubbard and Holcombe's *Minnesota in Three Centuries*, Vol. III; *House Executive Documents*, 1st Session, 35th Congress, Vol. II, Pt. I; Hodge's *Handbook of American Indians*, Pt. II.

length of Iowa's western frontier.

It should be borne in mind, as events rapidly follow, that the deeds of these Indians were not by any means spontaneous or the result of any single or isolated incident or circumstance. As an explanation of what occurred in Iowa in the spring of 1857, there has been advanced the theory that Inkpaduta was merely seeking revenge for the murder of his brother, Sidominadota. This explanation has been advanced so frequently that it has been long accepted by most people as an undoubted fact. In all probability, however, such was not the motive of the Indians: on the contrary the real cause must be sought in the innate character of the band that committed the tragic deed. In fact this unhappy incident in Iowa's pioneer history was but one of many justly charged against this particular band of wild Bedouins of the prairies.

The murder of Sidominadota in all probability did not cause Inkpaduta much concern. Moreover, it should be said at the outset that Inkpaduta and Sidominadota were not brothers—as has so often been claimed—since Inkpaduta was a Lower Sioux, a Wahpekuta; while Sidominadota was an Upper Sioux, a Sisseton. Hence they could not have been brothers. It is true that in some phases of Indian relationship they might have been spoken of as brothers, but the conditions making such a reference even remotely possible were not present in the case of these two Indian leaders. Hence the theory of blood revenge can not be accepted. Furthermore, the term "brother" with the Sioux was not limited to blood relationship. "The tribe consists of a group of men calling one another brother, who are husbands to a group of women calling one another sister." To call one another brother was a common practice and carried with it no idea of relationship as ordinarily interpreted.

Granting that the two were brothers, if Inkpaduta could not have avenged the death within a year he could not have done so thereafter according to the practice of blood revenge universally taught and practiced among the Sioux. In religious practice and ceremonial observance Inkpaduta was neither a heretic nor an outcast. The Sioux have never been noted for retentive memories in matters of revenge, but rather for their laxity.

Inkpaduta was superior to Sidominadota in rank; hence he would not have succeeded him and could not have taken up blood revenge as his successor. Moreover, these two men had bitterly disagreed, and Sidominadota had severed all relation and connection with Inkpaduta or any of his band and had grown to be one of the bitterest and most vindictive of enemies. Inkpaduta knew this. It is likely that Inkpaduta would have rejoiced at the news of his enemy's death: it is certain that the murder would not have caused him much if any concern. "With him it was every man for himself; he never had a sentiment so noble and dignified as that of revenge, and would not turn on his heel to retaliate for the slaughter of his nearest friend."[5]

Again, according to Siouan practice each band is absolutely separate: one band must not concern itself with the affairs of another. War would inevitably have followed such conduct. Although Inkpaduta was lawless in many respects, no instance in which he broke over the strict letter of this custom has come to light.

Finally, the bands were so widely separated and so busily engaged in dodging each other that "it is doubtful whether Inkpadoota ever heard the particulars of All Over Red's murder; it is certain that he would not have been concerned if he had."

Thus it seems evident that Inkpaduta could not have been on a mission of blood revenge: it seems more probable that his own character and that of the members of his group, coupled with an overemphasized conviction of wrongs suffered in years past, allied with the intense suffering of the moment, had produced an outburst of savage frenzy culminating in murder. This would seem to be more in keeping with the known character of the Indian and in line with his known conduct. The idea of blood revenge has made a strong appeal since it was advanced as an explanation by Major William Williams, but it can not be made to rest upon a foundation of known and recognised facts in connection with the Spirit Lake Massacre.[6]

---

5. Powell's *On Kinship and the Tribe* in the *Third Annual Report of the Bureau of American Ethnology*; Hubbard and Holcombe's *Minnesota in Three Centuries*, Vol. III.

6. Hubbard and Holcombe's *Minnesota in Three Centuries*, Vol. III. For further support of the view that Sidominadota's death was not a cause as here set forth see J. W. Powell's *Kinship and the Tribe* in the preface to the *Third Annual Report of the Bureau of American Ethnology*; Senate Documents, 1st Session, 32nd Congress, Vol. III, Doc. No. 1; Pond's *The Dakotas or Sioux in Minnesota as They Were in 1834* in the *Collections of the Minnesota Historical Society*, Vol. XII; Dorsey's *Siouan Sociology* in the *Fifteenth Annual Report of the Bureau of American Ethnology*.

CHAPTER 10

The Smithland Incident

The approach of Inkpaduta and his band to the white settlements was unobserved—due probably to the fact that the severity of the winter had driven into the settlement all the traders and trappers who were commonly the purveyors of such news along the frontier. Although the Indians appeared at Smithland on the Little Sioux in southeastern Woodbury County unannounced, no alarm was felt since they had been there before and seemed quite friendly. Even now they bore, outwardly at least, every indication of friendship for the whites. Quietly and inoffensively they begged from the settlers who, pitying their evident starving condition, gave as liberally as they could to satisfy their needs rather than their demands.[1]

It seems that the Indians had been at the settlement but a brief time when they discovered that the whites had not been able to complete the harvesting of the past season's corn crop on account of the coming of the early and deep snows. Much of the corn had been buried, where the settlers had been content to leave it for husking in early spring. Upon making this discovery the Indians with a will set about gathering corn from the fields. Very naturally the settlers objected and demanded that the Indians desist, which they did after some jangling and expressions of ill feeling. They did not, however, cease their demands for food.

The settlers now assumed a plainly unfriendly attitude toward the Indians, which in turn gave impetus to a change in the temper and attitude of the Indians toward the whites. They soon became sullen and insolent, with a manifest tendency to commit a variety of malicious acts—probably for the purpose of trying the temper of the settlers.

1. Smith's *A History of Dickinson County, Iowa*; Flickinger's *Pioneer History of Pocahontas County, Iowa*.

Only acts of a trivial character, however, were actually committed; and so the wiser heads in Smithland were successful in warding off for some time any serious trouble.

Several days after the arrival of the Indians a large drove of elk appeared in the timber on the river bottom. This meant plenty to the nearly famished Indians, and they at once began preparations for the hunt in which all were to participate. When the hunt had gotten well under way an Indian was attacked by a settler's dog which apparently had become over zealous in the chase. The Indian retaliated by killing the dog. Then the owner of the dog sought to even matters by administering a rather severe beating to the Indian, at the same time forcibly disarming him. To a young Indian brave such treatment was an insult calling for retaliation. When the other settlers learned of this reckless action on the part of one of their number they grew alarmed, for they knew Indian character well enough to conclude that the incident was not a closed one by any means.

Meanwhile the petty pilfering and thieving by the Indians continued. Especially annoying were the squaws who, constantly haunting the cabins and other buildings of the settlement, would sometimes carry away grain and hay. Occasionally a settler catching a squaw in the act would give her a whipping—which only increased the tension of the situation. Finally, a settlers' council was called, the result of which was an effort to disarm the Indians as an assurance of safety. Failing to realise the full purport of what was being done, the Indians offered little opposition. The guns were hidden, and for a while the settlers breathed easily. But in their alarm, they had really taken a very unwise course. They probably thought that the Indians would soon come forward and offer some reasonable and peaceful settlement of any wrongs that had been committed. In this, however, the settlers exhibited little appreciation of the character of the Sioux Indian.[2]

Not a little enraged, the Indians committed other depredations upon the settlers; and it was not long before the settlers awoke to a realisation of the mistake they had made. But they soon committed a worse blunder in seeking to correct the first. A militia company of twenty-one men was organised among the men of Smithland and

---

2. Flandrau's *Inkpaduta Massacre of 1857* in the *Collections of the Minnesota Historical Society*, Vol. III; Mrs. Sharp's *Spirit Lake Massacre*; *House Executive Documents*, 1st Session, 35th Congress, Vol. II, Pt. I; *Senate Documents*, 1st Session, 35th Congress, Vol. III; *The Spirit Lake Massacre and Relief Expedition* in the *Roster and Record of Iowa Soldiers*, Vol. VI.

vicinity under the leadership of Seth Smith, the founder of the settlement. Captain Smith was selected as leader of the organisation not for his known military ability, but because he owned a "magnificent suit of regimentals, with its quivering epaulettes, gaily bedecked cocked hat and flashing sword." Surely these would strike terror to the souls of the Indians.

The party was quickly and quietly prepared for a demonstration of military power, after which they marched to the Indian camp and there paraded before the Indians. When the demonstration was ended, Captain Smith demanded of the Indians that they leave at once. This seemed impossible to the Indians, who are said to have replied that the weather was so cold and the snows so deep up north that nothing to eat could be secured by them in that direction. They added, however, that they would like to go on down the river to the camps of the Omahas and treat with them. This the whites did not seem to think would be advisable: they evidently thought that the Indians would visit them again upon their return to the north. When denied the privilege of passing on to the Omahas the Indians flatly refused to leave at all—an action that may have been due in part to the fact that not all of the Indians were then in the camp.[3]

The settlers, finding themselves sufficiently strong after this demonstration of military preparedness, began a series of annoying acts directed toward the Indians, who seemed to submit stoically to these impositions. Finally, one morning the settlers were not a little gratified to discover that the Indians had gone. But the joy was only temporary; for the Indians later reappeared with guns—possibly the very ones that had been taken from them by the settlers. How they secured these arms was not known; but it was evident that the reclamation of their property had a marked effect upon their conduct. They now became defiant and openly committed theft to satisfy their wants; for they knew that they were now better prepared for resistance than were the whites.

It was shortly before this time that General Harney had conducted his march through the Indian country in Kansas and Nebraska, thence westward into Wyoming, and back northeastward to or near Fort Pierre in Dakota. Every Sioux knew of him and held him in a sort of superstitious awe or dread. They thought of him as one guided and guarded by the Almighty in his work as an avenger. Aware of the regard with which the Sioux held Harney, it was proposed by the

---

3. A. Warner and Company's *History of the Counties of Woodbury and Plymouth, Iowa*.

settlers to use him as a means of ridding themselves of their Indian guests. Accordingly a settler donned the soiled uniform of an army officer and at sunset appeared in the edge of the timber on the bank of the Little Sioux opposite the Indian camp. His appearance there was called to the attention of the Indians, along with the suggestion that the stranger was Harney, in all likelihood, in close pursuit of them. The ruse, it is said, was effective: that same night the Indians fled up the river from Smithland. As they fled it became increasingly evident that they were thirsting for revenge. From suffering indignities themselves they now turned to the infliction of atrocities upon whomsoever chanced to cross their path. While the more level-headed settlers at Smithland regretted the tricks played upon the Indians, all congratulated themselves upon being rid of their unwelcome guests.[4]

---

4. Smith's *A History of Dickinson County, Iowa*; Fulton's *Red Men of Iowa*.

CHAPTER 11

From Smithland to Okoboji

After leaving Smithland the next place visited by Inkpaduta and his band seems to have been Correctionville—a place about twenty miles up the course of the Little Sioux. Here the Indians appear to have been friendly at first; but they were not long in the settlement before their begging and thieving led to opposition from the whites. Indeed, during the later portion of their stay they used their guise of friendship only for the purpose of securing an entrance to the cabins of the settlers, and having been admitted helped themselves to whatever was most convenient and best suited to their needs, such as food, guns, and ammunition.

The ugliness of their real character for the first time appeared in their treatment of a settler by the name of Robert Hammond. It seems that Hammond resisted their thieving after he had admitted them to his cabin, with the result that he was badly beaten. This episode appears to have started the Indians upon their fiendish career. Having left Hammond helpless in his cabin, they turned, when some distance away, and literally shot the cabin door off its hinges. This was done, presumably, as a warning of what was likely to happen if they were further interfered with. They then left the settlement and continued their journey northward.

As he proceeded up the course of the Little Sioux, Inkpaduta followed the policy of sending out scouting and foraging parties into the surrounding country. At nearly every cabin found by these parties everything in the line of guns, food, and ammunition was either carried off or destroyed. Not infrequently the stock of the settler—hogs, cattle, or horses—was killed and left untouched: the Indians seemed now to be seeking to destroy rather than to take for their own use.

The next settlement reached by the band was Pilot Rock in Cherokee County. While pausing here for a brief time scouts were sent out in all directions through the surrounding country. Very little transpired at Pilot Rock other than the taking of food and arms. Here the Indians found no opposition upon the part of the settlers; and when they had satisfied themselves they left the community.

Another settlement visited was that of the Milford Colony, which was located a little north of the present town of Cherokee. Cattle and hogs were shot, doors torn from their hinges, and furniture ruined. Bedding was torn into shreds, and feather ticks were ripped open and the contents scattered upon the prairie. Here the Indians remained for three days; and while the settlers suffered only from fright and the destruction of property, they were only too happy to note the red men's preparations for leaving.

The Indians had tarried at Milford Colony evidently for rest and recuperation, finding here more supplies than they had encountered elsewhere. This was doubtless due to the fact that the settlers, having but lately come west from Milford, Massachusetts, were well provided against possible future needs. For three days the Indians feasted and appeared to deliberate. Upon the evening of the third day two of the Milford pioneers returned from a business trip to Sac City. The arrival of Parkhurst and Lebourveau seemed to arouse the Indians' suspicion. They demanded to be told from whence the settlers had come. Not having received the desired information they probably concluded they were being pursued and that night left the settlement. After the departure of the Indians, the Milford pioneers deserted the colony and sought refuge at various places—at Ashland, at Onawa, and at Smithland.

As they came to isolated cabins north of this settlement the Indians resorted to various modes of terrorising the pioneers. At the cabin of Lemuel Parkhurst they amused themselves for an hour or more by striking their tomahawks into the floor and logs of the cabin, while flourishing scalping knives about the heads of the affrighted occupants. Mrs. Parkhurst finally pacified them by preparing a meal which she set before them. Having consumed this meal, they proffered the peace pipe, shook hands, and departed.

At the cabin of James A. Brown they seemed to be seeking entertainment rather than food. After compelling Brown to mount a haystack, two Indians climbed up—one armed with a rifle, the other with a pitchfork. They amused themselves by testing the steadiness of Brown's nerve. He was alternately lunged at by the possessor of the fork and levelled at by the holder of the gun. After thus amusing themselves for ten or fifteen minutes, the Indians allowed him to get down and go to his cabin. They then went to the stable, killed an ox, and attempted to steal a horse; but the animal was so vicious that they finally gave up the attempt and left. These are but incidents illustrative of the behaviour of the Indians as they passed to the north of Cherokee and up the Little Sioux.[1]

Arriving in the northwestern corner of Buena Vista County, their conduct became, if possible, still more vicious. Wherever they appeared they were sullen, as contrasted with their tendency to talk and seek entertainment at points further down the river. Waste, violence, and cruelty now characterized their actions. At the home of a Mr. Weaver they not only wantonly shot all his hogs and cattle, but also roughly handled him and the members of his family. Satisfied with this, they moved off to the northwest.

They were next heard of at the home of H. H. Waterman in O'Brien County. The visit to the Waterman cabin, however, seems to have been from a scouting detachment rather than from the band as a whole. In Waterman's own words "Seven big strapping Sioux bucks stopped at my house; they were so tall I had to look up at them". They told him of the Smithland affair. Although they seemed much excited, Waterman paid little attention to their story for he recognised them as the same Indians that had called upon him more than once before. He did, however, become alarmed when they began stealing his property—to which he finally objected. But they took everything they could lay hands on; and ended by beating Waterman in the back and stringing him up by the thumbs. Apparently satisfied, they committed no further mischief, but departed in the direction from which they had come.[2]

After the episode at the Waterman cabin the band concentrated at the site of the present town of Peterson in southwestern Clay County, where they found white settlers—at which they were apparently much surprised. Peterson was only a short distance away from the cabins of Weaver in Buena Vista County and Waterman in O'Brien. Here it would seem they began in earnest the campaign of terror which was to end in massacre at the lakes and in the attack upon Springfield. They were no longer satisfied with thieving and pillaging;

---

1. W. S. Dunbar and Company's *Biographical History of Cherokee County, Iowa*; Fulton's *The Red Men of Iowa*.
2. Peck and Montzheimer's *Past and Present of O'Brien and Osceola Counties, Iowa*, Vol. 1.

but the torturing of people and the taking of human life now seemed to be the pronounced bent and purpose of their raid. The mere presence of white people seemed to infuriate them to frenzied acts, and the wonder is that the general massacre of the settlers did not begin at Peterson rather than at Okoboji.

As already noted there were at Peterson by February, 1857, the families of James Bicknell, Jacob Kirchner, and Ambrose S. Mead. Although the news of Indian depredations had reached these families before the coming of the Indians themselves, conditions were such that no steps could be taken to offer resistance. The Bicknell cabin, being located the furthest to the south and west, was reached first. This probability had been anticipated, for by the time the Indians arrived the inmates had fled to the shelter of the Kirchner home across the river. At the Bicknell home everything was either taken or destroyed. Early on the following morning the Indians crossed the river and appeared at the Kirchner home, where were huddled closely together for mutual protection the families of Bicknell and Jacob Kirchner. Here the Indians repeated their atrocities, leaving only the cabin and the lives of the settlers.

Although the Meads have been spoken of as a part of the Peterson settlement, they were not properly so since they were located some little distance up the course of the stream and were nearer the open prairie. It seems that they had not been warned of the coming of the Indians. Mr. Mead was absent at Cedar Falls; but before going he had arranged with a family by the name of Taylor to jointly occupy the Mead cabin with Mrs. Mead and the children. When the Indians appeared Mr. E. Taylor resisted their meddling in matters about the cabin. This enraged them and they threatened to kill him unless he desisted from objecting to their pillaging. Fearing that they might carry out the threat, Taylor managed to elude the watchfulness of the Indians and started south with a view to procuring help. Mrs. Mead meanwhile had been knocked down and otherwise abused for resisting.

The whole affair at the Mead cabin ended by the Indians attempting to carry off the women and children as prisoners. They succeeded in carrying away Hattie, the eldest of the Mead children, but when they attempted to take Emma Mead, who was about ten years of age, she resisted so strongly that they contented themselves with beating her all the way back to her cabin home and then letting her go. The Taylor child was kicked into the fireplace where he was fearfully burned; while his mother and Mrs. Mead were carried away to camp. On the following morning the prisoners were allowed to return to their home. The Indians evidently feared pursuit or did not care to be burdened with prisoners at this time.[3]

Mr. Taylor made good his escape and started across the country to the Sac City settlement for aid. After some privation, he was successful in reaching the settlement. A relief party consisting of a company of men under Enoch Ross as captain made the march up the Raccoon River to Storm Lake and across country to the Mead home on the Little Sioux. Of course the Indians were gone by this time, but the company started up the river in pursuit. It is written by someone that a member of the party when out on a reconnaissance, discovered the Indians, and at once hurried back to report his discovery. Upon reaching the main party he found an active quarrel going on among the members; and when he reported his news the company at once disbanded and hurried home. Other accounts have related that the Indians were pursued to within a few miles of Spencer, when the company was stopped by a terrific blizzard and compelled to turn back without having accomplished its purpose of punishing the Indians.[4]

While the Sac County relief party was forming and on its way across the country, the Indians had moved up the river to the little group of cabins where Sioux Rapids now stands. No damage was done at this settlement, the band seeming to be content with asking and receiving. Before the relief party arrived, the Indians had reached Gillett's Grove where again they seemed disposed to create trouble.

In the summer and fall of 1856 the Gillett brothers had settled in what was perhaps the finest body of timber along the whole course of the Little Sioux. Through this grove, dividing it nearly equally, flows the Little Sioux. Each of the two brothers had built a cabin upon his claim, one on either bank of the stream. In preparing for the winter they thought in the main only of their need of food and shelter: they troubled themselves little concerning an Indian visitation, reasoning that such an event was quite unlikely as Indians had not been seen since their arrival. Moreover, fishing in that region was poor and game was extremely scarce.

Great therefore was the surprise of the Gillett brothers when in

---

3. Gillespie and Steele's *History of Clay County, Iowa*; Mrs. Sharp's *History of the Spirit Lake Massacre*; Smith's *History of Dickinson County, Iowa*.

4. William H. Hart's *History of Sac County, Iowa*; Gillespie and Steele's *History of Clay County, Iowa*.

the late winter they learned of the arrival of an Indian party. Although the cabins were well placed for purposes of shelter, the Indians readily located them and at once paid them a visit. The red men were well received and their wants attended to by the settlers. Seeming well pleased they left with protestations of friendship. A few days later a second and different group appeared, led by the same Indian as the first. As the days passed this red man's visits became unpleasantly frequent, but thus far no offensive attitude had been assumed by the Indians. When, however, he began paying unwelcome attentions to Mrs. Gillett it was decided to put an end to his coming.

One day, after the Indian had been peculiarly annoying, Gillett followed him and at some distance from the cabin shot him. The next morning the brothers visited the spot where the Indian had fallen, and finding the body beheaded it. Having committed this outrage they became frightened and decided upon flight to save themselves from Indian vengeance. Accordingly, they hastily packed a few belongings and started across the country toward Fort Dodge. It was later learned that when the Indians discovered the body of the murdered man they destroyed as much of the Gillett property as they could lay hands upon. The influence of this murder in provoking the terrible deeds committed by the Indians a few days later when they reached the lakes can not be definitely determined.[5]

When the Gilletts fled from their homes they knew not whence they were going except that they were seeking to escape from Indian retribution. They finally decided to make an attempt to reach Fort Dodge, although they realised that this would be an exceedingly difficult task since they knew only in a general way the direction in which that station lay. In their wanderings they finally reached the little settlement at Sioux Rapids, where after some counselling it was decided to send couriers to Fort Dodge for relief. Abner Bell, E. Weaver, and one of the Wilcox brothers were chosen to make the journey.

It was near the first of March when the men from Sioux Rapids reached Fort Dodge with the intelligence of the Indian depredations along the Little Sioux. At first their story was not believed; but as other reports of Indian depredations in this region continued to come in the people of Fort Dodge came to the conclusion that there must be some truth in what they had been told by the men from Sioux Rapids. Then they became alarmed as they saw evidence of some great plan

---

5. *The Spirit Lake Massacre and Relief Expedition* in the *Roster and Record of Iowa Soldiers*, Vol. VI; Smith's *History of Dickinson County, Iowa*.

of Indian revenge against the whole of the exposed frontier. Later the story of Bell and his fellow couriers was confirmed by reports from the Gilletts themselves, from Christian Kirchner, and from Ambrose S. Mead.

An attempt was made to organise a relief party at Fort Dodge, but the effort was soon abandoned by its promoters. The distance was greater than seventy miles, the snow was deep, the cold intense, and the treeless prairies were being constantly visited by terrific storms, all of which combined to make the success of such an expedition seem like the last thing that could be expected. Doubt was strong that such a party would ever be able to reach its destination or offer succour to the settlers on the frontier even though it should be fortunate enough to reach them. It was finally decided that any attempt at relief would probably end in a needless sacrifice of human lives. In the light of future events it may be said that this decision was indeed a wise one.[6]

---

6 John F. Duncombe's *Spirit Lake Relief Expedition of 1857* in the *Proceedings of the Pioneer Lawmakers' Association of Iowa for 1898*; *Annals of Iowa* (Third Series), Vol. III.

CHAPTER 12

The First Day of the Massacre

Nothing is known of the Inkpaduta band from the time of the episode at Gillett's Grove until its appearance at the lakes on the evening of Saturday, March 7, 1857. From events that followed, it is inferred that they were in a fiendish temper at the time of their arrival and that this temper developed in intensity during their stay upon the Okoboji shores. The Indians celebrated their arrival by holding a war dance. Mrs. Sharp refers to this ceremony as a scalp dance; but such it could not have been, since with the Sioux as with other Indians such a dance is held only when scalps have been taken. It is known positively that none had been taken up to the time of their arrival at the lakes.

What must have been the feelings of the settlers when the Indians, arriving near sundown, began the celebration of the war dance of the Sioux! As the hideous painted forms of the red men in a half squat position, in short, quick jumps kept time to the weird accompaniment of the dance, lifting both feet from the ground at once, the settlers must have felt that something unusual was brewing. And when the cadence of the dance was momentarily stopped and the sharp cutting notes of the war whoop rent the frosty air one can scarcely imagine that they could have remained wholly ignorant of its purpose. And yet it is said that the settlers slept that night as they had slept before the appearance of the band; and on the ensuing morning they went quietly and calmly about the duties of their homes wondering, perhaps, when the Indians would leave.[1]

The people at the lakes had received no inkling of the events that had been transpiring to the south, for they were isolated from all other white settlements. They had come to this region so late and under such circumstances that none of the settlers to the south knew they

[1]. Pond's *The Dakotas or Sioux in Minnesota as They Were in 1834* in the *Collections of the Minnesota Historical Society*, Vol. XII.

were there. Then, too, the character of the season and the difficulties of transportation were such that no one would think of making a journey in that direction. To the people who had settled along the Little Sioux relief lay in the direction from which they had come—which was also the direction of their source of supplies. Thus it happened that no warning of impending danger from Indian attacks was given to these advanced settlements. Having no information concerning the conduct of red men in the valley to the south, the settlers at the lakes did not anticipate any unfriendly acts upon the part of the Indians who were now in their midst.

The Indians selected as a site for their camp a spot directly across the trail which led from the Gardner cabin to the Mattock cabin and from thence became the highway of communication between all of the cabins of the settlement. Thus its location was strategic in an attack upon the settlers. For purposes of conducting their war dance it was necessary that the *tepees* should be so pitched as to surround a hollow square. It was directly across this square that the trail ran. Thus the Gardners were cut off from the remainder of the settlement. That there was design in so placing the camp can not positively be asserted; but its location did have the effect of isolating the Gardners.

The day before the arrival of the Indians, Luce and his three companions had come in from Shippey's, where Thatcher and Burtch had been left with the exhausted oxen. The evening of their arrival had witnessed a slight moderation in the temperature which was still felt on the morning of the seventh. Everyone had begun to feel that possibly spring might not be far distant.

During the absence of Luce and Thatcher it had been decided by the people of the settlement that Gardner should undertake a trip to Fort Dodge upon their return. Wants had arisen during their absence which it was believed could be satisfied by going to Fort Dodge as the nearest outpost for supplies. It was also deemed desirable to make the trip before the breaking of winter should render the roads impassable. Thus, when Luce and Thatcher returned with the news that relief was near, Gardner at once began preparations to start upon his trip two days later or on the morning of Sunday, March eighth. The purpose of the trip was not only to secure food, but also to purchase implements which would be needed in the spring's agricultural activities.[2]

---

2. *The Spirit Lake Massacre and Relief Expedition* in the *Roster and Record of Iowa Soldiers*, Vol. VI, Mrs. Sharp's *Spirit Lake Massacre*; Smith's *History of Dickinson County, Iowa*.

The morning of March eighth dawned cold but clear and bright, forecasting for Gardner the likelihood of a pleasant first day's journey. Having learned from the accounts of Luce something of the condition of the prairie, Gardner arose early in order that as much as possible of his journey might be accomplished during the first day. Not only did Gardner himself arise early, but every member of his family did likewise in order that each might contribute something toward speeding him upon his journey.

Breakfast having been prepared and placed upon the table by Mrs. Gardner and her daughter Mrs. Luce, the members of the family were gathering about the table when the latch of the door was lifted and a tall Indian stepped within the cabin with protestations of hunger and friendship. Mrs. Gardner at once prepared an additional place at the table which the Indian was invited to occupy. The Indian accepted this hospitality and seated himself with the family; and all were soon engaged in partaking of the morning's meal.

It soon developed that this Indian visitor was but a forerunner of more who were to follow. Before the meal had been finished the door was again opened and fourteen Indian warriors, besides women and children, crowded into the cabin. All demanded food, the while protesting friendship as the first comer had done. The Gardners at once set about the satisfaction of this demand as far as possible from their limited store. At first the Indians seemed concerned solely with the gratification of their appetites. But when their hunger had been appeased a member of the party suddenly became insolent. Then others in a sullen overbearing manner demanded various things other than food.

The Indian who had been the first to enter the cabin now demanded that he be given ammunition. Another demanded gun-caps; and yet another asked for powder. Mr. Gardner, willing to appease the Indians if possible and rid himself and family of the intruders, secured his box of gun-caps and prepared to distribute them to all. This did not prove to be satisfactory to one of the number who snatched the box from his hand, appropriating all the caps for himself. Upon the wall hung the powder-horn which another buck attempted to secure, but was prevented from doing so by Mr. Luce who at this moment interfered. This interference angered the Indian who drew up and levelled his gun as if intending to shoot. But Luce was too alert for the Indian and struck the weapon from his hand. The Indians did not seem inclined to carry matters further and withdrew from the cabin—but in a very bad frame of mind.[3]

As they were slowly and sullenly withdrawing from the Gardner cabin, Bertell E. Snyder and Dr. Harriott, from the cabin across the strait, appeared with letters which they wished to send with Gardner to Fort Dodge. They had been unaware of the presence of the Indian camp until they had come to it that morning. Gardner expressed his fears of future trouble to these men who only ridiculed the thought, refusing to believe that there was any possibility of danger. Nevertheless, Gardner advised that a warning be sent to the settlers urging them to concentrate at the Gardner cabin should trouble arise. To Harriott and Snyder this did not seem necessary: they left for home, protesting that there was no occasion for uneasiness. Gardner, however, told them that under the conditions then developing he did not plan to go to Fort Dodge.

In the meantime the Indians had not returned to their camp, but were seen to be prowling about in the vicinity of the Gardner cabin. On their way home Harriott and Snyder met and did some trading with a group of the red men by whom they had been intercepted. So sure were the two men that the Indians were friendly that they did not consider the fact of their presence worth mentioning as they passed the Mattock cabin. As a further indication of their confidence in the friendly character of the red men, it is noted that in a letter written by Dr. Harriott, presumably after his return from the Gardner cabin, he states that Indians had camped nearby but they were very friendly and had occasioned no uneasiness among the settlers.

At the same time the fears of the Gardners were increased by the sight of Indians in the nearby timber and by occasional calls at the cabin where new demands were made, many of which could not be met. Although the Indians seemed to maintain a certain gravity of demeanour and apparently were only seeking to gratify their physical wants, Gardner remained firm in his conviction that trouble was brewing and that the remaining settlers should be warned of the impending danger. After much counselling it was decided that Luce and Clark should go at once by a roundabout path along the lake shore to warn the other settlers and to advise that they gather in the Mattock cabin as the one best adapted for defence.

Luce and Clark set out upon their mission about two o'clock in

---

3. Concerning the events at the Gardner cabin we must, of necessity, rely upon the statements of Mrs. Abbie Gardner Sharp who remained the only living witness of the scene. See Mrs. Sharp's *History of the Spirit Lake Massacre.*

the afternoon. They were to make their way first of all to the Mattock cabin, since it was nearer the Indian camp. Plans decided upon by Gardner, Luce, and Clark were also to be told to the Mattock people so that they might have ample opportunity to prepare for the proposed concentration of the settlers. After this they were to go as far and as rapidly as possible on their work of warning the settlers on the east lake before nightfall would of necessity end their mission.[4]

The fears of the people at the Gardner cabin had been considerably increased by the attitude of the Indians when they took their leave shortly after noon. During the whole of the forenoon they had done no damage to property, and their only overt act had been their behaviour within the cabin in the early morning. But they seem now to have suffered a change of mind, for as they moved away toward their camp they drove before them the Gardner-Luce cattle—about six in number—shooting them as they proceeded. Apparently there was no motive in doing this—unless, perhaps, it was the fiendish satisfaction in the taking of life. They did not seem to want the cattle as food, since they left them untouched.

About mid-afternoon a number of shots were heard in the direction of the Mattock cabin. As the afternoon wore away there came no evidence as to the meaning of the firing. The suspense became fearful as all manner of suggestions were offered in explanation of the shooting. Gardner reasoned that it could not have concerned Luce and Clark since they had had plenty of time to be further on their journey than the cabin of Mattock. Mrs. Luce became frantic, for she had believed from the first that her husband would never return. If the Indians should kill anyone it would surely be Luce on account of his foiling the savages in their purpose in the morning; and in this intuition she was right. Luce and Clark had not gone far on their mission when they were intercepted and shot by the Indians. This fact, however, did not develop until weeks later when their dead bodies were found along the lake shore not a great distance from Luce's home. Thus no warning of peril reached the Mattock family.

For two hours time dragged on slowly and fearfully at the Gardner home: all eyes watched either for Indians or for the return of the messengers. Neither came. When the sun had sunk to the horizon Gardner stepped outside to look about. Suddenly he came running

---

4. Smith's *History of Dickinson County, Iowa*; Carpenter's *The Spirit Lake Massacre* in the *Midland Monthly*, Vol. IV; Gue's *History of Iowa*, Vol. I; Mrs. Sharp's *History of the Spirit Lake Massacre*.

back calling that the Indians were coming. Upon entering the cabin he began barring the door, determined after the experience of the morning not to allow the red men to enter. Mrs. Gardner objected that they should have faith in the good intentions of the Indians and that it was better for one not to shed the blood of another. Yielding to her importunities, Gardner desisted from barricading the door. The family now awaited in terror the second coming of the Indians.

Looking through the windows they observed nine warriors hurrying toward them from the direction of the camp. With no more formality than during their morning visit they again entered the cabin. One glance sufficed to tell the frightened family that the anticipated trouble was upon them. The first demand of the Indians was for flour—not only for a part of what the Gardners had but for all. The scarcity of flour had been one of the reasons for the planned trip to Fort Dodge; and yet, at the risk of causing his family to suffer privation, Gardner turned to the flour barrel to gratify the demands of the Indians. As he turned a buck raised his gun to shoot. It seems that either Mrs. Gardner or Mrs. Luce made a move to stay the act of the Indian, but failed. Gardner fell to the floor, the third victim of the Indian massacre at Okoboji. Having made a beginning, the Indians no longer restrained the impulses of their savage nature. After the killing of Gardner their stay at Okoboji became a carnival of murder.

As soon as Gardner fell, the quest for flour was lost sight of and the Indians turned upon the two women who had attempted to protect the object of their rage. Mrs. Luce and Mrs. Gardner were seized and held by several Indians while others beat them into insensibility and death with the butts of their guns. This was but the work of a moment. Indeed, so quickly had it been done that Abbie Gardner did not see the act herself; in her later relations of the affair she relied wholly upon stories related to her frequently by the Indians in their flight following the massacre. Without pause Mr. and Mrs. Gardner and Mrs. Luce were scalped—an act of savagery which the children were compelled to witness. When the Indians entered the cabin, Abbie was striving to quiet the younger child of her sister, while the other Luce child clung to one side of her chair and at the other side crouched Abbie's brother, Rowland Gardner, Jr.

Having destroyed the parents, the Indians now turned to the destruction of the children. Rowland Gardner and the two Luce children were torn away from Abbie and beaten to death against the posts of the door and the trunks of trees in the yard. Dropping the dead bodies upon the ground, the Indians appeared to counsel concerning the further disposition of the house and its only living inmate. At the close of their deliberation Abbie was seized by one of the Indians and, much to her surprise, was not killed but led away in the direction of the Indian camp. Her last sight of her family showed them strewn lifeless and bleeding about the doorstep of her home.[5]

Before the Gardner cabin was deserted by the Indians it was completely ransacked. Chests were broken open and their contents scattered about the house and yard. All available food stores and clothing were carried away to the camp. Abbie had abundant opportunity to learn this when later about their evening camp fires bucks and squaws alike, arrayed in the clothing of the murdered people, wildly recounted the incidents of the day. Although she had been carried away from her home without any provision for clothing against the winter's cold, she was not allowed to share in the wearing of the stolen goods. Shivering from cold and fright, she witnessed the fiendish joy with which the events of that memorable day were told and retold by the Indians.

As the evening wore on preparations for the scalp dance began. Soon the rhythmic cadence of the hideous dance song started, and the scalps of the day, elevated on the ends of long poles, could be seen swaying back and forth marking time with the movements of the women who bore them. At every shriek of the dancing women, the captive girl doubtless thought her time had come. In the darkness, lighted occasionally by the flaring of a firebrand, the distorted and hideously painted faces of the savages swinging alternately backward and forward in the dance must have seemed to the prisoner a veritable dance of demons. The dance lasted far into the night, with no sleep for the child who was momentarily expecting to fall a victim of savage fury. Toward morning the dance ended and the savages sought a brief respite in sleep to strengthen them for the work of the succeeding day. At the breaking of the early dawn the Indians were again astir, making preparations for a continuation of their bloody work.[6]

While the inmates of the Gardner cabin were being massacred similar events were transpiring at the home of the Mattocks. What actually happened at this cabin is not known, since no living witnesses,

---

5. Richman's *The Tragedy at Minnewaukon* in *John Brown among the Quakers*; Mrs. Sharp's *History of the Spirit Lake Massacre*; Carpenter's *The Spirit Lake Massacre* in the *Midland Monthly*, Vol. IV.
6. Pond's *The Dakotas or Sioux in Minnesota as They were in 1834* in the *Collections of the Minnesota Historical Society*, Vol. XII.

other than red men, survived to tell the tale. From the position of the bodies when found, it is inferred that the Mattocks must have sensed the situation; but thinking that their own home was lacking in security had started for the cabin of Harriott, Snyder, and Granger across the strait. Mrs. Sharp states that when the Indians brought her to their camp, which had been moved during the day and pitched near the Mattock home, the cabin was in flames and shrieks of human beings were issuing from it.[7] But this could hardly have been true unless there were persons staying at the Mattock cabin unknown to others in the settlement, since all the people were later accounted for in the bodies found.

Snyder, Harriott, and Harshman apparently discovered what was happening across the strait, and with rifles in hand came to the rescue. This is inferred from the fact that their bodies were found in company with those of the Mattocks. Resistance had evidently been made by the men: it is not unlikely that they were attempting to cover the retreat of Mrs. Mattock and her children, since they were in advance, while Mattock, Snyder, Madison, Harshman, and Harriott were in the rear with the gun in each case lying by the side of the dead owner. Harriott's gun had its stock broken as if it had been used for a club after other means of defence had been exhausted. Further evidence that resistance was offered to the Indians is to be found in the fact that one young Indian was badly injured, possibly by Dr. Harriott. No one, however, was spared in the attack by the Indians at that point: the dead bodies of eleven persons were found on the path between the two cabins. These were later identified as Mr. and Mrs. Mattock, their five children, Dr. Harriott, Bertell Snyder, Robert Madison, and Joseph Harshman.[8] To make the destruction more complete, fire was set to the Mattock cabin which was soon in ruins.

It is said that, leaving the Gardner cabin shortly after noon, the Indians had gone to Mattock's cabin where they wished to get some hay with which to feed their ponies. While they were in the act of taking the hay objection was raised. A *parley* over the matter seems to have been carried on for some time before the Indians arrived at the killing point. Mattock sent to the Red Wing cabin for help, and Harriott, Snyder, and Harshman responded. Meanwhile the Indians appeared to withdraw, and it was probably decided by Mattock, as a measure

---

7. Mrs. Sharp's *History of the Spirit Lake Massacre*.
8. See Mrs. Sharp's *History of the Spirit Lake Massacre*, where the statement is made that five men, two women, and four children were killed at the Mattock cabin.

of added safety, to take the members of his family to the Red Wing cabin. They were in the act of doing so, Mrs. Mattock and the children ahead and the men in the rear guarding the retreat, when they were fired upon by the Indians from ambush. All were killed outright except Harriott, who resisted and before being disposed of had badly wounded at least one Indian.[9] In their relation of the event the Indians spoke of all having left the cabin before it was destroyed by fire.

Across the strait at the Red Wing or Granger cabin, Carl Granger, who for some reason remained at his cabin when the others crossed to the Mattock home, was brutally slain and scalped. The Indians killed him by splitting his head open with an axe which had evidently been taken from the wood pile near by.[10]

Thus the close of the first day of the massacre witnessed a toll of twenty lives. Three groups of settlers had been wholly wiped out—with the exception of one child who was carried away into captivity.

---

9. Hughes's *Causes and Results of the Inkpaduta Massacre* in the *Collections of the Minnesota Historical Society*, Vol. XII. But there is a third view as to the outcome of the conflict at the Mattock cabin. This version is sponsored by Major William Williams who was a member of the relief expedition sent from Fort Dodge. Major Williams believed that the Indians purposely concealed their losses. In his report to Governor Grimes, made upon his return to Fort Dodge under date of April 12th, he stated that "the number of Indians killed or wounded must be from fifteen to twenty."— (Gue's *History of Iowa*, Vol. I.) This estimate would seem to be entirely too high. Only under exceptionally favourable conditions would it have been possible for five men, suffering every possible handicap, to have killed or wounded so many concealed enemies. Again, there were in all probability not more than fifteen or twenty warriors in the party of the red men. The loss or crippling of such a number would have meant practical annihilation. Later when the party was encountered in its flight from the scene of the massacre, various individuals who had the opportunity of recognising the individual members of the band reported them to be the same in membership as at the beginning of the raid at Smithland. Thus the statement of Major Williams could not have been accurate. Mrs. Sharp speaks of only one Indian as being injured and of no deaths—which is more probable.

10. Mrs. Sharp's *History of the Spirit Lake Massacre*.

CHAPTER 13

The Second Day of the Massacre

Although the scalp dance had continued far into the small hours of the previous night, the Indians were astir early on the morning of the ninth of March. They were determined upon completing the fiendish work which they had so well begun on the previous day. No council was held so far as the only white inmate of their *tepees* could discern. At the same time every Indian seemed to know where to go and what was to be done. There was no confusion of plans or hitch in their execution at any point.

It was on the morning of March ninth that a portion of the Inkpaduta band started for the Howe and Thatcher cabins which were nearly three miles from the Indian encampment. As already noted, the settlers about the lakes had established a sort of mutual exchange system among themselves for the purpose of husbanding their food supplies during the absence of Luce and Thatcher on the expedition to Waterloo and other points in eastern Iowa. This morning Mrs. Howe discovered that the supply of meal was so nearly exhausted that it would be necessary to procure an additional supply from one of the neighbours. Thus it was that on this Monday morning Howe started on what proved to be a fateful trip to the home of either Gardner or Mattock. With his sack thrown over his shoulder he took the path along the south shore of the east lake. He was wholly ignorant of the recent arrival of the Indians.

As Howe walked briskly along he may have been revolving in his mind possible plans for his work in the coming season; or he may have been speculating as to when his neighbour Thatcher would return from the trip back east. Possibly he was cherishing the hope that the privations of the winter might have ample compensation in an abundant harvest. Whatever his thoughts may have been as he walked along the lake, they were soon brought to an end by the Indians, who in all probability quickly disposed of their victim. The details of the murder are not known; but the badly mutilated body was later found and given burial by the Fort Dodge relief party.

After murdering Howe the Indians stealthily hastened on to his cabin. Here the wife and children were as unprepared for the Indians as was the husband and father. Mrs. Howe was no doubt busy in the performance of her Monday morning duties. Engrossed with these activities she, in all likelihood, did not discover the approach of the red men until they were upon her. After killing Mrs. Howe the Indians proceeded to dispatch the remaining members of the family—a grown son and daughter, and three younger children. It seemed obvious to the members of the relief party, from the conditions which they found at the Howe cabin, that there had been no resistance offered to the Indians. No scalping was done here or at any other place after the red men had left the Mattock cabin. Nor did the savages stop to plunder or destroy after taking the lives of this family, but hurried on to the next stage in their work—which consisted of dealing death to the members of the Noble and Thatcher families.

Arriving at the cabin of Noble and Thatcher the Indians secured admission by professing friendship. Here they made demands which could not be granted; and then, as at the Gardner home, they resorted to insult. Their insolence was resisted by Noble and one Ryan—a son-in-law of Howe who had but lately come from Hampton and was staying with the Nobles. This was evidently what the Indians desired, for without further provocation they shot both Ryan and Noble. The former was killed instantly; but Noble was able to walk to the door, where he fell dead after exclaiming "Oh, I am killed!" The two children were then torn from their mothers and dragged by the feet out of the house where they were dashed to death against the oak trees of the door yard. This seems to have satisfied the Indians' desire for human blood, for they desisted from killing Mrs. Noble and Mrs. Thatcher. For some time the Indians busied themselves in destroying hogs and cattle and in chasing the poultry. Finally, they returned to the cabin where they ransacked its contents, destroying what they did not happen to want. In the end Mrs. Noble and Mrs. Thatcher were seized and led away as prisoners.

Obviously the horrible work at the Howe cabin had not been completed to the satisfaction of the Indians, since upon their return trip they stopped and resumed the destruction of what life was still in evidence. Here a fearful sight met the eyes of the two captive women. Scattered about the door yard they saw the mutilated bodies of the members of the Howe family; while Mrs. Noble found the dead body of her mother under a bed where she had evidently crawled for the purpose of shielding herself from further attacks after she had been terribly beaten with a flat-iron. In the yard Mrs. Noble found her thirteen year old brother Jacob, sitting propped up against a tree. He had been horribly beaten and evidently left for dead; but having managed to crawl to a tree he had raised himself to a sitting posture. Although conscious, he was unable to speak. Mrs. Noble urged him to make his way into the house and conceal himself in the clothing of a bed and there await rescue. The boy made the effort, but was discovered by the Indians and killed.[1]

Having completed their destructive work at the Howe cabin, the Indians hastened to their own camp. When Mrs. Noble and Mrs. Thatcher were brought into the camp, Abbie Gardner was permitted to visit them in the *tepee* set aside for the latest captives. For about an hour the three captives were permitted to talk over their experiences, after which they were separated. Thenceforth each captive was required to remain in a *tepee* wholly separated and isolated from the others.

The captives were now subjected to training through which the Indians evidently hoped to remake them into real pale-faced squaws. From the beginning they were required to paint their faces and dress their hair as Indians. They were frequently subjected to torturing ordeals which seemed to have no purpose other than that of noting what the reaction would be. At times they were, as far as the captives could discern, made ready for death so that the red men might see how they would behave under such trying conditions. Guns and revolvers would be loaded and with drawn triggers pointed at them as with intent to shoot, but no shooting occurred. These feints at shooting furnished the Indians a great deal of what appeared to be real

---

1. *The Spirit Lake Massacre and Relief Expedition* in the *Roster and Record of Iowa Soldiers*, Vol. VI; Mrs. Sharp's *History of the Spirit Lake Massacre*; Smith's *History of Dickinson County, Iowa*; Gue's *History of Iowa*, Vol. I. Mrs. Noble and Mrs. Thatcher in later relations of the massacre spoke of their children as having been killed at their own cabin. If such were the facts then their dead bodies must have been carried to the Howe home; for there they were found by the members of the rescue party rather than at the place of death. This fact has led to the statement that five small Howe children were killed in addition to Sardis and Jonathan. There were, however, only three smaller children in the Howe family—Alfred, Jacob, and Philetus.

amusement. For days they would recite again and again the details of the massacre at the lakes. But this treatment was only a foretaste of what was in store for the captives. For weeks, until they were released by death or ransom, they were to be subjected to nearly every annoyance that the ingenuity of the Indians might invent.[2]

---

2. Mrs. Sharp's *History of the Spirit Lake Massacre*; Neill's *History of Minnesota*.

CHAPTER 14

From Okoboji to Heron Lake

Following the massacre little was done by the Indians except to search the vicinity of the lakes for the homes of other settlers. And so for a brief time scouting parties were at work; but obviously no other cabins were found, since the parties returned empty-handed. On the morning of Tuesday, March tenth, the camp was broken, West Okoboji was crossed on the ice, and after a move of three miles to the northwest, camp was again pitched in what was known as the Madison Grove. The Indians seemed inclined to move very deliberately. This may be accounted for by the fact that they knew they were not pursued. At the Madison Grove they remained but one night, and at early dawn of the eleventh they moved north to a grove beyond the cabin of William Marble on the southwest shore of Spirit Lake.

From Gillett's Grove the journey for the Indians had become easier inasmuch as they had procured horses and sleds. These must have been obtained by scouting parties while the main body was encamped at Lost Island Lake. Since the Indians had not learned how to hitch the horses to the sleds Abbie Gardner, Mrs. Noble, and Mrs. Thatcher now undertook the task of teaching them how to handle horses and sleds with the thought that travelling might be made easier. In this they were mistaken; for no sooner had the red men learned their lessons than the bucks took to riding while the squaws and captives were required to walk and carry the heavy packs for the whole party. The horses and sleds were for pleasure and not for the transportation of freight and workers.

So deliberate were the movements of the band that although the camp was broken up early in the morning of Wednesday, the eleventh, it was not pitched at the new place, which was only a few miles to the north of Marble's cabin, until late in the afternoon of the same day. As the Indians proceeded they made numerous side trips, partly for scouting purposes and partly for the pursuit of game. Frequently the squaws and captives found it necessary to pause in their march in order that the bucks might make these side excursions. Under more favourable conditions this would have been most welcome as a relief from fatigue, but now each stop was anticipated as a period of intense suffering from cold and exposure.

As the sun approached the western horizon the Indians began to exert themselves in quest of a suitable camping place for the night. After no little inspection of their surroundings, they decided to camp north of the Marble grove. In reaching this spot they had so circled the Marble cabin that they were not seen by the Marbles; nor had the captives seen the cabin of their white neighbours. Although the captives could discern that a council was held that evening, they had no means of ascertaining its purpose.

Thursday, March twelfth, was a day of inactivity in the camp: the Indians spent the time in gorging themselves upon what food remained from their raids upon the larders and barnyards of the unfortunate white settlers. Nor is the statement fully substantiated that on Thursday a friendly Indian visited the Marbles and informed them that the settlers to the south had all been killed a day or two previously. Even though the suspicion of the Marbles had possibly been aroused, the depth of the snow would have made it difficult if not impossible for them to get out and attempt a verification of the Indian's statement. Moreover, it does not appear that the Marbles took precautions against possible surprise.[1]

Upon the morning of Friday, the thirteenth, the Indians are said to have arisen early and with great care removed from their faces the paint which until now had indicated that they were on the warpath and which would have served as a warning to the Marbles whom they were now planning to visit.[2] Approaching the cabin they signalled protestations of friendship. Upon being invited to enter they set their guns down just without the door. This little procedure attracted the attention of Mrs. Marble, who had never before seen an Indian leave his gun outside the cabin. The Marbles had just risen from the breakfast table when the Indians were seen to emerge from the timber and approach the house. Having entered the cabin the guests asked for food—a request which Mrs. Marble at once set about to gratify. While

---

1. Mrs. Sharp's *History of the Spirit Lake Massacre*.
2. Agnes C. Laut's *Heroines of Spirit Lake* in *Outing Magazine*, Vol. LI.

she was doing so the Indians, noting Marble's gun, bantered him for a trade. Marble accepted the banter, and soon a deal was completed for one of the Indian guns. The outcome of the trade seemed to be a matter of no little elation for the Indians who hilariously turned to the food which had been placed before them.

After eating, the Indian with whom the trade had been made proposed that the relative worth of the guns should be determined by their actual use and indicated a desire for target practice. Although Mrs. Marble protested the advisability of such a contest her husband agreed to the proposal. When a suitable wooden slab had been secured and set up the practice shooting was begun. All went well, the Indians appearing to enjoy the sport immensely, until the impact of the shots caused the target to fall. The Indians indicated to Marble that he should replace the slab. Laying down his gun, Marble stepped out from the group. This guileless act on the part of Marble gave the Indians their opportunity for treachery. When the white men had gone but a short distance the Indians, as if by preconcerted action, raised their guns, took aim at Marble, and fired. Marble instantly fell dead.

Meanwhile, Mrs. Marble had been standing at the window watching the target work. When she saw her husband lay down his gun and start to replace the mark she divined that treachery would follow. And so she left the window and started forward to warn her husband when the volley was fired into his back. Fleeing from the cabin, Mrs. Marble started for the timber; but she was soon overtaken and dragged back to the scene of her husband's death and by signs told that she was to be held as a captive. Following the shooting the cabin was pillaged and Marble was stripped of a leather belt containing a thousand dollars in gold which he had planned to use in improving his claim at the earliest opportunity.[3]

With Mrs. Marble the Indians quickly returned to camp. Again, as after the taking of Mrs. Noble and Mrs. Thatcher, the captives, now four in number, were permitted to meet in the same *tepee*, while the Indians busied themselves in the adjustment of other matters. The meeting was brief and once again the captives were completely isolated from each other. That evening the events of the day were cel-

---

3. Gue in his *History of Iowa*, Vol. I, says that Marble fired first at the target, and when he went out to see what had been the result of his shot the Indians fired on him; while Carpenter in his article on *The Spirit Lake Massacre* in the *Midland Monthly*, Vol. IV, states that when Marble's gun became empty and he was defenceless he was shot.

ebrated by a dance.

The massacre of Marble was the last act in the Indian attacks upon the white settlements at the lakes. Only four individuals had survived to tell the story of the frightful deeds committed since the morning of Sunday, March eighth. Of the four, only two were destined to return to the homes of friends or relatives and relate their tales of suffering and Indian cruelties.

When the work of destruction of the settlements along the shores of East Okoboji, West Okoboji, and Spirit Lake was completed with the shooting of Marble, the total number of human lives taken reached thirty-two. The list comprised the following persons: Robert Clark, Rowland Gardner, Francis M. Gardner, Rowland Gardner, Jr., Carl Granger, Joseph Harshman, Isaac H. Harriott, Joel Howe, Millie Howe, Jonathan Howe, Sardis Howe, Alfred Howe, Jacob Howe, Philetus Howe, Harvey Luce, Mary M. Luce, Albert Luce, Amanda Luce, William Marble, James H. Mattock, Mary M. Mattock, Alice Mattock, Daniel Mattock, Agnes Mattock, Jacob M. Mattock, Jackson A. Mattock, Robert Madison, Alvin Noble, John Noble, Enoch Ryan, Bertell E. Snyder, and Dora Thatcher.[4]

The tale is told that, before leaving the region of the lakes, the Indians left a record of their deeds. They are reputed to have stripped the bark from the trunk of a large tree in the Marble grove and upon the white surface recorded in black paint a detailed description of their exploits. The number of cabins they had visited was shown as six, while the largest, presumably the Mattock cabin, was represented as in flames. The number of persons whose lives had paid the forfeit of their visit was also to be seen—each individual being so drawn as to show the position in which he had been left by his murderers. An attempt was even made to distinguish white men from red men—the white people being shown as pierced by arrows. This pictographic reproduction of the massacre is said to have remained clearly visible for many years after the massacre and was frequently visited by interested or curious persons who came to the region.[5] (See note following)

---

4. This is the list as it appears on the east tablet of the State Memorial near the Gardner cabin with the exception of the omission of the names of those not killed at the lakes but who were massacred in the vicinity of Springfield, Minnesota.—*The Spirit Lake Massacre and Relief Expedition* in the *Roster and Record of Iowa Soldiers*, Vol. VI.

5. Mrs. Sharp's *History of the Spirit Lake Massacre*; *The Spirit Lake Massacre and Relief Expedition* in the *Roster and Record of Iowa Soldiers*, Vol. VI.

Note:—R. A. Smith, in his *History of Dickinson County*, appears sceptical concerning the real character or meaning of this attempt at Indian pictographic writing, and in commenting upon it notes that "many of the writers who have mentioned this incident have made more of it than the facts would warrant. The three or four published accounts which have been given to the public agree in stating that the picture record gave the position and number of victims correctly, and also represented those killed as being pierced with arrows. Now this is mainly fiction. The first discovery of the tree on which the hieroglyphics were delineated was by a party consisting of O. C. Howe, R. U. Wheelock and the writer sometime in May. . . . It was a white ash tree standing a little way to the southeast of the door of the Marble cabin. . . . The rough outside bark had been hewed off for a distance of some twelve or fifteen inches up and down the tree. Upon the smoothed surface thus made were the representations. The number of cabins (six) was correctly given, the largest of which was represented as being in flames. There were also representations of human figures and with the help of the imagination it was possible to distinguish which were meant for the whites and which the Indians. There were not over ten or a dozen all told, and except for the hint contained in the cabins, the largest one being in flames, we could not have figured any meaning out of it. This talk of the victims being pierced with arrows and their number and position given, is all nonsense. Mr. Howe and the writer spent some time studying it, and, while they came to the conclusion that it would convey a definite meaning to those understanding it, they could not make much out of it."

Upon leaving the Marble grove, Inkpaduta and his band moved leisurely in a northwestward direction. From the time of their departure from this point, the lot of the captives grew steadily more difficult to bear. The snows of winter melted under the influence of the spring sun on occasional days and caused the prairie trails to become two or three feet deep in slush, except on the exposed knolls which the winds had swept free from snow. In such places an opportunity was afforded the burden bearers to stand on reasonably solid footing. Not infrequently they would be compelled to flounder through gullies and ravines ten or twelve feet deep in soft, yielding snow; while an occasional stream must be waded waist deep in icily cold water. This made the plight of the unfortunate white women doubly hard.

Mrs. Thatcher, who had not been in good health at the beginning of her captivity, found the bearing of the burdens imposed upon her and the long, wearisome marches under such conditions nearly unendurable, but she sustained her strength with the hope that relief would come in time. The sublimity of her faith in rescue was of great inspiration to her companion sufferers who otherwise would soon have lost all hope. But, despite their faith and hope, the captives daily noted that their journey was leading them steadily farther away from the bounds of civilization. No stop longer than over night was made by the Indians at any point in their march for nearly two weeks, when they arrived at Heron Lake, Minnesota, about thirty miles northwest of Spirit Lake and seventeen miles in the same direction from Springfield, Minnesota.

The encampments of the Indians from the time of leaving Spirit Lake had been of the most temporary character, but upon reaching Heron Lake preparations were made for a camp of many days duration. After completing the camp, Inkpaduta's band at once prepared for a raid upon the white settlements in the vicinity. The warrior members of the band bedaubed their faces with paint, while the squaws hastened their departure by putting the weapons in condition and aiding in various minor ways. When all preparations had been completed, each warrior "with rifle in hand and scalping knife in belt" sallied forth to the taking of more human lives. The squaws and papooses were left at the camp to guard the captives, and upon the departure of the war party the women took every possible means of acquainting the captives with the fact that the expedition was one against the whites. It soon developed, from the direction taken by the party, that Springfield was their objective point.[6]

The food which the Indians had taken from the cabins of the massacred settlers was now nearly exhausted. Hence, upon the departure of the warriors there was rejoicing among the squaws who saw in the expedition the possibility of more feasting. But what of the feelings of the captives? Who can picture the condition of the mind of Abbie Gardner when she realised that the Indians were bound for Springfield? There in the home of Dr. Strong was her sister, Eliza, who

---

6. Mrs. Sharp's *History of the Spirit Lake Massacre*; Hamilton Freeman, July 13, 1857; *The Spirit Lake Massacre and Relief Expedition* in the *Roster and Record of Iowa Soldiers*, Vol. VI.

except for herself, was the only surviving member of the family that had come into the West. In all probability Eliza was doomed to the same fate as Abbie had seen meted out to her father, mother, relatives, and friends. The possibility was too horrible for contemplation. The mental anguish of the young girl became almost more than could be endured; but the hope of some saving miracle working for the life of her sister sustained her for the days of waiting that were to elapse before the return of the war party.

CHAPTER 15

News of the Massacre Reaches Springfield and Fort Ridgely

Morris Markham, who had followed the Okoboji settlers to the lake region, spent the winter in trapping along the lakes and in the marshes of the Upper Des Moines. He had brought with him a yoke of oxen which, during the early days of the winter, had strayed away and were thought to be somewhere in the valley of the Des Moines. But they could not be located; and finally the effort to trace them was abandoned. No information concerning their whereabouts had been received until the sixth of March, when Luce brought word that the oxen were to be found at Big Island Grove in Emmet County. On the following morning Markham left for Big Island Grove where he discovered and identified his property. After spending a few hours in visiting the settlers he started upon the return trip to the cabin of Noble and Thatcher. Owing to the state of the weather and the conditions of travel, he did not attempt to bring the oxen back at this time, but returned alone and on foot.

Owing to his imperfect knowledge of the country and to the darkness that had settled down before he had come within known territory, Markham missed the cabin he was seeking and found himself instead at the Gardner home. As he approached the cabin he was surprised to find it deserted. No light could be seen nor was any sound to be heard. Looking more closely he saw the mutilated bodies of the Gardners scattered about the yard; and upon entering the open door of the cabin he beheld the badly pillaged condition of the once happy home.

It was nearly eleven o'clock on the Monday night following the attack upon the Gardners when Markham reached the scene of desolation and horror. Since he had been walking from early morning and had travelled more than thirty miles he felt the need of rest and food, and so without delay set out for the Mattock cabin. He had not gone far when he was startled by the barking of a dog in the low brush just ahead. Stopping and peering through the shrubs he saw directly across his path the camp in which the Indians were then sitting in solemn council over the events of the day. The barking of the dog for some unexplainable reason passed wholly unheeded by the Indians who continued in consultation over their fiendish deeds. Markham slipped by them and hastened as rapidly as he could across the ice of the east lake to the place he called home.

Upon his arrival at the Howe cabin the same scene of violence, confusion, and desolation greeted him. Sickened at the horrible sight, cold, hungry, and exhausted he pushed on to the home of Noble and Thatcher, hoping that there all would be well. Instead, he found only an empty cabin and murdered friends. Afraid to pass the remainder of the night in a cabin which had been so fearfully visited, he dragged himself to a nearby timbered ravine where he remained until dawn. Fearful that if he lay down he would fall asleep and freeze to death—for the night was bitterly cold—he kept moving through a limited section of the ravine.[1]

With the coming of daylight Markham set out for the nearest settlement, which was Granger's Point on the Des Moines River. With feet already badly bruised and frozen he journeyed on to spread the tidings of what he had discovered. Famished and half frozen, he struggled for eighteen miles through obstacles that would have deterred all but the most heroic. Completely exhausted from continuous exposure for thirty-six hours, he finally reached the home of George Granger, where he related the story of what he had seen.

Two trappers who happened to be staying temporarily at the Granger home started at once down the Des Moines Valley for Fort Dodge. Upon arriving at Fort Dodge they told the tale of the terrible massacre at the lakes, but their story was so confusing and incoherent that they were not believed. Those who had authority refused to act upon this recital of events; and thus it came about that the first warning of trouble along the frontier went unheeded.[2]

---

1. Carpenter's *The Spirit Lake Massacre* in the *Midland Monthly*, Vol. IV; Mrs. Sharp's *History of the Spirit Lake Massacre*; *The Spirit Lake Massacre and Relief Expedition* in the *Roster and Record of Iowa Soldiers*, Vol. VI; Smith's *History of Dickinson County, Iowa*.

2. *The Spirit Lake Massacre and Relief Expedition* in the *Roster and Record of Iowa Soldiers*, Vol. VI; Smith's *History of Dickinson County, Iowa*.

Resting for only a brief time at the Granger home, Markham accompanied by George Granger started north to Springfield to warn that group of settlers against the Indians who had stricken Okoboji. It had occurred to them that the red men might also visit the Minnesota settlement; and they hoped to reach the place before the Indians appeared and thus prevent a repetition of the affair at the lakes.

At Springfield these bearers of bad tidings had a wholly different reception than that accorded the men who carried the news to Fort Dodge. No sooner did the people at this place become aware of the outbreak than they took measures looking toward protection from a similar attack. The coming of Markham and Granger was indeed fortunate, for if the information had not reached them when it did it is not unlikely that the settlers of Springfield would have met a fate similar to that of the people at Okoboji.

While some of the settlers fled at once upon receipt of the news, others remained; and a few gave their lives as the price of refusal to believe that danger was imminent. Among these was the Indian trader and settlement storekeeper, William Wood, who steadfastly refused to believe that a massacre would be attempted at Springfield. His refusal to believe that the community was in danger was doubtless due to the fact that he had traded with the Indians for years and did not note, in his recent dealings with them, any cause for alarm.[3]

The thought uppermost in the minds of most members of the settlement was to send a relief party to the lakes at once. After some deliberation this was deemed unwise: soberer second thought convinced them that it would be better to take measures for their own protection. At the time there were fifteen able-bodied men and about twelve adult women in the village.[4]

This number, it was argued, would make a reasonably efficient fighting force in case of attack—although they realised that they would be able to resist for only a brief time, since they were in no condition for a prolonged defence. And so it was decided to send messengers to the United States military authorities at Fort Ridgely for aid.

Two young men, Joseph B. Cheffins who had come thither with the trader William Wood, and a young German, Henry Tretts, were

3. *The Spirit Lake Massacre and Relief Expedition* in the *Roster and Record of Iowa Soldiers*, Vol. VI; Hubbard and Holcombe's *Minnesota in Three Centuries*, Vol. III; Hughes's *Causes and Results of the Inkpaduta Massacre* in the *Collections of the Minnesota Historical Society*, Vol. XII; Mrs. Sharp's *History of the Spirit Lake Massacre*; Carpenter's *The Spirit Lake Massacre* in the *Midland Monthly*, Vol. IV.
4. Hubbard and Holcombe's *Minnesota in Three Centuries*, Vol. III..

selected to bear the message for help to the Lower Agency of the Sioux.[5] These men carried with them a written statement of facts which was signed by individuals at Springfield who personally knew the agent of the Lower Sioux at Red Wood.[6] Cheffins and Tretts left Springfield at once, but they were not able to reach the Lower Agency until the eighteenth.

The trip was one of unusual privation. Owing to the exigencies of the situation, the men had left hastily and without making adequate preparation for the hardships of such a journey. The direct distance between the two points was not greater than seventy miles, but owing to difficulties encountered they had been obliged to detour and thus the distance travelled was more than one hundred miles. Under the most favourable conditions they made but little better than fifteen miles per day. The trip was undertaken on foot through deep snow and for most of the way under the disabling effects of a dazzling sun. When the Lower Agency was reached they could scarcely see—so severely were they suffering from snow blindness. They were also physically exhausted, for they had travelled almost continuously with but very little rest. After their arrival they were forced to remain in bed for two days before they were able to begin the return journey to Springfield.[7]

---

5. Hubbard and Holcombe's *Minnesota in Three Centuries*, Vol. III.
6. Flandrau's *The Ink-pa-du-ta Massacre of 1857* in the *Collections of the Minnesota Historical Society*, Vol. III.
7. Daniels's *Reminiscences of Little Crow* in the *Collections of the Minnesota Historical Society*, Vol. XII; Hubbard and Holcombe's *Minnesota in Three Centuries*, Vol. III; Flandrau's *The Ink-pa-du-ta Massacre of 1857* in the *Collections of the Minnesota Historical Society*, Vol. III.

CHAPTER 16

Relief Sent from Fort Ridgely

Charles E. Flandrau was at this time the agent for the Lower Sioux, and as soon as he was informed of the situation to the south he proceeded at once to Fort Ridgely, which was located on the Minnesota River fourteen miles southeast of the agency. Here he immediately had an interview with Colonel E. B. Alexander of the Tenth Infantry who was then in command of the post. As the result of this conference, Colonel Alexander, on the morning of the nineteenth, ordered Company D of the Tenth Infantry, under the command of Captain Barnard E. Bee[1] and Lieutenant Alexander Murry, to prepare for an expedition to Springfield and if need be to Spirit Lake. So expeditiously did the military authorities operate that at half past twelve, less than three hours and a half after the order was issued, Captain Bee with a company of forty-eight men was on the march to the scene of reported trouble.[2]

Realising that if they wished to make any considerable progress the company must travel by some other means than on foot, the expedition started in sleds drawn by mules. The original intention was to

---

1. This was the Barnard E. Bee who was later to win fame as a general of the South during the Civil War. During that conflict, he it was who fastened the sobriquet of "Stonewall" upon the Confederate General Thomas E. Jackson in his now famous charge to his men—"For God's sake stand, men. Stand like Jackson's brigade, on your right, there they stand like a stone wall." Bee was killed in an attempt to hold his brigade in line of battle against a murderous fire in the first battle of Bull Run, July 21, 1861.—Hubbard and Holcombe's *Minnesota in Three Centuries*, Vol. III; Heitman's *Historical Register and Dictionary of the United States Army*, Vol. I.
2. Hubbard and Holcombe's *Minnesota in Three Centuries*, Vol. III; Flandrau's *The Ink-pa-du-ta Massacre of 1857* in the *Collections of the Minnesota Historical Society*, Vol. III; report of Captain Barnard E. Bee in *House Executive Documents*, 1st Session, 35th Congress, Vol. II, Pt. I.

strike directly across the country in order to reach the afflicted people as soon as possible. But this route had to be abandoned, for it was soon found to be impracticable owing to the depth of the snow. Captain Bee in reporting upon the march stated that he took, "by advice of experienced guides, a long and circuitous route down the valley of the Minnesota, as far as South Bend, for the purpose of following, as long as possible, a beaten track."

Concerning the difficulties encountered on the trip Captain Bee reported that "the season was unpropitious for military operations; the snow lay in heavy masses on the track which I was following, but these masses were thawing and could not bear the weight of the men, much less that of the heavy sleds with which I was compelled to travel.

"The narrative of a single day's march is the history of the whole: wading through deep drifts; cutting through them with the spade and shovel; extricating mules and sleighs from sloughs, or dragging the latter up steep hills or over bare spaces of prairie; the men wet from morning till night, and sleeping on the snow. Such were the obstacles I encountered while still on the beaten track, the terminus of which was a farm belonging to a man by the name of Slocum. From this point to the Des Moines was an unbroken waste of snow."[3]

The route mentioned by Captain Bee would have taken him down the valley of the Minnesota for forty-five miles to Mankato—every mile of which would have carried him east of his objective point, Springfield. From Mankato, it must have been necessary to double back for twenty-five miles following the course of the Watonwan to Madelia, a few miles southwest of which was the farm of Isaac Slocum. This was as far as any road could be followed, since the region beyond was a wilderness. Indeed Slocum's was the westernmost white settlement in that section of the country. Captain Bee was still nearly fifty miles to the northeast of Springfield.

At the mouth of the Little Rock River, only a few miles below Fort Ridgely, Captain Bee secured a young half-breed guide, Joseph La Framboise, who was reputed to know the country well. But under the conditions then existing no guide could be expected to be infallible. The difficulties encountered only attested too well what could be looked forward to in the future. Agent Flandrau and his interpreter Philander Prescott, a French Canadian voyageur, also accompanied the party.

---

3. Report of Captain Barnard E. Bee in *House Executive Documents*, 1st Session, 35th Congress, Vol. II, Pt. I, No. 2.

According to Flandrau "the first day's march was appalling." Indeed, at the close of this first day's struggling he was willing to call the whole undertaking hopeless, because so "much time had elapsed since the murders were committed, and so much more would necessarily be consumed before the troops could possibly reach the lake, that I felt assured that no good could result from going on".[4] On the following day Flandrau and Prescott, with "a light sleigh and a fine team", forged ahead to Slocum's farm in the hope of learning more details of what had taken place at the lakes. Finding the road beyond this point impassable they turned back. At South Bend, on March twenty-second, they met Captain Bee's expeditionary force. Feeling the absolute impossibility of pushing beyond Slocum's, they advised him to turn back.[5] Although Captain Bee admitted the apparent hopelessness of the task, his military training prompted him to reply:"My orders are to go to Spirit Lake, and to do what I can. It is not for me to interpret my orders, but to obey them. I shall go on until it becomes physically impossible to proceed further. It will then be time to turn back".[6] And so he pressed on.

On the morning of March twenty-sixth Captain Bee and his company of men left Slocum's for Springfield.[7] Thus it happened that on the same morning that Inkpaduta and his party left Heron Lake, taking the direction of Springfield, the Fort Ridgely relief party left Slocum's, pushing toward the same point. But mark the difference in their relative rate of progress. While Captain Bee, encumbered with the ponderous army equipment, found progress nearly impossible, Inkpaduta, unimpeded by equipment of any kind save rifles and scalping knives, easily covered the distance from Heron Lake to Springfield in one day.

---

4. Flandrau's *The Ink-pa-du-ta Massacre of 1857* in the *Collections of the Minnesota Historical Society*, Vol. III
5. Hughes's *Causes and Results of the Inkpaduta Massacre* in the *Collections of the Minnesota Historical Society*, Vol. XII; *House Executive Documents*, 1st Session, 35th Congress, Vol. II, Pt. I.
6. Flandrau's *The Ink-pa-du-ta Massacre of 1857* in the *Collections of the Minnesota Historical Society*, Vol. III. 7. Report of Captain Barnard E. Bee in *House Executive Documents*, 1st Session, 35th Congress, Vol. II, Pt. I.

CHAPTER 17

Preparations for Defence at Springfield

Springfield had been located and platted by the Indian traders, George and William Wood, who built their post on the west side of the Des Moines; while the settlers who came later, mostly from Iowa, selected claims and built cabins on the east side of the river. The cabins of the settlers were not closely grouped, but were scattered up and down the river valley for seven or eight miles. Owing to this isolation the settlers could not be of much service to each other in the matter of defence. Moreover, the difficulty of successful individual defence was appreciated; and so at the conference which followed the arrival of Markham and Granger, it was decided to concentrate so far as possible.

In this conference the Wood brothers did not participate, as they scouted even the possibility of trouble—so confident were they of the friendliness of the Indians and of their own ability to keep them from hostile acts. According to Jareb Palmer, the Woods believed that only two houses had been robbed at the lakes, that the robbery had been laid to the Indians for no good reason whatever, and that in all likelihood it "had been done by the whites, as there had been some difficulty at the Lake in regard to claims."[1]

Having decided to concentrate, the Springfield settlers selected the cabins of James B. Thomas and William T. Wheeler as the points of defence. The Thomas cabin was distant about one and a half miles from the Wood brothers' store, and the Wheeler cabin about three-quarters of a mile beyond that of Thomas. Various reasons led to the selection

---

1. Palmer's *Incidents of the Late Indian Outrages* in the *Hamilton Freeman* (Webster City), July 23, 1857.

of these cabins, the principal of which were their size and the great strength with which they had been built. In the end it appears that not all of the settlers were gathered in these two cabins. The Joshua Stewart family, consisting of Mr. Stewart, Mrs. Stewart, and three children, were originally at the Thomas cabin; but owing to the physical condition of Mrs. Stewart, who had been overwrought by the fear of Indian attack, and the too crowded condition at the Thomas home, it was necessary for the family to return to their own home. This they did after a stay of two or three days at the Thomas cabin.[2] The Stewart cabin was located about one-half mile from that of Thomas.

At the Thomas cabin there remained nineteen individuals—the major portion of the settlement. These included Mr. and Mrs. James B. Thomas and six children, the oldest of whom was about thirteen; Mrs. E. B. N. Strong and two children; Mrs. William L. Church, two small children, and a sister, Miss Drusilla Swanger; Miss Eliza Gardner, a daughter of Rowland Gardner who was massacred at Okoboji; John Bradshaw, Morris Markham, and David N. Carver.[3] At the Wheeler cabin were collected Mr. and Mrs. J. B. Skinner and two children; Mr. and Mrs. William Nelson and one child; Mr. and Mrs. Robert Smith; John Henderson; and the little son of Adam P. Shiegley.[4] Meanwhile a number of people had fled from the settlement as soon as the news of the massacre at the lakes had arrived.

Thus, collected in two or three groups the Springfield settlers continued to live for several days without any sign of the approach of hostile Indians. In time their vigil relaxed, and at intervals a settler would leave the cabin to secure some much needed article. At no time for many days was anyone able to note any real cause for alarm in what was seen or heard.

The Thomas cabin, about which most of the events centred, was located in the edge of the timber which bordered the river. The design of the dwelling was that of the double type, each section being about sixteen feet square and joined by what was known in pioneer phraseology as a "dog trot"—a narrow and somewhat open connecting passageway. One part was used as a kitchen and a general living-room;

---

2. Hubbard and Holcombe's *Minnesota in Three Centuries*, Vol. III; Palmer's *Incidents of the Late Indian Outrages* in the *Hamilton Freeman* (Webster City), July 23, 1857.

3. Hoover's *The Tragedy of Okoboji* in the *Annals of Iowa* (Third Series), Vol. V.; Palmer's *Incidents of the Late Indian Outrages* in the *Hamilton Freeman* (Webster City), July 23, 1857.

4. Hubbard and Holcombe's *Minnesota in Three Centuries*, Vol. III; Palmer's *Incidents of the Late Indian Outrages* in the *Hamilton Freeman* (Webster City), July 23, 1857.

while the other part was reserved as a sitting room, which on occasion served as a spare bedroom. The one room faced the prairie; while the other looked out upon the timber of the river. The windows had been so placed that through them a view in all cardinal directions might be secured—which in addition to the port-holes was deemed a wise precaution. About ten rods from the cabin, and in the edge of the timber, was the stable, near which were a hay rack and some stacks of hay. Beyond these was a ravine which descended rapidly to the river.[5] Out upon the open prairie, nearly three-fourths of a mile away, was the cabin of Adam Shiegley.

On the tenth day of March—before the arrival of Granger and Markham—Jareb Palmer and Nathaniel Frost had gone to the Slocum farm for the purpose of bringing home some supplies which had been abandoned some time previously in the drifts a few miles from the farm house. After an absence of nine days they returned on March nineteenth. The first house of the settlement reached by them was the store of the Wood brothers.

Upon entering they found two strange Indians, "each of whom had a double barrelled gun, a tommyhawk and knife; one of them a very tall Indian was painted black; they were very busy trading and did not seem inclined to talk much, but said they were from Spirit Lake and that there were twenty lodges of them, all of whom would be at Springfield in two days. They purchased a keg of powder, some shot, lead, blankets, beads and other trinkets."[6] When they had completed their varied purchasing, which amounted in all to more than eighty dollars, they paid for them in gold, which act aroused the curiosity of Frost and Palmer, as gold was an almost unknown form of money in that region.[7]

Before these Indians had completed their trading and departed, two friendly Indians, Umpashota, or Smoky Moccasin, and Black Buffalo, entered and greeted them in a cordial manner. The two groups were soon engaged in conversation which grew excited and ended in the abrupt departure of the strangers. On the same day, Smoky Moccasin, for some reason that did not appear clear, moved his *tepees* to Cour-

---

5. Palmer's *Incidents of the Late Indian Outrages* in the *Hamilton Freeman* (Webster City), July 23, 1857.

6. Palmer's *Incidents of the Late Indian Outrages* in the *Hamilton Freeman* (Webster City), July 23, 1857.

7. The gold with which they paid for their purchases was presumably a portion of that which was taken from Marble's body.— See Hubbard and Holcombe's *Minnesota in Three Centuries*, Vol. III.

salle's trading post.[8] On the following day when he was interrogated by George Wood as to what he knew of the visiting Indians, Smoky Moccasin admitted that he had been told that "they had raided the Spirit Lake settlements, and killed all the inmates, except four young women prisoners without having one of their number injured in any manner." When questioned further he "said he feared they were lingering somewhere in the neighbourhood and intended more mischief. 'At any rate' said the Moccasin, 'I am going to remain close to my camp for awhile.'"[9]

In spite of this evidence of Indian activity and the promise of a visitation the Wood brothers remained unconvinced that danger lurked near, and ridiculed the fears of the settlers on the east side of the river. But they were not the only ones who were now doubting Markham's story: the failure of the Indian attack to develop had caused several of the settlers to ask why they had grown so alarmed. Among them gradually developed a feeling that they would like to hear a version of the story from one of their own number. Thus it transpired that Jareb Palmer volunteered to go to the lakes if some other man would accompany him. Markham, anxious to prove the correctness of what he had told, expressed his willingness to make the return trip. On Saturday morning, March twenty-first, the pair set out, carrying supplies for a journey of two days. They planned to go first to the Marble cabin, and if all was well there they would go on down to the lower settlements on Okoboji. They had been instructed by the Springfield people to return at once if they found that the Marble cabin had been plundered and that the evidence of Indian attack was plain.

Having no definite route which they could follow with assurance, the men struck out boldly to the southwest across the trackless prairie in the general direction of the lakes. Without incident or loss of way they reached Spirit Lake and made their way to the Marble cabin, which was found deserted. A closer examination revealed the fact that trunks had been broken open and the contents of the house scattered everywhere. The body of Mr. Marble, however, was nowhere to be seen. Signs about the cabin seemed to suggest that the place had been visited some five days before the arrival of the men from Springfield,

---

8. The Moccasin's camp had been about six miles up the river to the north of Springfield, while the trading post here referred to was nine miles distant. Coursalle, or "Joe Gaboo", was a well-known half-blood Sisseton Sioux. At all times Indians in small numbers were grouped about him; they were always friendly.—Hubbard and Holcombe's *Minnesota in Three Centuries*, Vol. III.

9. Hubbard and Holcombe's *Minnesota in Three Centuries*, Vol. III.

although there were fresh moccasin tracks along the lake shore which appeared to be only one day old. After examining the situation carefully the men decided to return at once, as enough had been seen to convince them that Indians had been there. Palmer was firmly convinced that Markham's story was only too true. The return trip was made during the afternoon and the early evening of the same day without incident.[10]

---

10. Palmer's *Incidents of the Late Indian Outrages* in the *Hamilton Freeman* (Webster City), July 23, 1857; Hubbard and Holcombe's *Minnesota in Three Centuries*, Vol. III.

CHAPTER 18

Inkpaduta Attacks Springfield

The morning of March twenty-sixth dawned bright at Springfield; and the settlers at the Thomas cabin were astir early making preparations for the expected attack. The messengers from Spirit Lake had returned and no one longer doubted the strong possibility that Springfield would be visited by the Indians. While the supply of food, firearms, and ammunition which they had procured was sufficient for a resistance of some days, there was a shortage of wood. And so, on the morning of the twenty-sixth a number of the settlers were out chopping and hauling wood. As they carried on their preparations they hoped that the soldiers from Fort Ridgely would soon appear bringing the needed relief and protection. Cheffins and Tretts had been gone nearly two weeks; surely relief could now be expected any day or hour. Happy in the expectation that relief must be near the settlers slackened still more the vigil which they had been keeping and became somewhat careless. The forenoon wore away without incident, and a generous supply of wood was accumulated which would last for several days.

While preparations were thus going forward, Inkpaduta and his band of red men were hastening from Heron Lake toward Springfield. The wily Inkpaduta did not wish to make a precipitate attack, for his spies sent out on the nineteenth had probably informed him of how the settlers were preparing for opposition. As his party stole into the timber along the Des Moines near the Thomas cabin, he sent scouts forward to reconnoitre. Thus while the unsuspecting settlers were at work the spies of Inkpaduta were stealthily lurking in the near-by timber stalking their white brothers as they would some wild beast of the forest.

The settlers were unable to complete the task which they had undertaken by noon, and as everything seemed so very favourable it was thought advisable to continue the work without interruption. Accordingly, they did not pause to eat the mid-day meal that had been prepared for them, but continued working until about two o'clock in the afternoon. They then withdrew into the cabin to eat their long deferred dinner. While thus engaged they were startled by a cry from Willie Thomas, who was outside at play and who now thought that Henry Tretts was coming.[1]

Immediately the people in the cabin rushed out hoping that the report was true and that the messengers sent to Fort Ridgely were in fact returning. In the distance a man was observed to be approaching. He was clad in civilian dress and to all outward appearances bore a close resemblance to one of the messengers. In fact, so close was the resemblance that David Carver exclaimed, "Yes, it's Henry Tretts!" But the words had scarcely been uttered before a volley of shots came from hitherto unseen guns in the direction of the timber. As near as could be determined fully a dozen guns had been discharged from the underbrush near the stable and haystacks. The supposed white man was only a decoy Indian dressed in white men's clothing and sent out for the sole purpose of drawing the settlers from the cabin. While he was slowly approaching the cabin, Inkpaduta and his men had crept up the ravine to the rear of the stable and posted themselves for action when the ruse worked out as planned.

In confusion the surprised settlers—men, women, and children—scrambled back into the cabin. Doors and windows were closed and barricaded, while women screamed. Bradshaw and Markham, as soon as the doors had been secured, seized their rifles and stood ready to shoot any Indian who might have the hardihood to show himself. The window shutters had been fastened open on the outside thus making it necessary to use the table to close one window; while puncheons were torn from the floor to cover other windows and aid in rendering the cabin bullet proof.

Meanwhile, the Indians kept up a constant fire; but Bradshaw and Markham kept them well in hiding by shooting at any who happened to show themselves. While the men were busy reloading, an Indian was seen to emerge from the brush near the stable and start for

---

1. Carpenter's *The Spirit Lake Massacre* in the *Midland Monthly*, Vol. IV; Mrs. Sharp's *History of the Spirit Lake Massacre*; Hubbard and Holcombe's *Minnesota in Three Centuries*, Vol. III. See also a different version in Palmer's *Incidents of the Late Indian Outrages* in the *Hamilton Freeman* (Webster City), July 30, 1857.

the house. Mrs. Church hastily seized a loaded gun and, thrusting it through a porthole, fired. After the firing the Indian was nowhere to be seen and it was concluded that he had either been badly wounded or killed by the shot. Three or four Indians next appeared from a hazel thicket, but the emptying of the contents of a number of guns into their midst caused them to disappear. All of this had taken place in four or five minutes after the first volley fired by the Indians. In that brief time the Indian attack had been repelled, windows shuttered from within by temporary means, and all doors barricaded securely against a rush attack.

During the attack no one had had time or thought for anything except the necessity of repelling the Indians. When a lull came it was found that several persons had been wounded. Mr. Thomas was bleeding profusely from a wound in his left arm where a bullet had broken a bone. Later this wound, owing to lack of attention, became so irritated and infected that amputation was necessary. David Carver was suffering greatly, for a bullet or buckshot had passed through the fleshy part of his right arm, penetrated his side, and affected his lung; while Miss Swanger, who had been hit on the shoulder, was suffering considerably from pain and was very weak from the loss of blood. It was she who has been alluded to as saying that she was too weak to fight but could pray, and so fell "upon her knees, fervently petitioning the God of Battles to help until the fight closed."[2] Willie Thomas, who had given the alarm, was missing and no one seemed able to account for him until his older brother stated that after the door had been closed he heard groaning from the doorstep. It was presumed that the boy had been killed. At all events no one felt that it would be wise to open the door at this juncture. It later developed that he had been shot through the head and had probably died in a brief time.

There were now left in the cabin only three able-bodied men who could be counted upon for effective defence. These men were Jareb Palmer, John Bradshaw, and Morris Markham. Dr. Strong had gone to the Wheeler cabin that forenoon to dress the wounds of Smith and Henderson and had not returned at the time of the attack.[3]

---

2. Hubbard and Holcombe's *Minnesota in Three Centuries*, Vol. III; Laut's *Heroines of Spirit Lake* in the *Outing Magazine*, Vol. LI; Mrs. Sharp's *History of the Spirit Lake Massacre*.

3. Dr. Strong has been considerably maligned as one who upon the first alarm had become so terrified that he summarily fled south, leaving his wife and children to the mercies of an Indian attack. For a more charitable view see Palmer's *Incidents of the Late Indian Outrages* in the *Hamilton Freeman* (Webster City), July 30, 1857.

The heavy firing by the Indians did not continue for more than seven or eight minutes when it became desultory in character. Occasionally an Indian would be seen skulking through the edge of the timber, but not one allowed himself to come within range of the cabin. It is presumed that they had counted upon a complete surprise as at Okoboji and were not supplied with the ammunition necessary to conduct a continuous attack. The firing, however, continued until sunset. It was later discovered that the Indians had withdrawn at this time, although this fact was not known to the inmates of the cabin. The desultory nature of the Indian fire had allowed the settlers to prepare, and soon six guns were projecting from as many port-holes and covering as many possible lines of approach. This evidence of readiness in the cabin may have led the Indians to defer or abandon their attack.[4]

Meanwhile, the Wood brothers were paying dearly for their misplaced confidence in the peaceful intentions of the red men. It was reported—but the statement has never been confirmed—that when the firing upon the Thomas cabin began William Wood, thinking no harm would come to him, started to cross the river with a view to investigating the cause. When he reached the west bank of the stream, he ran into a group of Indians who at once riddled him with bullets. It is further asserted that a pile of brush was then collected, his lifeless body thrown upon it, and the whole set on fire. This conclusion is drawn from the fact that in a pile of wood ashes, not far from the river's edge, a group of the Fort Ridgely soldiers later found charred human bones and with them a twenty dollar gold piece.[5] The body of George Wood was found, while that of William Wood was never discovered—unless the charred bones indicated his fate. Since the Wood brothers were the only persons in the settlement who had gold coin it was thought that the remains in the ashes were those of William Wood.

George Wood, who had remained at the store in his brother's absence, possibly witnessed his brother's fate and attempted to forestall a similar one for himself by striving to reach the settlers' cabins. But he was too late. He succeeded in reaching the river and in crossing it, but

---

4. For somewhat varying accounts of the attack upon the Thomas cabin see Palmer's *Incidents of the Late Indian Outrages* in the *Hamilton Freeman* (Webster City), July 30, 1857; Carpenter's *The Spirit Lake Massacre* in the *Midland Monthly*, Vol. IV; Gue's *History of Iowa*, Vol. I; Mrs. Sharp's *History of the Spirit Lake Massacre*; Hughes's *Causes and Results of the Inkpaduta Massacre* in the *Collections of the Minnesota Historical Society*, Vol. XII; Hubbard and Holcombe's *Minnesota in Three Centuries*, Vol. III; *The Spirit Lake Massacre and Relief Expedition* in the *Roster and Record of Iowa Soldiers*, Vol. VI.
5. Hubbard and Holcombe's *Minnesota in Three Centuries*, Vol. III.

while trying to secrete himself in the underbrush he was seen by the Indians and shot. His body was subjected to no further violence.[6]

It would seem that during the afternoon, while the attack was being made upon the Thomas cabin, Inkpaduta selected three of his band to raid the remaining cabins or at least to investigate them for plunder in case they should be found abandoned. It was probably this trio of Indians who attacked and killed George and William Wood.

The first cabin visited by the three Indians was that of Joshua Stewart. Mr. Stewart was called to the door by one of the number and requested to sell a hog. Some gold coins were displayed by the Indian as evidence that the hog would be paid for when purchased. Mr. Stewart being willing to sell, stepped back into the house to secure his cap and coat. When he reappeared and stepped out into the yard, he was instantly shot by the two Indians who had not appeared to be concerned in the deal. Upon hearing the shots, Mrs. Stewart and the children ran out of the cabin. They, too, were instantly shot down by the Indians and their bodies horribly mutilated with knives.

According to Captain Bee, it was here that "the savages revelled in blood. When I visited the spot, the father lay dead on his threshold, the mother, with one arm encircling her murdered infant, lay outside the door, and by her side was stretched the lifeless body of a little girl of three summers".[7] But Johnny, a lad of perhaps ten years, eluded the Indians and made his escape. In his own relation to the people at the Thomas cabin he stated that he hid behind a log in the yard while the savages did their work of murder and plunder. After they left he ran to the cabin of Robert Smith, but was frightened away; from there he made his way to the Thomas cabin where he arrived at dusk and was taken in by the inmates—who, however, came near shooting him for an Indian prowler.[8]

---

6. For the attack upon the Wood brothers see Hubbard and Holcombe's *Minnesota in Three Centuries*, Vol. III; Hughes's *Causes and Results of the Inkpaduta Massacre* in the *Collections of the Minnesota Historical Society*, Vol. XII; Mrs. Sharp's *History of the Spirit Lake Massacre*.

7. Report of Captain Barnard E. Bee in *House Executive Documents*, 1st Session, 35th Congress, Vol. II, Pt. II.

8. All of the particulars of the events which happened at the Stewart home we owe to the relation of Johnny. He was later adopted into the home of Major William Williams at Fort Dodge and in 1915 was living in Byron, Minnesota, and at that time was one of the four living survivors of the raid. Read accounts in Hubbard and Holcombe's *Minnesota in Three Centuries*, Vol. III; Palmer's *Incidents of the Late Indian Outrages* in the *Hamilton Freeman* (Webster City), July 30, 1857; Gue's *History of Iowa*, Vol. I; Mrs. Sharp's *History of the Spirit Lake Massacre*.

After completing their ghastly work at the Stewart home, the Indians returned in the direction of the Wood store, which they probably planned to pillage. When passing the Wheeler home, they attempted no further molestation than to shoot an ox and empty the contents of their guns into the cabin. One of the charges narrowly missed Mr. Henderson who was lying helpless as the result of his recent amputations. For some reason the Indians did not take the trouble to determine whether any people were really occupying the house.[9] From here the Indians appear to have gone directly to the Wood store, where they finished their work and then departed for Heron Lake. At the time, however, the departure of the Indians was not known to the terrified inhabitants of the settlement.

At the Wood store on the west side of the river guns, powder, shot, and lead were found in reasonably large quantities and appropriated. But this was not all; food and dry goods were also found and taken. It is said that when they returned to Heron Lake "they had twelve horses, heavily laden with dry goods, groceries, powder, lead, bed-quilts, wearing apparel, provisions, etc.... Among this plunder were several bolts of calico and red flannel. Of these, especially the flannel, they were exceedingly proud; decorating themselves with it in fantastic fashion. Red leggings, red shirts, red blankets, and red in every conceivable way, was the style there, as long as it lasted."[10]

---

9. Hubbard and Holcombe's *Minnesota in Three Centuries*, Vol. II; Mrs. Sharp's *History of the Spirit Lake Massacre*.
10. Mrs. Sharp's *History of the Spirit Lake Massacre*. For Mrs. Marble's impressions see an article from the *St. Paul Pioneer*, May 31, 1857, republished in the *Hamilton Freeman* (Webster City), July 13, 1857.

CHAPTER 19

The Settlers Flee from Springfield

When quiet had reigned for some little time and darkness had fallen, there being no signs that the Indians would reopen their attack, the inmates of the Thomas cabin began to discuss the best course to pursue. It was the general belief that they would again be attacked if they remained: in fact they reasoned that to remain would be to invite an attack. But would not the soldiers from Fort Ridgely soon bring relief? And yet they had no means of knowing whether their messengers had ever reached that post. Having reached the fort, might not their story have been received in the same manner in which the people of Springfield had greeted the tale of Markham? No idea had been gained as to the numerical strength of the Indians: although they seemed to be about twelve in number, there was a possibility that they might be ten or twenty times as many, and well prepared to carry the attack through to a conclusive end.

Some suggested flight; but there seemed to be many obstacles to such a course. Nothing was known of the whereabouts of the Indians: they might be lurking near the cabin awaiting the appearance of its inmates for the purpose of picking them off as they came out. Again, they were more than fifty miles from any adequate place of refuge; while the nearest settlement was no less than fifteen miles away. But worst of all the snow was deep and there was not even a known trail upon the wintry wastes that could be followed with certainty. Moreover, there were among them three badly wounded people whose suffering would only be intensified by the cold and exposure incident to such a flight. And there were children in the party: would they be able to endure such a journey as flight would compel them to undergo? From the hardships encountered by Markham in his trip from the lakes it was known that a journey of fifty miles under the existing conditions of weather would be a hard trial of endurance, even for the strongest and most rugged person.

In the course of the discussion someone called attention to the fact that the Indians had driven away the Thomas horses. How were they to move Carver who was unable to walk and Thomas who was so weak that at best it was believed he could live but a short time? Carver was willing to be left behind if by so doing the safety of the others could be assured; but none of his companions were willing to consider such a proposition. When the thought of flight was about to be abandoned someone recalled that the Indians had not taken the Thomas oxen. If they had not been killed, they must be safe in the stable. Markham, who had twice before volunteered to risk his life, offered to go to the stable, and if the oxen were there hitch them to the sled and drive to the door.[1] Meanwhile, in the cabin preparations were to be made for flight.

When Markham returned to the cabin he reported that everything seemed to indicate that the Indians had given up the attack and left the vicinity. He had been gone nearly half an hour, which led the people in the cabin to fear that he too had fallen a victim of Indian lust. And so they were overjoyed when he finally appeared at the door with the ox-drawn sled. Feather ticks were first taken to the sled and upon them the wounded Thomas, Carver, and Miss Swanger were placed. Around them were packed such articles as were deemed necessary upon the journey.

The night sky was obscured by clouds and the darkness was intense, which would make it possible for the fleeing settlers to elude the watchfulness of the Indians if any happened to be lurking in the vicinity of the cabin. About nine o'clock the nineteen frightened and wretchedly equipped refugees left the Thomas cabin.[2] Ahead of the oxen walked Markham, Bradshaw, and Palmer, with rifles in their hands, ready to protect the women, children, and wounded from possible attack. Then came the ox-drawn sled piled with feather beds, the wounded, blankets, bed-quilts, and provisions. Upon either side and behind the sled walked the women, carrying or leading the children.

Progress was slow since no distinct trail could be discerned in the

---

1. Palmer's *Incidents of the Late Indian Outrages* in the *Hamilton Freeman* (Webster City), July 30, 1857; Mrs. Sharp's *History of the Spirit Lake Massacre*.
2. Charles Aldrich in an address at the unveiling of a commemorative tablet in the Hamilton County Court House in Webster City, Iowa, on August 12, 1887, states that they started about midnight. It does not seem, however, that such a late hour could have been possible under the circumstances.—See the *Annals of Iowa* (Third Series), Vol. III.

darkness. Frequently they would stop and by signs and consultation assure themselves that they were moving in the proper direction. Often they missed the way and were compelled to alter their course. At two o'clock in the morning, having made an advance of only five miles, they concluded to halt and await the dawn.[3] Where they were they did not know. Blankets and bed-quilts were spread upon the snow; and upon these the women, children, and wounded lay down, while the men stood guard. With the coming of day the refugees again pushed forward, but found that they could make little headway because of the deep snow drifts through which the men had to break a way for the oxen and sled.

In less than an hour the party, finding further progress well-nigh impossible, decided to halt. After some deliberation it was decided to send Palmer ahead about ten miles to Granger's Point for help. Palmer, having succeeded in making his way to the Point without incident, returned with George Granger, who very willingly brought his ox team to the rescue of the stranded settlers. A Mr. Addington also accompanied Palmer upon the return trip. When about a mile to the north of Granger's place a man was observed on the open prairie. Addington jumped off the sled and started toward him. The man turned and ran, but was soon overtaken. He was found to be Dr. Strong of Springfield who had fled from the Wheeler cabin that same morning, supposing that his wife and children had been killed in the attack upon the Thomas cabin.

In the meantime the stranded settlers, thinking they saw Indians in pursuit, had left their wounded companions in the sled and taken to the open prairie in flight—an effort which greatly exhausted the women. Returning to the sled the march onward to Granger's Point was resumed. After remaining here for two days to recuperate they continued their journey southward toward Fort Dodge.[4]

It will be recalled that the Wheeler cabin had received but one volley from a group of three Indians who passed without stopping. The inmates had doubtless heard the continuous firing in the direction of the Thomas cabin during the afternoon and had surmised that something serious must have happened. As all was quiet at the cabin on the following morning, the anxiety of Mrs. Robert Smith to know what

---

3. Palmer's *Incidents of the Late Indian Outrages* in the *Hamilton Freeman* (Webster City), July 30, 1857.
4. Palmer's *Incidents of the Late Indian Outrages* in the *Hamilton Freeman* (Webster City), July 30, 1857; Hubbard and Holcombe's *Minnesota in Three Centuries*, Vol. III. For a wholly different view of Dr. Strong see Gue's *History of Iowa*, Vol. I.

had really transpired at the Thomas cabin overcame her fears. With the fortitude characteristic of pioneer women, she determined to visit the cabin as early as possible. When she arrived at the cabin she found the body of Willie Thomas lying at the side of the doorstep. Greatly alarmed she investigated no further, but returned at once to the Wheeler cabin. Her hasty conclusion was that all the inmates of the Thomas cabin had been murdered by the Indians. Thus Dr. Strong, having heard the report of Mrs. Smith, concluded that his family had been murdered and that his own safety was all that was left for him to consider; and so he fled toward the settlements in Iowa.

The flight of Dr. Strong left Mr. Skinner as the only able-bodied man at the Wheeler house. He and the three women—Mrs. Skinner, Mrs. Nelson, Mrs. Smith—decided to escape if possible before receiving a second visit from the Indians. Mrs. Smith strongly protested against the plan of leaving her husband, but he bade her go and save her own life.[5] The problem of escape with these people was a vastly more difficult one than with the party at the Thomas cabin, since they had no team or other means of transportation. From the first it was evident that the disabled men must be abandoned—a plan in which the men themselves willingly acquiesced.

After providing for the comfort of those who were to be left behind, Mr. Skinner and the three women set out. Smith attempted to follow, but was compelled to return to the cabin after again overcoming the objections of his wife at going without him. The only individual, other than Smith and Henderson, who could not be taken was the little son of Adam P. Shiegley. After the departure of the grown-ups this boy made his way to the home of a settler who had not been disturbed and was there well taken care of until found by his father who later came in search of his son. Two days later, on Sunday, March twenty-ninth, the Wheeler party arrived at Granger's Point where they joined the people from the Thomas cabin.[6]

---

5. One version of the flight of these refugees tells us that Smith and Henderson were not, at first, left behind but were taken for some distance on hand sleds. This proved impracticable and the men were abandoned. Miss Agnes C. Laut has this plainly in mind when she refers to Mrs. Smith as the "one dame, who abandoned an injured husband on a hand sleigh" and hence does not need to "be preserved as a heroine of the West." This, however, is unfair to Mrs. Smith.—See Miss Laut's *Heroines of Spirit Lake* in the *Outing Magazine*, Vol. LI.

6. For varied versions of the flight of the Wheeler refugees see Mrs. Sharp's *History of the Spirit Lake Massacre*; Gue's *History of Iowa*, Vol. I; Hubbard and Holcombe's *Minnesota in Three Centuries*, Vol. III.

CHAPTER 20

Relief Arrives from Fort Ridgely

On the morning of March twenty-sixth the relief expedition from Fort Ridgely was laboriously seeking to make its way through nearly impassable drifts of snow. Captain Bee had scarcely struck camp that morning when two white men from the Des Moines River—probably Nelson and Frost from Springfield—came in for supplies. They reported that the Indians, to the number of thirty lodges, were encamped at Coursalle's Grove about eight or nine miles to the north of Springfield. Coursalle, known as "Gaboo" among the borderers and settlers, was a half-blood Sisseton who was well-known throughout the surrounding country as a trapper, trader, and intermediary between the whites and the Indians. With this information Captain Bee pushed forward with renewed energy, hoping to reach Coursalle's before the Indians should leave.

After encountering and overcoming nearly insurmountable obstacles of roads and weather Captain Bee finally reached the trader's post. The grove and its vicinity were thoroughly reconnoitred with no success other than the rounding up of Coursalle and his family. Coursalle grudgingly gave the information that Inkpaduta's band had in truth wiped out not only the settlements at the southern lakes, but also those at Springfield. From Springfield the Indians had gone to Heron Lake, twenty-five miles to the west, and were headed for the Yankton country on the Missouri. Further knowledge concerning their whereabouts Coursalle said he did not have.

Coursalle seemed so confident that the Indians were still at Heron Lake that Captain Bee decided to pursue and punish them before going to Springfield with his command. Having been told that only the dead were to be found at either Spirit Lake or Springfield, he concluded that little could be gained and perhaps everything lost if he should hasten to the scenes of the massacres and allow the perpetrators of the horrible deeds to escape without punishment. Hence "at retreat" that evening he called for no less than twenty volunteers to go on an expedition early the next morning for the purpose of punishing the Indians. The response from the men was unanimous, and when early morning came Captain Bee and Lieutenant Murry with the guides, Coursalle and La Framboise, together with all the men of the command, started out. It was expected that upon the approach of the soldiers the Indians would probably attempt flight. To prevent their succeeding in this, the teamsters were taken along to lead the mules, numbering thirteen in all, to be used as mounts in the pursuit of the fleeing Indians.[1]

The road taken under the guidance of Coursalle led them in a direct line across the open prairie from the trading post to the lake. This open route was taken because it shortened the distance to fifteen miles between the two points. The approach to the lake proved easy, and by ten o'clock the lake had been reached and wholly surrounded by Captain Bee's men so that it would have been difficult for anyone to have escaped unnoticed. The instructions were that when the camp and Indians were found a single shot should be fired as a signal for the ingathering of the troops. In about a half hour after the deploying of the men a shot was heard in the direction taken by La Framboise. He had found the place of their camp, but the Indians themselves had gone. The camp gave every evidence of the destruction of the settlements "with all its traces of plunder and rapine; books, scissors, articles of female apparel, furs, and traps, were scattered on the ground".[2] The guides, after examining the ashes of the camp fire and other signs, pronounced the camp to be about three or four days old. If such were the truth, it was plain that further pursuit would be useless.

There was, however, one more hope which was eagerly seized by Captain Bee. Coursalle suggested that possibly the band had moved to another lake about four miles to the northwestward. This lake being much larger and its borders more heavily timbered the Indians might have gone on to it for better concealment. Such a possibility appealed to Captain Bee, who was not long in detailing Lieutenant Murry with ten men and Coursalle as guide to make a dash to that point by means of mule mounts. If signs there should prove as old as at the first lake

---
1. Hubbard and Holcombe's *Minnesota in Three Centuries*, Vol. III.
2. Report of Captain Barnard E. Bee in *House Executive Documents*, 1st Session, 35th Congress, Vol. II, Pt. II, Doc. No. 2.

the members of the party were instructed to lose no time in returning, since further pursuit would be useless. The dash was made as planned; and signs in abundance were found, but Coursalle pronounced them to be at least twenty-four hours old. Such being the case Lieutenant Murry returned to the main command.

It has been charged that Coursalle lacked good faith in that he purposely declared the signs many hours older than they were in order to assure the escape of the Inkpaduta band.[3] Captain Bee, however, stated in a public letter that "Gaboo was in front of my men" and "his whole demeanor convinced me that he had come out to fight", for his life had been threatened by the band.[4] It was also further charged that Mrs. Coursalle was observed wearing Mrs. Church's shawl; but this was discredited by several competent observers. The fact remains, however, that Captain Bee's men approached much nearer the band than they knew—which gives colour to the view that Coursalle either practiced deception or was not wise in wood and camp lore.

How near the troops came to the Indian band is disclosed in the testimony of both Mrs. Sharp and Mrs. Marble who were with the Indians as captives. They both state that at three o'clock in the afternoon Lieutenant Murry's men reached the same place that the Indians had left at about nine in the morning. Furthermore, the Indians were even then within reach, being encamped on a low stretch of ground bordering a small stream just over a slight rise of ground west of the lake. They were so located that while the Indian lookout was able from the treetops to see for miles around, the camp itself could not easily be seen.

Mrs. Sharp relates that as soon as the lookout reported the approach of the soldiers of Lieutenant Murry:

> The squaws at once extinguished the fires by pouring on water, that the smoke might not be seen; tore down the tents; packed their plunder; and .... one Indian was detailed to stand guard over us, and to kill us if there was an attack. The rest of the warriors prepared for battle.... The excitement manifested by the Indians was for a little while intense; and although less manifested ours was fully as great, as we were well aware that the Indians meant all they said when they told us we were to be shot, in case of an attack. We therefore knew that an attack

---
3. Mrs. Sharp's *History of the Spirit Lake Massacre*.
4. Quoted from the *St. Paul Pioneer and Democrat* for May 16, 1857, in Holcombe's *Minnesota in Three Centuries*, Vol. III.

would be certain *death to us*, whatever the results might be in other respects. After an hour and a half of this exciting suspense ... a sudden change came to us. The soldiers, it seems, just here decided to turn back.[5]

Upon Lieutenant Murry's return, it was decided to give up the pursuit. This decision was based in part upon the report made by Lieutenant Murry and Coursalle and also on the fact that the supplies were nearly exhausted. From this point Captain Bee's command went to Springfield. Here Smith and Henderson were found in the Wheeler cabin where they had been left two days previously. They were in good spirits despite their desolation. They had been visited by Mr. Shiegley who was in search of his boy. These men related to Captain Bee the story of events so far as they knew it, telling of the flight of their companions in the direction of Granger's. Captain Bee at once sent a man in search of the fugitives who were to be invited to return. They were to be assured that the Indians were gone and that a guard of soldiers would be stationed at Springfield for their protection. The messenger, however, failed to overtake the refugees and in a few days returned. Meanwhile, Captain Bee sent a detail of twenty men under Lieutenant Murry to Spirit Lake to bury the dead. Murry went no farther than the Marble cabin where he found and buried Marble's body and then returned to Springfield.

In a final adjustment of matters, Captain Bee left a detail of twenty-eight non-commissioned officers and privates at Springfield under Lieutenant Murry. This detail, while only temporary, remained until April twentieth when it was relieved by a second detail which, under Lieutenant John McNab, remained until late in the fall of 1857. Captain Bee reported at Fort Ridgely on April eighth, after an absence of about three weeks.[6]

---

5. Mrs. Sharp's *History of the Spirit Lake Massacre*.
6. Hubbard and Holcombe's *Minnesota in Three Centuries*, Vol. III.

CHAPTER 21

Organisation of Relief at Fort Dodge and Webster City

When the citizens of Fort Dodge and Webster City were convinced by repeated tales of Indian horrors that assistance was needed they organised a relief party to fend off the savage forays of the Sioux. The trials and sufferings of this little volunteer band have few if any parallels in the pioneer history of the Mississippi Valley. Unprepared for such a venture as the journey proved to be, they nevertheless met its ordeals with a courage that attests the hardihood of the pioneers who chose the task of advancing the frontier.

Early in November, 1856, Orlando C. Howe (a lawyer and later a professor of law at the State University of Iowa), R. U. Wheelock, and B. F. Parmenter, guided by a well-known and widely experienced western trapper, Wiltfong, came from Newton, Jasper County, Iowa, to the lake region on a land-hunting tour. They were particularly attracted by the natural beauty of the region and before leaving staked out claims to the southeast of Marble's place on what is now the site of the town of Spirit Lake. Like many other prospective settlers at that time they did not plan to remain during the winter season; and so, after visiting for some days among the settlers on the south and east shores of the Okobojis, they returned to Jasper County. The route homeward led them to Loon Lake, where they are said to have found Inkpaduta's band encamped. The band seems to have been peaceful enough at the time of the visit; indeed, they made a rather favorable impression upon these prospective settlers.

Although the season had been severe Howe, Wheelock, and Parmenter expected the usual breaking of winter during the closing week of March, when they anticipated that travel across the prairies would be difficult if not impossible owing to the overabundance of snow. It was to forestall delays caused by the melting snows that they started about the first of March for the lake region with ox wagons heavily laden with seed, food supplies, and agricultural implements. From the very start they made but indifferent progress owing to the deep snows and continued intensity of the cold. Tarrying but a short time at Fort Dodge to replenish their supplies and renew former acquaintances, they proceeded up the west side of the Des Moines Valley to their destination. Following the trail up this side of the valley, they missed the two trappers who came down from Granger's Point carrying the news of the massacre to Fort Dodge. When within two or three miles of their destination, and somewhere to the southeast of Gar Lake, on the evening of March fifteenth their oxen became too exhausted to proceed further. Temporarily abandoning the load and the oxen, the men went forward on foot to the settlements along the East Okoboji Lake.

About midnight, after spending several hours in groping their way through the timber along the lake, they came to the Noble and Thatcher cabin. Failing to receive a response after repeated rapping upon the door they pushed the door open and entered only to find everything in confusion. Hesitating to remain for the night amid such evidences of violence, they left at once and made their way along the trail in the direction of the cabin of Joel Howe. At this cabin likewise on account of the darkness they did not discover that there were dead bodies lying in the yard. Entering they found the cabin deserted; but the hour was so late that they decided to remain and make further investigations on the morrow.

The following morning they soon discovered the dead bodies in the yard and other evidences of an Indian visit. From here they crossed the east lake to the Mattock cabin, which they found in ashes; while the clearing around the cabin was strewn with the bodies of the slaughtered members of the family. They now had all the evidence necessary to convince them that an Indian war party had visited the settlement and wiped out the white population. Without further delay they started for the settlements to the southeast along the Des Moines. So anxious were they to spread the news as speedily as possible that Parmenter remained behind to follow more slowly with the oxen, while the other two men rushed on ahead on foot. On Saturday evening, March twenty-first, they arrived at Fort Dodge with the news of the Indian massacre at the lakes. So well-known was Howe in that vicinity that no one hesitated to believe the information which he brought of the Indian raid on the frontier.[1]

When Howe and Wheelock had recited the story of conditions as they found them at the lakes, it coincided so nearly with information already brought to the community that no one could doubt the urgent need for immediate action. And so it was resolved to hold a meeting for the purpose of determining the course to be followed. This meeting was called for the next afternoon (which was Sunday) in the schoolhouse of the village. When the meeting convened practically every able-bodied man in Fort Dodge and vicinity was present. Major William Williams presided as chairman, and Charles B. Richards acted as secretary.[2] Howe and Wheelock were called upon to relate their tale of horrors at the lakes. The recital gave rise to great excitement: the people realised their own proximity to danger.

It was the unanimous sentiment of the meeting that immediate and resolute action should be taken to deal with the situation. The chairman, Major Williams, read a commission held by him from Governor Grimes empowering him in any emergency that might arise to take such action as seemed best in the light of existing circumstances.[3] It was thereupon resolved that at least two companies of volunteers should be called for and sent to the lakes to rescue the living, bury the dead, and if possible overtake and punish the perpetrators of the massacre. Nearly eighty men volunteered at once to join the proposed expedition.

Before the meeting adjourned a messenger, in the person of a Mr. White,[4] was named to carry the news of the massacre to Homer, Border Plains, and Webster City, and to ask the co-operation of these communities in the recruiting of members for the expedition. To make the plea for assistance as effective as possible, Howe was requested to

---

1. For information concerning the journey and findings of Howe, Wheelock, and Parmenter see *The Spirit Lake Massacre and Relief Expedition* in the *Roster and Record of Iowa Soldiers*, Vol. VI; Mrs. Sharp's *History of the Spirit Lake Massacre*; Smith's *History of Dickinson County, Iowa*,; Carpenter's *The Spirit Lake Massacre* in the *Midland Monthly*, Vol. IV; Flickinger's *Pioneer History of Pocahontas County, Iowa*; Gue's *History of Iowa*, Vol. I.

2. *Address of Capt. Charles B. Richards*, at the placing of a memorial tablet in the Hamilton County Court House, in the *Annals of Iowa* (Third Series), Vol. III.

3. Carpenter's *The Spirit Lake Massacre* in the *Midland Monthly*, Vol. IV; *Address of John N. Maxwell* in the *Annals of Iowa* (Third Series), Vol. III; Smith's *History of Dickinson County, Iowa*.

4. *Letter from Sergt. Harris Hoover* in the *Annals of Iowa* (Third Series), Vol. III; Hoover's *The Tragedy of Okoboji* in the *Annals of Iowa* (Third Series), Vol. V.

accompany the messenger to these places. The response at Webster City was as spontaneous as at Fort Dodge. Upon the arrival of the messengers a meeting was called in the village schoolhouse, so that all might hear the story of the Indian outrages. Volunteers were called for, and by nine o'clock on the morning of the twenty-third a company of twenty-eight men had been selected to undertake the expedition. Only young men were encouraged to volunteer, since it was thought that the older men would not be able to undergo the trials of the trip to and from the lakes. But when both young and old insisted upon going a sort of selective draft was resorted to. On Monday morning, March twenty-third, all who had volunteered were ranged in a row and J. D. Maxwell, the county judge, was called upon to make the selection, which he did to the satisfaction of all.[5]

But there were problems other than the securing of volunteers to be met and solved—such as the procuring of tents, provisions, wagons or sleds, and teams, without which the expedition would have little hope of success. By contributions the company was provided with a varied collection of fire-arms, a wagon, two or three yoke of oxen, food, and some extra clothing and blankets. Among those who gave liberally were "W. C. and S. Willson, A. Moon, the Brewers, Charles T. Fenton, S. B. Rosenkrans, the Funks, E. W. Saulsbury and B. S. Mason."[6] At this time the village of Webster City could boast of but few people who were able to provide much assistance; but each did his best and in the end the volunteers were reasonably well outfitted for the journey.

Departure from Webster City was delayed until one o'clock in the afternoon of the twenty-third, owing to the difficulty of securing the necessary equipment for the men. Even then they were not adequately equipped. Indeed, it was impossible to foresee and prepare for the trials to be faced on the expedition. Moreover, not one of these people had had any experience in contending with the elements under such conditions as then prevailed.

The Webster City company arrived at Fort Dodge about nine o'clock in the evening of the same day and was given a rousing welcome. No better testimonial to the spirit and determination of the men, untrained as they were, can be given than to say that they made the march of more than twenty miles in eight hours over nearly impassable roads. The snow had thawed just enough to cause it to yield

---

5. Hoover's *The Tragedy of Okoboji* in the *Annals of Iowa* (Third Series), Vol. V.
6. *Address of John N. Maxwell* in the *Annals of Iowa* (Third Series), Vol. III.

readily under the tread of the men—making the march one continuous flounder from Webster City to Fort Dodge.[7]

In the evening, immediately following the arrival at Fort Dodge, officers for the company were chosen by ballot. The company as then organised was designated as Company C and was officered as follows: John C. Johnson, Captain; John N. Maxwell, First Lieutenant; Frank B. Mason, Second Lieutenant; Harris Hoover, Sergeant; and A. Newton Hathaway, Corporal. The privates were William K. Laughlin and Michael Sweeney of the Webster City settlement; and Thomas Anderson, Thomas B. Bonebright, James Brainard, Sherman Cassady, Patrick Conlan, Henry E. Dalley, John Erie, Emery W. Gates, John Gates, Josiah Griffith, James Hickey, Humphrey C. Hillock, M. W. Howland, Elias D. Kellogg, A. S. Leonard, F. R. Moody, John Nolan (or Nowland), J. C. Pemberton, Alonzo Richardson, Patrick Stafford, and A. K. Tullis of the country immediately adjacent to Webster City.[8]

Captain Johnson was not a Webster City man but came from Bach Grove. In view of the later incidents of the trip his enlistment was somewhat pathetic. He arrived in town, after the beginning of the meeting, which he attended with a friend. He was so impressed by the spirit of the occasion that he volunteered, being one of the first who expressed a willingness to go. He at once sent word to his mother concerning the mission upon which he was going, saying that he probably would not see her for some time—not thinking that it might be his lot never to return.[9]

While news of the massacre was being carried to Homer, Webster City, and Border Plains, the citizens of Fort Dodge and vicinity were hard at work organising their groups of volunteers, so that by the time the Webster City unit had arrived they were ready for some form of united action. Here too it was thought best to select only the younger men, since the inclemency of the weather as well as the marching conditions at this time would be a severe drain upon the physical endurance of the strongest. In addition it was recognised that the young men would not have in many instances the care of dependent families. Fully eighty men had stepped forward in response to the call for volunteers, and from these two companies were organised.

---

7. *The Narrative of W. K. Laughlin* in the *Annals of Iowa* (Third Series), Vol. III.
8. *The Spirit Lake Massacre and Relief Expedition* in the *Roster and Record of Iowa Soldiers*, Vol. VI; *Annals of Iowa* (Third Series), Vol. II. See also the west tablet on the State Memorial Monument near the Gardner cabin, Arnold's Park, Okoboji, Iowa.
9. *Address of John N. Maxwell* in the *Annals of Iowa* (Third Series), Vol. III; *The Spirit Lake Massacre and Relief Expedition* in the *Roster and Record of Iowa Soldiers*, Vol. VI.

Early on Monday morning each of the two companies selected officers. Charles B. Richards, who had acted as secretary of the first general meeting, was selected as Captain of Company A; while John F. Duncombe was chosen to head Company B. Captain Richards at once selected Franklin A. Stratton as First Lieutenant, L. K. Wright as Sergeant, and Solon Mason as Corporal; while Captain Duncombe named James Linn as First Lieutenant, Smith E. Stevens, Second Lieutenant, William N. Koons, Sergeant, and Thomas Callagan as Corporal of Company B.[10]

The Roster of Company A at the time of its organisation on March 23rd comprised the following privates: George W. Brizee, William E. Burkholder, Henry Carse, —— Chatterton, Julius Conrad, L. D. Crawford, J. W. Dawson, William De Fore or William A. De Foe, John Farney, William N. Ford, John Gales, William McCauley, E. Mahan, Michael Maher, B. F. Parmenter, W. F. Porter, L. B. Ridgeway, George P. Smith, Roderick A. Smith, Winton Smith, Owen S. Spencer, C. Stebbins, Silas Van Cleave, D. Westerfield, and R. U. Wheelock.

In Company B were enrolled the following: Jesse Addington, D. H. Baker, Hiram Benjamin, Orlando Bice, R. F. Carter, Richard Carter, Michael Cavanaugh, A. E. Crouse, John Hefley, Orlando C. Howe, D. F. Howell, Albert S. Johnson, Michael McCarty, G. F. McClure, Robert McCormick, John N. McFarland, A. S. Malcolm, Daniel Morrissey, Jonas Murray, Daniel Okeson, John O'Laughlin, W. Searles, Guernsey Smith, Reuben Whetstone, John White, Washington Williams, and William R. Wilson.[11]

These companies when organised were equipped in the same manner as at Webster City—that is, by contributions from those older men who, finding age a bar to joining the expedition, contributed whatever they found possible "near the end of a severe winter in a frontier town one hundred and fifty miles from any source of supply."[12] Scarcely was there a man or woman in the little hamlet or in the surrounding country who did not offer something—guns, ammunition, food, gloves, wearing apparel, blankets, or other articles that might prove

---

10. *Roster and Record of Iowa Soldiers*, Vol. VI; Duncombe's *Spirit Lake Expedition* in the *Annals of Iowa* (Third Series), Vol. III. 11. The roster as here given is that found in the *Roster and Record of Iowa Soldiers*, Vol. VI, and is also to be found on the west tablet of the Memorial Monument at Arnold's Park, Okoboji, Iowa. Harris Hoover in his *Expedition to Spirit Lake* in the *Hamilton Freeman* (Webster City), August 20, 1857, differs somewhat

12. *Address of Capt. Charles B. Richards* in the *Annals of Iowa* (Third Series), Vol. II.

useful on the journey. The equipment of arms varied from the worst conditioned shotgun to some of the finest type of Sharps rifle to be found on the frontier.[13] All of Monday, after the muster in, was spent in collecting the equipment for the expedition. After some little effort two or three ox teams and wagons were secured to haul the food supplies, bedding, and camp equipment. A team and wagon was allotted to each company, so that all supplies for each organisation might be kept separate and distinct. The imperfect means of transportation permitted the taking of only limited supplies; and no grain or forage could be taken upon which the oxen might subsist. It was thought, strangely enough, that the cattle might be able to forage for themselves at the various camping or stopping places along the route.

After the companies had been organised as separate units and the Webster City contingent had arrived, a closer co-ordination of the forces was effected. A general meeting of the three organisations was called and the matter of co-ordination discussed. In the end it was decided to organise as a battalion. Major William Williams, the only person who had had military experience and who had been empowered by Governor Grimes to act in such an emergency, was chosen to command the battalion thus created. This was a recognition of the undoubted ability and vigour of the first postmaster, first mayor, and first citizen of Fort Dodge—especially since his age of sixty years was far beyond that considered desirable for members of the expedition.[14] The future proved the wisdom of the selection, for his command of the situation had much to do with shaping the later developments more fortunately than otherwise might have been the case. George B. Sherman was selected as quartermaster and commissary; and in order to enable him to better perform his duties he was detached from Company A into which he had already been mustered. Dr. George R. Bissell of Fort Dodge was selected as surgeon, and he proved a most worthy and helpful member of the expedition. Thus organised, the battalion numbered at the time of leaving Fort Dodge a total of ninety-one officers and enlisted men.

---

13. *Mr. Duncombe's Address* in the *Annals of Iowa* (Third Series), Vol. III.

14. Hoover in his *Expedition to Spirit Lake* in the *Hamilton Freeman* (Webster City), August 20, 1857, speaks of Major Williams as "afflicted with rheumatism, and the frost of 70 winters whitening his brow" as resolutely setting "forward at our head." This Major Williams resented and took occasion to reply in the succeeding issue of the *Freeman* that "I can't agree to be made so old. I was 60 last December (1856), and never have I been afflicted with rheumatism in my life .... I don't wish to be considered so old."

CHAPTER 22

The March from Fort Dodge to Medium Lake

Though somewhat delayed by inability to secure transportation, the relief battalion from Fort Dodge and Webster City got under way about noon on Tuesday, March twenty-fourth, within four days after receiving the news of the massacre.[1] The first day's march did not record much progress, as the men had advanced only about six or seven miles when they encamped at the mouth of Beaver Creek. By this time they had begun to realise that they were no more than raw recruits with no knowledge or appreciation of active service. With snow nearly four feet deep on the level, and with ravines, gulches, and low places completely filled, they encountered from the beginning almost endless difficulties in marching and in the transportation of supplies. Not a man was intimately acquainted with the surrounding country. Frequently they found themselves plunged into snow-filled creek beds where with the oxen they floundered vainly for some time in more than fifteen or twenty feet of drifted snow before they gained the lesser depth beyond. The difficulties were greatly increased by the lack of sufficient transportation facilities.

Having halted for the night each company built a monster camp fire around which the men gathered, each endeavouring to prepare his own supper since neither company was provided with a cook. "It was quite amusing to see 'the boys' mix up meal, bake 'slap jacks', fry meat, wash dishes and act the 'housewife' generally, but 'tis said 'practice makes perfect' and the truth of the adage was substantiated in the case under consideration for before our return some of the boys became quite expert in the handicraft above mentioned.

1. *Address of John N. Maxwell* in the *Annals of Iowa* (Third Series), Vol. III.

"One of our Lieutenants—a jolly good fellow, by the way—averred that he could throw a 'griddle-cake' out of the roof of a log cabin, which he temporarily occupied, and while it performed divers circumgyrations in mid-air, could run out and catch it 't'other side up' on the spider." [2] Emery W. Gates of Company C is said to have successfully demonstrated his ability to perform this feat while the expedition was in camp at McKnight's Point.[3] He was later appointed cook of his company, in which capacity he rendered most acceptable service.

After finishing their first meal the men made ready for the night. Each man had been provided with one blanket, and in this he rolled himself for sleep that came to but few. Many found the pillowing of the head upon the ground or snow not conducive to slumber, while a few were prevented from sleeping by the heavy slumber of others. "My first night on this expedition", says Captain Duncombe, "will never pass from my memory. It is as vivid now as it was at the time. I, too, slept on a snowbank and had as my next neighbour one of those horrible snorers who could make a danger signal louder than a locomotive whistle and more musical than a calliope in the procession of a circus."[4]

The morning of the twenty-fifth saw the men awake and astir early in the preparation of a breakfast that failed to satisfy. On this second day the line of march led them up the course of the Des Moines—the plan being to travel upon the ice of the river in order to avoid the dangerous pitfalls of the land. The point which they hoped to reach was Dakota City just above the junction of the east and west forks of the Des Moines. In attempting to use the ice as a roadway, the men were compelled to cross and recross the river no less than fifteen or twenty times. In the end this plan of march proved impracticable since the ice in places was not strong enough to sustain the weight of the men; whenever a weak place was reached it was necessary to leave the river and struggle along over the ravines which broke the banks of the river.

Matters became much worse as the day developed into one of

---

2. Hoover's *Expedition to Spirit Lake* in the *Hamilton Freeman* (Webster City), August 20, 1857; *Address of Capt. Charles B. Richards* in the *Annals of Iowa* (Third Series), Vol. III.

3. *A Paper by Michael Sweeney* in the *Annals of Iowa* (Third Series), Vol. III; *The Narrative of W. K. Laughlin* in the *Annals of Iowa* (Third Series), Vol. III; Hoover's *Expedition to Spirit Lake* in the *Hamilton Freeman* (Webster City), August 20, 1857.

4. Duncombe's *Spirit Lake Expedition* in the *Annals of Iowa* (Third Series), Vol. III.

considerable warmth. The water running down from the hillsides collected in the depressions and turned the snow of the ravines into slush. With dazzling brilliancy the sun shone upon the white snow, and many of the men suffered so severely from snow-blindness as to become practically helpless. The rays reflected from the snow also burned the hands and faces of the men.[5] By night the battalion had covered no more than the ten miles to Dakota City. Here they camped as best they could. Some were able to secure places in stables, and a few were taken into the homes; but by far the greater number were compelled to sleep in their blankets on the open prairie. By this time some of the men were showing evidence of exhaustion, while others were suffering a very marked decline in spirits.

On the march north from Dakota City the real difficulties of the expedition developed. Beyond this point the snow was piled so high that frequently the groves and timber along the river could not be reached. When such conditions were encountered the command was compelled to keep to the open prairie. This was not, however, practicable for any considerable time on account of the cutting wind that swept across the snow fields. Having to choose between two evils, they elected what appeared to be the lesser and kept within the shelter of the timber regardless of the difficulties.

To overcome the difficulties on the third day out from Fort Dodge and the first day north of Dakota City, it was found necessary to send the men ahead in double files to break a road for the ox teams and wagons which followed. By marching and counter-marching the snow was beaten down so that it was made possible for the oxen to drag the wagons through the deep drifts. This did not, however, always solve the transportation problem, for even with such help the oxen were frequently unable to move the wagons. When the oxen became stalled in a snow bank a long rope was attached to the wagon so that all hands could take hold and pull together with the oxen. By almost herculean efforts the wagons were thus dragged through the drifts of snow. Often the snow would accumulate in great piles in front of the wagons, which caused many pauses in the march. The marching and counter-marching, the dragging of wagons by man power, and the clearing away of snow continued during the two days out from Dakota City. Under such conditions the advance of the command was painfully slow.

But the drifts were not the worst obstacle. When ravines or stream

---

5. *Address of Capt. Charles B. Richards* in the *Annals of Iowa* (Third Series), Vol. III.

heads were encountered in the line of march the oxen could do little but flounder in the snow which was then four or five times as deep as on the level ground of the prairie. They could scarcely secure a footing, for here the soft snow had usually been converted into almost bottomless slush. At such times the men would "wade through, stack arms, return and unhitch the teams, and attach ropes to them and *draw them through*"; this done, they "performed a similar operation on the wagons".[6] It was necessary to resort to this method of advance every mile or two.

In the face of such conditions, it became very evident that the timber at McKnight's Point could not be reached on scheduled time.[7] When the companies came to appreciate more fully the difficulties before them, Captain Duncombe, Lieutenant Maxwell, and R. U. Wheelock were sent ahead as scouts to pick out a better road and if possible secure a camping place near timber and water.[8] To guide the advancing column, beacon fires were built; but these were of little or no use to the men in the rear. The main body of marchers, wet, hungry, and suffering acutely from the cold, toiled on until darkness made further progress seem an impossibility. Major Williams therefore called a halt and "put it to a vote whether we should camp where we were, or still persist in getting to the Point. A majority voted to camp where we were, although several preferred to keep on, fearing we would freeze to death anyway, and that it was as well to keep moving. We were on the bleak prairie.... We had no tents to shelter us; so, to many the outlook was extremely forbidding, but all acquiesced in the will of the majority."[9]

The place selected for the camp was a high ridge from which the snow had been blown by the winter's winds. Each company went into its own camp. The tarpaulin covers for the wagons were removed and stretched around the wagons so as to form a shelter from the wind. Upon the ground under the wagons the men placed their oil-skin

---

6. Hoover's *Expedition to Spirit Lake* in the *Hamilton Freeman* (Webster City), August 20, 1857. See also Duncombe's *Spirit Lake Expedition* in the *Annals of Iowa* (Third Series),Vol. III; *Address of John N. Maxwell* in the *Annals of Iowa* (Third Series),Vol. III; *A Paper by Michael Sweeney* in the *Annals of Iowa* (Third Series),Vol. III.
7. McKnight's Point was on the West Fork of the Des Moines, on the Fort Ridgely road, about two miles to the southeast of the mouth of Bridge Creek.—See map in Parker's *Iowa As It Is*, 1857.
8. Hoover's *The Tragedy of Okoboji* in the *Annals of Iowa* (Third Series),Vol.V; Duncombe's *Spirit Lake Expedition* in the *Annals of Iowa* (Third Series),Vol. III.
9. *A Paper by Michael Sweeney* in the *Annals of Iowa*(Third Series),Vol. III.

coats to serve as a floor upon which to pile the bedding. Wet boots were used for pillows. Then, huddled closely together under the wagons so that when one turned all had to do likewise, the weary volunteers "turned in" for the night. Being some distance from the timber they could obtain no wood with which to kindle fires—without which the men were unable to warm themselves, dry their clothing, or cook their food. For supper they had nothing to eat save crackers and uncooked ham; and the same diet made up the breakfast on the following morning.[10]

Early Friday morning the companies continued the march toward McKnight's Point, where they arrived about noon. Here they found Duncombe, Wheelock, and Maxwell awaiting them. In nearly two days the battalion had covered a distance of something over twelve miles from Dakota City to McKnight's Point. Even at this slow rate of progress they arrived in a thoroughly exhausted condition.

Captain Duncombe had reached the Point the evening before in a very benumbed condition and nearly unconscious from the exposure and suffering occasioned by the intensity of the cold. In explaining his condition, however, a story was later told by a member of the expedition to the effect that as the Point was neared by the three scouts Duncombe became exhausted and appeared to be unable to proceed. Wheelock had with him what was thought to be a cordial, some of which he offered to the captain. The "cordial" proved to be laudanum, which so affected Duncombe that had it not been for Wheelock and Maxwell, who kept him awake and moving, he would have been overcome. When within two miles of the Point, Maxwell started for help. Too exhausted to walk, he lay down on the snow and rolled himself over and over till he reached the grove; while Wheelock remained with Duncombe to keep him awake and moving. At the grove Maxwell found a cabin in which were Jeremiah Evans and William L. Church. Hearing Maxwell's story, they at once set out to rescue Duncombe and Wheelock. In rolling over and over in the snow Maxwell had made a trail which the rescuers had no trouble in following to the suffering men. After being dragged to the cabin, Duncombe fell asleep and could not be aroused. But by the time the expedition arrived on the following day he had awakened and appeared to be little or none the worse for his unusual experience.[11]

10. *A Paper by Michael Sweeney* in the *Annals of Iowa* (Third Series), Vol. III.
11. For this incident see Duncombe's *Spirit Lake Expedition* in the *Annals of Iowa* (Third Series), Vol. III; Hoover's *The Tragedy of Okoboji* in the *Annals of Iowa* (Third Series), Vol. V.

By Saturday a number of the men were ill from exposure, but uncomplainingly continued the trying march. Major Williams, although the oldest man of the expeditionary force, bore his privations extremely well, giving no evidence of exhaustion. If anything the trials of the march had aroused in him a still stronger and sterner fighting spirit. Some of the force, apparently bearing the trials well, were reported as complaining. One of these men is said to have been a veteran of the Mexican War and often made the boast that he had been the third soldier to enter the Mexican fortress of Churubusco when it was stormed and taken by the American forces. But now he declared the continuance of the march "would result in the destruction of the entire command".[12]

Calling a meeting of the battalion, Major Williams addressed the men upon the duties and obligations of the expedition, and he ended by declaring: "You now understand this is not to be a holiday campaign, and every man in the battalion who feels that he has gone far enough is at liberty to return."[13] No one was willing to accept the offer. It appears, however, that Daniel Okeson and John O'Laughlin, who had been accepted under protest on account of their age, were now discharged from Company B on account of disabilities incident to their years. Under protest they accepted discharge and returned to Fort Dodge.

The battalion's ranks, however, were not depleted by these dismissals, as Jeremiah Evans and William L. Church at once enlisted—the former in Company B and the latter in Company C.[14] Evans had been a settler at McKnight's Point for some time, and it was at his cabin that the advance scouts were received and cared for. Church, whose home was at Springfield, Minnesota, had been on a trip to Fort Dodge for supplies and had stopped at the Evans cabin on his return up the river on the Fort Ridgely trail. Upon his arrival he had been told of the massacre at the lakes and also that a relief expedition was being organised at Fort Dodge to rescue the whites who might have escaped and to punish the Indians who had done the deed. Upon hearing this he had resolved to await the coming of the expedition and enlist for service.

At McKnight's Point a halt of a half-day on Friday afternoon was taken for purposes of recuperation. Here a number of deserted cab-

---

12. Duncombe's *Spirit Lake Expedition* in the *Annals of Iowa* (Third Series),Vol. III.
13. Carpenter's *The Spirit Lake Massacre* in the *Midland Monthly*,Vol. IV.
14. *Roster and Record of Iowa Soldiers*,Vol.VI.

ins furnished shelter for the men. It was at this halt that Company C selected Emery W. Gates as cook. Following his appointment it is said that Gates prepared for the men one of the best meals they had ever eaten; and they agreed that their stay here was one "grand, good time".[15]

Company A also celebrated, but in an entirely different manner. To divert the minds of those who were suffering from the hardships of the march, Captain Richards decided to hold a mock court-martial. The victim, a man by the name of Brizee, was of course unaware of the fake character of the affair and took the proceeding with great seriousness. It seems that the tar box of Company A's wagon had been lost, and for this Brizee was held responsible. The formal trial procedure—the organisation of the court, the summoning of witnesses, the taking of testimony, and the rendering of a formal decision—was carried through and Brizee was declared guilty. In all solemnity he was sentenced to be shot. It is said that he was very much frightened and most earnestly implored a pardon which was finally granted.[16]

On the morning of Saturday, the twenty-eighth, the three companies bade goodbye to McKnight's Point and started for Shippey's Point, which was located on the west fork of Cylinder Creek about two miles above the junction of the main stream with the Des Moines. Since leaving Dakota City the expedition had followed as nearly as possible the Fort Ridgely road up the Des Moines Valley—a route which it was planned to continue as far as practicable. At McCormick's place about two miles below Shippey's, they met Angus McBane, Cyrus C. Carpenter, William P. Pollock, and Andrew Hood, who had heard of the massacre at the Irish Colony and were hastening south to Fort Dodge to report.[17] These men at once joined Company A.

It was at Shippey's Point that J. M. Thatcher and Asa Burtch were found anxiously awaiting the coming of the battalion. Thatcher was nearly frantic over the reported fate of his family, but had been induced by Burtch to await the coming of the relief party—in Company B of which the two men now enlisted.[18] The load of supplies—

---

15. *The Narrative of W. K. Laughlin* in the *Annals of Iowa* (Third Series), Vol. III.
16. Duncombe's *Spirit Lake Expedition* in the *Annals of Iowa* (Third Series), Vol. III
17. For the enlistments of these individuals see the *Roster and Record of Iowa Soldiers*, Vol. VI.
18. In the *Roster and Record of Iowa Soldiers*, Vol. VI, it is stated that Thatcher and Burtch enlisted either at Fort Dodge on March twenty-third or at Shippey's on March twenty-eighth. The latter place and date seem far more probable than do the former.

mostly flour, which Luce and Thatcher had been taking to the lakes from the eastern part of the state—was confiscated for the use of the battalion as the supplies of the party were growing uncomfortably low and Sherman, the commissary, was becoming nervous.

On Sunday morning the onward march was resumed with the Irish settlement on Medium Lake as the objective point for the day. As the expedition moved further to the north, the difficulties of the march became greater because the snow increased in depth. From Shippey's Point the march followed the Dragoon Trail, although no team had been able to make its way over this road for weeks. To the tired men the drifts seemed mountain high, while the depth of the snow in the low places seemed fathomless. The "colony" was finally reached without incident.

The settlement at Medium Lake comprised about twelve or fifteen Irish families who had come from Illinois in the fall of 1856. They had selected claims along the Des Moines River, but had made no permanent improvements. Instead, they had built temporary cabins in a grove at the southwest corner of Medium Lake where they planned to spend the winter.[19] In time this temporary settlement developed into the town of Emmetsburg, which to the present day has retained a large percentage of people of Irish nativity. Here also were many people who had fled from the perils of an Indian attack and had come together for the winter. They were found living in rudely constructed cabin shelters or in dugouts.[20] Destitute of provisions, they were as far as possible being supported from the slender stores of their Irish neighbours upon whose pity they had thrown themselves.

While here the expeditionary force was augmented by new recruits: thereafter it comprised one hundred and twenty-five men. Since most of these persons did not formally enlist their names do not appear upon the official muster roll of the battalion. Not only did the companies receive recruits at Medium Lake, but it was here that they were able to exchange their worn out oxen for fresh teams. They were also able to replenish somewhat their commissary department, for the new members brought with them as much food as the settlement was able to spare.

---

19. *A Paper by Michael Sweeney* in the *Annals of Iowa*(Third Series),Vol. III; *The Narrative of W. K. Laughlin* in the *Annals of Iowa* (Third Series),Vol. III.
20. *The Narrative of W. K. Laughlin* in the *Annals of Iowa* (Third Series),Vol. III.

CHAPTER 23

From Medium Lake to Granger's Point

On Monday morning the expedition set out very much refreshed; for the men had not only feasted the evening before but that morning they "butchered a cow that had been wintered on prairie hay. The beef was not exactly porterhouse steak, but it was food for hungry men."[1] The day's march was a hard one, and when Big Island Grove near the Mud Lakes was reached the men were so exhausted that they threw themselves on the ground, rolled up in their blankets, and went to sleep without supper.

Ex-Governor Carpenter, in relating his experiences as a member of the expedition, says that there was after the lapse of forty-one years a picture before him "of Capt. Charles B. Richards and Lieutenant F. A. Stratton ... with two or three of the men, cutting wood, punching the fire, and baking pancakes, until long after midnight; and as they would get enough baked for a meal they would waken some tired and hungry man and give him his supper: and the exercises in Company A were but a sample of what was in progress in each of the companies."[2] Thus the greater portion of the night was spent by the solicitous officers in caring for their men.

After leaving Medium Lake evidences of the presence of Indians were observed from time to time. What appeared to be *moccasin* tracks were frequently seen. Cattle had been killed in such a manner as to leave no doubt that the work had been done by Indians. At Big Island Grove many signs of Indians were found. On an island in the middle of the lake the Indians had constructed a look-out in the tree-tops

---
1. *Address of John N. Maxwell* in the *Annals of Iowa* (Third Series), Vol. III.
2. Carpenter's *The Spirit Lake Expedition* in the *Annals of Iowa* (Third Series), Vol. III.

from which they were able to see the country for miles around. Better evidence still of the fact that their visits were recent was the report that the campfires were still glowing, and that fishing holes were found in the ice.[3]

Many members of the expedition believed that the Indians, after raiding the settlements at the lake, would cross over to the Des Moines and proceed south on a war of extermination; and the signs at Big Island Grove were very readily accepted as a substantiation of this belief. It is probable, however, that this was a mistaken conclusion. Sleepy-Eye had frequently rendezvoused at Big Island Grove, and the arrival of the expedition may have followed closely his departure on the spring hunting trip. It is not probable that Inkpaduta's men went east of the lakes or south of Springfield.

On the evening of the arrival of the expedition at Big Island Grove, Major Williams decided that since they were evidently in the Indian country the march should thereafter be made with more caution. Accordingly, he called for volunteers for an advance scouting party of ten men whose work would be to precede the main expeditionary force and keep a sharp look-out for the near approach of Indians and to observe, interpret, and report any signs that might be discovered. They were to maintain an advance of perhaps three miles over the main column. Major Williams selected as the commander of this advance guard William L. Church, who of all the members of the expedition was the most familiar with the country in which they were now moving, since he had passed through it a number of times after settling at Springfield. Those who had volunteered as his companions were Lieutenant Maxwell, Thatcher, Hathaway, F. R. Mason, Laughlin, A. S. Johnson, De Foe, Carpenter, and another man whose identity seems to have been forgotten shortly after the return of the expedition to Fort Dodge.[4]

The members of the advance guard were astir early Tuesday morning; and while they breakfasted, rations for three days were made ready for each man. These rations when totalled amounted to forty pounds of corn meal and twenty pounds of wheat flour. In addition the men were allowed each a piece of corn bread about six inches square,

---

3. Carpenter's *The Spirit Lake Expedition* in the *Annals of Iowa* (Third Series), Vol. III; *Address of John N. Maxwell* in the *Annals of Iowa* (Third Series), Vol. III; *The Narrative of W. K. Laughlin* in the *Annals of Iowa* (Third Series), Vol. III.

4. There seems to have been some disagreement as to who had charge of the advance guard. For the view taken by the present writer see Smith's *History of Dickinson County, Iowa*.

which was supposed to be divided among the meals of the succeeding three days; but a number of the men, deciding that the easiest way to carry the bread was to eat it, immediately set about doing that very thing. The scouting party left the main body of the expedition about six o'clock on a beautiful winter's morning—although it was in fact the closing day of March. Orders were given to the men to scout north, northwest, and northeast of the route to be followed by the main body. Lieutenant Maxwell and Laughlin, being true plainsmen, took the lead, while the remaining eight were soon envying "the ease and celerity with which" they "with their long legs and wiry frames, pulled through the snow and across the snow-drifts".[5]

The advance had made about twelve miles when the men paused on the bare ridge of the Des Moines water-shed for the mid-day meal. Mason was stationed as sentry, while the others ate in the sheltered lea of the ridge. At some distance from the other members of the party, Mason had been at his post only a short time when he saw far to the northwest a black spot come into view. It soon became evident that the spot was moving. The attention of the other members of the party was called to the discovery. After sighting with their ramrods for some minutes, they too concluded that the object was really on the move. Furthermore it was agreed that the moving object must be a party of Indians; and so an attack was planned.

The squad advanced on the run to meet the party, which was probably two miles away. But no sooner had the whites started toward the "Indians" than the latter were observed to hold a hurried consultation. Between the two parties was a willow-bordered creek toward which each started for the apparent purpose of ambushing the other. The advance guard, having reached and passed the creek first, scaled the knoll or ridge of ground just beyond. Having reached the crest of the swell, the expeditionists prepared to fight. The opposing force halted and likewise seemed to prepare for defence. Before beginning the attack, however, the arrival of Church and a second man was awaited. When these men had come up, breathless but ready for the fray, the order to advance was given. Suddenly Church gave a shout and sprang forward exclaiming: "My God, there's my wife and babies!" The "Indians" turned out to be none other than the refugees from Springfield, Minnesota. The meeting was both dramatic and pathetic. For days relatives and friends of the refugees had believed them dead—victims

---

5. Frank R. Mason's *Recollections* in the *Annals of Iowa* (Third Series), Vol. III; Carpenter's *Spirit Lake Expedition* in the *Annals of Iowa* (Third Series), Vol. III.

of Indian barbarities. Now some were reunited with their loved ones, while others received word that their kin were lying in the snows of the lake region or had been carried away in captivity by the Indians.[6]

A pathetic sight, indeed, were these terrified fugitives. "In the haste of their flight they had taken but few provisions and scanty clothing. The women had worn out their shoes; their dresses were worn into fringe about the ankles; the children were crying with hunger and cold; the wounded were in a deplorable condition for want of surgical aid. Their food was entirely exhausted; they had no means of making fire; their blankets and clothing were wet and frozen.... The refugees were so overcome ... that they sank down in the snow, crying and laughing alternately, as their deliverers gathered around them."[7] The wounded were in a terrible condition. "Mr. Thomas was travelling with his hand dangling by the cords of his arm, having been shot through the wrist."[8] They were "almost exhausted from the toilsome march, lack of food, exposure to the inclement weather, and the terrible anxiety of the previous week."[9]

From the story of the refugees it seems that while painfully making their way southward, and almost ready to perish from cold, starvation, and physical exhaustion, they saw appear upon the summit of a ridge far to the southeastward a group of men whom they, too, supposed to be Indians. It happened that the men of the advance guard were wearing shawls as a protection from the cold, and so they really did have the appearance of blanket-clad Indians. The refugees were wild with terror for they felt that their end had certainly come. There was only one man in the party who really had the courage and was able to fight. Loading the eight rifles which were in the possession of the party, John Bradshaw prepared to meet the enemy single-handed, ready to sacrifice his life if necessary in the defence of the helpless members of the party. It is said that he stood rifle in hand until Church, breaking from the ranks of the advance guard, ran forward shouting for his wife and children. Not until then was it evident to the refugees that friends rather than enemies were approaching.[10]

Mason and Smith were chosen to carry the news back to the main

---

6. For an account of the discovery of the Springfield fugitives see that of *Frank R. Mason's Recollections* in *Annals of Iowa* (Third Series), Vol. III.
7. A quotation from Carpenter in Gue's *History of Iowa*, Vol. I.
8. *Frank R. Mason's Recollections* in the *Annals of Iowa* (Third Series), Vol. III; Smith's *A History of Dickinson County, Iowa*.
9 & 10. *A Paper by Charles Aldrich* in the *Annals of Iowa* (Third Series), Vol. III.

body of the expedition, which at this time was nearly eight miles to the rear. Mason declares that he was so excited that notwithstanding his fatigue he ran the whole distance. When the messengers were within two miles of the expedition their coming was observed by Captains Duncombe and Richards who rode out to meet them. Major Williams was sent for and a consultation held. Mason, Duncombe, Richards, and Dr. Bissell were ordered by Major Williams to push forward as rapidly as possible to the aid of the refugees. At four o'clock in the afternoon the start was made, and so well did the men make the return trip that the fugitives from Springfield were reached about nine o'clock. The advance guard and the fugitives were found in the shelter of the creek willows over a mile from where they had been left. Camp had been pitched—if such it could be called. Meanwhile, a storm had come up and it was raining furiously, which only increased the sad plight of the starving and ragged refugees who were without adequate shelter.[11]

When the main expeditionary body arrived about midnight strenuous efforts were made to provide some sort of comfort for the distressed and starving fugitives. The only semblance to a tent in the expedition's equipment—one made of blankets patched together—was provided them, and their wounds were dressed by Dr. Bissell. Being so near the scene of the massacre, it was feared that even then Indians might be in the vicinity of the camp. And so guards were placed to prevent a surprise attack. Since the men were greatly exhausted by the day's efforts, they were relieved of guard duty each hour. Thus little rest came to any of the men that night. In the morning the refugees were again fed and provided with blankets by the expeditionary force from its already slender store. Being thus outfitted, they were given a guard and sent on to the Irish Colony. Mr. Church left the expedition at this point to accompany his wife and children to Fort Dodge and Webster City.

Learning from the fugitives the facts concerning the presence of the Indians at Springfield, Major Williams decided to push toward that point as rapidly as possible. When the march was resumed on the morning following the meeting with the refugees from Springfield, the expedition moved in the direction of Granger's Point. John Bradshaw, Morris Markham, and Jareb Palmer did not continue with the refugees, but enlisted as members of the expeditionary force, each hoping for a chance to even up matters with the red men.

---

11. *Frank R. Mason's Recollections* in the *Annals of Iowa* (Third Series), Vol. III.

The march to the Granger settlement was enlivened by a little incident that aided much in detracting from the trying ordeal of the march. In the morning additional precautions were taken to guard against a surprise by Indians: a small group of men were selected by Major Williams to scout just ahead of the main body and ascertain if Indians might chance to be in the timber along the streams and about the lakes. The scouts were given orders to fire their guns only in case they found Indians. The advance had continued about three miles when the crack of a gun was heard, followed by a number of reports in quick succession from the timber just ahead. Immediately two men emerged from the timber on the run. Captain Duncombe who was about a mile in advance of his command thought the runners to be Indians, and he at once gave chase hoping to head them off before they could enter another grove a short distance beyond and for which they were evidently making. Being mounted, Duncombe soon approached near enough to recognise two of the expedition scouts.

It was soon learned that while passing through the timber two old hunter members of the squad chanced to see some beavers sunning themselves on the ice. Unable to resist the first impulse, they emptied the contents of their guns at the unsuspecting animals. The men seen running out of the timber were only chasing some of the animals that had not been killed by the initial volley. Meanwhile, the whole expeditionary force had been halted, and with loaded guns put in readiness for the attack. Some members, unable to control themselves, did not wait for the command, but broke ranks and ran toward the imagined Indians with guns ready for firing. After some little time the expedition was again restored to a state of order and the march resumed.

Upon reaching Granger's Point that evening, they were very inhospitably received by a man and boy who were occupying the cabin. Little information and absolutely no assistance could be secured from them. They reported that they had no food, withdrew into the cabin, and barred the door. Within a brief time, however, a horseman arrived, who proved to be a United States regular from Captain Bee's command which had but lately arrived at Springfield. He brought the information of Bee's arrival, of the flight of the Indians westward, and of Bee's sending a detail to Spirit Lake to bury the dead. He said, however, that the detail had visited only one cabin on Spirit Lake and had there found one body which they buried. They had made no attempt to reach the lower lakes on account of bad weather and roads and the shortage of provisions.

That night Major Williams called a council, and upon a review of the facts it was decided to abandon the chase. But since the bodies of the massacred were yet unburied, it was thought that a detail of volunteers should proceed to the lakes on that mission.[12]

---

12. *Address of Capt. Charles B. Richards* in the *Annals of Iowa* (Third Series), Vol. III; *Address of John N. Maxwell* in the *Annals of Iowa* (Third Series), Vol. III; Duncombe's *Spirit Lake Expedition* in the *Annals of Iowa* (Third Series), Vol. III.

CHAPTER 24

The Burial Detail

When morning came the conclusions of the council were reported to the command, and volunteers, not over twenty-five in number, were called for to serve on the burial detail. The report met with a most cordial response and the full quota of volunteers was obtained at once. Those who signified their willingness to serve were: Captain J. C. Johnson and Captain Charles B. Richards, Lieutenant John N. Maxwell, and privates Henry Carse, William E. Burkholder, William Ford, H. E. Dalley, Orlando C. Howe, George P. Smith, Owen S. Spencer, Carl Stebbins, Silas Van Cleave, R. U. Wheelock, R. A. Smith, William A. De Foe, B. F. Parmenter, Jesse Addington, R. McCormick, J. M. Thatcher, William R. Wilson, William K. Laughlin, Elias D. Kellogg, and another whose name is not known.[1]

These men were placed by Major Williams under the immediate command of Captain Johnson of Company C; and on the morning of April second the detail, supplied with two days' rations, took up its march for the lakes. From the outset their undertaking was precarious; with limited rations the men had no assurance that they would be able to secure any more supplies. Nevertheless, they courageously undertook the humanitarian task with the hope that somehow the future would care for itself.

The burial detail was to proceed to the lakes, perform the sad task of burying the dead, and rejoin the main command at the Irish settlement on Medium Lake. Accompanied by two mounted men—Captain Richards and another whose name is now lost—the detail set out upon its journey; but at the crossing of the Des Moines, the first stream reached, the horsemen were unable to force a passage. The men

---

1. *Roster and Record of Iowa Soldiers*, Vol. VI; Smith's *History of Dickinson County, Iowa*.

crossed safely on a log; but the horses could not be forced to swim the channel, and after an hour's work Captain Richards, and his companion gave up the effort and returned to the main command.[2]

Without incident the members of the party reached the southeastern shore of the east lake about two o'clock in the afternoon. Making their way to the Noble and Thatcher cabin, they found the bodies of Enoch Ryan and Alvin Noble at the rear of the house. Each body had been riddled with bullets. The yard and adjacent prairie were thickly sprinkled with feathers which had come from the destroyed feather ticks for which the Indians had had no use. The bodies were buried at the foot of a large oak tree near the house. While some of the party were interring the dead at this cabin, others walked on to the Howe cabin where seven bodies were found lying about the cabin doorstep. Among the mangled remains found in the yard Thatcher identified his infant child. The burials at the Howe cabin were completed late in the afternoon; but darkness prevented the men from proceeding to the other cabins. Returning to the Thatcher cabin they there planned to pass the night. The body of the Thatcher child was interred near the head of a ravine not far from the Thatcher cabin. This was in keeping with the desire of the father that his child should be buried upon his own property. Returning to the Howe cabin the following morning, they found the body of a boy of about thirteen years of age lying at the side of a fallen tree in the dooryard. This apparently was Jacob, the brother of Mrs. Noble, whom she vainly tried to get into the house. The burial detail reported the interment of eight bodies at the Howe cabin.

From Howe's cabin they proceeded to the settlements on the west lake. At this juncture the party was divided, and one section under Captain Johnson took the lake shore trail, while a second under Lieutenant Maxwell crossed the lake directly in line with the Mattock cabin. The Johnson party is said to have found the body of Joel Howe near the trail and to have buried it near the spot where it was found—a place which was lost sight of until its alleged discovery in August, 1914, by a young man, Lee Goodenough of Knoxville, Iowa, while attending a Young Men's Christian Association camp, (see note following). At the Mattock cabin the dead were found widely scattered through the clearing and along the trail toward the Granger home across the strait. Every evidence of a desperate resistance was

---

2. *Address of Captain Charles B. Richards* in the *Annals of Iowa* (Third Series), Vol. III; Smith's *History of Dickinson County, Iowa*.

noted. Dr. Harriott was found with his broken rifle still grasped in his hand. Eleven bodies were collected and buried at this place.

> Note. The reputed finding of the body of Joel Howe may well be questioned. The evidence presented tends to show that the headless skeleton found by Mr. Goodenough could not have been that of Howe. Of the party that took the trail route to the Mattock cabin from Howe's, H. E. Dalley is the only one who in late years has survived, and in fact he was about the only one of the Johnson party who survived the fearful storm of the fourth and was able to give a coherent tale of what they had done. The leader of the party and its second most active member both were lost in the storm. Mr. Dalley in relating the facts of the burial of Howe has always maintained that Howe's body, complete and not headless, was found but not buried at the same spot. Instead the party carried the body to the Mattock place where it was interred. He has ever sturdily maintained that this act of the party is the most vivid recollection of the whole experience. Lieutenant Maxwell has also maintained that the body was not headless when found. There is a discrepancy between the number of bodies disinterred in the vicinity of the Mattock cabin and the number of people reported to have been killed there.
>
> The place and conditions under which the skeleton was found also lend an air of controversy. The skeleton is said to have been found about eighteen inches deep under a cow-path and at the head of a small ravine worn back about thirty feet from the lake shore. In soil conditions as they exist at the lakes, such a ravine would not have been the result of years of work, as is implied, but would have been the work of a freshet. That the wearing back was the result of the work of years is implied in the statement that "Turning at the head of this recession is a cattle path." Here the inference is plain that the cattle for years had turned to avoid the ravine. Once started, the spring freshets and summer rains would have rapidly worn the ravine back to a greater distance than thirty feet. All those stating that the body was buried where found say it was buried upon the summit of a bluff. The conclusion is evident that a thirty foot backward recession of a ravine would hardly have occurred in the face of a bluff. By its finders the body is said to have been buried only

about eighteen inches deep. With the eroding effects of a cattle path would it have been still that depth below the surface after a lapse of nearly a half century? One would think that such could hardly be. For discovery and interment of the remains of Joel Howe, see *Annals of Iowa* (Third Series), Vol. XI.

Across the strait at the Granger cabin they found the body of Carl Granger horribly mutilated, as by cutting or slashing with some sharp instrument about the face. Near him lay his dog which had evidently remained faithfully by him to the last. The dog's body was also terribly mangled.

The Gardner home was the last place to be visited. Here six bodies were found and buried about fifty yards to the southeast of the cabin on a spot said to have been designated by Eliza Gardner when she met the rescue party. As yet the bodies of Luce and Clark had not been found; indeed they were not found until the following June when they were discovered near the outlet of the east lake. Their burial place is not known.[3]

By the time the work of interment was completed at the Gardner cabin, it was late in the afternoon. The rations of the party were all but gone; but the night was coming on, and so the party decided to remain and camp to the north of the Gardner cabin. Fortunately Wilson's memory came to the rescue of the party in their stress for food: he now recalled that in the fall when a visitor at the Gardner cabin he had seen Gardner bury a box of potatoes beneath the stove to insure them against being frozen during the winter. Upon investigation there was discovered nearly a bushel of the potatoes which satisfied the hunger of the men that evening and on the following morning.

After this potato breakfast on the morning of April fourth, sixteen of the twenty-three men composing the detail began the return trip; while seven of the party having interests to look after at the lakes, decided to remain a few days longer. Those who decided to remain were R. A. Smith, Orlando C. Howe, R. U. Wheelock, B. F. Parmenter, Asa Burtch, J. M. Thatcher, and William R. Wilson. Howe and Wheelock remained to make sure of their load of supplies which Parmenter had been compelled to abandon when his two companions started ahead

---

3. There will probably always be more or less controversy as to the number of bodies found and buried. The present writer has sought to be conservative in accepting evidence. See Smith's *A History of Dickinson County, Iowa; Address of John N. Maxwell* in the *Annals of Iowa* (Third Series), Vol. III; *The Narrative of W. K. Laughlin* in the *Annals of Iowa* (Third Series), Vol. III; Mrs. Sharp's *History of the Spirit Lake Massacre*.

of him to Fort Dodge with the news of the massacre.[4]

It appears, however, that the split in the party is to be attributed to something besides business demands. There was a disagreement over the best route to be taken on the return trip. While breakfasting that morning the discussion had arisen. The majority favoured as direct a route as possible across the open prairie to the Irish Colony. Others of the party did not consider such a route to be safe, arguing that it would be better to retrace the route by which they had come—which route would lead them to Granger's Point and thence to the Irish Colony. Meanwhile, a storm was gathering which seemed to add force to the arguments of those in favour of a known road.

The matter could not be settled by argument; and so, after breakfast Captain Johnson, gave the command to fall in. "After the men had fallen in he gave the further order, 'All who favour starting at once across the prairie, step three paces to the front; the rest stand fast'. . . . What little provision was left in camp was speedily packed and the party made ready to depart at once."[5] Captain Johnson and Burkholder urged united action upon the seven who stood fast; but the appeal was unavailing, for the seven men remained steadfast in their conviction that the course as planned was wrong. They offered to join the party if they would take the Granger route; but Johnson and Burkholder stood as firmly against that proposition as the seven were opposed to their plans. Thus the two groups parted company—good friends but each firmly convinced that the other was in the wrong. The members of the party that left took all the food, and were allowed to do so because those who remained behind counted upon securing their store from the wagonload of supplies which had been left somewhere out on the prairie.

The men who remained set out at once to locate the wagon and bring in the needed food. It appears that there was no difficulty in finding the wagon with its cargo of supplies. When each man had loaded himself with a supply, they returned as rapidly as possible for the gathering storm had broken and snow was falling heavily. In a short time, it became a blinding, driving whirlwind of snow. Reaching the cabin, they laid in a supply of fuel. Being well armed, they felt no alarm at the prospect of an Indian attack. All that could be done while the storm raged was to await patiently its abatement. Only after two

---

4. Smith's *A History of Dickinson County, Iowa; Roster and Record of Iowa Soldiers,* Vol. VI.

5. Smith's *A History of Dickinson County, Iowa.*

days did the fury of the storm abate sufficiently to permit the men to leave the cabin in safety.

The morning of the second day after the beginning of the blizzard dawned clear and intensely cold, although the weather had moderated somewhat since the previous evening. The snow was frozen with a hard crust and upon it the party from the Gardner cabin made their way rapidly in the direction of Granger's Point. When they arrived at the Des Moines they found the river completely frozen, which made the crossing easy. Thus with little trouble they were again at Granger's Point where they had left the main body five days previously. They now procured a team and wagon, loaded their baggage, and, after resting a day, started for the Irish settlement. At this point they found some of the wounded from the Springfield settlement who had not been able to proceed with the main command. Here also was Henry Carse who, as will be seen, suffered so terribly on the night out from the Gardner cabin. Resting a day at the Irish settlement, they resumed their journey to Fort Dodge. What had been a small party on leaving the Gardner cabin had more than doubled in number when the Irish colonists were bidden goodbye.

When Cylinder Creek was reached the party succeeded through great effort in effecting a crossing. The undertaking required the whole of an afternoon, but by nightfall the men succeeded in reaching Shippey's Point two miles beyond. "From here the party proceeded on their way to Fort Dodge, which they reached without further adventures than such as are incident to swimming swollen streams and living on short rations, which, in some instances, consisted of a handful of flour and a little salt, which they mixed up with water and baked over a campfire. A few of the party shot, dressed and broiled some muskrats and tried to make the rest believe they considered them good eating, but that diet did not become popular."[6]

★★★★★★

The early part of the day upon which Captain Johnson and party left the Gardner cabin, after the disagreement of the morning, was quite warm, and the rapidly melting snow added greatly to the difficulties of travelling. Being forced to wade through sloughs several feet deep in slush the men were soon wet to the shoulders. But they plodded on cheerfully for they were on the way home after the completion of an arduous duty. While they were in this cheery frame of mind, the blizzard broke upon them in all its fury about four in the

---

6. Smith's *A History of Dickinson County, Iowa.*

afternoon. With the storm came a rapid fall in temperature, and it was not long before the clothes of the members of the party were frozen stiff from feet to shoulders—rendering progress next to impossible.

With the oncoming of the storm began the first disagreement among the men after leaving the Gardner cabin in the morning. Again, it was a matter of the best route to be taken. Jonas Murray, a trapper who had volunteered as guide, claimed to be thoroughly familiar with the country. Not all, however, were willing to accept his guidance. Spencer and McCormick were the first to break away from his leadership. This they did when Mud Creek was reached only about eight or nine miles from the point of starting. Crossing far to the north of where Murray maintained was the proper place, these men struck directly east for the settlement which they reached within a short time after the storm broke upon them.[7]

The other members of the party lost much valuable time in wandering southward along the course of Mud Creek. Finally a crossing was effected, but much farther to the south than several thought it should have been. Against the protests of a number, Murray continued to lead the party still farther south. Near sunset Maxwell and Laughlin found a township corner pit, at which they proposed to camp for the night since they feared the loss of direction in the oncoming darkness. But Murray, Johnson, and Burkholder, thought it best to continue and so the party pressed on.[8] Ahead of them was a lake to the east of which was a great stretch of uncommonly high grass which seemed to afford good shelter. Maxwell, Laughlin, and seven others started to walk around this lake to the east; but Johnson, Burkholder, Addington, G. P. Smith, and Murray went around in the opposite direction. Finding a shelter Laughlin called to Johnson's party which could then only be dimly seen through the sedge. Apparently he was not heard, for the men struck out toward the southeast and were not again seen before the Irish settlement was reached. Laughlin's party decided to remain where it was rather than attempt to follow.

As soon as the halt was made the men tumbled down in a shivering heap and huddled closely together to keep from freezing. In crossing sloughs several men had removed their boots to keep them dry, while others had cut holes in the leather in order to let the water out.

---

7. *The Narrative of W. K. Laughlin* in the *Annals of Iowa* (Third Series), Vol. III.
8. Smith's *A History of Dickinson County, Iowa; Address of John N. Maxwell* in the *Annals of Iowa* (Third Series), Vol. III; *The Narrative of W. K. Laughlin* in the *Annals of Iowa* (Third Series), Vol. III.

Carse had removed his boots, but found it impossible to replace them for they were frozen stiff. He then tore his blanket into pieces and wrapped his feet as well as he could, but even then he suffered fearfully from the cold. Maxwell and Laughlin, realising the danger of freezing to death, did not permit themselves to sleep the whole night through: they kept constantly on the move and compelled the others to do the same. Whenever any man fell asleep the others would pick him up, arouse him, and force him to remain awake and on the move regardless of his objections. Some of the men begged that they be allowed to sleep, protesting that moving about in their ice stiffened garments was worse punishment than they could bear. Thus all night long the awful vigil was kept. It was largely due to the tireless watching of Maxwell and Laughlin that no one froze to death, although the temperature that night was said to have been thirty-four degrees below zero at points in Iowa much farther south.[9]

The next day opened clear and cold. About eight miles to the east was seen a grove of timber. Every man expressed himself as willing and able to travel; and so without breakfast (for they had no food) the party started in that direction, believing that the timber bordered the Des Moines. Maxwell was the last to leave camp, and when about three miles from the timber he found Carse sitting on the sunny side of a small mound trying to pull on his frozen boots. The blanket wrappings of his feet had already become so worn in travelling over the ice and snow that he could go no further. Maxwell endeavoured to take Carse along with him, but every time he tried to guide him toward the timber Carse obstinately insisted on taking the opposite direction. It soon became evident that the man had grown delirious and that nothing could be done with him on the open prairie. Henry E. Dalley, seeing the difficulty, came to Maxwell's assistance. The two were able to get Carse to the timber, by which time he was unconscious and blood was streaming from his mouth.[10]

Laughlin and Kellogg, who had reached the timber first, had set about the building of a fire when it was discovered that not a member of the party had matches. Laughlin's ingenuity, however, came to the rescue. He had a gun and powder, and was wearing a vest with a

---

9. *The Spirit Lake Massacre and Relief Expedition* in the *Roster and Record of Iowa Soldiers*, Vol. VI; *Narrative of W. L. Laughlin* in the *Annals of Iowa* (Third Series), Vol. III; *Address of John N. Maxwell* in the *Annals of Iowa* (Third Series), Vol. III

10. *Address of John N. Maxwell* in the *Annals of Iowa* (Third Series), Vol. III; *The Narrative of W. K. Laughlin* in the *Annals of Iowa* (Third Series), Vol. III.

heavy, quilted cotton lining. Removing some of the cotton from his vest he loaded the gun with a powder charge and rammed it down tight with cotton. He then discharged the gun into a piece of rotten wood which, after some attention, began blazing. Dalley soon arrived with the helpless Carse. When the blanket wrappings were removed from Carse's feet the skin of the soles came with them. Dalley finally succeeded in stopping the bleeding and in reviving him. It was only a few nights before that Carse had befriended Dalley by taking him under his own blanket.

The boy—for such he was, being less than twenty years of age—was poorly clad and had suffered much from the trials of the expedition. His youthful strength and courage, however, carried him safely through to the end. Meanwhile, Kellogg had seated himself at the base of a tree and before anyone had observed his need for attention he too had become unconscious from exposure. Before he could be revived it was necessary to cut his icy clothing away from his body as the only practicable means of removing it. When this had been done he gradually regained consciousness and seemed but little the worse for his experience.[11]

Laughlin and Maxwell, having attended those who were needing help and noting that all were as comfortable as conditions would permit, started out to cross the river with a view to locating the Irish settlement. They found the river frozen thick enough to support them, with the exception of a few spots over which they improvised a bridge of poles. Making their way to the margin of the timber, they saw the settlement in plain sight not over three miles away. Help was at once secured which enabled them to get the disabled members of the party across the river and to safety in the homes of the settlement. Here they found Major Williams awaiting their coming.

Without delay Major Williams sent men down the Des Moines to look for Johnson and his companions. They remained out during the whole of the day; and when they returned near dark reported that they had discovered no trace of the men, but had found a cabin in which a good fire was burning. The major concluded that the men had been at the cabin and had then gone southward, following the course of the river. Three of the five men in the party—Smith, Addington, and Murray—came to the settlement the following morning but could give little information concerning Johnson and Burkholder. Smith had been the last to see them; and his story left no doubt in the

---

11. *The Narrative of W. K. Laughlin* in the *Annals of Iowa* (Third Series), Vol. III.

minds of most of his hearers that the two men had perished somewhere to the west of the Des Moines River.

The two unfortunate men having become completely exhausted by wading streams and sloughs had finally sat down declaring that they were unable to go any farther. They were sheeted with ice from head to feet. Their feet were badly frozen and, unable to walk, they insisted, against Smith's advice, upon removing their boots. Realising that they could not replace the boots they cut their blankets in strips with which to wrap their feet. At this time they were in sight of the timber along the Des Moines River, which they were urged to exert every effort to reach. But they were unable to rise from the ground. "After vainly trying for a long time to get them to make another effort to reach the timber, Smith at last realised that to save his own life he must leave them. After going some distance he looked back and saw them still on their knees in the snow, apparently unable to rise. It is not likely they ever left the spot where Smith left them, but, overcome with cold, they finally sank down and perished side by side."[12] Nearly eleven years later two skeletons were found near the place where Smith said he left his companions. By the guns and powder flasks lying near them the skeletons were identified as being those of Johnson and Burkholder.[13]

---

12. *Address of John N. Maxwell* in the *Annals of Iowa* (Third Series), Vol. III; *The Narrative of W. K. Laughlin* in the *Annals of Iowa* (Third Series), Vol. III; Gue's *History of Iowa*, Vol. I.

13. Captain Johnson had come to Bach Grove on the Boone River Troy Township, Wright County, from Pennsylvania. Mention has been made of the manner of his enlistment. Upon his failure to return, his mother disposed of the claim and returned to Pennsylvania. When the bodies were found, Angus McBane of Fort Dodge took charge of the remains and sent them to his mother for burial. The remains of Burkholder were taken charge of by his brother-in-law, Governor C. C. Carpenter. They were given a military funeral at Fort Dodge, conducted by Major Williams. All the members of Company C that could be brought together at that time attended.—*A Paper by Michael Sweeney* in the *Annals of Iowa* (Third Series), III.

CHAPTER 25

Return of the Relief Expedition

From Granger's Point the return of the main body of the command was uneventful until the Irish settlement was reached and passed. It will be recalled that when the burial detail was outfitted nearly all of the scanty rations then remaining were turned over to them because of the probable hardships which would be encountered in venturing into the hostile lake region. Thus the main command was hard pressed in the matter of providing itself with adequate supplies. By the end of the first day the command had reached the cabin of an old trapper near the shore of Mud Lake. The experiences of the first night out are illustrative of the extremity to which members of the expedition were driven upon their homeward journey.

At the trapper's cabin were found the frozen carcasses of some beaver, which it was thought could be utilized as food. But frozen beaver even when roasted failed to satisfy the hunger of the men. Captain Richards tells of one member of his company, George W. Brizee, who, as a result of exposure was suffering from a severe case of toothache and very sore feet.

Finally, the pain in his feet grew easier. But "his tooth reminded him that it needed his attention; and after lying down and trying to sleep, frequently reiterating that he knew he should die, he got up and went out and returned with a hind-quarter of beaver and began to roast it over the coals; and in a half-reclining position he spent the entire night roasting and trying to eat the tough, leathery meat, first consigning his feet to a warmer climate, and then as his toothache for a time attracted most of his attention, giving us a lecture on dentistry; when his tooth was relieved for a short time he would, with both hands holding on to the partially roasted quarter of beaver, get hold with his teeth and try to tear off a piece! The picture by the weird light of the fire was a striking one".[1]

The party did not tarry long at the Irish settlement, which was reached on the evening of the next day, since it was evident that the settlers had barely sufficient food to keep themselves alive and would surely suffer if the command remained for any length of time.[2] The day of leaving Medium Lake was a cloudy one and rather warm—just such a day as is sure to start the water running from rapidly melting snow. Only a short distance had been travelled when rain began falling—first as a drizzle, but by the time Cylinder Creek was reached it was a downpour. The prairies were flooded, while Cylinder Creek was about half a mile wide, completely covering its rather narrow bottom, which was under from two to five feet of water, while the main channel had a depth of fifteen to twenty feet and was from sixty to eighty feet wide. Obviously the problem of crossing would be a serious one. Arriving at the border of the valley about two o'clock in the afternoon the command vainly sought a passage. Then suddenly the wind veered sharply to the northwest and became a gale—the rain changing into a blinding fall of snow. This was the fearful blizzard of April fourth that overtook the Johnson party on its return from the Gardner cabin.

Captains Richards and Duncombe, not despairing of being able to effect a crossing of the main channel, undertook to improvise a boat out of a nearly new wagon box. With very little effort this wagon box was caulked water tight with bedquilt cotton. Solon Mason and Guernsey Smith were the men chosen to assist in getting the boat across the channel. But the wind blew so hard that, although Richards and Duncombe bailed water as rapidly as they could, the party scarcely reached the opposite side of the channel before the make-believe boat sank—the men barely saving themselves from drowning.

1. *Address of Capt. Charles B. Richards* in the *Annals of Iowa* (Third Series), Vol. III.
2. Captain Richards speaks of their attempt to secure supplies at the settlement upon their return as follows: "The settlers at the Colony were on short rations and could spare nothing. We decided to buy a steer and kill for the party, but we had no money and the owner refused to sell without pay. We offered to give the personal obligation of all the officers, and assured him the State would pay a good price; but this was not satisfactory. We therefore decided to take one *vi et armis*, and detailed several men to kill and dress the steer. They were met by men, women and children, armed with pitchforks to resist the sacrifice, and not being able to convince them either of the necessity of the case or that they would get pay for the steer, I ordered Lieut. Stratton and a squad of men with loaded guns to go and take the steer; when ...the hostile party retired."—*Address of Capt. Charles B. Richards* in the *Annals of Iowa* (Third Series), Vol. III.

Thus the attempt to take all across in that manner failed.[3] Having no blankets and unable to assist their comrades on the opposite side, there was nothing to do but hasten on to Shippey's Point which was two or three miles distant.[4] This point they reached about nine o'clock at night. Here they were liberally fed, and by sitting around the fire all night were able to dry their clothes by exposing first one side and then the other to the fire.

When morning came the storm had abated somewhat, and so it was decided to return to the creek in an effort to locate the command. Mason had not gone far when he succumbed to the cold and had to be taken back. It seems that in crossing the Cylinder he had lost both overcoat and cap. Upon their arrival at the east side of the bottom the men could see nothing on the other side to indicate the presence of their comrades. After spending some time in trying to accomplish a crossing, they gave up the attempt and returned to Shippey's. There they remained until about the middle of the afternoon when they again returned to the creek. This time they were no more successful than before. Resigned to the thought that the remainder of the command had either perished or returned to Medium Lake, they wandered back to Shippey's. Shortly after their return, Hoover and Howland came in and reported that when they left the command all were safe on the west side, though suffering considerably while waiting for the channel to freeze.

Early on Monday morning, while the blizzard was yet raging and the cold was still intense, the little group at Shippey's once more started for the creek in an effort to locate their companions. Reaching the creek, the little group saw the men on the opposite side making preparations to cross—the storm by this time having abated so that a

---

3. Duncombe's *Spirit Lake Expedition* in the *Proceedings of the Pioneer Lawmakers' Association of Iowa for 1898*; *Address of Capt. Charles B. Richards* in the *Annals of Iowa* (Third Series), Vol. III.

4. Captain Richards is quoted as follows in Gue's *History of Iowa*, Vol. I, concerning the attempt to cross at this point:—"The wind was now blowing a terrific gale and the cold was intense, so that our wet clothing was frozen stiff upon us.... When help and material for a raft came, so strong and cold was the wind, and so swift the current, filled with floating ice, that all of our efforts to build a raft failed. It was now dark and still growing colder, and the roar of the blinding storm so great that we could no longer hold communication with our companions on the other side. We were benumbed with cold, utterly exhausted, and three miles from the nearest cabin. We were powerless to aid our comrades, and could only try to save ourselves. It was a terrible walk in the face of the terrific blizzard, our clothes frozen, our feet freezing, and our strength gone."

crossing might be attempted. The creek was now solidly frozen so that the task of crossing was easy. The way to Shippey's was soon made. Here they told the story of how they had saved themselves from the terrors of the awful storm.

From this story it appears that no thought of returning to the Irish settlement had been entertained by those who had been left behind. Major Williams and two or three others had, indeed, returned, hoping that they would there find the burial detail and guide them to the Cylinder Creek camp. Those at the latter place resolved to remain and await the dying down of the storm before making any further attempt at crossing; and they set to work to improvise a shelter. Again the tarpaulin wagon covers were brought into use and supplemented with blankets, which when fastened together were stretched around and over the wagon frames and then staked down to the frozen ground. This improvised shelter was completely closed excepting a small flap opening on the south or lea side which served the purpose of a door. Then with blankets and other covers a common bed was made; and into this the party crowded, wet from head to feet. Here they remained from Saturday night until Monday morning when a few ventured out to examine the state of the weather.[5] Finding conditions satisfactory they began the crossing after having tarried "*over forty hours, without food or fire, on the open prairie, with the mercury at 32° below zero.*"[6]

It is little wonder that when they started to make the crossing the men had scarcely "strength enough to reach the opposite shore.... Every man's mouth was open wide, his tongue hanging out, and in some instances blood running from nose or mouth."[7] Governor Carpenter, in commenting upon this terrific test of endurance notes that "since that experience upon Cylinder Creek, I have marched with armies engaged in actual war. During three and a half years' service, the army with which I was connected, marched from Cairo to Chattanooga, from Chattanooga to Atlanta, from Atlanta to the Sea, and from the Sea through the Carolinas to Richmond.... But I never in those weary years experienced a conflict with the elements that could be compared with the two nights and one day on Cylinder Creek."[8]

After refreshing themselves at Shippey's the men held a consultation and reached the decision that henceforth the command should

---

5. *Address of Ex-Governor Carpenter* in the *Annals of Iowa* (Third Series), Vol. III.
6. Hoover's *The Tragedy of Okoboji* in the *Annals of Iowa* (Third Series), Vol. V.
7. *Frank R. Mason's Recollections* in the *Annals of Iowa* (Third Series), Vol. III.
8. *Address of Ex-Governor Carpenter* in the *Annals of Iowa* (Third Series), Vol. III.

break up into small details—a plan that seemed necessary on account of the increasing difficulty of securing food. Each group was to find its way home in the best manner it might be able to devise. Every man was ordered to rid himself of all surplus baggage, retaining only his blanket. Thus the expedition really came to an end with the crossing of Cylinder Creek. But the hardships of the men were not ended; before a number of the squads reached home they endured trials almost as severe as those encountered before crossing the Cylinder.

The experience of the little group which Frank R. Mason undertook to guide is perhaps typical of the hardships of the journey south from Shippey's. Mason had frequently been north of Fort Dodge hunting in the timber along Lott's Creek, and for that reason he was selected by a Webster City group to pilot them home. With his party he struck out boldly across the prairie in a line which he thought would lead to a clearing in the timber where he knew they would receive a hearty welcome. As darkness came on the men began to show exhaustion; but the looked-for timber along Lott's Creek did not appear. One of the men, Hathaway by name, became wholly exhausted and had to be carried. Within a short time he became delirious; and then the united efforts of three of the party were needed to keep him under control, with only indifferent success. Finally passing into a stupor he was more easily managed.

When Mason and his companions reached the timber at about eleven o'clock the expected cabin could not be found. The men grew impatient and at times were inclined to criticize Mason as an incompetent guide. Having reached a slight elevation or ridge, and despairing of locating the cabin, they prepared to spend the night. Snow was cleared away until the bare ground was reached and upon this they threw themselves. They had had no food since the start; indeed they had not brought any with them, for they had expected to reach the cabin before nightfall. When they had lain sleepless for nearly an hour, voices were heard and out of the darkness appeared human forms.[9] The newcomers were Mr. and Mrs. Elwood Collins who were returning from an evening spent at a neighbour's home.

The finding of the men is thus described by Mrs. Collins:

> Husband and I, after having stayed later than usual at a neighbour's, started for home. . . . All at once the outline of dark objects appeared before us. . . . I at first thought we might be

---

9. *Frank R. Mason's Recollections* in the *Annals of Iowa* (Third Series), Vol. III.

upon a company of Indians! We were too near to retreat.... I then heard groans of distress, and I thought sobs.... We had a lantern, and as the light shone upon the place my pity was truly stirred. There, with the snow crushed beneath them, were eight men; some sitting, some reclining, and others lying flat upon their backs![10]

Having been piloted to the clearing the men slept that night in the cabin loft. In the morning they breakfasted hastily and resumed their journey to Webster City. Hathaway and Gates had to be left at the cabin as they were not able to proceed. This day's experience was but a repetition of the previous one. As darkness fell the men were again exhausted, but by crawling on hands and knees they managed to reach the cabin of a Mr. Corsau where they were taken in for the night. On the following day they were taken by Corsau to Webster City. Thus ended, for this Webster City group, the fearful experience of attempting to relieve the settlers of the lake region from Indian attacks.

For the Fort Dodge men the task of making their way home was easier, as it did not necessitate the crossing of as many streams—which at this time were in flood condition. At the same time their trip was not lacking in incidents of trial. They arranged the march from cabin to cabin so that they might have no difficulty in procuring food, for they, too, made no attempt to carry supplies. More than once the men experienced trials similar to those encountered by the Mason party, and like them they too found the place searched for before hope was gone. Within three or four days after leaving Cylinder Creek, all parties had straggled in—weary, worn, and wasted. They were met with a hearty welcome from friends who had thought them in all probability lost on the northwestern prairies. All who had volunteered in the expedition returned home in safety, except Johnson and Burkholder who perished in the snow.

---

10. *Letter from Mrs. Collins* in the *Annals of Iowa* (Third Series), Vol. III.

Chapter 26

The Death of Mrs. Thatcher

From March twenty-sixth to April tenth, while the relief expedition from Fort Dodge and Webster City was making its way painfully to and from the scene of the massacre at the lakes, Inkpaduta and his band continued their flight. When Lieutenant Murry's men had been sighted by the look-out, warning of their approach was communicated through the Indian camp. The warriors crouched among the willows along the creek ready to spring out upon their pursuers, while the squaws and children made hurried preparations for a hasty retreat if need be. Meanwhile, a warrior stood guard over the helpless white captives with orders to shoot them the moment the soldiers should attack. But Coursalle and La Framboise, who were guiding Murry's men, declared that the signs were so old that pursuit would be hopeless; and so the soldiers returned to the main command. No sooner had they started on their return than Inkpaduta fled from his temporary camp and began the long journey to the Big Sioux, the James, and the region beyond.

The Indians were now thoroughly alarmed at the nearness of danger, and for two days and nights they kept up a continuous flight. No stops were made to prepare food: if they ate at all it was while they were on the move. Such a sustained flight would have been arduous enough for untrained marchers under the most favourable conditions, but for the women captives it was terrible. Not only were they compelled to wade through snow and slush but they were burdened with loads which might well have been regarded as too heavy for men to bear.

Mrs. Marble states that upon leaving Heron Lake she and her associates "were forced to carry heavy packs, and perform the degrading and menial services in the camp ... that the pack ... consisted of two bags of shot, each weighing twenty-five pounds, and a lot of camp furniture, increasing the weight of the pack to 100 pounds. On top of this heavy load . . . was placed the additional weight of an Indian urchin of some three or four years of age."[1]

The *papoose* which she was supposed to carry seemed to consider that it was entitled to as many liberties and as much attention when carried by her as it would have enjoyed if in the care of its mother. Mrs. Marble objected to making friends with the baby, and watching her opportunity would scratch it in the face until the Indians, hearing its cries, finally concluded it didn't like her and took it away.

Abbie Gardner, though but a girl, was also burdened with a pack—though its weight was somewhat less than that carried by Mrs. Marble. It was made up of "eight bars of lead, one pint of lead balls, one *tepee* cover made of the heaviest, thickest cloth, one blanket, one bed-comforter, one iron bar, three feet long and half an inch thick . . . one gun, and one piece of wood several inches wide and four feet long, to keep the pack in shape."[2]

This burdening of the captives was the more objectionable to them since the Indian men were encumbered with nothing but a gun. As a matter of course the squaws carried packs, but they were accustomed to such burden-bearing and knew how to save themselves from its ill effects. Moreover, the squaws were frequently equipped with a sort of crude snowshoe which greatly aided them in walking. The white captives sank deep into the snow at every step. They dared not stop to rest, for whenever they slackened their pace the Indians would level guns at them and resort to various other devices to keep them moving.

The food which the Indians had secured at Okoboji and Springfield supplied them for about four weeks. Following this they made little or no effort to secure food by hunting. If game crossed their path they would kill it—if they could do so without much effort. But there was no organisation of hunting parties. After the confiscated supplies were exhausted, they contented themselves with muskrat and skunk; and as a luxury, Mrs. Sharp relates, they indulged in dog. As spring opened they were able to secure a few ducks and geese, which seemed very plentiful, but of which the Indians obtained only a few. Such delicacies, however, were never shared with the captives: they were not even allowed to assist in their preparation.

---

1. Republished article from the *St. Paul Pioneer* of May 31, 1857, in the *Hamilton Freeman* (Webster City), July 13, 1857.
2. Mrs. Sharp's *History of the Spirit Lake Massacre.*

The treatment of the horses secured at Okoboji and Springfield was still worse. There was neither hay nor grass—little or nothing upon which the horses might feed. Even so they were given but slight opportunity to feed. Before the Big Sioux had been reached nearly all of the horses taken in the raids at the lakes had died of starvation.[3]

Continued pursuit and ultimate capture by the soldiers seem to have soon lost their terrors for the Indians. Although they kept constantly on the move, progress was not very rapid—largely owing to the huge drifts of snow over and through which they were compelled to travel. Their first stopping-place, after nearly two weeks of uninterrupted marching, was at the great red pipestone quarry in southwestern Minnesota. This was but little more than one hundred miles northwest of Heron Lake. Here they remained for a day quarrying pipestone and fashioning pipes. A further cause for delay was the fact that the snow was rapidly melting and travel, even for the Indians, was very difficult.

The Indians were now in a sacred region to which all the Sioux were wont to make frequent journeys—a region closely associated with the superstitions of their race. Here the footprints made by the Great Spirit when he alighted upon the earth could be seen. It was while he stood here that a stream of water burst forth from beneath his feet and flowed away to nourish the plain. Here it was that the Great Spirit fashioned a pipe and smoked: huge volumes of smoke issued forth serving as a signal for all the tribes to assemble from far and near. When so assembled, the Great Spirit, blowing the smoke over all, bade them meet here always in peace even though they might be at war elsewhere. Moreover, if they wished to receive his favour, the calumet must be fashioned from the rock upon which he stood. Having thus enjoined his people, the Great Spirit disappeared in a cloud. It is said that ever afterward when the Indians met at the pipestone quarry, they met in peace though elsewhere they might be at war.[4]

After leaving the pipestone region so much time was consumed by the Indians in camping that it might be said they camped more than they marched. This is explained by the fact that they felt themselves now wholly free from the danger of pursuit. Spring was rapidly approaching and the smaller game was becoming more plentiful; and

---

3. Mrs. Sharp's *History of the Spirit Lake Massacre.*
4. *Ibid.* This stone is more familiarly known in mineralogy as catlinite—being so named from George Catlin, the noted traveller, who first studied it. See Hodge's *Handbook of American Indians*, Vol. I.

so they did not feel the need of hastening to the buffalo ranges in Dakota.

The burdens of the captives grew increasingly more difficult. Although snow no longer impeded their march, the rains were frequent and the rivers and creeks were flowing wide over the valleys. When it rained they were without shelter. The streams were crossed by the Indians on the backs of the few ponies that yet survived. But the captives had to wade at the risk of losing their lives: they could not swim.

Notwithstanding the hardships through which they were compelled to pass, all but Mrs. Thatcher were faring much better than might have been expected. Mrs. Marble, Mrs. Noble, and Abbie Gardner were willing to appear resigned to their lot and did all that was requested of them: they even appeared ready and willing to perform the many menial duties which fell to their lot. With Mrs. Thatcher, however, it was different. She had from the first rebelled at the service imposed by her Indian captors; nor did she hesitate to show them very plainly her frame of mind. This attitude on her part proved to be most unfortunate.

From the beginning of her captivity Mrs. Thatcher had been ill with phlebitis, which before the end of two weeks had developed into virulent blood poisoning.[5] Indeed, so serious was her condition that for a large portion of the march she had been relieved of much of her pack. At the pipestone quarry and on the march after leaving that region the medicine man of the band had undertaken to treat her—and the treatment seemed to help her. To such an extent had she been relieved that the Indians considered her again able to bear a pack. Thus it happened that when they arrived at the crossing of the Big Sioux near the present village of Flandrau, Mrs. Thatcher was laden as heavily as were the other three captives.

This crossing had been for generations the fording place of the red peoples in their pilgrimages to the pipestone quarry. Normally the river at this point is wide but shallow. But "the vast amount of snow which covered the ground that memorable winter had nearly gone, by reason of the rapid thawing during the last few weeks, causing the river to rise beyond all ordinary bounds, and assume majestic proportions."[6] Throughout the greater portion of the upper course of the Big Sioux it flows between perpendicular and continuous cliffs of red jasper rocks peculiar to the region, but at or near this traditional crossing place the stone cliffs were neither high nor continuous.

---

5 & 6. Mrs. Sharp's *History of the Spirit Lake Massacre.*

Moreover, at this particular time so many tree trunks had become lodged by the spring freshets that at one point a bridge crossing was formed. Upon this the Indians proposed to cross, instead of attempting the more dangerous method of fording. At the prospect of crossing the swollen stream, the captives were terrified, believing that they would again be compelled to wade. They despaired of being able to get across. The situation seemed quite hopeless.

As soon as the determination to cross had been reached, an Indian warrior—the one who had seized the box of caps from Gardner—removed the pack from Mrs. Thatcher's back and transferred it to his own.[7] This in itself was ominous, and Mrs. Thatcher was not slow to perceive that some unusual disposition was to be made of her. As she was ordered forward to the driftwood bridge she spoke to her companions, bidding them goodbye and saying as she did so: "If any of you escape, tell my dear husband that I wanted to live for his sake."[8]

When she had made the middle of the stream, the Indian carrying her pack suddenly tripped her into the river. Retaining her presence of mind she was able by desperate efforts to keep herself afloat. A number of times she succeeded in making her way to the banks of the stream where, grasping the roots of trees, she strove to pull herself out of the water. But each time she was met by an Indian who clubbed her loose and with a long pole pushed her into the main current. Finally, as she came to shore and grasped the roots of a tree for what proved to be the last time, an Indian who had always been peculiarly brutal in his treatment of the captive raised his gun and shot her through the head, killing her instantly.[9]

Mrs. Marble relates that the death of Mrs. Thatcher "was hailed by the Indian women with loud shouts of joy and exultation.—The feelings of the surviving prisoners at this horrid murder, cannot be imagined. They beheld in Mrs. Thatcher's death, the fate reserved for them, when overpowered by fatigue, they would be unable to proceed."[10]

The death of Mrs. Thatcher was a sad blow to the remaining captives: it was particularly distressing to Mrs. Noble. These two women

---

7. Robinson's *A History of the Dakota or Sioux Indians* in the *South Dakota Historical Collections*, Vol. II.
8. Gue's *History of Iowa*, Vol. I; Mrs. Sharp's *History of the Spirit Lake Massacre*.
9. Gue's *History of Iowa*, Vol. I; Robinson's *A History of the Dakota or Sioux Indians* in the *South Dakota Historical Collections*, Vol. II; Mrs. Sharp's *History of the Spirit Lake Massacre*.
10. Republished article from the *St. Paul Pioneer*, of May 31, 1857, in the *Hamilton Freeman* (Webster City), July 13, 1857.

had been lifelong friends and had married cousins. The families had come to the frontier together, had lived in the same cabin, and had planned to build homes as nearly together as possible. Mrs. Noble was so depressed and so bereft of any hope that in the evening she proposed to the other captives that they steal away to the Big Sioux and drown themselves. Mrs Marble, however, succeeded in convincing her that such an act would be useless. But from this time Mrs. Noble seemed to be wholly indifferent as to her treatment or possible fate at the hands of her captors. The captives were now made to realise as never before the heartlessness of their captors: they lived in the expectation that any day might see for them the end of life.

Before them lay many days of the most wearisome travel. It is true that walking had become easier, for spring had really come and the trails were much improved. With spring had come also the blossoming of the prairies; but in this there was neither charm nor beauty for the captives as they wearily plodded on knowing not whither they were bound. After crossing the Big Sioux the journey was continued in a nearly direct line westward. Other bands of Sioux or Yanktons were now frequently seen; and notwithstanding the reputation of Inkpaduta, he and his band were usually very cordially met by other Indians. Indeed, they were more than cordially greeted from time to time at these chance meetings. The fact that they seemed to be known by all bands they chanced to meet suggests that they were not strangers to the region. The story of how they obtained their captives, which was always told, seemed to be received with every sign of approbation.

By May fifth Inkpaduta and his band had reached Lake M'da Chan-Pta-Ya Tonka (Lake with a Grove of Big Trees). This body of water lies to the east of the present town of Madison, South Dakota, at the headwaters of Skunk Creek, and for that reason it has sometimes been called Skunk Lake.[11] Situated about thirty miles west of Flandrau, South Dakota, it is now known as Lake Madison. At the time it was visited by Inkpaduta it was on the margin of the buffalo range. Hunting was now quite the order of the day, and food became plentiful. The dressing and preparing of skins occupied the time of the squaws.

---

11. B. M. Smith and A. J. Hill's *Map of the Ceded Part of Dakota Territory*, 1861.

CHAPTER 27

The Ransom of Mrs. Marble

In view of the events which followed the camping of the Indians at Skunk Lake, it may be well to take note of the attempts made by the Indian agent and by the Territory of Minnesota to rescue the captives and punish the Indians. When the news of the massacre reached St. Paul and other Minnesota towns it created no little excitement. The Sioux were blamed as a nation, and this gave rise to a demand for their punishment without just regard for the identification of the actual perpetrators of the deed.

Charles E. Flandrau, the agent of the Mississippi Sioux who was then located at the agency on the Yellow Medicine, solved the problem of the identity of the murderers to his own satisfaction, and late in April began the publication of articles in a number of the most widely circulated newspapers in Minnesota in which he explained to the people of the Territory the real identity of the Indians concerned. While doing this he was also conferring with Colonel E. B. Alexander, commander of the Tenth United States Infantry then stationed at Fort Ridgely, Minnesota, concerning the best course to be pursued in the attempt to rescue the captives and apprehend the Indians. It was very clear to both that only such a course could be adopted and followed as would be reasonably sure to guarantee the safety of the white women who presumably were still held in captivity by Inkpaduta's band. It was felt by both Agent Flandrau and Colonel Alexander that the release of the captives must be secured by resort to some means other than force; but neither of these men was able to devise the proper means. While they were seeking a solution of the difficulty, news was brought of the ransoming of Mrs. Marble.

It seems that two Indian brothers from the Yellow Medicine Agency, who had been Christianized by the Rev. Stephen R. Riggs, had gone into the district beyond the Big Sioux to take part in the spring hunt along with other members of their tribe. While in the vicinity of Skunk Lake, the brothers, Ma-kpe-ya-ka-ho-ton (Sounding Heavens) and Se-ha-ho-ta (Gray foot) by name, sons of Spirit Walker, Chief of the Lac qui Parle Wahpetons, heard that Inkpaduta had lately passed through the region.[1] They were also told that his band held as captives three white women who had been taken in a raid which they had but lately made upon the settlements at the lakes. The first feeling of the brothers was one of pity for the captives, since they well knew the ferocious character of the Inkpaduta band. Discussing the matter between themselves, they decided to visit the camp of Inkpaduta for the purpose of securing the release of the captives. The plan met with disapproval when it was submitted to their companions who feared the consequences. But the brothers were so strongly convinced that they could secure the release of at least one of the prisoners, and possibly of all, that they refused the advice of their fellows and set out on the trail of Inkpaduta.

Anticipating that the release of the captives might only be secured through ransom, the brothers had collected from their companions as much in the way of personal belongings as could be spared. Adding this to their own supply they thought they had sufficient property to accomplish their purpose. Being Indians themselves, and therefore well acquainted with the Indian attitude of mind, they did not take their possessions with them when they went to Inkpaduta's camp to negotiate. Instead they concealed the property in the brush on the lake shore not far distant. At first they were not received with any show of cordiality, for they were known to be Christian Indians: Inkpaduta suspected them as spies, and they were constantly watched, since they were supposed to be in direct communication with United States soldiers. Frequently, as they would move about the camp, an alarm would be raised that soldiers were coming.[2]

The first night spent by the brothers in the camp was wholly taken up with the recital of the well-worn tale of the massacre. At daybreak the brothers broached the reason for their coming. All forenoon the proposition was argued. Grayfoot, acting in the capacity of spokesman

---

1. *The Ink-pa-du-ta Massacre of 1857* in the *Collections of the Minnesota Historical Society*, Vol. III; Robinson's *A History of the Dakota or Sioux Indians* in the *South Dakota Historical Collections*, Vol. II.
2. Robinson's *A History of the Dakota or Sioux Indians* in the *South Dakota Historical Collections*, Vol. II.

of the brothers, did not hesitate to tell Inkpaduta the enormity of the crime he had committed.[3] But Inkpaduta remained unimpressed; and not until mid-afternoon did he give any sign of wavering. Finally he proposed that the brothers take only one of the captives. This, he added, would show his good faith in the matter. It was also quite evident that this proposition was made for the purpose of getting rid of his unwelcome and tenacious visitors as soon as possible. The price demanded for the release of even one of the captives was so high that there was nothing to do but accept the offer—especially since it was clear that a longer parley was useless. The price for the one was to be "one gun, a lot of blankets, a keg of powder, and a small supply of Indian trinkets."[4]

It appears that Inkpaduta did not value any one of the captives more highly than the other, and so he was willing that the brothers should exercise the privilege of choice. In a *tepee* only a short distance away the white women were engaged in some of the menial tasks of the afternoon. Grayfoot walked over to the tent and looked in. At first he decided upon Mrs. Noble, being touched by her appearance of unhappiness. But when he beckoned her to follow him from the tent, she became angry and refused to comply. This apparently did not discourage Grayfoot, for he turned to Mrs. Marble and repeated the signal. Mrs. Marble, having resolved upon ready compliance with the demands of the Indians, at once followed him from the *tepee*. It should be said that there was little thought of selecting Miss Gardner for she was regarded as relatively safe from harsh treatment by her captors on account of her youth.[5] With Mrs. Marble, Grayfoot and Sounding Heavens, accompanied by two of Inkpaduta's Indians, returned to the camp upon the Big Sioux.

Upon reaching this camp Mrs. Marble was informed by a Frenchman, who happened to be in the camp, of the real purpose of the Indian brothers. The brothers now hastened to the *tepee* of Spirit Walker at Lac qui Parle where they arrived on May twentieth, the journey having occupied ten days. Here Mrs. Marble was given clothing and as good care as the means of Spirit Walker and his squaw would permit. Word was taken in a few days to the missionaries, Riggs and William-

---

3. Robinson's *A History of the Dakota or Sioux Indians* in the *South Dakota Historical Collections*, Vol. II.
4. Republished article from *St. Paul Pioneer*, of May 31, 1857, in the *Hamilton Freeman* (Webster City), July 13, 1857.
5. Robinson's *A History of the Dakota or Sioux Indians* in the *South Dakota Historical Collections*, Vol. II.

son, at the upper agency that one of the Spirit Lake captives was at the *tepee* of Spirit Walker. They at once hastened to the chief's lodge where they found Mrs. Marble happily situated and somewhat reluctant to leave her new-found and kind friends. Upon leaving the lodge she was placed in the care of Agent Flandrau who started with her at once for St. Paul where they arrived on May thirtieth.

In writing of Mrs. Marble's arrival in St. Paul the *St. Paul Pioneer* describes her as being:

> About twenty-five years of age; of medium size, and very pleasant looking. She is a native of Darke county, Ohio, and moved to Michigan about ten years ago. She has been twice married. Her first husband's name was Phips. After his death, she married Mr. Marble, with whom she removed to Linn county, Iowa, and ultimately to Spirit Lake in Dick(in)son county. Mrs. M. is in a very destitute condition,—her husband has been murdered and as to whether her parents are alive or not, she is ignorant. We trust those who are blessed with a supply of this world's goods will contribute liberally in aid of this unfortunate woman. The privations she has undergone, and her present destitute condition commend her to the consideration of the benevolent.[6]

The Indian brothers in notifying Agent Flandrau of their ransom of Mrs. Marble took occasion to remind him that they deemed the act worthy of a somewhat liberal reward, for, quoting the language of their letter:

> It was perilous business, which we think should be liberally rewarded. We claim for our services $500 each. We do not want it in horses, they would be killed by jealous young men. We do not wish it in ammunition and goods, these we should be obliged to divide with others. The labourer is worthy of his own reward. We want it in money, which we can make more serviceable to ourselves than it could be in any other form. This is what we have to say.[7]

To the agent this claim presented a problem difficult to handle, since he could see no way in which to secure the amount demanded.

---

[6]. Republished article from *St. Paul Pioneer*, of May 31, 1857, in the *Hamilton Freeman* (Webster City), July 13, 1857

[7]. Flandrau's *The Ink pa du-ta Massacre of 1857* in the *Collections of the Minnesota Historical Society*, Vol. III.

At the same time he did not for a moment consider the demand unjust—indeed he was surprised at its reasonableness. Having no public money at his disposal, if he met the demand it would necessarily be from private funds of his own or from the generosity of others. His own private funds amounted to but little more than five hundred dollars; and so an equal amount had to be secured from other sources.[8] But where should he go to solicit funds? When his own ingenuity failed to solve the problem he called missionary Riggs into conference. They decided upon a bold stroke of finance, which was nothing less than the issuance of a Territorial bond for the amount required. This proved a happy solution of the difficulty, and although they acted without legal authority they issued the paper in good faith.[9]

---

8. Flandrau's *The Ink-pa-du-ta Massacre of 1857* in the *Collections of the Minnesota Historical Society*, Vol. III.
9. The text of this bond appears in Flandrau's *Ink-pa-du-ta Massacre of 1857* in the *Collections of the Minnesota Historical Society*, Vol. III.

Chapter 28

The Death of Mrs. Noble and the Ransom of Abbie Gardner

From Mrs. Marble was obtained the information as to the whereabouts of the other captives. Without delay Agent Flandrau and the Rev. Stephen H. Riggs began to lay plans for their rescue. A dominant motive in Agent Flandrau's desire to reward the brothers was to stimulate interest in the rescue of those who remained in the hands of the Indians. In this he was successful; for at once a number of whites and Indians proffered their services. It was not, however, deemed desirable that the rescue should be undertaken by any but red men. Accordingly all whites who applied were at once rejected.

The elimination finally left three volunteers—Paul Ma-za-ku-ta-ma-ni (sometimes called Little Paul) one of the staunchest native followers of Rev. Riggs,[1] An-pe-tu-tok-cha (John Other Day),[2] and

---

1. Ma-za-ku-ta-ma-ni was at this time the President of the Rev. Riggs' Hazelwood Republic. This Republic was a rather unique attempt at self-government upon the part of Christianized Indians of the Yellow Medicine Agency under the guidance of the Rev. Mr. Riggs. It was "a respectable community of young men who had cut off their hair and exchanged the dress of the Dakotas for that of the white man. They elected their president and other officers for two years, and were recognised by the Indian agent as a separate band of the Sioux."—Hubbard and Holcombe's *Minnesota in Three Centuries*, Vol. II.

2. John Other Day won his title to fame in the annals of Minnesota by the part he took in the terrible Sioux Massacre of 1862. Certainly nothing else is needed to prove the worth of a Christian Indian than this act of his. The whites and Christian Indian refugees were in deadly peril of massacre at the Yellow Medicine Agency when to "John Other Day was entrusted the agency people and the refugees sixty-two souls in all, and as the revelry still came up from the stores on the bottom he moved off to the east with his white friends, crossed the Minnesota and skillfully covering the trail bore them away to safety without rest or delay he hurried back, (continued next page),

Che-tan-maza. Equipped with the following outfit these Indians were told to use it to the best advantage in securing the release of the two remaining captives:

	$
Wagon and double harness	110.00
Four horses	600.00
Twelve three-point blankets, four blue and eight white	56.00
Twenty-two yards of blue squaw cloth	44.00
Thirty-seven and a half yards of calico	5.37
Twenty pounds of tobacco	10.00
One sack of shot	4.00
One dozen shirts	13.00
Ribbon	4.75
Fifty pounds of powder	25.00
Corn	4.00
Flour	10.00
Coffee	1.50
Sugar	1.50

This bill of goods totalling $889.12, was purchased by Agent Flandrau of the traders at the Yellow Medicine Agency on credit, as he could not from his own private funds make cash payment to that amount. Thus equipped the Indians left the Yellow Medicine Agency on May twenty-third bound southwestward in an effort to locate Inkpaduta and negotiate with him for the release of his captives.[3]

As soon as Mrs. Marble and her purchasers left the camp on Lake Madison it was evident to Inkpaduta that it would not be long until soldiers would again be on his trail. He felt sure that the captive's return to civilization would result in redoubled energies to apprehend him. Hence, as soon as his two envoys to the hunting camp on the Big Sioux returned, he was once more on the move. He went first to Lake Herman, which was only a short distance from Lake Madison. From Lake Herman his course led northwestward and then up the valley of the James or Dakota River.

About two weeks after the breaking of camp at Lake Madison they

---

to the scene of the massacre to save more lives and assist in bringing the miscreants to justice."—Robinson's *A History of the Dakota or Sioux Indians* in the *South Dakota Historical Collections*, Vol. II.

3. Flandrau's *The Ink-pa-du-ta Massacre of 1857* in the *Collections of the Minnesota Historical Society*, Vol. III.

fell in with a band of Yanktons. In this band was a one-legged fellow, Wanduskaihanke (End of the Snake) by name, who, having an eye for business and having heard of the ransom of Mrs. Marble, decided to buy the remaining captives, take them to the Missouri River forts, and there offer them for sale. A bargain was soon struck with Inkpaduta, who now seemed anxious to rid himself of his charges, and the transfer of property at once took place. But for some reason not clear the Yankton instead of continuing with his band remained with Inkpaduta's party, which now moved directly north, headed for the Earth Lodges of the Yanktons. Apparently the Indians under Inkpaduta paid no further heed to the captives.

Thus matters had stood for some days when one evening, as Mrs. Noble and Miss Gardner were preparing for the night's rest, Roaring Cloud, a son of Inkpaduta, entered. The captives suspected that trouble was at hand and anxiously waited to see what form it might take. Roaring Cloud had no sooner entered than he ordered Mrs. Noble out of the tent. She refused to comply. Enraged, he grasped her by one arm and with his other hand seized a stick of wood which happened to be close by. Dragging her out of the *tepee*, he struck her three or four heavy blows on the head, thus ending her life. On the following morning, as the squaws were breaking camp, the warriors gathered about the dead body and amused themselves by shooting arrows into it.

That the Indians with their remaining captive now journeyed well into the range of the buffalo is evidenced by the testimony of Mrs. Sharp who said that they "crossed one prairie so vast and so perfectly devoid of timber, that for days not even a hazel-brush, or a sprout large enough for a riding-whip could be found." As they "attained the more elevated points the scene was really sublime. Look in any direction, and the grassy plain was bounded only by the horizon. . . . The only things to be seen, except grass, were wild fowls, birds, buffalo, and antelope. The supply of buffalo seemed almost as limitless as the grass. This was their own realm, and they showed no inclination to surrender it, not even to the Sioux."[4]

Within two days after the killing of Mrs. Noble the Indians crossed the James somewhere near the mouth of Snake Creek and encamped a short distance to the south of the site of the present town of Ashton. Not far removed was a permanent camp of about one hundred and

---

4. Mrs. Sharp's *History of the Spirit Lake Massacre*. Mrs. Noble seems to have been killed in the southeastern corner of what is now Spink County, South Dakota.

ninety lodges of Yankton Sioux.

The arrival of the white captive created a stir in the Yankton camp. Their great curiosity was probably due to the fact that she was the first white person that many of them had ever seen. Her hair and skin were examined with intense admiration. "No sooner was one company out of the *teepe* (sic) than others came; and so they kept it up from morning until night, day after day".[5] The excitement over the white captive had scarcely died away when it was renewed by the arrival of the three Indian emissaries from the Yellow Medicine, who came garbed in civilized attire, "coats and white shirts, with starched bosoms."[6] They had taken up Inkpaduta's trail at Lake Madison and had closely followed it all the way without overtaking the band.

Considerable time was spent in parleying for the captive, but the Yankton owner remained firm in his refusal of the terms offered. At the close of the second day he stated that he would have to submit the question of sale to a tribal vote, since he lacked the power to negotiate it himself. This brought to light the fact that there were two parties in the tribe—one favouring immediate sale, the other maintaining that it would be better to take the captive to the Missouri River country.

While these negotiations were in progress groups of Yanktons visited Abbie Gardner. With great gusto they dwelt upon the situation that existed in the council from time to time. Each group had its own version as to her future disposition. "One would say that I would be taken to the river and drowned.... Another would tell me that I would be bound to a stake and burned, showing the manner in which I would writhe and struggle in the flames. Another declared that I was to be cut to pieces by inches; taking his knife and beginning at my toes, or fingers, he would show how piece after piece was to be cut off".[7] Finally the captive was relieved by a Yankton squaw who told her that there was no truth in these explanations, since the council had decided that she was to be freed by sale to the stranger Indians who would take her back to the whites. Thus on the fifth day of the council the party for immediate sale won, and the tribal vote expressed a willingness to close the bargain as soon as possible.

The price paid for the ransom of Abbie Gardner was probably "two horses, twelve blankets, two kegs of powder, twenty pounds of tobacco, thirty-two yards of blue squaw cloth, thirty-seven and a half

---

5, 6 & 7. Mrs. Sharp's *History of the Spirit Lake Massacre.* 8. *Ibid.* See also Flandrau's *The Ink-pa-du-ta Massacre of 1857* in the *Collections of the Minnesota Historical Society*, Vol. III.

yards of calico and ribbon, and other small articles".[8] Although there is no little disagreement as to how much was actually paid for her ransom, it is certain that none of the many articles with which the Indians were provided to secure the release of Mrs. Noble and Miss Gardner were ever turned back or accounted for by the three Indians. From this it may fairly be presumed that all were used in bringing about the ransom.

After the purchase price had been paid and the captive turned over to her new caretakers, they were all urged by the Yanktons to remain and attend a feast to be given in their honor. Abbie Gardner, however, was anxious to make her return to civilization as speedily as possible. She had also observed in the preparations which were being made that roast dog was to be served at the feast, and so declined to attend, urging upon her guides an immediate departure. In spite of her failure to appreciate the honour of a dog feast, the Yankton chief, Ma-to-wa-ken, ordered that the wagon be piled high with buffalo skins and meat. So well filled was the wagon that only Miss Gardner could be accommodated in addition to the load.[9] As a further assurance of good will the chief sent two of his best men along as a guard. They were to accompany the group to the Wahpeton Agency before turning back. Evidently this was a safeguard against attack from Inkpaduta's men, for it appears that a number of his party followed for four days before turning back to the camp on Snake Creek.[10]

The return trip of Abbie Gardner was strikingly different from her forced flight, since now she was the only member of the party who rode while all the others walked. The first adventure of the journey which proved to her the good intentions of the Indians was at the crossing of the James River. When the party arrived at the stream, the girl was placed in a frail little boat not more than five or six feet in length—just large enough for herself. In her fright she recalled the Yankton's tales of her early killing by her purchasers. But she was soon happily assured of their good intentions. Having placed her in the frail boat, they attached a strong rawhide thong cable to one end. When these preparations for crossing were completed, the Indians divested themselves of most of their clothing, plunged into the stream, and led or guided the canoe and its occupant safely across to the opposite bank. From this time on the girl's confidence in her guides grew with every evidence of their goodwill toward her.

The return journey was without any unusual incident. After a

---

9 & 10. Lee's *History of the Spirit Lake Massacre*.

week of uninterrupted travelling, they came to a region thickly populated with Indians, and to the great joy of Abbie Gardner there were a large number of log houses in addition to the primitive and loathsome *tepees*. She thought these were inhabited by white people when she first sighted them, but later she discovered that such was not the case: they were all inhabited by Indians. After two more days of travel, she reached the home of a half-breed family who could talk English. It was here that she learned that her guides had been sent out by the authorities to bring her in. While they tarried here for a day and a half Abbie made a suit for herself out of cloth furnished by the half-breed girls at whose home she lodged.[11] The next stop was at the Yellow Medicine mission on the confines of civilization. Here the girl was given into the temporary care of the missionaries, Dr. and Mrs. Thomas S. Williamson. The date of her arrival at this point was on or about the tenth day of June. Her joy was altogether unbounded when she found herself once more lodged in the home of a person of her own race; for she now fully realised that her deliverance was actual and not a fanciful dream.

✶✶✶✶✶✶

While this expedition was being successfully carried out, Agent Flandrau had gone to St. Paul with Mrs. Marble, whom he tells us he took thither in his own wagon. As soon as they arrived Mrs. Marble was turned over to a Mrs. Long, the wife of Steve Long, proprietor of the Fuller House then located at the northeast corner of Jackson and Seventh Streets. Mrs. Long was instructed to outfit her in the most becoming and "effective widow's weeds obtainable in the market".[12] When this had been satisfactorily accomplished, Mrs. Marble was presented to the people at a public meeting or reception in the hotel. Before the reception came to a close over one thousand dollars had been contributed toward her future support. This was turned over to Governor Medary to be used in whatever manner the governor thought best. Mrs. Marble was detained in St. Paul for only a brief time, due to her great desire to return to her friends and relatives in the East. At the time of her leaving, Governor Medary gave her two hundred and fifty dollars of the money contributed and placed the

---

11. Mrs. Sharp's *History of the Spirit Lake Massacre*. Concerning this costume Mrs. Sharp has since remarked that "the style and fit might not have been approved by Worth, but it was *worth* everything to me."

12. Flandrau's *The Ink-pa-du-ta Massacre of 1857* in the *Collections of the Minnesota Historical Society*, Vol. III.

remainder in a St. Paul bank. Later the bank failed and nothing could be realised on the deposit.[13]

******

At the time of Abbie Gardner's arrival at the Yellow Medicine station, the annuity Indians were in revolt because of the non-payment of annuities then due. These annuities were being held up until the Indians would agree to co-operate in apprehending Inkpaduta and his band. A massacre seemed imminent at any moment; but within two days after her arrival the Indians tentatively agreed to co-operate and all became peaceful. The return of quiet among the Indians enabled a certain Mr. Robinson to join in the trip to St. Paul. The journey was by means of a team and a cumbersome lumber wagon which, owing to the almost unbroken roads, did not permit of either rapid or comfortable travel.

Sunday, or the day following their start, was spent at Redwood, Lower Agency, just above Fort Ridgely. Word was carried in advance to Captain Bee, who at this time was in command at the post. Upon the receipt of the news the captain at once sent his horse and buggy with the urgent request that the girl return with his orderly to spend Sunday at the post with his family. But her Indian rescuers were suspicious of an attempt to deprive them of their reward and would not consent to her going unless they accompanied her. Of course such an arrangement could not be made, and so the acceptance of Captain Bee's kind invitation was impossible.

Since Abbie Gardner could not spend Sunday at the fort, the officers, Captain Bee and Lieutenant Murry, resolved to express their admiration for the girl's fortitude and courage in another way. Previous to her arrival at the post on the following day, these officers solicited from the soldiers a purse containing several dollars in gold, which with a gold ring were presented to her upon her arrival. The presentation was made by Mrs. Bee on behalf of the contributors to the fund. Lieutenant Murry presented her, as a personal testimonial of his regard for her wonderful bravery, an elegant shawl and a dress pattern of the finest cloth that could be obtained at the post trader's store.[14]

From Fort Ridgely the rescue party followed the cross country trail to Traverse des Sioux, then the head of navigation on the Minnesota River. Here they embarked on a steamer; and on June 22nd they

---

13. Flandrau's *The Ink-pa-du-ta Massacre of 1857* in the *Collections of the Minnesota Historical Society*, Vol. III.
14. Mrs. Sharp's *History of the Spirit Lake Massacre*.

reached Shakopee where a large crowd awaited their coming. Again Abbie Gardner was presented with a purse of money amounting to some thirty dollars. The news of her coming had preceded her down the river to St. Paul, and when she arrived there on the evening of the same day she was again met by a large number of people. Accompanied by her rescuers and the Yankton messenger, she was hurried to a carriage and taken to the Fuller House. The landlady, the same who had cared for Mrs. Marble, immediately took her in charge with the same purpose in view as on the previous occasion—that of making her presentable for a public reception.

Previous to her arrival it had been arranged that Abbie Gardner should be formally and publicly turned over to the governor by her rescuers. Thus, at ten o'clock on the morning of Tuesday, June twenty-third, in the public receiving room of the Fuller House the ceremony took place in the presence of a large number of ladies and gentlemen who were specially invited to be present. There was much speechmaking, in which Governor Medary, Agent Flandrau, Ma-za-ku-ta-ma-ni, and An-pe-tu-tok-cha took the prominent parts. Ma-za-ku-ta-ma-ni reminded Governor Medary of the great regard in which his people held the whites and how on account of their desire to manifest this respect he and his companions had been willing to undertake the perilous mission—which they really believed at the outset might prove to be a fatal undertaking. An-pe-tu-tok-cha followed his companion with a relation of the salient features of the journey to and from the Yankton camp and with a description of the difficulties met and overcome in the council while the negotiation for the captive's ransom was pending.

Governor Medary in reply cautioned the Indians against fraternizing or holding any form of communication with the lawless elements of the plains Indians; and he assured them that the great service they had rendered would be rewarded in a proper manner, and that an account of their mission would be sent to the Great Father at Washington as soon as possible.[15]

At the close of the ceremony Agent Flandrau presented Abbie Gardner with a magnificent Indian war bonnet—the gift of the Yankton chief, Ma-to-wa-ken, from whom she had been purchased. The bonnet had been entrusted to the keeping of Ma-za-ku-ta-ma-ni with instructions to have it presented to the girl when she should be

---

15. For these speeches see Lee's *History of the Spirit Lake Massacre*; Mrs. Sharp's *History of the Spirit Lake Massacre*.

safely delivered to their White Father, the governor. Following these formalities an elaborate state dinner was served in honour of the released captive and her rescuers.

On the following day, which was June twenty-fourth, Abbie Gardner, under the escort of Governor Medary and accompanied by a certain L. P. Lee, embarked on the steamer *Galena* for Iowa, for the purpose of finding her sister Eliza, who had been so fortunate as to escape the massacres at Okoboji and Springfield. Governor Medary accompanied her as far as Dubuque. In case the sister could not be located, he proposed to take Abbie to Columbus, Ohio, and adopt her into his own family.[16] From Dubuque Mr. Lee conducted Miss Gardner to Fort Dodge where she was left in the care of Major William Williams, who promised to have her taken as soon as possible to the home of her sister. It seems that Eliza Gardner had married William R. Wilson of Company B of the Fort Dodge relief expedition and was then living at Hampton, Iowa.

At Hampton anxiously awaiting the captive's return was not only her sister, but also Mr. Thatcher who was hoping that he might yet hear something favourable concerning Mrs. Thatcher. To Abbie Gardner fell the sad duty of conveying to him the last words spoken by Mrs. Thatcher as she started to cross what turned out to be a river of death.[17]

---

16. Lee's *History of the Spirit Lake Massacre*.
17. Mrs. Sharp's *History of the Spirit Lake Massacre*, Lee's *History of the Spirit Lake Massacre*.

CHAPTER 29

Pursuit and Punishment of Inkpaduta

Immediately after the departure of Abbie Gardner, Agent Flandrau and her rescuers returned to the Yellow Medicine Agency. Here Agent Flandrau proceeded to make a settlement with the Indians who had so well demonstrated their good faith. Without difficulty the matter was adjusted upon the basis of a four hundred dollar cash payment to each or a total of twelve hundred dollars.[1] The legislature of Minnesota Territory had acted in the matter while these Indians were on their mission; and the payment was now made on behalf of Governor Medary.

By the first of May sentiment had begun to crystallize in favour of some form of action by the Territorial legislature looking toward the rescue of the captives. Before such action could be taken, Mrs. Marble was brought in. This only increased the interest in the welfare of those yet remaining in the hands of the Indians somewhere on the Dakota plains. An insistent popular demand arose for immediate action; and this demand was met by an appropriation of ten thousand dollars.[2] But the news of this action had not reached Agent Flandrau at the time he sent his Indians to the rescue. The Territory willingly honored all obligations contracted by him for the purpose of the ransom, even paying the principal and interest upon the ingeniously contrived but extra-legal bond. In securing the release of Abbie Gardner and Mrs. Marble somewhat more than three thousand dollars were expended

---

1. Flandrau's *The Ink-pa-du-ta Massacre of 1857* in the Collections of the Minnesota Historical Society, Vol. III.
2. Flandrau's The *Ink-pa-du-ta Massacre of 1857* in the Collections of the Minnesota Historical Society, Vol. III.

out of the ten thousand appropriated.[3]

As soon as Agent Flandrau had outfitted his Indians and had seen them off on their journey for the rescue of Mrs. Noble and Abbie Gardner, he went to Fort Ridgely to confer with Colonel Alexander as to the best plan of operating against Inkpaduta. In any event the plan was to be put in operation only on receipt of word that the captives were safe from further harm. Colonel Alexander was very enthusiastic over the suggested punishment of Inkpaduta's band, and he signified his willingness to detail no less than five companies to proceed to the Skunk Lake region and close in upon the Indian outlaws from as many directions. This plan it was believed would, destroy all possibility of escape. But before arrangements had been fully matured, Colonel Alexander was ordered by the War Department to get his forces under way immediately and unite with those under General Albert Sidney Johnston who was marching west to quell the Mormon disturbances in Utah. Unfortunately the successor to Colonel Alexander had but little interest in the matter, and Agent Flandrau's scheme had to be given up, at least for a time.

Following quickly upon the order received by Colonel Alexander was one sent by the Secretary of the Interior to Agent Flandrau "to investigate and report the facts in the case, and the measures"[4] which in his judgment would be most effective in ferreting out and punishing the marauders. This order somewhat irritated the agent as he had already reported fully upon the facts and had suggested the best measures to be taken in dealing with the outlaws. In commenting upon this incident the agent wrote some years later that he "had become so thoroughly convinced of the imbecility of a military administration, which clothed and equipped its troops exactly in the same manner for duty in the tropical climate of Florida, and the frigid region of Minnesota, that I took advantage of the invitation, to lay before the authorities some of my notions as to what was the proper thing to do".[5]

Agent Flandrau does not appear to have considered the request for a report as being urgent, since he sent no reply until August twenty-seventh, nearly two months later. In the report he took occasion to suggest a remedy for the causes of the failure of Captain Bee's detail to capture Inkpaduta's band before it made the attack on Springfield.

---

3. Lee's *History of the Spirit Lake Massacre.*
4 & 5. Flandrau's *The Ink-pa-du-ta Massacre of 1857* in the *Collections of the Minnesota Historical Society*, Vol. III.

As has already been stated the slow progress of the detail was not alone due to the depth of the snow, but also to the unwieldly character of the men's equipment. Concerning this situation the agent observed that "the ordinary means of transportation in the army is, as you well know, by heavy wagons drawn by mules. In the winter these wagons are placed upon sleds, and where there are roads for them to go upon, they can do well enough.

But, as I have before said, it will be very seldom if ever, that troops will be called upon to act in a country where there are roads of any kind made in the snow, consequently these sleds and mules are useless." In lieu of this sort of equipment, he recommended that troops, to be effective in winter, should be equipped with snowshoes. In concluding he asked that men be placed on the frontier "who will at all times and under all circumstances, be *superior* to the enemy they have to contend with, and I would have no fear of a recurrence of the difficulties of last spring".[6]

The annuities due the Sioux Indians in accordance with the treaties of Traverse des Sioux and Mendota were customarily paid them at the upper and lower agencies during the closing week in June of each year. Upon such occasions the Indians flocked to these points by the thousands from Minnesota and Dakota. They came prepared to celebrate; and this they commonly did for several days both before and after the payment was made. It was not alone the annuity Indians who assembled, but the undesirable whites of the frontier also came to pick up whatever money might be obtainable. At this particular time—late in June, 1857—in addition to about six thousand annuity Indians, many such desperate characters had gathered at the agencies and may be considered responsible for much that happened.

When all had gathered in at the two agencies, the Superintendent of Indian Affairs, W. J. Cullen, called a conference at the Upper Agency. This council, attended by representatives from all bands of the Upper Sioux and a few from the lower tribes, was addressed by Superintendent Cullen. He told them plainly that they would be held responsible for the conduct of the lawless characters of their nation, and that in view of this responsibility they should without delay devise some means of apprehending Inkpaduta. Leaving them to deliberate and report later, he proceeded to the Lower Agency, where he called a like council of the Mdewakanton and Wahpekuta bands to meet on July

---

6. Flandrau's *The Ink-pa-du-ta Massacre of 1857* in the *Collections of the Minnesota Historical Society*, Vol. III.

twelfth. At this meeting he made the same demands as at the Upper Agency and with like result.

Within a brief time Cullen received deputations from both branches of the Sioux informing him that they neither could nor would comply with his demands unless United States soldiers were sent with them. He communicated the demand to Major Sherman, then commanding at Fort Ridgely, who replied that soldiers could not be furnished for such an undertaking since there was not a sufficient number then at the post to make it advisable to spare any; and "the policy of sending soldiers to co-operate with Indians . . . would only expose troops to treachery on the part of the Indians." Then, too, "a body of Indians on an expedition of that kind would rely on troops to do the work of capturing and killing . . . in case they should have an engagement with the party they were seeking".[7]

Admitting the soundness of this answer Superintendent Cullen informed the Indian envoys that United States troops could not be furnished for such a purpose, and he stated that unless the Indians decided to undertake such an expedition alone and unaided, other measures than those already taken would be resorted to from necessity. No further action coming from the Indians, Superintendent Cullen determined to withhold the annuities.[8]

On the thirteenth the Indians again declined to go in pursuit of Inkpaduta without the aid of United States troops. On the fourteenth they began consolidating their bands and it became evident to all that trouble was afoot. Matters were growing more critical every day. The whites became alarmed and began to leave their farms. Many fled to the post or left the country altogether. The situation reached a climax on the evening of the fifteenth when a Sisseton, without provocation, stabbed a soldier of Major Sherman's command. The Indian escaped and fled to the Sisseton camp where he was received and protected. This incident evidenced the determination of these Indians to protect rather than punish law-breakers.[9]

The crisis was made more acute by the demand for the release of the Indian to the military authorities. Major Sherman made the demand and was refused. The officer sent by him was received "with two hundred of their guns pointed towards him". Delivery of the culprit was, however, promised for the next morning. At that time "they came down from their lodges, numbering about twenty-five hundred warriors, all armed and painted, evidently prepared for fight.

7, 8 & 9. *House Executive Documents*, 1st Session, 35th Congress, Vol. II, Pt. I.

Many surrounded and came into the camp; they asked a council".[10] They were told that their request could not be granted until they surrendered the culprit and laid their guns aside. By deceit they then sought to draw out the Indian agents and army officers one by one to talk, with the intention of killing them when they had been drawn into a council. In this plan they were frustrated, and on the following day they surrendered the culprit. The Indians were probably emboldened by the panic which then existed throughout the whole of southern and western Minnesota. They construed the situation as "an open confession of cowardice, fear and weakness" upon the part of the Indian and military authorities, and they were ready to flout both at any opportunity.[11]

At this time Little Crow appeared and tendered his best offices in quieting the disturbance and expelling the malcontents. While these rebellious proceedings were taking place at the Upper Agency, he had been at the Redwood Agency. Owing to his intercession and influence, the Indians at the Lower Agency sent word within a day or two that they were willing to undertake the pursuit and punishment of Inkpaduta. In this resolve they were also joined by the Sissetons. Because of Little Crow's undoubted influence in bringing his tribesmen to terms, it was decided to place him in command of the expedition if such an appointment was acceptable to its members—which proved to be the case. But the Indians were in no condition to embark on such an expedition, since they were without food or supplies of any kind. Upon their assurance of good faith in the prosecution of the expedition they were promised the needed supplies.

Thus equipped the Indian expedition started in pursuit of Inkpaduta on the nineteenth day of July. To hold them to the faithful performance of their promise, Superintendent Cullen sent his interpreter, Joseph Campbell, and six half-breeds along to report upon operations. One hundred and six warriors under Little Crow made up the personnel of the company, in addition to Campbell and the half-breeds.[12] The membership came from the whole Sioux nation represented at the agencies, being recruited from the seventeen bands of the Upper Sioux and the eight bands of the Lower Sioux.

After an absence of sixteen days the Little Crow expeditionary force returned to the Upper Agency on the fourth of August. They

---

10. *House Executive Documents*, 1st Session, 35th Congress, Vol. II, Pt. I.
11. Hubbard and Holcombe's *Minnesota in Three Centuries*, Vol. II.
12. *House Executive Documents*, 1st Session, 35th Congress, Vol. II, Pt. I.

reported that on July twenty-eighth, on arriving at Skunk Lake, they found six lodges of Inkpaduta's people. These were divided into two encampments of three lodges each, about three miles apart. Prior to the arrival of the expedition the lodges were deserted by their occupants who fled to the Big Drift Wood Lake, twenty miles away. They had evidently fled to this lake for the better protection it would afford, owing to the rank growth of reeds in its shallow waters. When the pursuers came up with the fleeing Indians fighting began at once, but it had continued only a half hour when darkness put an end to the conflict. In the morning three prisoners were taken, two squaws and a boy, and three men were found killed and one wounded. Of those killed one was identified as Mak-pi-a-pe-ta or Fire Cloud, a twin son of Inkpaduta. It was also learned from the captives that a defection had arisen in Inkpaduta's band, as a result of which Inkpaduta and a few followers had broken away and gone to the Snake Creek camp of the Yanktons. Not feeling strong enough to make demands upon a camp of over a thousand Yankton friends of Inkpaduta the expedition had returned to report.[13]

But Superintendent Cullen was not satisfied with what had been done and he plainly spoke his mind. His insistence irritated not only Little Crow, but other leaders of the Sioux at both agencies. Cullen, however, was determined and he called a council of the Sissetons and Wahpetons at the Upper Agency on August tenth. The Indian representatives were sullen and Superintendent Cullen was tactless, with the result that many sharp replies were exchanged to the disadvantage of both parties. Wahpuja Wicasta accused the superintendent of being dissatisfied because they, the Indians, had failed to bring back a piece of Inkpaduta that he, Superintendent Cullen, might taste of it and thus pronounce upon its genuineness and prove their good faith in the pursuit of the outlaw.[14]

Ma-za-ku-ta-ma-ni, representing the soldier lodge which had been formed, spoke bitterly concerning the wrongs done the Indians and accused Superintendent Cullen of breaking faith in his relations with the soldiers and in his failure to reward the efforts which they had honestly put forth, (see note following). Superintendent Cullen failed to accomplish his purpose and in the end had to admit the need for action upon the part of the military arm of the government. Such action he now recommended, as well as the payment of the annuities long overdue. It is a reflection upon the effectiveness of the military to note that no further

---

13. *House Executive Documents*, 1st Session, 35th Congress, Vol. II, Pt. I.

action was taken to punish the outlaw and his band.

> Note:—This speech is one of the very few well-known oratorical efforts of a Siouan leader and as such it is here appended:"The soldiers have appointed me to speak for them. The man who killed white people did not belong to us, and we did not expect to be called to account for the people of another band. We have always tried to do as our Great Father tells us. One of our young men brought in a captive woman. I went out and brought the other. The soldiers came up here, and our young men assisted to kill one of Ink-pa-du-tah's sons at this place. Then you (Superintendent Cullen) spoke about our soldiers going after the rest. Wakea Ska (White Lodge) said he would go, and the rest of us followed. The lower Indians did not get up the war party for you; it was our Indians, the Wahpeton and Sisiton. The soldiers here say that they were told by you that a thousand dollars would be paid for killing each of the murderers. Their Great Father does not expect to do these things without money, and I suppose that it is for that that the special agent is come up.
>
> We wish the men who went out paid for what they have done. Three men are killed as we know. I am not a chief among the Indians. The white people have declared me a chief, and I suppose I am able to do something. We have nothing to eat, and our families are hungry. If we go out again we must have some money before we go. This is what the soldiers have wished me to say. . . . All of us want our money now very much. We have never seen our Great Father, but have heard a great deal from him, and have always tried to do as he has told us. A man of another band has done wrong, and we are to suffer for it. Our old women and children are hungry for this. I have seen ten thousand dollars sent to pay for our going out. I wish the soldiers were paid for it. I suppose our Great Father has more money than this."—*House Executive Documents*, 1st Session, 35th Congress, Vol. II, Pt. I.

For a few years Inkpaduta was lost sight of. Apparently he had ceased his activities along the frontier. For five years he remained in seclusion. In the summer of 1862 a portion of the band appeared at the Yellow Medicine Agency, hoping to share in the annuities of that

---

14. *House Executive Documents*, 1st Session, 35th Congress, Vol. II, Pt. I.

year. Agent Galbraith, hearing of their presence, sent Lieutenant T. J. Sheehan with a few soldiers to drive them away from the agency. But their friends had warned them; and when the detail surrounded the camp to the south of Lake Benton the Indians were gone. The trail was followed for some distance, but it suddenly ended leaving not a trace of its continuance.

It must not be supposed, however, that Inkpaduta contented himself with a life of complete inactivity. He is presumed to have joined with Little Crow in a plan for the expulsion of all whites from the Dakota country which was to culminate in the massacres of 1862. During the progress of this revolt his presence was several times reported, and toward its close he is said to have gone westward and united with the Santees of the Missouri. In a few years he succeeded in uniting this tribe with the Yanktons and then secured the leadership.

But he had now grown too old to be aggressive, and so his leadership was more nominal than real. According to Holcombe "Inkpadoota's last appearance in an historical scene was at the Custer massacre, in the Little Big Horn, in Eastern Montana, in June, 1876. On the morning of the day that General Custer made his ill-fated ride upon the Indian camp, Inkpadoota, then seventy-five years old, and stone blind, was sitting on the banks of the Little Big Horn ... with two of his grandsons, and the three were fishing in the stream. The little boys were the first to see Major Reno's command as it came riding up the valley to hold the Indians on the south, while Custer should come upon them from the north. They ran as fast as they could encumbered with their blind and decrepit grandsire, and gave the alarm in time for Gall and Grass to come down and drive back Reno, and then hasten back and exterminate Custer and his force.

At this time, and for ten years before, Inkpadoota had been blind, and no longer regarded as a leader of anybody, for he could not walk without a guide. He and his two surviving sons fled with Sitting Bull to Canada, finally locating at the Canadian Red Pipestone Quarry, in Southwestern Manitoba. Here, in 1894, Dr. Charles Eastman, the well-known Indian authority, found the descendants of Inkpadoota . However, the bloody-minded old savage himself had died miserably some years before".[15] Thus ended the life of an implacable foe of the white race, who for nearly forty years had terrorized the northwestern frontier from the Mississippi River in Iowa to the far away Rockies of Canada.

---

15. Hubbard and Holcombe's *Minnesota in Three Centuries*, Vol. III; *South Dakota Historical Collections*, Vol. II & Vol. VI.

Of the original band but little more remains to be said. While the excitement was at its highest in the closing days of June, 1857, incident to the non-payment of the annuities, Agent Flandrau, then at the Lower Agency, received a note from Sam Brown, a trader on the Yellow Medicine. The note brought the information that Inkpaduta and several of his band were then at the Upper Agency. The agent immediately sent a messenger to Fort Ridgely requesting help. He was given a detachment of fifteen men under Lieutenant Murry. While these troops were on the way from Fort Ridgely to the Redwood Agency, Agent Flandrau recruited a volunteer force of perhaps twenty-five men to assist in the operations against Inkpaduta. Among these volunteers was the well-known scout and interpreter, Joseph Campbell, who was almost an indispensable adjunct of any such expedition. When these preparations had been completed, the Indian messenger was sent back to the Upper Agency with the request that a guide be sent out to meet and lead them to the outlaw's camp.

At dusk the united forces started for the Yellow Medicine. About midway between the two agencies there was a high mound or butte which overlooked the whole of the surrounding country for miles. The trail being followed was that of the Sioux and according to their custom it passed over the summit of the elevation. When the party had reached the summit they found An-pe-tu-tok-cha or Other Day who had been sent by Brown to guide them to the camp. When found he was quietly sitting by the side of the trail, engaged in his favorite pastime of smoking. Upon being accosted he gave not the slightest evidence of recognition or interest. When he finally replied to questions put to him he admitted that a few of Inkpaduta's Indians were near the Yellow Medicine, up the river about five miles, and numbered perhaps six lodges. Further than this he either did not have, or did not care to give, information. When questioned as to methods of attack he declared the best plan would be to "charge down on the camp, and when they see the soldiers, they will know who they are after, and any of *Ink-pa-du-ta's* people that are there, will run or show fight, the rest will remain passive."[16] This plan, after being confirmed by Campbell as best, was adopted.

With Other Day as guide, the march was resumed. The party reached the river, about one mile below the camp, just at dawn. The camp was pitched on a plateau or open prairie about a quarter of a

---

16. Flandrau's The *Ink-pa-du-ta Massacre of 1857* in the *Collections of the Minnesota Historical Society*, Vol. III.

mile from the river. To reach the shelter of the river it would be necessary for one fleeing from the camp to pass across the open space and go down a precipitous descent of about fifty feet. When within a half mile of the camp, a charge was ordered by Lieutenant Murry. Nearly simultaneously with this command an Indian, leading a squaw, ran from one of the lodges toward the river. Other Day at once called out that there was the man, and rifles instantly cracked. Obviously the fugitive was not hit, for he safely made the shelter of the brush along the river in the face of a continued fire.

In his hurried flight the Indian was not unarmed, for he carried a double-barrelled shot-gun. This fact made it extremely dangerous to go into the brush after him or even to attempt a reconnaissance. That he intended to defend himself was evident, for as soon as he reached the shelter of the brush he began firing on the attacking party. Each shot from him was greeted with a volley from the soldiers, which soon put an end to his firing. When found the body of the man was riddled with bullets. Upon investigation the individual proved to be none other than Roaring Cloud, son of Inkpaduta, the Indian who had so atrociously attacked and murdered Mrs. Noble.

The squaw whom he led at the beginning of his dash for the river was taken prisoner in the hope that she might assist in identifying the Indian who had been killed, as well as give information about other inhabitants of the camp. Taking her prisoner, however, proved most unfortunate, for it produced a great commotion at the Upper Agency which only added fuel to the excitement over the deferred annuities. On the return it was necessary to pass through the camps of over seven thousand Indians. According to Agent Flandrau "the excitement among them was terrible. The squaw kept up a howling such as a squaw in distress only can make. The Indians swarmed about us, guns in hand, and scowled upon us in the most threatening manner.... I then began to realise the desperate temerity of the enterprise. Our salvation was simply the moral force of the government that was behind us. We reached the Agency buildings in safety, and took possession of a log house, where we remained several days in a state of sleepless anxiety, until relieved by Major Sherman with the famous old Buena Vista battery.... We felt ... like the man who was chased by a bear, and finally seized his paws around a tree; he wanted somebody *to help him let go*."[17] With the coming of the battery the Indians became quiet.

---

17. Flandrau's *The Ink-pa-du-ta Massacre of 1857* in the *Collections of the Minnesota Historical Society*, Vol. III.

CHAPTER 30

The Memorial Tributes of Iowa

From what has preceded one might conclude that Minnesota Territory alone was sufficiently interested in the welfare of the captives and the punishment of the marauders to take official action relative thereto. Although such was not the case, it is true that Minnesota Territory through its legislative body was the first to take official notice of the situation and attempt a remedy. To be sure the Governors of Iowa had for several years been insistent in making demands upon the Federal government for the protection of the northwestern frontier; but nothing was accomplished. Both the Iowa legislature and Congress remained obdurate.

The delay on the part of Iowa was in large part due to the belief that the frontier troubles demanded action by the Federal authorities rather than by the State.[1] After the presentation of numerous petitions and following considerable debate, the Thirty-fifth Congress enacted a relief measure on June 14, 1858, by which the sum of twenty thousand dollars was appropriated "for defraying the expenses of the several expeditions against Ink-pa-du-tah's band, and in the search, ransom, and recovery of the female captives taken by said band in eighteen hundred and fifty-seven".[2] This fund was to be expended under the direction of the Secretary of the Interior, who in turn designated the Superintendent of Indian Affairs, W. J. Cullen of St. Paul, Minnesota, as the disbursing agent of the Department.

Under the provisions of this act claims aggregating $7180.36 were

---

1. Letter of Governor James W. Grimes to the Iowa Delegation in Congress, January 3, 1855, in the *Annals of Iowa*(Third Series), Vol. II; Letter of Governor James W. Grimes to President Franklin Pierce in the *Annals of Iowa* (Third Series), Vol. III.
2. *United States Statutes at Large*, Vol. II, Ch. 163, 1st Session, 35th Congress, June 14, 1858.

presented by Iowans to Superintendent Cullen.[3] Upon the submission of required proof and the auditing of claims submitted, Superintendent Cullen recommended a payment of $3156.36 to apply on supplies furnished the Iowa relief expedition, and $1657.00 for services rendered by individual members of the expedition, making a total of $4813.36.[4] These claims were duly certified to the Secretary of the Interior, and the auditors of the Department, after eight months of examination of proof, advised the payment of $3628.43—a cut of $1184.93 from the Superintendent's recommendations.[5]

The act of the Thirty-fifth Congress was later supplemented by a second and a third act by the Thirty-sixth Congress under dates of June 19 and 21, 1860—the first[6] of which set aside $16,679.90, and the second[7] $18,988.84 for the further reimbursement of the State. These measures were further supplemented during the same Congress by an act, under date of March 2, 1861, indemnifying the "citizens of Iowa and Minnesota for the destruction of property at or near Spirit Lake by Ink-pa-du-tah's band of Sioux Indians", to the amount of $9,640.74.[8] By these acts the Federal government had set aside a total of $65,308.48 to indemnify the citizens of Iowa and Minnesota for lives lost, property destroyed, and expenses incurred in connection with the rescue of the captives and the punishment of the outlaws. Further than this Congress refused to act, the consensus of opinion in Congress being that the States concerned should supply any further needed relief.

Almost two years after Congress had officially recognised the need of the State for assistance in handling the Indian frontier problem, the Iowa legislature took action. On March 12, 1860, a bill was enacted into law whereby "the sum of three thousand dollars, or so much thereof as shall be necessary" was appropriated for the aid of those

---

3. *Copies of Claims Submitted* in Auditor's office, in the Public Archives, Des Moines, Iowa; *Statement from the Office of the Northern Superintendent of Indian Affairs, St. Paul, Minnesota*, in the Public Archives, Des Moines, Iowa.

4. *Statement from Office of Northern Superintendent of Indian Affairs, St. Paul, Minnesota*, in the Public Archives, Des Moines, Iowa.

5. Letter to Governor Lowe from Superintendent W. J. Cullen, August 12, 1859, in the Public Archives, Des Moines, Iowa.

6. *United States Statutes at Large*, Vol. 12, Ch. 157, 1st Session, 36th Congress, June 19, 1860.

7. *United States Statutes at Large*, Vol. 12, Ch. 163, 1st Session, 36th Congress, June 21, 1860.

8. *United States Statutes at Large*, Vol. 12, Ch. 72, 2nd Session, 36th Congress, March 2, 1861.

members of the relief expedition who had drawn largely upon their private means to finance the undertaking, but who had not been afforded the expected relief by the Federal government.

Under the provisions of this act the governor was made the auditor of all claims presented in accordance with its provisions. He was directed to secure copies of all claims filed with the Federal government and, when satisfied by the evidence submitted that such as were yet unpaid were just, he might issue an order upon the Treasurer of State to pay the claims.[9] This law was supplemented on March twenty-second by a second act looking toward the relief of persons specifically named in the law,[10] although no additional funds for such purpose were provided. Under the provisions of these acts there was disbursed under order of the governor a total of $1126.02, which was distributed among eighty-two claimants.[11]

Before the matter had been finally closed the strife between North and South eliminated from the public mind an interest in all things save the momentous struggle then in progress. Thus it happened that the Spirit Lake Massacre and the relief expeditions were lost from view for more than a generation. But there was one individual with an abiding interest who for thirty years cherished the hope of commemorating in some way the heroic struggles of that little group of men who went from Webster City in March, 1857, to relieve the settlers at the lakes.

In the summer of 1887 Charles Aldrich, long a resident of Webster City, proposed placing a brass tablet in some suitable place in that city in memory of Company C of the relief expedition. The decision was quickly reached to place the memorial in the Hamilton County court house and to ask the board of supervisors to appropriate three hundred dollars to meet the expense. A petition was circulated in the city and throughout the county requesting such action. Owing to the good will and work of Charles T. Fenton, president of the board, the petition was granted and a committee was appointed to secure and place the memorial.[12]

---

9 & 10. *Laws of Iowa*, 1860.
11. *Claims and Vouchers Filed with Governor of Iowa* in Auditor's Office, in the Public Archives, Des Moines, Iowa. As late as January, 1870, in his first biennial message to the legislature, Governor Merrill stated that the State had recently received from the Federal government the "sum of $18,117 to reimburse outlay for the defence of the northern border of the State, subsequent to the massacre at Spirit Lake in 1857."— Shambaugh's *Messages and Proclamations of the Governors of Iowa*, Vol. III.
12. *Annals of Iowa* (Third Series), Vol. III.

August twelfth was the date set for the unveiling and dedication of the tablet. Mr. Aldrich planned an elaborate program which was to be given in the court room of the newly erected building; but more than two thousand people attended the ceremony, and so the exercises were held on the lawn in front of the court house. Brief addresses were made by Governor William Larrabee, ex-Governor C. C. Carpenter, Mayor McMurray, Captains Richards and Duncombe, Lieutenant John N. Maxwell, Privates William Laughlin and Michael Sweeney, and Mr. Charles Aldrich. The speeches were so planned as to offer a complete review of the attempt to carry relief to the settlers at Spirit Lake and Lake Okoboji.

The tablet consisted of "a slab of Champlain marble, upon which is artistically mounted a plate of polished brass containing the names of the Hamilton county members of the expedition and a number of other suitable inscriptions."[13] Thus did Hamilton County place "in a position of honor in the Hamilton County court house a lasting attestation to the patriotic spirit of appreciation which animates her citizens."[14]

Encouraged by the response in his home county, Mr. Aldrich set about the stimulation of sentiment in the State at large favouring the erection by the State of some fitting memorial to those pioneers whose lives were sacrificed in March, 1857. This proved a long drawn out and arduous task. The public had all but forgotten the incident; memories had to be refreshed, and a desire for commemoration aroused. This proved too great an undertaking for one person, and so Mr. Aldrich turned to the legislative body of the State. Here he obtained only an indifferent response.

But with the awakening in Hamilton County the interest in the project spread; and when the Twenty-fifth General Assembly convened in January, 1894, it became evident that favourable action might be hoped for.

By far the most active and efficient work was done by Mrs. Abbie Gardner Sharp, who came to Des Moines at the very beginning of the session and remained until near its close. In her efforts to secure action she was most ably seconded by Senator A. B. Funk of Spirit Lake. On January twenty-ninth a bill was simultaneously introduced in the Senate and House of Representatives, providing for the proper interment of the remains of the victims of the massacre and the erec-

---

13 & 14. *A Worthy Tribute* in the *Fort Dodge Messenger*, Vol. 23, No. 39, August 18, 1887.

tion of a suitable commemorative monument.[15] The bill carried an appropriation of five thousand dollars which was to be expended under the supervision of a commission of five persons appointed by the governor. Suitable grounds were to be selected near the scene of the massacre. These grounds were to "be purchased, reinterments made and monument erected before the 4th day of July, 1895."[16] So well had the matter been canvassed among the members of the legislature that there were but few negative votes on the measure. The bill was approved by the governor on March 30th, and went into effect on April 4, 1894.

On April tenth Governor Frank D. Jackson appointed as members of the commission Hon. J. F. Duncombe and ex-Governor C. C. Carpenter of Fort Dodge, Mrs. Abbie Gardner Sharp of Okoboji, Hon. R. A. Smith of Spirit Lake, and Charles Aldrich of Des Moines. Within a short time the commission met at Fort Dodge and later at the Gardner cabin on Lake Okoboji. The commission effected an organisation by selecting ex-Governor Carpenter as chairman and Mrs. Sharp as secretary. They quickly decided on the selection of the lot adjacent to and south of the Gardner cabin. This site was immediately presented to the State by its owners, the Okoboji South Beach Company. On June 20, 1894, the P. N. Peterson Granite Company of St. Paul, Minnesota, was awarded the contract for the erection of the memorial. The specifications provided that the monument should be "a shaft 55 feet high above the foundation, in alternate blocks of rough and polished Minnesota granite, with a die 6 × 6 feet, upon which should be placed four bronze tablets—for the sum of $4,500. The inscriptions placed upon the tablets may be described as follows: On the east, the list of murdered settlers; on the west, a complete roster of the relief expedition commanded by Major William Williams; on the south, historical memoranda relating to the loss of Capt. J. C. Johnson and Private W. E. Burkholder, the list of settlers who escaped from Springfield (now Jackson), Minn., etc.; and on the north, the coat of arms of Iowa, with these words: 'Erected by order of the 25th General Assembly of the State of Iowa.'"[17]

---

15. S. F. 115 was introduced by Senator A. B. Funk of Spirit Lake, and H. F. 230 by Representative J. G. Myerly of Estherville. Senator Funk's measure was later substituted in the House for the House measure, upon motion of Representative Myerly.—*Senate Journal*, 1894; *House Journal*, 1894.
16. *Laws of Iowa*, 1894.
17. *Report of the Okoboji and Spirit Lake Monument Commission* in the *Annals of Iowa* (Third Series), Vol. III.

So diligently did the contracting company apply itself in the erection of the memorial that early in March, 1895, four months before the expiration of its contract, the monument was ready for inspection. On March 14, 1895, the commission met at Okoboji and inspected and accepted the work. Upon July twenty-eighth over five thousand people came by wagon and excursion train, from a radius of over fifty miles, to witness the formal dedication of the memorial and its presentation to the State. The gathering was significant in that it marked the opening of a new era in the appropriate marking of historic sites not only in Iowa but in the Middle West. In the words of the Hon. R. A. Smith, it was "meet and fitting that to the pioneer the same as the soldier should be accorded the meed of praise and recognition ... a just, though long delayed, tribute to the memory of the brave and hardy, though unpretentious and unpretending, band of settlers who sacrificed their lives in their attempts to build them homes on this then far away northwestern frontier."[18]

Upon the platform were seated ex-Governor C. C. Carpenter and Hon. R. A. Smith, members of the relief expedition; Mrs. I. A. Thomas, Rev. Valentine C. Thomas, and Jareb Palmer, who fortunately escaped the massacre at Springfield; Judge Charles E. Flandrau, the Indian agent who made possible the project to rescue Abbie Gardner, and Chetanmaza, the Siouan Indian whose intrepidity secured her release; Mrs. Abbie Gardner Sharp a survivor of the massacre at Okoboji; and various State officials. The memorial was presented to the State by ex-Governor C. C. Carpenter upon behalf of the commission under whose direction it had been erected, and was accepted for the State by Lieutenant Governor Warren S. Dungan and Hon. W. S. Richards.

Thus the people of Iowa, through their law-making body, paid a fitting though somewhat tardy tribute to the memory of the pioneers who, imbued with the true American spirit of progress, were willing to brave the hardships of the frontier that those who came later might share the blessings of a richer civilization. In the words of one of the speakers of the occasion:

> Let us hope that this awakening is not ephemeral or temporary. ... The story told by this memorial shaft is but a faint expression of the toils endured, the dangers braved and the sacrifices made by the unfortunate victims whose remains lie buried here.[19]

The memorial "not only commemorates the great tragedy which

---

18 & 19. Smith's *A History of Dickinson County, Iowa*.

crimsoned the waters of these lakes, but it will keep alive the memory of a species of American character which will soon become extinct. As we look away to the west, we are impressed that there is no longer an American frontier; and when the frontier shall have faded away, the pioneer will live only in history, and in the monuments which will preserve his memory."[20]

---

20. Smith's *A History of Dickinson County, Iowa.* It should also be noted that on April 9, 1913, there was approved a law which declared that "on and after the passage of this act, the survivors of the Spirit Lake Relief Expedition of 1857 . . . shall receive a monthly pension of $20.00 per month, during the lifetime of each such survivor".—*Laws of Iowa*, 1913. Under the provisions of this law there was paid out of the State treasury the sum of $2,189.33 for the biennial period ending June 30, 1914, and $4,677.33 for the biennial period ending June 30, 1916.—*Report of the Treasurer of State*, 1914, & 1916.

CHAPTER 31

Changes of Sixty Years

When one looks back over the sixty years, (as at time of first publication), that have elapsed since Ma-za-ku-ta-ma-ni delivered his bitter invective against white infidelity at the Upper Agency on the Yellow Medicine, one can only wonder at the transformation which has been wrought in what was popularly known east of the Alleghenies as the Great American Desert. In sixty years the frontier has moved steadily westward until today it is gone not alone from the Mississippi Valley but from the American continent. What was a vast expanse of prairie in 1857 has become a country of prosperous homes.

Where then not a town was to be found today may be seen numerous large cities throbbing with industrial life, while towns and villages dot the landscape everywhere. Loneliness and desolation have given way to that condition where man's habitation is found at every turn. In sixty years this area has changed from the frontier of civilization to the very centre of its arts and industries. In a country where Indians were met with by the thousands in 1857, one may now travel for days across the plains without catching a glimpse of a red man. The Indian has all but gone from a land where he once roamed free and uncontrolled.

Similarly time has dealt with the people of a different race who played major or minor parts in the tragedy at Spirit Lake and Springfield in 1857. Indeed, time has not always dealt kindly with them, and in more than one instance they have suffered much from its ravages. No one who survived the terrible experience of March, 1857, on the borders of the northwestern lakes was able to regain title to the claims of murdered relatives. The Gardner, Thatcher, and Marble claims were all pre-empted by the settlers of 1858 without regard to their former holders. Those pre-empting were perhaps acting within their legal rights; but the first comers, under the customs of the frontier, were entitled to the claims which they had staked out.

So widely have the survivors of the events of 1857 scattered that today, (1918), but one individual, Mrs. Abbie Gardner Sharp, remains at or near the scene of the massacre. While living with her sister Eliza at Hampton, Iowa, Miss Abbie Gardner became acquainted with Casville Sharp, a young relative of the Noble and Thatcher families. On August 16, 1857, they were married. About a year after the marriage, Mr. and Mrs. Sharp visited the scene of the tragedy at Okoboji in the hope of securing some settlement for the Gardner claim. Although a small amount was paid Mrs. Sharp by J. S. Prescott who had pre-empted the claim, the sum was only nominal and in no sense an adequate compensation for the property lost.

Mrs. Sharp continued to live in Iowa; but not until 1891 did she regain the site of her childhood home at Okoboji. At that time a company interested in the promotion of the Okobojis as a pleasure resort acquired title to some thirteen acres of land at Pillsbury's Point, West Okoboji. This area included the Gardner cabin. The syndicate at once plotted the land for sale as sites for summer cottages. Out of the proceeds derived from the sale of her history of the massacre, Mrs. Sharp acquired the lot upon which stands the original log cabin home—the scene of the massacre.[1] The summer tourist at Okoboji may yet (in 1918) enter the original log cabin and learn from Mrs. Sharp the story of her captivity and rescue.

Mrs. Marble, the only other survivor of the massacre at Lake Okoboji and Spirit Lake, likewise found her husband's claim preempted upon her return. Less fortunate than Mrs. Sharp, she was unable to secure any compensation. For some years she was lost to the knowledge of her Iowa and Minnesota friends. At length, in the early eighties, she was located at Sidell, Napa County, California. Meanwhile, she had married a Mr. Silbaugh. Since then little information has been obtained concerning her, other than that of her death a number of years ago.[2] Thus Mrs. Sharp is now the sole survivor of the

---

1. Mrs. Sharp's *History of the Spirit Lake Massacre.*
2. Judge Charles E. Flandrau in *The Ink-pa-du-ta Massacre of 1857* in the *Collections of the Minnesota Historical Society*, Vol. III, has this to say of Mrs. Marble after leaving St. Paul, Minnesota: "The bank (where her money had been placed) failed, and that was the end of Mrs. Marble so far as I know, except that I heard that she exhibited herself at the East, in the role of the rescued captive, and the very last information I had of her, was, that she went up in a balloon at New Orleans. I leave to future historians the solution of the problem, whether she ever came down again?"

massacre at the lakes, (as at time of first publication).

With the survivors of the Springfield massacre it has been different. All who survived were able to regain their claims, since they returned within a brief time to the scene of the massacre and before their holdings had been pre-empted by settlers in the rush of 1857-1858. In 1913 occurred the death of Mrs. Irene A. Thomas whose cabin was made the rendezvous of the settlers at Springfield, and whose son Willie was the first known victim of the Indian attack. Her husband, it will be recalled, had one arm so badly shattered as to necessitate amputation upon reaching Fort Dodge. A remaining son, Valentine C. Thomas, who was a young boy at the time of the massacre, later served as a minister in Marshalltown, Iowa, where he died in August, 1915. Mrs. Eliza Gardner McGowan was at that time still living in Fort Wayne, Indiana. It will be recalled that following the return of the relief expedition to Fort Dodge she married William R. Wilson, a member of the expedition. For many years Mr. and Mrs. Wilson lived at Hampton and Mason City, Iowa. Some time after Mr. Wilson's death, Mrs. Wilson married a Mr. McGowan and removed to Fort Wayne.

It may be remembered that Johnnie Stewart escaped by hiding in the dooryard of his home while the members of his family were being ruthlessly slaughtered by the Indians. After the Indians left he crawled to the Thomas cabin, which he reached at dusk, was recognised and taken in. In 1915 he was living at Byron, Minnesota; and, from the latest information obtained he is still living at that place, (as at time of first publication). There also survives a Mrs. Gillespie of Blaine, Washington, who at the time of the Springfield attack was Miss Drusilla Swanger, sister of Mrs. William L. Church.

As we of another generation seek recreation at Okoboji, let us pause in retrospection. Let us, "when we contemplate the dangers braved, the hardships and privations endured, and the final suffering and sacrifice which fell to the lot of the victims whose dust and ashes have been gathered together and interred in this historic spot", be conscious that we are paying "a deserved tribute to courage and self-denial, endurance and self-sacrifice".[3]

---

3. Smith's *A History of Dickinson County, Iowa*.

A History of Dickinson County, Iowa

Contents

Introduction	213
Dickinson County Location and Physical Features	215
Treaty of 1851	230
The First Attempt at Settlement in 1856	240
The Indians Arrive at the Lakes	248
Incidents of the First Day of the Massacre	261
Discovery of the Massacre	267
Adventures of the Party That Remained Behind	278
Terrible Sufferings	285
The Attack and Defence	300
The Pursuit	309
Government Apathy	326
Effect of the Massacre Elsewhere	332
The Trip to the Lakes	336
The First Family After the Massacre	347
The Spirit Lake Claim Club	363
The Troops Ordered Back to the Lakes	371
Emigration in 1859	380

Introduction

There has for some time existed a feeling that a connected account of the Indian trouble on the northwestern border of Iowa should be given to the public, or rather that what facts are preserved should be so grouped that a person reading them could form a reasonably intelligent idea of them. Any person following this line of investigation will soon come face to face with the fact that the sources of information are extremely limited. The writer has endeavoured to give as correct and concise an idea of the points treated as was possible under the circumstances, and it seems appropriate to combine them with the early history of Dickinson County, inasmuch as that was the storm centre around which, so far as Iowa is concerned, these events seemed to culminate.

In doing this work he has quoted freely from such sources as were accessible and known to be reliable, and notably so from the writings of Hon. C. E. Flandrau, Hon. Harvey Ingham, Hon. A. R. Fulton and Mrs. Abbie Gardner Sharp, giving at all times the proper credit. The writer was a member of the Relief Expedition in 1857, and assisted in burying the victims of the massacre at that time, and much of what is written in that regard came under his own personal observation. He was also a member of the first party that effected a settlement subsequent to the massacre and has given those events as nearly correct as he can remember them after the lapse of near half a century.

Many will remember that in the centennial year Governor Kirkwood recommended that the several counties procure a summary or synopsis of their pioneer history, and to the writer herewith was assigned the task of preparing one for Dickinson County. The article was published in the Spirit Lake Beacon of that year running through ten numbers. Had that paper not been preserved the present work would not have been attempted. In writing up the county history proper he has departed somewhat from the usual method; whether wisely or unwisely remains to be seen. It has come to be the practice too much in works of this kind to give a glowing write-up for those who are able and willing to pay well for it and ignore others whose work may have been more valuable in building up and developing the country but who do not feel that they have money to invest that way.

It has been the aim of the writer to evade this objection and to avoid everything that looked like favouritism or booming anybody's business. In this he realises that he may have gone to the other extreme. In fact this defect, if defect it be, became more apparent as the work neared completion and it was too late to remedy it. Such as it is it must go to the public who will doubtless judge it at its true value.

CHAPTER 1

Dickinson County Location and Physical Features

Dickinson County is the third county in the state from the west line and in the north tier of counties bordering on the Minnesota line. It is twenty-four miles in length east and west, and nearly seventeen miles in width north and south, and therefore embraces an area of about four hundred square miles, about eight *per cent* of which is covered with lakes.

It is the most elevated county in the state as it lies on the "height of land" or great watershed between the Mississippi and Missouri Rivers and is drained by the upper branches of both the upper Des Moines and Little Sioux Rivers, which empty respectively into each of the before named streams. Its altitude is about seventeen hundred feet above tide water. The marked physical feature which distinguishes Dickinson from the other counties of northwestern Iowa is her numerous lakes. First and last, many descriptions of these lakes have been written up and published, but by far the most interesting and readable is that contained in Prof. T. H. MacBride's report of the geology of Dickinson and Osceola Counties. Writing on this subject he says:

> The lakes of our region lie almost all in Dickinson County. Not that Osceola is destitute of similar topographic features, but for some reason the peculiar conditions that resulted in lakes of size were developed farther east.... But in Dickinson County the lakes are the features of the topography, many of them deep enough to promise permanency, and several so large as to have long attracted popular attention by their beautiful blue waters and the charming outlines of their shores. Minne Waukon or

Spirit Lake, is as we have seen, historic, nay, is it not prehistoric? Even for the red man these beautiful gems of the prairie had name and fame. He hung them around with legends of his own and named them in his own poetic, mystic fashion. Okoboji, place of rest; Minnetonka, great water; Minne Waukon, lake of demons, *lac d'esprits*, were every one apparently familiar to all the tribes and nations of the Sioux, and were doubtless known by name at least to all the eighteenth-century trappers and *voyageurs*.

Okoboji, evidently distinguished by the red man, was by white explorers generally reckoned part of Spirit Lake, and is so entered on the earlier maps. The two bodies are in fact part of a remarkable system extending in chain-like fashion for twenty miles or more in Iowa and probably almost as far in Minnesota. Nevertheless, the greater lakes have now no natural connection with each other; they are in general quite unlike and have, in some details at least, a different geological history. In all cases the water level seems dependent entirely upon rainfall. The few springs discoverable are small and insignificant, while of affluent streams there are practically none; none at least that bring in perennial waters.

The overflow of the Minnesota lakes, it is claimed, reaches our Spirit Lake, and certain smaller lakes to the west and north are also on occasion tributary. But all the lakes, whether in Iowa or Minnesota, are subject to similar fortune. In rainy seasons full, they send their waters to the common outlet; in drier years there is no surplus and the outlet fails. In fact the lakes are each and all simply great pools left on the surface by the retreating glacier, marking points where the ice was somewhat thicker or the amount of detritus carried somewhat less abundant. They owe not their existence to erosion; no recent change of level has formed an outlet for their waters; such as they are, such were they when the latest geologic epoch closed.

The present form and condition of the outlet would not suggest that the principal lakes, at least, have ever been much deeper than at present. The outlet valley is largely constructional and while there has been erosion, considerable in the vicinity of Milford, still erosion has not in time past much affected the level of the lakes, does not at the present day seem to affect them at all. Those familiar with the situation for the last four or five decades assert that Spirit Lake had formerly a natural outlet southward. There is no sign of it at present. On the other hand the out-thrust of the ice from winter to winter has tended to form a species of dyke almost entirely around the lake, especially along its sandy beaches, and this alone would seem to have been sufficient to close up any connection, slight and shallow at best, between Spirit Lake and the waters south of it.

At any rate there is along the south shore of Spirit Lake a pronounced terrace, which is natural and due to the causes mentioned. There are, however, evidences, chiefly afforded by terrace construction, that the water level in the lake has been higher in days gone by than now, perhaps ten feet higher. In such event there would be an overflow southward. Probably the level of the lake has oscillated through the centuries. With a succession of dry seasons the water would become so reduced that out-flow would cease entirely. The sand pushed up in winter by the ice would then form a dam higher and higher and which at length only a very considerable rise in the waters of the lake could surmount.

Then probably some exceptionally rainy season would wash out the obstacle and again reduce the level of the lake, making possible again the construction of the dyke. In the maintenance of the barrier vegetation very much assisted. Today various aquatic plants hold the shallower parts of all the lakes in possession undisputed and greatly check the movements of their waters. In fact by reason of abundant vegetation many of the smaller lakes are now in danger of being completely filled. The plants, many of them rooted to the bottom, at once absolutely prevent erosion, and at the same time hold all solid matter coming in from whatever source from without. For this reason the general outlet of the system, the south end of the south Gar Lake, is not deepening, but seems to be actually rising year by year. But it is time we should describe the lakes more in detail.

Minne Waukon or Spirit Lake, the largest body of water in Iowa, occupies the greater part of the township of the same name. Its extreme length from north to south is a little more than four miles, in Iowa. The extreme width is about the same, but owing to irregularity of contour the area is not more than ten square miles, while the circumference is nearly sixteen. The depth of the lake is said to be thirty feet; the bottom, so far as

VIEW ON SPIRIT LAKE

DRIVE BETWEEN SPIRIT LAKE AND SUNKEN LAKE.

can be learned, is almost even, so that from the deepest part to the shores the diminution in depth is remarkably gradual. The shores are for the most part comparatively low, the water-line sandy, affording unlimited beach. Hard by on the west lie Marble Lake, Hottes Lake, and Little Spirit Lake, separated by only the shortest distance from the main body of water, but draining one into the other and north—at length, however, tributary to Spirit Lake. Those interested have in recent years cut a channel to bring Little Spirit Lake and its congeners into more direct communication with the larger water, apparently with small success.

In dry years no lake has anything to spare. Strangest of all, in the middle of the series, in the south half of section 17, lies Sunken Lake, distant from Spirit Lake only a few rods, and parted from it by a wall of drift some twenty or thirty feet high and at its summit scarcely a rod in width. So abrupt are the shores and so peculiar the situation that common rumour asserts the lake a matter of recent formation; some people even declare that so lately as twenty years ago trees stood where now the water is ten feet deep. The name Sunken Lake records the popular estimate and explanation of the remarkable phenomenon. It seems probable, however, that Sunken Lake is as old as any of the others, and while a most remarkable bit of topography, sufficiently wonderful to demand, even peremptorily demand, an explanation, yet is it quite in harmony with its entire surroundings, and not without parallel in many only less conspicuous cases.

For instance, on the east side of East Okoboji Lake, in the southwest quarter of Section 15, Center Grove township, there are two small lakes even nearer the principal lake than in the case we have just considered and similarly walled off from the greater body of water by a pile of drift. Similar situations on a small scale may be pointed out in every part of Dickinson County. The only explanation is the unevenness of the lower surface of the ice-sheet which rested here, advanced no further, and as it melted retreating even farther and farther northward, left behind, perchance as blocks of ice, these pools of clear, fresh water. Sunken Lake may then represent an ice bowlder; this seems more probable since its walls are steep, Unbroken on every side.

South of Spirit Lake lies Okoboji, in its two sections stretching somewhat in the form of the letter U, open to the north, partly

WEST OKOBOJI.

NATURAL RIPRAPPING ON WEST OKOBOJI.

MINNE WASHTA

in Center Grove, partly in Lakeville township. West Okoboji, which represents the western side of the U, lies almost wholly in Lakeville. This is by many estimated the most beautiful water in the series. Its greater depth, more picturesque winding shores give it some advantage over Minne Waukon, although the latter shows the greater expanse of water. West Okoboji Lake, or simply Okoboji, as it is commonly called, extends nearly six miles in greatest length and almost three at the point of greatest breadth. The greater portion of the lake is, however, narrower, so that the total area does not exceed seven square miles, while its irregular contour measures nearly eighteen miles, as platted. The depth of the lake varies very much at different places and is variously reported. The bed of the lake probably resembles the topography of the adjacent country; it has its hills and its valleys. There seems no reason to doubt that there are many places where the depth is at least one hundred feet, but soundings of two or three times that depth are reported.[1]

The shores of Okoboji are for the most part high walls of bowlder-clay and drift; sandy beaches are less frequent. Everywhere the erosion of the waves has shaped the shores, undermining them and sorting their materials; the fine clays have been carried 'out to sea,' while the weighty bowlders are left behind every winter to be pushed up closer and closer by the ice, at length piled over one another in ramparts and walls, often riprapping the shore for long distances as if to simulate the work of civilized man. A beautiful illustration of this is seen along the southern shore of Lake East Okoboji, section 20. The less attentive observer would surely conclude that those stones were piled up by 'art and man's device,' a seawall to prevent further encroachments of the tide.

At the southern end of Okoboji, near Gilley's Beach, is another fine display of bowlders, notable not so much perhaps for their position as for their variety and beauty. Here are bowlders of limestone, bowlders of granite of every sort, porphyry, syenite, trap, greenstone, quartzite, what you will, the debris of all northern ledges. Similar deposits are visible all around the lake, more especially on the eastern side, probably because the prevailing winds being westerly, the waves have exerted their more constant energy along the eastern bluffs.

---

1. These particulars are from the reports of fishermen and boatmen about the lake.

His descriptions of East Okoboji, Minnie Washta, Centre Lake and Gar Lakes are equally fine, but must be excluded for lack of space. In conclusion he says:

> These lakes taken altogether form one of the attractions of Iowa. Their preservation in their pristine beauty is a matter of more than local interest.

Originally what now comprises the state of Iowa was occupied by several different tribes of Indians. These several tribes were descended from one or the other of two parent races, *viz.*: the Algonquins and the Dacotahs. The Algonquins were the most numerous and powerful of the native races. They originally occupied the valley of the St. Lawrence River from whence their migrations were gradually westward to the Great Lakes, and eventually to the Mississippi and even beyond. They were divided into a large number of tribes having their separate interests, but speaking a common language and owning a common ancestry.

The Algonquin tribe which figured the most prominently in the history of Iowa were the Sacs and Foxes. These were originally two different tribes, but Indian history informs us that they were united about the year 1712 and moved towards the Mississippi River. The names Sacs and Foxes were given them by the whites. The Indian name of the Sacs was the "Outagamies" and that of the Foxes was the "Musquawkies." Very little is known of them for the first hundred years after they moved to the Mississippi. When Lieutenant Pike, in 1805. made his first voyage of discovery up the river he saw a great deal of them and learned considerable about them. He estimated their number at that time to be not far from five thousand. Judge Fulton says that:

> According to a communication submitted to Congress by President Monroe, in relation to the Indians, in 1825, the Sacs and Foxes were estimated at six thousand four hundred, more than one-half of whom resided west of the Mississippi.

They were the hereditary enemies of the Sioux, who were a native tribe which the Sacs and Foxes strove in vain to dispossess. They had previously conquered and driven out the Iowas and taken possession of their country. They had also been successful in their wars with other tribes, but they met more than their match in the fierce and terrible Sioux, and were in a fair way to be finally overcome by them when the United States authorities interfered and endeavoured to put a stop to the hostilities, in which they were but partially successful. The most prominent chief of this tribe known to the whites was the renowned "Black Hawk." Other chiefs of prominence were Pashepaho, Keokuk, Appanoose, Poweshiek, Wapello, Kishkekosh and many others. Judge Fulton gives a list of one hundred and fifty-seven names of members of this tribe copied from the daybook of one of the old traders.

In 1845 and 1840 they were removed to a reservation in Kansas. A short time later a "lingering remnant" of the tribe, becoming dissatisfied with their Kansas home, wandered back to their old haunts on the Iowa River, where they were allowed to gain a foothold and follow the free and easy life of their ancestors in the midst of a progressive and highly civilized community. They have readopted their ancient name and are now known to their white neighbours as "Musquawkies."

Another of the Algonquin tribes, which at one time had a home in Iowa, was the Pottawattamies. When they ceded their lands east of the Mississippi in 1833, they were placed on a reservation near Council Bluffs, where they remained until 1846, when another treaty was concluded with them by which they disposed of their land in Iowa and moved west of the Missouri. As with the Sacs and Foxes so with them after being on their reservation for a short time a few homesick stragglers under the lead of the well known Johnnie Green, wandered back to their old haunts in central Iowa, where they fished, hunted and strolled about undisturbed by their white neighbours until they passed out by life limitation or were merged with the Musquawkies.

The Illini, or Illinois, as they afterward came to be called, were a powerful confederacy made up of five distinct tribes of Algonquins, and at the close of the Seventeenth Century inhabited central Illinois and southern Iowa. It was members of this tribe that Father Marquette came in contact with on his memorable voyage down the Mississippi in 1673. Historical accounts relate that he made the entire trip from the Fox River in Wisconsin to the point where he discovered "the footprints in the sand" near the mouth of the Des Moines River in Iowa without encountering a single native. After landing he followed the trail inland to an Indian village, and found to his great delight that the savages there spoke the same language as those he had left on the shore of Green Bay. Later on this powerful confederacy became much reduced by a sanguinary war with the Iroquois, and by the time of the Louisiana Purchase in 1803 were either exterminated or had joined other tribes and so had passed out of existence as a distinct nation.

Another strong tribe of the same race inhabiting the state of Iowa at the time of the French explorations, but which became extinct before the time of the Louisiana Purchase, were the Muscatines, or Mascoutins, as they were then called. But little is known of this tribe, although there is abundant proof of their once having occupied both sides of the Mississippi near where the city of Muscatine now stands. Judge Fulton closes a chapter regarding them, as follows:

> Having left the last traces of their existence on what is now Iowa soil we have perpetuated the memory of this vanished people by enrolling the appellation Muscatine in our Indian geographical nomenclature.

It would seem that a careful study of the history of the different tribes about this period would cause many people to revise their preconceived notions of the rights and wrongs of the American Indians. According to the most reliable estimates there were originally not far from half a million natives scattered through the territory of what is now the United States. The theory that this vast empire, capable of supporting its hundreds of millions of population, should have been preserved in its native wildness for the gratification of the savage instincts and propensities of these few thousand warriors is. at least debatable if not wholly untenable. The main occupation of these tribes was war among themselves. Upon the least provocation and on the flimsiest pretext they rushed into the most deadly and destructive warfare with each other. They fought for the love of fighting. Entire tribes were exterminated and others greatly diminished.

There is every reason to believe that the number of native inhabitants was largely diminished during the last half of the Seventeenth and the first half of the Eighteenth Centuries by reason of this bitter, unrelenting warfare. The number of Indians who have fallen first and last in the various actions with the whites is wholly insignificant when compared with the numbers slain in wars among themselves. Of course there have been many instances of dishonesty and bad faith in dealing with the Indians, but that doesn't change the main proposition that in the nature of things it was never intended that this vast continent should be shut off from civilization in order that a few tribes of blood-thirsty savages should be undisturbed in their favourite diversion of waging relentless warfare against each other.

The Dacotah tribes figuring in Iowa history are the Omahas, the

Iowas, the Winnebagos and the Sioux. It is doubtful whether the Omahas ever had a permanent residence on Iowa soil, but they frequently visited the state and were closely connected with the Iowas, who were of the same race and spoke the same language. Judge Fulton, in writing of the Iowas, uses the following language:

> The Iowas were once a strong and powerful tribe and were able under their brave and warlike chiefs to maintain successful warfare against their enemies. Their later seat of empire was in the Des Moines Valley. Their principal village was situated on the Des Moines River near the northwest corner of Van Buren County, where the old trading post of Iowaville was subsequently located. That spot may be regarded as historic ground, for there transpired events in the annals of savage warfare which transferred the sovereignty of the Des Moines Valley from the Iowas to the Sacs and Foxes.

The decisive battle in which the Iowas were so signally defeated by the Sacs and Foxes occurred some time between 1820 and 1825. During the latter year the government purchased their undivided interest in the country, whatever it might have been, and they were placed under government protection and settled on a reservation beyond the Missouri River. The only prominent chief of this tribe whose name has been perpetuated in Iowa is Mahaska.

Another Dacotah tribe at one time residing in Iowa were the Winnebagos. This tribe when first known were located west of Lake Michigan near Green Bay. Their history is a chequered one which cannot be repeated here. After the Black Hawk War they were removed from Wisconsin to the "Neutral Ground" in Iowa, where they remained until 1846 when they were again removed to a reservation in Minnesota near Mankato. They remained there until after the Sioux outbreak in 1802 when they were sent to a reservation on the Missouri in South Dakota. Of their chiefs those who have been remembered by the people of Iowa are Winneshiek, Waukon Decorah, and One Eyed Decorah. It was the latter who delivered Black Hawk a prisoner to the United States Indian Agent at Prairie du Chien at the close of the Black Hawk War.

The main branch of the Dacotah race are called Sioux. Many persons consider the terms Sioux and Dacotah as applying to the same people. This is not strictly true, since several of the Dacotah tribes, as the Iowas and Winnebagos, and some others, have never been called

Sioux. Still no great confusion of ideas can arise from using the terms as interchangeable. While the term Dacotah is the more comprehensive of the two, the term Sioux is the best known and the one with which the people are most familiar. These Indians originally occupied the western part of Wisconsin, the northern part of Iowa, the greater part of Minnesota, the whole of North and South Dakota, and much of the country west to the Rocky Mountains.

The first well authenticated meeting of the whites with the Dacotahs was in 1662, but for nearly fifty years previous to that time fabulous stories had reached the French on the St. Lawrence River of a wonderful people who dwelt far to the westward and who spoke a different language from any with which they were acquainted. These mysterious reports made such an impression on the mind of Champlain, the governor of New France, that he determined to investigate. Accordingly in 1634 he induced Jean Nicollet to undertake a journey of exploration in the region beyond what had then been discovered. Nicollet's account of his journey reads like a fairy tale, but he did not succeed in reaching the Sioux on that trip. A very interesting paper by Hon. Irving B. Richman, entitled, *First Meeting with Dacotahs*, says:

> The first meeting of the Dacotah Indians by white men took place at a spot not so remote from the hike regions of Iowa. In 1662 the French travellers, Radison and Grosseliers, held a council with a large company of the Dacotahs near the Mille Lacs, in what is now the state of Minnesota. They were even then a famous and dreaded nation. Says Radison in his quaint and Gallic way: 'They were so much respected that nobody durst not offend them.'

Eighteen years later or in 1680, the Mississippi River having been discovered in the meantime, Father Hennepin was sent out by La Salle to explore the upper regions of it. Judge Fulton, in his introduction to a chapter on the Sioux, uses this language:

> It was in 1680 that Father Hennepin and his two companions, Michael Ako and Anthony Anguella, were sent from Fort Crevecour, near Lake Peoria, by the renowned La Salle on their mission of discovery to the upper Mississippi. The tribes they found inhabiting the country now embraced in northern Iowa and the state of Minnesota were those belonging to the great Dacotah group or nation. While encamped on the banks of the Mississippi they were taken prisoners by a band of Sioux

warriors, and remained with them in their wanderings over the vast prairies and among the lakes of that region from April until September, having during that time been joined by that other intrepid French adventurer, Duluth. These were the first Europeans who met the people that occupied and roamed over the prairies of northern Iowa, or kindled their campfires about the headwaters of the Des Moines and on the borders of our beautiful lakes two hundred years ago.

The numerical strength of the Dacotahs was then estimated at about forty thousand and does not vary a great deal from that at the present time. The nation was divided into a large number of tribes and these tribes were again subdivided into numberless clans or bands, each under its petty chief or leader, who roamed over the prairies far and wide, living on game and fish and the spontaneous production of the soil. They lived mainly in rude tents called "*tepees*" and roamed about as inclination dictated. They had favourite haunts which they visited at stated periods and which were regarded by them as headquarters, where different bands would rendezvous for a while and then scatter again over the prairies and their places be occupied by other bands. Judge Fulton, in his *Red Men of Iowa*, says:

At the time of the celebrated voyage of exploration made by Lewis and Clarke in 1804 up the Missouri River, the band or tribe of the Great Sioux nation, known as Yanktons, lived on the upper Des Moines and Little Sioux Rivers and the region about Spirit Lake.

But little reliable information can be obtained calculated to throw light upon the history of the different bands that occupied this country previous to its purchase and settlement by the whites. Authorities seem to agree, however, that a band of Yankton-Sioux, known as the Wahpekutahs, occupied the country of northern Iowa and southern Minnesota during the earlier part of the present century, north of these in Minnesota were three other tribes of Sioux for whom agencies were subsequently established on the Minnesota River, which will be noticed more in detail further on.

The Sioux were the deadly enemies of the Sacs and Foxes, the Wahpekutahs being the most active in their hostilities and the most implacable in their hatred of their southern neighbours. So sanguinary was the warfare waged by the contending tribes that the United States government, in 1825, decided to interfere and if possible put a stop to it. By a treaty, bearing date August 19, 1825, a boundary was established between the Sioux on the north and the Sacs and Foxes on the south, as follows: Commencing at the mouth of the upper Iowa River on the west bank of the Mississippi and ascending the said Iowa River to its west fork, thence up the fork to its source, thence crossing the fork of the Red Cedar River in a direct line to the Calumet or Big Sioux River, and down to its junction with the Missouri River.

This action of the government only made matters worse, each party claiming that the other had trespassed by crossing over the line, and hostilities waged hotter than ever until in 1830, when the government interfered a second time and finally succeeded in negotiating a second treaty, whereby the several tribes ceded to the United States a strip of land twenty miles wide on each side of the former line, thus throwing the combatants forty miles apart. This strip was known as the "Neutral Ground." Many persons at the present time use the term without knowing its meaning. This scheme mended matters some but did not wholly prevent hostilities, which were kept up to a greater or less extent until 1845, when the Sacs and Foxes were removed from the state.

The last hostile meeting between the Sioux and the Sacs and Foxes was in Kossuth County, in April, 1852, between two straggling bands, both of whom at that time were trespassers and had no legal right on Iowa soil. This action possesses a dramatic interest out of all proportion to its importance as a historical event, from the fact that it was there that the "lingering remnants of two great nations who had for more than two hundred years waged unrelenting warfare against each other had their last and final struggle." The number engaged was about seventy on a side, and the result was a complete victory for the Sacs and Foxes.

At the same time of the treaty respecting the Neutral Ground, July 15, 1830, another treaty was negotiated by which the Sacs and Foxes, Western Sioux, Omahas, Iowas and Missouris united in conveying to the United States the portion of the western slope of Iowa described as follows: Beginning at the upper fork of the Des Moines River and passing the sources of the Little Sioux and Floyd Rivers to the fork of the first creek that falls into the Big Sioux or Calumet River on the east side, thence down said creek and the Calumet to the Missouri River, thence down said Missouri River to the Missouri state line above the Kansas River, thence along said line to the highlands between the waters falling into the Missouri and the Des Moines, passing to said highlands along the dividing ridge between the forks of the Grand River, thence along said highlands or ridge separating the waters of the Missouri from the Des Moines to a point opposite the source of the Boyer River, thence in a direct line to the upper fork of the Des Moines, the place of beginning.

By the terms of this treaty the United States agreed to pay to the Sacs and Foxes three thousand dollars each; to the Sioux, two thousand dollars; to the Yankton and Santee bands of Sioux, three thousand dollars; to the Omahas, two thousand five hundred dollars; and to the Otoe and Missouris, two thousand five hundred dollars, to be paid annually for ten successive years. In addition to these annuities the United States agreed to provide other advantages for some of the tribes joining in the treaty. This treaty was made by William Clark, Superintendent of Indian Affairs; and Colonel Willoughby Morgan, of the United States First Infantry. It went into effect by proclamation February 24, 1831. So much for the treaty by which the territory of western Iowa passed from the jurisdiction of the Indians to the government of the United States.

Chapter 2

Treaty of 1851

In 1851 another treaty was made with the Sioux by the provisions of which they agreed to relinquish to the United States their remaining title to all land in the state of Iowa, and also their title to all lands in Minnesota, except what constituted their reservation. A careful examination of the terms of this treaty and the preceding ones would seem to justify the conclusion that, so far as Iowa is concerned, this treaty was intended to be somewhat of the nature of a quitclaim deed given for the purpose of healing defects in a former conveyance. As before stated, there were four bands of these Sioux and they had their reservation on the Minnesota River. It was composed of a strip of land ten miles wide on each side of the river and extending from a short distance below Fort Ridgley to the source of that river. There were two agencies known as the Upper and Lower Agencies. The Lower Agency was located on the Minnesota River about five miles below the Redwood River and thirteen miles above Fort Ridgley, and the Upper Agency on the Yellow Medicine River, about three miles from its mouth. Two bands received their annuities at the Lower and two at the Upper Agency.

The Wahpekutahs, the band with which the history of this county is most closely identified, had their headquarters at the Lower Agency and were therefore known as Lower Sioux. Prominent among their chiefs was one Wamdisappi, or Black Eagle. He and his immediate followers were savages of such ferocity and were so quarrelsome and revengeful that they could not live at peace even with the members of their own tribe. It was largely through their intrigues and restlessness that the war with the Sacs and Foxes was kept up as long as it was, and after their removal these turbulent savages turned their attention to working up quarrels and dissensions in their own band. These quarrels finally culminated in Wamdisappi and the more turbulent of his followers leaving the main body and striking westward across the Big Sioux and establishing themselves on the Vermilion River, in what is now South Dakota, from which point they roamed over the country far and wide, often going as far south as the mouth of the Boone River and as far east as the Cedar and beyond. In writing of this band. Judge Flandrau has this to say of them:

> So thoroughly were they separated from the rest of the Wahpekutahs that when the last named Indians, together with the M'daywakautons, made their treaty at Mendota in 1851, by which they ceded the lands in Minnesota owned by them, the remnant of Wamdisappi's people were not regarded as being a part of the Wahpekutahsat all and took no part in the treaty.

The numerical strength of Wamdisappi's band has been variously estimated, some placing it as high as five hundred and others as low as one hundred and fifty. Doubtless the reason for this discrepancy is that there were a large number of Indians who would at times associate themselves with the outlaws in their predatory excursions, and then as the time for the payment of the annuities approached would unite themselves with the Agency Indians for the purpose of sharing in the annuities.

Among the followers of Wamdisappi was a chief known as Sidominadotah, or "Two Fingers," who eventually became leader of the band. While his headquarters were on the Vermilion, his favourite haunts were in the neighbourhood of the lakes and along the Des Moines and Little Sioux Rivers. They were known as far east as Prairie du Chien and as far south and southwest as Council Bluffs, and were universally regarded as a bad lot. Many and varied were the difficulties with the early settlers all along the frontier line. These difficulties were the source of a vast deal of annoyance, anxiety and apprehension on the part of the settlers.

Among others who had received indignities from this band was one Henry Lott, whom Judge Fulton characterizes as "a rough, unscrupulous border character," who in 1846 settled near the mouth of Boone River in Webster County. His chief occupation seems to have been selling poor whisky to the Indians. He was also accused of stealing horses, as in 1848 some horses stolen from the Indians were traced to his cabin. Other lawless acts were also charged to him. This so irritated and enraged the savages that they determined to drive him out of the country. It would be well to remember here that this was not on Sioux territory at all, but was south of the Neutral Ground, on land but recently vacated by the Sacs and Foxes. Lott was soon waited on by the chief and a party of his men and informed that he was regarded as an intruder and given a certain number of days in which to leave their hunting grounds. The Indians now went away, but Lott did not see proper to leave.

At the expiration of the appointed time the Indians returned, and, finding Lott still there, commenced to destroy his property. They shot his horses and cattle, robbed his bee hives, threatened his family and drove him and his stepson from home, carrying things with a high hand generally. After Lott and his stepson had left the house, a younger boy, Milton Lott, a lad of about twelve years of age, attempted to follow them. It was in December. The night was intensely cold, and after following them for some miles the boy became exhausted and froze to death. This embittered Lott against the Indians to an intense degree. After a short time he returned to the old place and remained there until after the death of his wife, which occurred a few years later, after which he changed his location, and in 1853 he and his stepson settled at Lott's Creek, on the east branch of the Des Moines River, in Humboldt County. They had been established there but a short time when Sidominadotah and his family of nine persons pitched their camp a short distance below on the other side of the river.

Burning with the desire to avenge the injuries they had received from this chief and his band five years before at the mouth of the Boone River, they conceived the diabolical plot of destroying the entire party. To accomplish this they went to the chief's lodge and reported that they had seen a herd of elk feeding on the bottom, and asked him to go with them and try to get one. He, suspecting nothing, prepared at once to accompany them. When some distance from the chief's lodge they shot him dead on the spot. After nightfall they returned to his lodge and murdered the balance of the family, including the aged mother of the chief, except two children, one a girl about ten years of age and a boy still older. The little girl had concealed herself in some bushes, and the boy they had left for dead on the ground, but he recovered.

This boy was afterward known to the frontier settlers as "Indian Josh," and lived some time with a family, on the west fork of the Des Moines in Palo Alto County, by the name of Carter. After finishing their terrible work, Lott and his stepson loaded what they could of their portables into a wagon and the balance they piled up in their cabin and set it on fire, then hitching their mules to the wagon they left the place. Following down the divide between the Des Moines and Boone Rivers, they continued their course in a southerly direction until they struck the great overland trail to California, which was then thronged with emigrants. Joining a party of these, they crossed the plains to California, where it is said Lott was shortly afterwards killed in a quarrel. The murder of the chief was not discovered for two weeks, and it was later still before it was known the Lotts were the guilty parties, and they were so far on their way by that time that no pursuit was attempted.

Inasmuch as everything calculated to throw light upon the relations existing between the settlers and the Sioux, during this interesting period, becomes more valuable as the difficulty in the way of securing correct information increases, the following extracts from Harvey Ingham's *Scraps of Early History*, published in the Upper Des Moines, will be read with interest:

> Fort Dodge was established as the frontier outpost of northern Iowa in 1850, just four years after Fort Des Moines was abandoned. Fort Des Moines was located in 1843 and occupied by troops until 1846, the years during which the Sacs and Foxes were being removed from the state. Between the occupancy of the two forts the Sioux came prominently into notice, driving out every white man who attempted to push into their territory and trying to stem the tide of emigration to the Northwest. The event which, more than any other, led to the establishment of the fort, was old Sidominadotah's attack upon Marsh, a government surveyor, in 1848. Sidominadotah is one of the conspicuous figures in our pioneer history. He was a brother of Inkpadutah and leader of a band of Wahpekutah outlaws. He was commonly called Chief Two Fingers, having lost the remainder of his right hand in battle.
>
> Major Williams knew him well and has left an accurate description of him. He says: Sidominadotah was a man about five feet ten in height, stout and well formed, very active, had a piercing black eye, broad face and high cheek bones.' The major adds an item to the description which certainly entitles Sidominadotah to be called the man with the iron jaw: 'Both rows of teeth were double all around in both jaws.' A dentist could have paid

off all of the old scores of the white race at one sitting. When killed he was forty-five or fifty years of age. He evidently was the leader of all the bands of the northern Sioux at that time, or, at least, held a prominent place among the leaders, for nearly all the attacks upon the whites who began to invade the territory north and west of Des Moines were led by him.

Here follows the detailed account of the attack on the surveying party when their instruments were destroyed, their supplies taken from them and they were obliged to abandon their work. Mr. Ingham's account continues:

> Marsh made a report to the government which, taken in connection with reports of other outrages, caused the order to bring troops into the Northwest..... Brigadier General Mason was ordered in 1849 to locate the new fort as nearly as possible to the northwest corner of the Neutral Ground. He chose the site where the city of Fort Dodge now stands and named the new post Fort Clarke. In 1851 General Winfield Scott changed the name to Fort Dodge, in honour of General Henry Dodge.
>
> *(Another reason for the change of name was that there was another Fort Clarke in the southwest, and a great deal of annoyance was occasioned by supplies that were intended for one going wrong and eventually reaching the other.)*
>
> Company E of the Sixth Infantry, U. S. A., came from Fort Snelling to occupy it. With this company Major Williams came as sutler. When the pioneer history of northwestern Iowa is written, Major Williams will be the central figure. He was part of all that happened in the early years.... When after three years and a half Fort Dodge was abandoned and the troops were ordered north to build Fort Ridgley, he remained, and buying the ground and buildings of the dismantled fortifications, founded the city which perpetuates its name. Fort Dodge was then and afterwards the central point in the upper Des Moines region. Major Williams was associated intimately with all the stirring events along the entire frontier.
>
> During the years of occupancy of the fort, Major Williams became acquainted with the various Sioux bands and their leaders. He has left very interesting descriptions of the latter. His estimate of the character of the outfit tallies with that before given of the Wahpekutahs. 'The Sioux Indians,' he says, 'who

inhabited this district of country, were the most desperate characters, made up of renegades from all the bands.' They were generally very active, stout Indians, and great horsemen. The majority of them were well armed with guns. They always had in their possession horses and mules with white men's brands. They generally encamped on high ground where they could not be easily surprised, and when any number of them were together, they encamped in a circle.

They were very expert hunters. Their famous leaders, Sidominadotah and Inkpadutah, were very stout, active men, also Titonka and Umpashota; in fact, all of them. Of Inkpadutah, who led in the Spirit Lake Massacre, and who was present in person at the raid on Mr. Call and the settlers south of Algona in 1855, he says: 'Inkpadutah was about, fifty-five years old, about five feet eleven inches in height, stoutly built, broad shouldered, high cheek bones, sunken and very black sparkling eyes, big mouth, light copper colour and pockmarked in the face.'

Umpashota is of scarcely less interest, as he is the Indian who visited with W. H. Ingham three days on the upper Des Moines when each one was figuring on who was in charge of the expedition, and his name is also associated with the legend of Spirit Lake.

Here follows a description of Umpashota (Smoky Day), also of Titonka, or Big Buffalo, and Ishtahaba, or Young Sleepy Eye :

Besides these there were Cosomeneh, dark, silent, stealthy; Wahkonsa, Umpashota's son, a dude, painting his cheeks, forehead and chin with stars; Modocaquemon, Inkpadutah's oldest son, who was shot for his part in the Spirit Lake Massacre, with low forehead, scowling face and thick lips; Mocopoco, Inkpadutah's second son, sullen and ill-favoured. . . . The soldiers were ordered to leave the fort in September, 1853. . . . .It was after the abandonment of the fort that the outrages most intimately associated with our early history were perpetrated. Of these, by far the most important in its after effects was the murder of Sidominadotah and his family by Henry Lott, at Bloody Run, in Humboldt County, in January, 1854. Major Williams records one fact in connection with the Sioux that is very singular. In all the raids made by them a very large negro was a prominent participant. The soldiers tried often to capture him, but failed.

He was one of the boldest and most reckless of the savages in every outrage that was perpetrated in these years.

More space has been given the foregoing extracts than was at first intended, but really reliable information is so difficult to obtain that it was deemed best to use what was available.

Upon the death of Sidominadotah, his brother, Inkpadutah, sometimes known as Scarlet Point or Red End, became chief of the band. This chief was known to be bold, reckless, cruel and bloodthirsty, and it is not difficult to imagine the effect such a tragedy as the one heretofore related would have upon a character such as he. It is a well known characteristic of all the aboriginal tribes that if they cannot take their revenge on the party from whom they received their injuries, they are ready to wreak their vengeance upon the first party they come in contact with, no matter how innocent. Many an honest and industrious frontiersman has had to pay with his life for the wrong done by some reckless, worthless, unscrupulous, border character just out of pure wantonness. It is the same old story so often repeated in our frontier history. In view of the condition of affairs just related, the relations between this band of Indians and the settlers will be readily understood to be anything but cordial.

It is but natural to presume that the arrogant and imperious character of Inkpadutah drove many of the more peaceably inclined Indians out of his band. It is possible, too, that the prospect of being deprived of their annuities sent a great number of this band back to the main tribe. At any rate the numerical strength of the band became rapidly depleted. 'What had been a tribe of respectable strength was soon reduced to a few families of stragglers. The strength of the band, after the death of Sidominadotah, has been variously estimated at from fifty to one hundred and fifty. In 1856 it dwindled down below the lowest figure.

Judge Flandrau, who was Indian agent at that time, says of them:

> By 1857 all that remained of Wamdisappi's band was under the chieftainship of Inkpadutah, or Scarlet Point, sometimes called Red End. In August, 1850, I received the appointment of United States Indian Agent for the Sioux of the Mississippi. The agencies for these Indians were on the Minnesota River at Redwood and on the Yellow Medicine River a few miles from its mouth. Having been on the frontier sometime previous to such appointment, I had become quite familiar with the Sioux

and knew in a general way of Inkpadutah and his band, its habits and whereabouts. They ranged the country far and wide and were considered a bad lot of vagabonds. In 1856 they came to the payment and demanded a share of the money of the Wahpekutahs, and made a great deal of trouble, but were forced to return to their haunts on the Big Sioux and adjoining country. To this Mrs. Sharp adds: 'According to the most authentic testimony collected by Major Prichette, Inkpadutah came to the Sioux Agency in the fall of 1855 and received annuities for eleven persons, although he was not identified with any band.'

It may seem singular to some that in preparing a history of Dickinson County so much time and space should be given to people and events wholly outside of the county. It may also seem that too much space has been given in endeavouring to set forth who Inkpadutah and his band were, their relations to the Agency Indians, also the strained relations between them and the settlers, and the cause thereof. This may he true, but it is the experience of the writer that many of the tourists who visit the lakes from year to year are entirely ignorant of the facts in the matter and. are also desirous of correct information on all of these points, and more questions are asked first and last involving a knowledge of them than any others. Many have expressed surprise that more has not been preserved, and that more is not known of the personal character and personal history of individual Indians who in an early day made these lakes their favourite rendezvous. This is accounted for in the strained and unfriendly relations existing between the settlers and the Sioux.

The fraternal relations which so long existed between the Sacs and Foxes on the one side and the pioneer settlers of eastern and central Iowa on the other, were entirely wanting on the northwestern frontier, and consequently very little is or can be known of the individual Indians who pitched their *tepees* in the groves, fished in the lakes and hunted on the prairies of northwestern Iowa. However, some enterprising real estate and hotel men have recently endeavoured to supply this lack of real knowledge on these points by fictitious inventions of their own. Of late a great many questions are asked about Okoboji. Who was he? Where were the headquarters of his band? How many warriors were amongst his followers? and a thousand and one other questions which nobody but inquisitive summer tourists would think of.

A large mound on the west side of the lake has been pointed out to the credulous and unsuspecting summer resorter as being the last resting place of the great chief, or, in other words, as the grave of Okoboji. Ambitious correspondents of the Capital City papers have, at different times, tried their hands at writing up glowing accounts of their visits to the grave of the mythical chief, and many doubtless believe that the representations made to them are true, and that the lake was actually named for a brave and powerful warrior who once lived in its groves and was buried in the mound on its western border, where his supposed resting place is pointed out by the obliging guide to the unsophisticated and inquisitive traveller. Now this is all pure fiction. There is not one particle of truth in it. So far as can be ascertained, no such chief as Okoboji was ever known to the Sioux, and no such Indian ever lived in the neighbourhood of the lakes.

It will be remembered that the death of Sidominadotah occurred in January, 1854, and that the chieftainship fell to Inkpadutah at that time. We know but little of the wanderings of Inkpadutah's band from then until the fall of 1856. The troubles in the neighbourhood of Clear Lake, which finally culminated in what is known as the "Grindstone War," were in the summer of 1854. Harvey Ingham, in an article in the Midland Monthly, has this to say of their movements in 1855:

> Major Williams expresses the opinion that but for the rapid influx of settlers an attack would have been made on Fort Dodge in 1855. As it was, Inkpadutah and his followers contented themselves with stripping trappers and surveyors, stealing horses, and foraging on scattered settlers, always maintaining a hostile and threatening attitude. Many pages of the Midland would be required for a brief enumeration of the petty annoyances, pilferings and more serious assaults which occurred. At Dakota City, in Humboldt County, the cabin of E. McKnight was rifled in the spring of 1855. Further north, within a few miles of Algona, the cabin of Malachi Clark was entered, and the settlers gathered in great alarm to drive out the Indians—a band of eighty braves led by Inkpadutah in person. Still further north, near where Bancroft stands, W. H. Ingham was captured by Umpashota, a leader under Inkpudatah in the massacre, and was held a prisoner for three days.

Judge Fulton writes of this same period as follows:

> During the same summer (1855) Chief Inkpadutah and his

band, comprising about fifty lodges, encamped in the timber near where Algona now stands. They occasionally pillaged the cabins of the white settlers in that vicinity. At last the whites notified them to leave, which they did reluctantly. They returned no more to that vicinity except in small hunting parties.

Chapter 3

The First Attempt at Settlement in 1856

Dickinson County was named in honour of Hon. Daniel S. Dickinson, formerly United States Senator from the state of New York. The student of political history will be at no loss to fix the date of the naming of the counties of Iowa, fully fifteen *per cent*, or about one-sixth, of which were named for prominent men in the councils of the nation about the middle of the Nineteenth Century. Benton, Buchanan, Calhoun, Cass, Clayton, Dickinson, Polk, Dallas, Wright and Woodbury, together with several others, all smack strongly of the same period, the forties and fifties. How long the country had been known, or what was known of the country at that time, it is difficult to find out. In endeavouring to investigate this subject we are at once brought face to face with the fact that but very little has been written and that very little is known about it. Spirit Lake has been known of for a hundred years, and how much longer, we don't know. The time when it passes from legend to history is the early part of the Nineteenth Century. An interesting and instructive paper written by Prof. Charles Keyes for the October, 1898, number of the Annals of Iowa, in discussing the origin and meaning of the word Des Moines, as applied to the Des Moines River, uses this language:

> At the beginning of the present century the Des to and from the Northwest. St. Louis was the great trading post of the region. The Indian and French *voyageurs* paddled their canoes upstream, passing through several little lakes near the headwaters and then on to the Hudson Bay region. This was a waterway practically unobstructed from the northern fur country to the

lower Mississippi.

The article which occupies six pages of the Annals of Iowa is illustrated with three maps, the largest one of which was copied from an old map made as early as 1720. This map shows the Des Moines as much larger than either the Mississippi or Missouri, and as having its source in a lake many times larger than the combined area of all the lakes in Iowa. The question at once arises, Did any of the early travellers in their journeys from the Mississippi Valley to the Saskatchawan country ever go so far to one side of their usual route as to pass through the lake region? It is more than probable that they did, but if so, when was it done and where is the record?

The famous Lewis and Clarke expedition up the Missouri River was made in 1804. The Louisiana Purchase was made in 1803, and this expedition was fitted out for the purpose of examining and reporting on the character and resources of the newly acquired possessions. They had for their guide and interpreter a Frenchman by the name of M. Durion, who had been much with the Indians and spoke the Dacotah language fluently. He imparted to them a vast deal of information relative to the country adjoining that through which they were passing. This information they made a record of and have given it to the public. While his statements are not strictly accurate in all particulars, they are sufficiently so to convince any person that he had a pretty good general idea of the geography of the country, whether he had ever seen it or not.

Judge Fulton, in the *Red Men of Iowa*, writing on this subject, says:

> Lewis and Clarke's French interpreter described other localities in the country of the Sioux nation now known to be within the boundaries of Iowa, with sufficient accuracy to warrant the conclusion that he had some knowledge of the geography of the country, though not strictly accurate in some respects. He described the Little Sioux as having its source within nine miles of the Des Moines, as passing through a large lake nearly sixty miles in circumference and dividing it into two parts which approach each other very closely, as being very irregular in its width, as having many islands, and as being known by the name of Lac D'Esprit, or Spirit Lake. This lake in the country of the Sioux, from the earliest knowledge of white men the chief seat of one of the Sioux tribes, is now known by the name of Spirit Lake and Lake Okoboji.

So far as can be ascertained, this is the first and oldest written account of the Spirit Lake region. The region must have been, and doubtless was, frequently visited by hunters, trappers and adventurers during the early part of the century, but they left no written account of their explorations or discoveries. The treaties relative to the "Neutral Line" and the "Neutral Ground," which were intended to define the boundary between the country of the Sacs and Foxes on the south and the Sioux on the north, were negotiated, the former in 1825 and the latter in 1830, but whether these lines were surveyed or even examined at the time, we are in total ignorance.

The first really authentic account we have of the lake region is that contained in the official report of the government exploring expedition by the younger Nicollet. During Van Buren's administration Nicollet was appointed by the Secretary of War to make a map of the hydrographic basin of the upper Mississippi River. The appointment was made on the 7th day of April, 1838. In the body of his report, speaking of the Little Sioux, he uses the following language:

> It has been heretofore designated as the Little Sioux, and has its origin from a group of hikes, the most important of which is called by the Sioux 'Minnie Waukon,' or 'Spirit Water,' hence its name of Spirit Lake.

Nicollet makes no mention of the Okobojis, but simply designates the whole group of them by the single name "Spirit Lake." In another portion of the report the following astronomical observation is recorded:

Place of observation: Spirit Lake, about the middle of the northern shore.	Altitude above the Gulf of Mexico	North Latitude	Longitude West from Greenwich		Authority
			In Time	In Arc	
			h m s		
	1310 feet	43° 30′ 21″	6 20 26	95° 6′ 30″	Nicollet

It will be readily seen that the point from which this observation was taken cannot be far from where Crandall's Lodge was afterwards located. It is not at all probable that many, if any, of the hundreds of visitors who every summer sport on the sandy beach or bathe in the crystal waters of that charming region are aware that they are treading on ground made historic by reason of its being the first of which any mention is made or record preserved in all northwestern Iowa.

NORTH SHORE OF SPIRIT LAKE
Where the observation by Nicollet and Fremont was taken.

THE GARDNER CABIN.

The old Nicollet maps, or imperfect copies of them, were much in evidence back in the fifties. They showed the larger portion of Spirit Lake as being north of the state line. The state line was not surveyed until several years after these maps were made and consequently the northern boundary of the state had not then been determined, Nicollet's assistant and companion in this expedition was a man with whose name the world has since become familiar, being none other than General John C. Fremont, then a young engineer in the service of the United States, afterwards the gallant "Pathfinder of the Rockies," the first republican candidate for the presidency, and a prominent major general in the Union army during the War of the Rebellion. It is more than probable that the observation before noticed was taken by him and the record made in his handwriting. If this be so, it can be safely asserted that John C. Fremont was the first explorer of the Spirit Lake region to give to the world an account of his discoveries. From this time on the lakes were frequently visited by hunters, trappers and adventurers up to the time when the state was admitted to the Union in 1846.

The foregoing accounts embody all that is known of the early explorations of the lake region. The fact that this region was the favourite resort of the Wahpekutah branch of the Yankton-Sioux has already been referred to. In the early days it was a well understood fact that the Indians regarded Spirit Lake with a kind of superstitious, reverential awe. The Indian name, "Minnie Waukon," signifying Spirit Water, is proof of this if there were no other, and the early trappers and adventurers agree in ascribing to them a belief in various legends and traditions to the effect that the lake was under the guardian watch care of a "Great Spirit," that its waters were continually troubled and that no Indian ever ventured to cross it in his canoe. That some belief of this kind existed is certain; to what extent is unknown. It may be regarded as a singular circumstance, but it is a fact, nevertheless, that no Indian canoe was ever found by the early settlers in the vicinity of the lakes. The veil of mystery, the shadow of uncertainty, the tinge of the supernatural, which rested on this enchanted region, early excited the interest and attracted the attention of the restless and hardy pioneers, who were thereby induced to strike out far beyond the confines of civilization and make homes for themselves and their posterity in this land of romance and this region of mystery.

On the 16th of July, 1856, Rowland Gardner, from Cerro Gordo County, in this state, and his son-in-law, Harvey Luce, came in and made claims and erected cabins adjacent to what was then known as the Gardner Grove. The Gardner house is still standing. It was occupied for several years by Rev. Samuel Pillsbury, and is now, (1902), occupied, during the summer season, by Mrs. Abbie Gardner Sharp. James Mattock and his family, with several others from Delaware County, in this state, settled in the grove south of the Okoboji bridge, which was then known as Mattock's Grove, taking its name from Esquire Mattock, one of the principal and most influential men in the settlement.

About the same time a party came in from Red Wing, Minnesota, consisting of William Granger, Carl Granger, Bert Snyder and Doctor Harriott, and located on the point on the north side of the Okoboji bridge. Their cabins stood upon what is now the right of way of the Chicago, Milwaukee & St. Paul Railroad, about half way between the lake shore and the depot. The Grangers claimed the point and the land along East Okoboji Lake; Harriott, the Maple Grove on West Okoboji Lake, and Snyder, Center Grove. Center Grove was known as Snyder's Grove for some time after the settlement subsequent to the massacre. Mr. Joseph M. Thatcher, from Hampton, Franklin County, but formerly from Howard County, Indiana, about this time settled at the north end of what is now called Tusculum Grove. His cabin formerly stood a little north of the present residence of H. D. Arthur. At the same time Joel Howe settled at the south end of the grove, near the present residence of Mr. Ladu. In September a Mr. Marble, from Linn County, this state, settled upon the west bank of Spirit Lake in the grove now owned by J. S. Polk. This grove was for years known as Marble Grove. These comprise all of the settlements made prior to 1857.

In order to avoid confusion a recapitulation may be desirable.

First. The party consisting of Granger brothers, Harriott and Snyder resided north of the straits, where the Okoboji bridge now stands. The track of the Milwankee Railroad runs through the site of their cabin. They were all young men without families except William Granger, ,and his family was not here. There was also stopping with them temporarily at the time of the massacre a young man by the name of Joseph Harshman,

Second. The family of Mr. Mattock, consisting of himself, wife and five children, resided at the south end of the Okoboji bridge. There were also residing with him a Mr. Mattison, who had taken a claim upon the west side of Okoboji Lake, on what was for a long time known as Madison Grove. The family of Mr. Madison remained in Delaware County during the winter, expecting to join him in the spring.

Third. The family of Mr. Gardner, consisting of himself, wife and four children (the oldest being the wife of Mr. Luce), and Mr. Luce, his wife and two children, resided in what was long known as the Gardner house, now occupied by Mrs. Sharp. There was also stopping temporarily with Mr. Gardner a young man from Waterloo by the name of Clark, also a young man by the name of Wilson, who afterwards became the husband of Eliza Gardner.

Fourth. The family of Joel Howe, consisting of himself, wife and seven children (the oldest being the wife of Mr. Noble), resided in a cabin near the present residence of Mr. Ladu, ,at the south end of Tusculum Grove.

Fifth. The family of J. M. Thatcher, consisting of himself, wife and one child; and the family of Mr. Noble, consisting of himself and wife and one child, resided in a cabin at the north end of Tusculum Grove, on the place now owned by H. D. Arthur. There was also boarding with Mr. Thatcher a trapper by the name of Morris Markham, a Mr. Ryan, who was a brother-in-law of Mr. Noble; and a brother-in-law of Mr. Thatcher by the name of Burtch.

Sixth. The family of Mr. Marble, consisting of himself and wife, resided in a cabin located in the grove on the ridge between Spirit Lake and Marble Lake.

From the above it will be seen that over forty persons, men, women and children, were dispersed in the various localities adjacent to the lakes. It has been deemed advisable to be thus particular in pointing out the location of the different families and the number of persons connected with each, from the face that the massacre in the spring of 1857 is the one important event in the early history of this county, and the one about which travellers and strangers make the most inquiries; and at the same time, the one about which they get the least reliable information.

It may assist our understanding of affairs at the lakes by knowing something of surrounding settlements. The same year that the first settlement was attempted here, namely, in 1850, some six or eight families had settled on the Des Moines River in Jackson County, near where the town of Jackson now stands. They called their settlement Springfield. It was about fourteen miles from Marble's, and about twenty miles from the balance of the lake settlements. In Emmet County

George Granger had built a good sized cabin four miles above where Estherville now stands, and there was a small cabin between his place and the river occupied by a couple of trappers. There were also two or three cabins in the neighbourhood of High Lake. There was no settlement at Estherville until 1857. There was a small settlement eighteen miles east of Estherville, at Chain Lakes, known as "Tuttle's Grove."

In the same year (1856) an Irish colony came from Kane County, Illinois, and settled on the Des Moines River in Palo Alto County. Between there and Fort Dodge there were cabins along the river from two to five miles apart occupied by settlers and trappers. To the south of the lakes the first settlement was at Gillett's Grove, about thirty miles distant, where two brothers by the name of Gillett had brought in a large herd of cattle, which they were wintering there. From Gillett's Grove to Peterson there were some eight or ten families scattered along the groves that skirt the river. Waterman, four miles below Peterson, was the only person between there and Cherokee. Below Cherokee there were settlements every few miles to the Missouri. There was no settlement to the north or west. From Cherokee west there was no settlement until the Floyd was reached some ten miles above Sioux City.

CHAPTER 4

The Indians Arrive at the Lakes

In the mouth of November, 1856, a party from Jasper County, in this state, consisting of O. C. Howe, R. U. Wheelock and B. P. Parmenter, under the guidance of a hunter and trapper by the name of Wiltfong, made a visit to the county and were so captivated by the romantic scenery, lovely climate and abundance of game that they decided to return the coming spring for the purpose of permanent settlement. They spent some time in the vicinity of the lakes and returned to their homes just in time to avoid the terrific storms with which the winter of 1856 and 1857 set in. It is to them and to Mrs. Abbie Gardner Sharp that we are indebted for what little we know of the condition of affairs in the vicinity of the lakes previous to the massacre. At the time they were here, in November, Inkpadutah and a part of his followers were camped at the southern extremity of Black Loon Lake, in Jackson County, Minnesota.

As near as could be ascertained at the time, the band consisted of not less than fifteen nor more than twenty warriors, with their squaws and *papooses* and the usual appurtenances of an Indian camp. This band has been pretty thoroughly described and their relations to the settlers can now be pretty well understood. They were known as a thieving, pilfering band of tramps and outlaws, hovering along the border dividing the whites from the Indians. They acknowledged the authority of neither. In their contact with civilization they had imbibed the evil and rejected the good. They possessed the vices of both races and the virtues of neither. It will require no stretch of the imagination to understand the feelings of bitterness, hatred and revenge on the one side, and that of distrust, apprehension and fear on the other, existing between the Indians and the settlers along the border. Under the circumstances it would be perfectly natural for the settlers to look to the general government for protection and defence. Other Indians besides Inkpadutah's band occasionally made excursions along the frontier, but they were without exception on friendly terms with the settlers.

Repeated appeals were made to the United States authorities, both before and after the massacre, for more adequate protection to the Iowa frontier. Governor Grimes, during his administration (1854-1858), addressed several urgent appeals to our senators and representatives in Congress setting forth the exposed and helpless condition of the border settlements. As early as January 3, 1855, he sent them a lengthy communication in which, among other things, he says:

> I have taken the responsibility to appoint Major Williams, of Fort Dodge, a kind of executive agent to act for me in protecting both the settlers and the Indians, and particularly to preserve the peace. I had no legal authority to make such appointment, but as there was no government agent in that section of the country, and as I was so remote from the scene of trouble and felt that there should be someone in the vicinity who would act prudently and who could act efficiently, I knew no better course than to appoint him as I have indicated.

The letter closes as follows:

> I trust, gentlemen, you will stimulate the department at Washington to take immediate steps to remedy the evil complained of. We have just cause for complaint. The government has undertaken to protect our frontiers from the Indians with the assurance that this stipulation would be fulfilled. That frontier is filled with peaceful citizens, but the Indians are suffered to come among them, destroying their property and jeopardizing their lives. I hope no time will be lost in allaying the apprehensions that exist in some parts of the state on this account. I am, gentlemen, very truly your obedient servant,
>
> James W. Grimes.
>
> To Hon. A. C. Dodge, Hon. George W. Jones, Hon. J. P. Cook and Hon. B. Henn, Delegation in Congress from Iowa. Washington, D. C.

No response whatever was made to this appeal.

Nearly a year later he made another attempt, this time addressing the president. The letter closes as follows:

> A year ago the General Assembly of this state unanimously asked

for the establishment of a military post on the Sioux River near the northwest corner of the state. I concur entirely in the propriety of that measure. I have no doubt that two companies of dragoons or cavalry stationed there would effectually prevent the incursions of the Indians and give quiet to the whole of northwestern Iowa. Without such a post they may be removed, but it does not occur to me how they may be permanently kept out. I am, very truly with great respect, your obedient servant,

James W. Grimes.

Hon. Franklin Pierce, President of the United States.

This letter was sent something more than a year previous to the massacre and shared the same fate as the former one.

Hon. Charles Aldrich, in the Annals of Iowa, commenting on the stupidity and stubbornness of the general government in withholding the necessary protection to the frontier, says:

> Governor James W. Grimes wrote letters to our United States senators and to the authorities at Washington some time before the outbreak of hostilities, asking that the general government take immediate steps for the protection of our exposed frontiers. Little or no attention was paid to his reiterated requests, and so when the Indians resorted to hostilities our Iowa border was wholly without protection. . . . .Had the earnest appeals of Governor Grimes been heeded, the Spirit Lake Massacre would not have occurred. What makes this neglect appear more stupidly and wickedly cruel was the fact that in those days the catching of a runaway negro under the infamous 'Fugitive Slave Law' was rife in the land, and detachments of the Federal Army or vessels of the United States Navy could be readily secured to return a slave to his master.

The winter of 1856 and 1857 is one long to be remembered by the early settlers of Iowa as the most severe one in the annals of its history. The first heavy storm occurred early in December, when snow fell to the depth of nearly two feet. This was followed by others in quick succession, until by the first of February the snow had reached a depth of four feet. These storms were accompanied with high winds and were of the most fearful and violent character. Nothing approaching then in intensity has been experienced in the state of Iowa since. The settlers at the lakes were but illy prepared for such a winter as this. We must remember that there was not a foot of lumber to be had within a hundred miles and all of the flour and provisions used had to be hauled twice that distance. The cabins of the settlers were unfurnished. They were without floors and had heavy puncheon doors hung upon wooden hinges. But few of the settlers had been able to get in a sufficient supply of provisions when the first storms came, and only succeeded in reaching home on snow shoes, dragging what little they could on hand sleds or sledges made for the occasion. The sufferings and privations endured at that time may be imagined, but they cannot be described.

Inkpadutah and his band left their camp at Loon Lake some time in December and went south down the Little Sioux as far as Smithland. Two other parties of Indians were known to have been hovering along the frontier at this time. One, a small party of agency Indians, pitched their camp in the neighbourhood of Springfield, now Jackson, Minnesota. Another party, under Ishtahaba, or Sleepy Eye, camped at Big Island Grove. There is no record that Inkpadutah's band had any trouble with the settlers on their way down the river. Whether they went by way of the settlements or not, is not known. There is no account of their being seen by the settlers here at all on their way down the river, and it is more than probable that they went from the head of Spirit Lake down the divide to Lost Island Lake.

Up to this time they were supposed to be friendly, that is, as friendly as usual. They were never cordial; always sullen and suspicious. The settlers at Smithland knew but little, if anything, of the previous troubles of this band of Indians with the settlers of the older localities, and they had no apprehensions of any serious difficulty. Various versions are given of the outbreak at this place. The one most generally accepted at the time was something as follows: Large numbers of elk had been driven in from the prairie by the deep snows and terrific storms. These the Indians surrounded and slaughtered in large numbers. This created excitement and indignation among the settlers, and some of them conceived the idea of driving the Indians away.

To accomplish this they got up a drunken frolic and invited the Indians in. They represented themselves as soldiers sent out by General Harney to drive them out of the country. At that time the operations of General Harney at Ash Hollow and other places had made his name a perfect terror to the Sioux, and they became very much alarmed and excited, so much so that they started at once on their return, leaving a portion of their guns and equipage in the hands of the supposed soldiers. When this transaction became known, the more level-headed citizens denounced it and did what they could to counteract what they feared would be the result. They gathered up the guns and other property which the Indians had left behind and sent them forward to them, and did what else they could to appease their indignation, but as will soon appear, however, all to no purpose.

Mrs. Sharp says:

> It seems that one day, while the Indians were in pursuit of elk, they had some difficulty with the settlers. The Indians claimed that the whites intercepted the chase. There is also a report that an Indian was bitten by a dog belonging to one of the settlers, that the Indian killed the dog and that the man gave the Indian a severe beating. It is also said that the settlers whipped off a company of squaws who were carrying off hay and corn to feed their ponies. The Indians becoming more and more insolent, the settlers in self-protection went to the camp and disarmed them, intending to return their guns the next day and escort them out of the country. But the next morning not a "red-skin" was to be seen. They had folded their tents like the Arabs, and as silently stolen away.

Judge Fulton says:

> One day while a party of them (the Indians) were in pursuit of an elk in the vicinity of Smithland, they had a difficulty with some white settlers. It is difficult to state with certainty the nature of the trouble, as different and conflicting accounts of it have been given. The Indians, however, claimed that their pursuit of the elk was intercepted by the whites, who forced them to give up their arms and availed themselves of the use of their guns in the pursuit of the game. This aroused the indignation of the Indians and they demanded provisions of the settlers. They continued encamped in the vicinity of Smithland for several days, during which time the whites became more and more annoyed by their presence. Finally the settlers resorted to strategy to get rid of them.
>
> At that time the name of General Harney was a terror to the Indians of the Northwest, owing to a recent severe chastisement some of them had received at his hands. One of the settlers donning the old uniform of an army officer made his appearance on the opposite side of the Little Sioux from the Indian encampment, while some of the other whites pointed him out

to the Indians as General Harney and told them he was in pursuit of them. This ruse had the desired effect and the Indians hastily moved up the river with their savage nature aroused to a desire for revenge.

These accounts, while none of them claim to be thoroughly accurate in detail, convey a pretty good general idea of the commencement of the troubles on the Little Sioux between the Indians and settlers. This affair occurred in February, 1857. The Indians after leaving Smithland followed up the Little Sioux River by way of the settlements and commenced their depredations by taking guns and ammunition from the whites, and as they advanced, the settlements becoming sparser, they became more insolent and fearless in their conduct toward the settlers. By the time they reached Clay County their depredations had assumed a most savage and atrocious character.

Their depredations at Peterson are described by Mr. W. C. Gilbraith in his history of Clay County, in the following language:

The Clay County settlers had heard of the depredations they were committing and were thoroughly alarmed for the safety of themselves and their property. When they came to the home of Mr. Bicknell and finding no one there, he with his family having gone to Mr. Kirchner's, across the river, they immediately appropriated everything which met their fancy. The next day they made their appearance at the Kirchner house, where they found the terror stricken settlers huddled together. Without any ceremony they captured all the arms to be found, killed the cattle and took what they wanted. After remaining in the Peterson settlement a day and a night, they pushed on, leaving the whites badly frightened but thankful that they had escaped with their lives.

This band of bloodthirsty Sioux then proceeded to the home of Ambrose Mead, who was absent at the time at, Cedar Falls. Previous to leaving for this place, he had arranged to have a Mr. Taylor and family remain with Mrs. Mead and children during his stay. When the Indians came, Mr. Taylor protested against their taking the property or disturbing the premises. Becoming angry at Taylor for his interference, they threatened to kill him if he did not keep out of the way. Fearing that they would carry out their threats, Taylor left the women and children and set out to secure assistance.

The Indians killed the stock, drove off the ponies and carried the women with them. But, fearing they would be pursued and overtaken, they decided to allow the women to return after taking such liberties as the helpless women could not prevent. They then directed their steps towards Linn Grove and Sioux Rapids, where they subjected the settlers to the same treatment they had given the Mead and Taylor families.

Mrs. Sharp, in her book, relates the same occurrence, as follows:

After remaining a few days in Cherokee, where they busied themselves with wantonly shooting cattle, hogs and fowls and destroying property generally, sometimes severely beating those who resisted, they proceeded up the Little Sioux to the little settlement in Clay County, now called Peterson. Here they tarried two or three days, committing acts of atrocity as usual. At the house of A. S. Mead (Mr. Mead being away) they not only killed his cattle and destroyed his property, but knocked down his wife and carried off to their camp his daughter Hattie (seventeen years old) and started away with a younger sister, Emma, but she resisted so hard and cried so loud that an Indian picked up a stick and whipped her all the way back to the house and left her. At the same house they knocked down Mr. E. Taylor, kicked his boy into the fireplace, burning him so badly that he still carries the scar on his leg, and took his wife off to their camp, but as yet they had committed no murder. After one night in an Indian camp, Mrs. Taylor and Hattie Mead were permitted to return home.

From Peterson they passed on up to Sioux Rapids, where similar scenes were enacted and similar outrages perpetrated. They killed the stock and destroyed everything capable of being destroyed. It was at the home of Abner Bell that their atrocities assumed the most fiendish aspect. From Sioux Rapids they went up to Gillett's Grove. The Gilletts were two brothers who had moved in late in the summer, bringing with them about a hundred head of cattle, intending to go largely into the stuck business. The Indians made more general destruction here than they had hitherto done. They killed every live animal on the place, took all of their bedding, clothing and provisions, and destroyed everything they could not take away. They even cut a new wagon to pieces to get the bolts.

The following highly sensational account is copied from Mr. Gilbraith's *History of Clay County*, and while it contains statements that are new and strange to those who supposed they were familiar with the story of the massacre of 1857, it must be accepted as history. There is nothing in it that is improbable or inconsistent with the circumstances as they then existed.

Mr. Gillett, one of the earliest settlers of the county, and for whom Gillett's Grove bears its name, recently visited friends in this county and the scene of his former home. During his visit he related an event which he hitherto had never made public. Mr. Gillett is now quite aged, and in a few more short years his race will be run, and, as he said, it would be useless to keep it a secret any longer, as the participants had passed over the silent river of death. The story is substantially as follows: He with his brother came to Clay County in the fall of 1856 and located at what is now known as Gillett's Grove, which is a beautiful grove filled with growing trees and through which courses the Little Sioux River. After deciding upon their location, they agreed to divide the grove equally, and one take the north and the other the south part.

This being settled, they at once set to work and in a short time had constructed neat log houses and prepared themselves comfortably for the winter. Being amply supplied with firewood, and their log houses being built not alone with a view to convenience, but as well for warmth, they had no fears of suffering from the storms or intense cold weather which were notable at that time in this section. The only fears they entertained were from the Indians. But at that time they did not make frequent visits to this particular section for the reason that there was but little game, poor fishing and no settlements. The newly acquired property holders, therefore, felt themselves safe and comfortable from any intrusions from the wild savages, whose treachery they so much feared.

Everything passed along quietly for several months, until one day a tribe under Chief Inkpadutah came and set up their *tepees* upon the bank of Lost Island Lake. The settlers upon learning of their arrival and location feared that the Indians would discover the location of their houses and visit them. Their fears were well founded, for in a few days several of the redskins paid them a visit. The white settlers treated them kindly and gave them provisions, and they left for their camping grounds expressing their friendship and thanks for the food given them. In a few days another lot of them came, headed by a stalwart brave who had been with the others a few days before.

After saying their usual "*How*," they were supplied by the whites and returned to the lakes. During both visits it was noticeable that one of them, the one who led the second group, had his eyes constantly fixed in admiration upon Mrs. Gillett. Wherever she went and whenever she moved, his eye was upon her. In a few days he returned; this time alone. He was given a seat and provided with a meal. He went away, but every two or three days he came, and although saying nothing, his looks indicated his admiration for Mrs. Gillett. His visits grew so constant and frequent that they became annoying, not only to Mrs. Gillett, but to the two families. He was constantly prowling around and appearing before them at the most unexpected moments, until he became a great nuisance.

He was given to understand that his visits were not desired, but to these reminders he paid not the least attention. He was always fed and well treated, for the reason that the settlers did not wish to give any offense to the tribe or incur their enmity. But, becoming emboldened by the kind treatment that had been extended to him, one day in the absence of Mr. Gillett, and mastering all of the English language he possessed, he made certain proposals to Mrs. Gillett, which she indignantly rejected, and warned him to leave. He left the house in a short time, but had not gone a great distance when Mr. Gillett returned home. His wife immediately informed him of the Indian's conduct. The husband took down his rifle, and learning the direction the Indian had taken, set out after him.

After a few minutes' walk he caught sight of him and drew up his rifle and fired. He did not wait to ascertain the result of his shot, but returned to his cabin and ate his supper. In the morning, in company with his brother, he visited the spot, and there found a dead Indian. The brothers, after severing the head from the body—which they subsequently sent to an eastern medical college—placed it in a hollow tree. They at once packed up their belongings and started for Fort Dodge, knowing full well that the Indians would discover the absence of the buck, and, knowing his fondness for Mrs. Gillett, would come there in search of him, and finding no trace of him, would suspicion they had killed him, and would revenge themselves upon the white settlers. They, therefore, deemed it prudent to make their escape before the arrival of the searching party, which they did.

According to the above account, the Indians remained in camp at Lost Island several days. Accepting it as true, it throws some light upon the origin, or rather the commencement, of the massacre here at the lakes. It is easy to understand the pitch of frenzy to which the passions of the savages would naturally be raised when they made the discovery that one of their number had been slain by Gillett, as related by him, and the fact that he had made good his escape before the act was discovered would only increase their determination to wreak their vengeance upon the first luckless white settler that came in their way.

We have always been led to observe the close connection between the murder of Sidominadotah and his family by Lott in 1854, and the Spirit Lake Massacre of 1857, and that the latter was the legitimate outcome of the former, but accepting Gillett's story as true, it must be regarded as an important factor in precipitating the massacre at that time. Except for that it is possible that the settlers at the lakes would have fared no worse than their neighbours down the river. It may be regarded as singular that Gillett should have kept the affair a secret for thirty-five years before giving it to the world, but that might be accounted for on the theory that he knew he would be blamed for not warning the other settlers of the danger he had precipitated by his somewhat rash act.

From the Little Sioux messengers were sent to Fort Dodge setting forth their situation and imploring relief. At first the citizens of Fort Dodge were inclined to be sceptical and suspicious that the reports of the depredations were largely exaggerated. They could not believe the Indians were rash enough or foolish enough to thus defy the power of the government and the people. They knew the destitute condition of the settlers along the frontier at the commencement of winter and many branded the story as a ruse to induce them to send supplies or take other measures for their relief. But the reports kept coming thicker and more of them.

Mr. Duncombe, in his account of the Spirit Lake Expedition, says:

> In January, 1857, word was brought to Fort Dodge that a large band of Indians, under the lead of Inkpadutah, had followed

down the Little Sioux River to a point near Smithland; that this band was composed of Sioux half-breeds and straggling renegades of the Sioux tribe, and that they had become exceedingly insolent and ugly. The next information received at Fort Dodge was in the latter part of February, when Abner Bell, a Mr. Weaver and a Mr. Wilcox came to Fort Dodge and gave Major Williams and myself the startling intelligence of acts and depredations of these scoundrels, said to be about seventy in number, including about thirty warriors. These three men had left the Little Sioux River, and coming through the awful storms and almost impassable snows for sixty miles without a house or landmark on the way, sought aid from our people.

They gave a sad and vivid description of the shooting down of their cattle and horses, of the abuse of their children, the violation of their women and other acts of brutishness and cruelty too savage to be repeated. They pictured in simple but eloquent words the exposures of the dear wife, mother and children, their starving condition and their utter helplessness. These reports were repeated from day to day by other settlers from the Little Sioux, who from time to time came straggling into Fort Dodge. These repeated accounts of the acts of the Indians led every one familiar with the Indian character to become fully satisfied that they were determined on some great purpose of revenge against the exposed frontier settlements, and this caused much alarm among the people.

Among the number giving this information were Ambrose S. Mead, L. F. Finch, G. M. and W. S. Gillett and John A. Kirchner, father of John C. and Jacob Kirchner, who are now citizens of Fort Dodge. These depredations commenced at the house of Abner Bell, on the 21st day of February, A. D. 1857. On the 24th of February, 1857, the house occupied by James Gillett was suddenly attacked by ten or more armed warriors and the two families living under the same roof, consisting of the heads of each family and five small children, were terrorised and most villainously abused. After enduring outrages there, they managed to escape at midnight and late the following evening arrived at the residence of Bell, poorly clad, and having been without food for over thirty-six hours.

The sufferings of these people and their little children will be appreciated by those who remember the driving storms, piercing winds and intense cold of the unparalleled winter of 1856 and 1857, to my knowledge the longest and most severe of any winter for the last forty-three years. From Gillett's Grove, near the present beautiful and prosperous city of Spencer, the Indians proceeded to Spirit Lake and the lakes near by. No preparation could be made for resistance on account of the sparsity of the population and the scattered homes. In fact, it is improbable that any family knew that depredations were being committed by these red devils until they were themselves attacked when wholly unprepared for any such event.

The settlers along the Little Sioux also applied for help to the settlers on the Coon River at Sac City and below. Quite a company was raised there and made their way across to Peterson by way of Storm Lake, but they were too late to accomplish anything. The Indians were gone and they were not prepared to follow them. They accordingly returned to their homes.

The Indians arrived in the neighbourhood of the lakes about the seventh of March, and camped in the Okoboji Grove at a distance of about fifteen rods from the Mattock cabin. The date of their arrival at the lakes was about two weeks after the trouble near Sioux Rapids, which interval of time they doubtless spent in the camp at Lost Island. The idea suggests itself at this point that possibly the party of Indians at Lost Island was much larger than at the lakes. Nearly every account referring to the Indians committing their depredations along the Little Sioux gives their numbers at from thirty to forty warriors, and some even more. Mr. Duncombe, who received his information direct from the settlers, in his account puts it between thirty and forty. Mr. Gilbraith, in his *History of Clay County*, says from sixty to seventy, while the actual number engaged in the massacre at the lakes was but fifteen. It may be possible that the Indians divided their forces at Lost Island, one party going direct to the Des Moines, while the other came by way of the lakes.

Either this, or the settlers along the Little Sioux largely overestimated their number. As before stated, the Indians went into camp near the Mattock cabin about the seventh of March. Their *tepees* were arranged in a circle on both sides of the road running from Mattock's place to Gardner's. The inhabitants here had received no intimation of the depredations committed by them along the Little Sioux and had no apprehension of danger, and were, therefore, taken entirely by surprise. A letter found in the Granger cabin, written by Doctor Harriott to his father, Judge Harriott, dated March sixth, throws some light on the matter. In this letter he refers to the fact that the Indians were camped there, that they were on friendly terms with them, and that they had done some trading with them. Other matters were referred to in the letter which showed that they had no suspicion of danger.

Chapter 5

Incidents of the First Day of the Massacre

Some time previous to this Harvey Luce and J. M. Thatcher went out for supplies, going as far east as Waterloo. On their return they were accompanied by Enoch Ryan, a brother-in-law of Noble; Robert Clark, a young man from Waterloo; Jonathan Howe, a son of Joel Howe; and Asa Burtch, a brother of Mrs. Thatcher. They travelled with an ox team and their progress through the deep snow was necessarily slow. Upon arriving at Shippey's, in Palo Alto County, some ten miles below Emmetsburg, their cattle were so nearly exhausted that they found it necessary to stop for a few days to rest and recruit them. It was decided that Burtch and Thatcher should stay and take care of the cattle and come on as soon as they were able, while the others took their way over the snow on foot to the lake, arriving there on the sixth of March, just in time to share the fate of their unfortunate neighbours, while Burtch and Thatcher escaped by being left behind.

Late in the fall Eliza Gardner made a visit to Springfield to the family of Doctor Strong, intending to return home after a short time, but the deep snow and, the unparalleled severity of the winter made communication between the two places almost impossible and she was compelled to stay where she was. This accounts for her absence at the time of the massacre, and for her being at the home of Mr. Thomas at the time of the attack on Springfield. The incidents of the massacre can never be fully known. All the details we have are those furnished by Mrs. Sharp and they are necessarily very meagre, as she saw but little of them. It seems that Mr. Gardner had been contemplating a trip to Fort Dodge for provisions as soon as Mr. Luce returned from his trip to Waterloo.

Mr. Luce returning on the sixth, Gardner determined to start on the eighth, and commenced making arrangements accordingly. On that morning the family arose earlier than usual that he might have the advantage of an early start. As they were about to sit down to breakfast, a single Indian came in and demanded food. He was given a place at the table with the family. Soon others made their appearance until Inkpadutah and his fourteen warriors, together with their squaws and *papooses*, were crowded into the cabin. After dispatching the food that had been provided for the family, they became sullen and insolent, demanding ammunition and numerous other things. One of them snatched a box of caps from Gardner. Another attempted to seize a powder horn from the wall, but was prevented by Mr. Luce. The Indian then attempted to shoot Luce, but was prevented by Luce seizing the gun pointed at him.

At this time two young men from the Granger cabin, Harriott and Snyder, knowing that Gardner intended starting for Fort Dodge, called to send letters down by him to be mailed. Gardner told them at once that he could not go and leave his family, that he believed the situation was serious and that the Indians were bent on mischief. He also wanted the settlers to get together at the strongest place and make preparations for defence. Harriott and Snyder did not believe there was any danger. They thought it a pet of the Indians that would soon pass away. So they did some trading with the Indians and started back to their own cabin, taking no precautions whatever for their own safety. the Indians prowled about the premises until about noon, when they started back towards their camp, driving Gardner's cattle ahead of them, shooting them on the way. This was the first time the cabin had been clear of Indians since they first came in the morning.

It was a serious question now what to do. They wanted to notify the other settlers, and still if any of the men left it would so weaken their own party that it would not be possible to make an effective defence if the Indians returned, which they were liable to do any minute. It was finally agreed that Luce and Clark should go out and warn the rest and return as soon as possible. Accordingly, about two o'clock they set out for the Mattock cabin. Anxiously the inmates of the cabin awaited, further developments.

We will let Mrs. Sharp tell the rest. She says:

About three o'clock we heard the report of guns in rapid succession from the house of Mr. Mattock. We were then no longer in doubt as to the awful reality that was hanging over us. Two long hours we passed in this fearful anxiety and suspense, waiting and watching with conflicting hopes and fears for Mr. Luce and Mr. Clark to return. At length, just as the sun was sinking behind the western horizon and shedding its brilliancy over the snowy landscape, father, whose anxiety would no longer allow him to remain within doors, went out to reconnoitre. He, however, hastily returned saying: 'Nine Indians are coming now only a short distance from the house and we are all doomed to die.' His first thought was to barricade the door and fight till the last, saying, 'While they are killing all of us I will kill a few of them with the two loaded guns left in the house.'

But to this mother protested, having not yet lost all faith in the savage monsters and still hoping they would appreciate our kindness and spare our lives. She said, 'If we have to die, let us die innocent of shedding blood.' Alas for the faith placed in these inhuman monsters! They entered the house and demanded more flour, and as father turned to get them what remained of our scanty store, they shot him through the heart. He fell upon his right side and died without a struggle.

When first the Indian raised his gun to fire mother or Mrs. Luce seized the gun and drew it down, but the other Indians instantly turned upon them, seized them by their arms and beat them over their heads with the butts of their guns; then dragged them out of doors and killed them in the most cruel and shocking manner. They next seized the children, tearing them from me one by one while they reached their little arms to me, crying piteously for protection that I was powerless to give. Heedless of their cries, they dragged them out of doors and beat them to death with sticks of stove wood.

After ransacking the cabin and taking whatever they could make use of and destroying the rest, they started for their camp near the Mattock cabin, taking Abigail (Mrs. Sharp) with them as a prisoner. This occurred just at nightfall. Upon arriving at the camp the Mattock cabin was in flames and the bodies of the murdered victims scattered about it. Nothing can be known as to what transpired here, as all was over and the cabin burning before the arrival of the Indians with their prisoner. Mrs. Sharp makes note of the fact that shrieks were heard issuing from the burning building indicating that one or more luckless victims were suffering the agonies of death from burning. It is conjectured that after the first surprise was over some resistance was made at this point. The bodies of two of the men from the Granger cabin, Harriott and Snyder, were found here; also that of young Harshman. Doctor Harriott, when found, had a loaded revolver in his hand with one barrel discharged. One or two Sharps rifles were found near the bodies of the men as they lay. In short, everything indicated a complete surprise at first and then an attempt to rally and make a defence, but too late.

The Indians celebrated their bloody achievement that night by holding a war dance among the bodies of their luckless victims. Their threatening gestures accompanied by their terrific howls and their monotonous *"Hi Yi, Hi Yi,"* were kept up until far into the night. On the next morning a portion of the force started for the Howe and Thatcher cabin, nearly four miles distant. They met Mr. Howe on the bank of the lake, about a quarter of a mile from his cabin. He had a grain bag with him when found by the burial party, and it is supposed that he had started for either Gardner's or Mattock's for flour. They killed him and severed his head from his body. The skull was found some time after by George Ring on the bank of the lake. They then went to the house of Mr. Howe, where they dispatched the rest of the family, consisting of Mrs. Howe, a grown up son and daughter, and five younger children, and the child of Mrs. Noble.

BURNING OF MATTOCK CABIN.

From here they went to the Thatcher cabin. Here were two men, two women and two children, Mr. Noble, wife and one child, Mrs. Thatcher and one child and Mr. Enoch Ryan. As usual they feigned friendship until the men were off their guard, and then shot them both simultaneously. The cabin had but one door and that faced the south, the men were on the north side of the cabin when they were shot. After killing the stock and plundering the house, they took the two women (Mrs. Noble and Mrs. Thatcher) prisoners and started back to camp.

On their way they again stopped at the house of Mr. Howe. Here Mrs. Noble found her mother lying dead under the bed, where she had doubtless crawled after being left by her murderers. Her brother Jacob, some thirteen rears old, who had been left for dead or dying, was found sitting up in the yard, conscious, but unable to speak. To her questions he responded only with a shake of the head. She told him that if the Indians did not come to him and finish the murder, to crawl into the house and get into one of the beds, as perhaps help would come and he might be saved, but the savages killed him before her eyes. While Mrs. Noble was taking note of these things, the Indians were busy with their work of plunder and destruction, after which they, with their prisoners, returned to camp. This was on the ninth of March, and as will appear later on, the day preceding the night in which Markham had his hairbreadth escape by wandering into the very centre of their camp before he was aware of their presence.

On the morning of the tenth they broke camp and crossed West Okoboji on the ice to Madison Grove, where they again went into camp, staying one night only. The next day, the eleventh, they took their way north to Marble Grove, on the west side of Spirit Lake, where they went into camp some distance north of Marble's house. Marble had heard nothing of the troubles below and was wholly unsuspicious of danger. As usual, they asked for food. After partaking of it, they bantered him to trade rifles. After some dickering a trade was made. They then proposed shooting at a mark. Accordingly, a mark was set up, and after Marble had shot at it, the Indians turned on him and riddled him with bullets.

They then proceeded to appropriate such things as they could make use of and to destroy the balance, after which they took Mrs. Marble with them to their camp, thus bringing the number of prisoners up to four. At night a war dance was held to celebrate the achievements of the day, at which they recounted with pantomimic gestures and energetic action the wonderful deeds in which they had so recently participated.

Before leaving this place the Indians removed the bark from an ash tree and delineated on the white surface by signs and characters a hieroglyphical representation of their recent exploits. Many of the writers who have mentioned this incident have made more of it than the facts would warrant. The three or four published accounts which have been given to the public agree in stating that the picture record gave the position and number of victims correctly, and also represented those killed as being pierced with arrows. Now this is mainly fiction. The first discovery of the tree on which the hieroglyphics were delineated was by a party consisting of O. C. Howe, R. U. Wheelock and the writer sometime in May. They were the first party to take a trip on the west side of Spirit Lake after the massacre. The tree was first noticed by Mr. Howe, and he called the attention of the rest of the party to it. It was a white ash tree standing a little way to the southeast of the door of the Marble cabin. It was about eight inches in diameter, not over ten at the most. The rough outside bark had been hewed off for a distance of some twelve or fifteen inches up and down the tree.

Upon the smoothed surface thus made were the representations. The number of cabins (six) was correctly given, the largest of which was represented as being in flames. There were also representations of human figures and with the help of the imagination it was possible to distinguish which were meant for the whites and which the Indians. There were not over ten or a dozen all told, and except for the hint contained in the cabins, the largest one being in flames, we could not have figured any meaning out of it. This talk of the victims being pierced with arrows and their number and position given, is all nonsense, Mr. Howe and the writer spent some time studying it, and, while they came to the conclusion that it would convey a definite meaning to those understanding it, they could not make much out of it.

After leaving Marble's place, the Indians travelled slowly to the northwest, camping in the groves that border on the small lakes in that direction, never stopping more than one night in a place, until they arrived at Heron Lake, about thirty-five miles northwest of Spirit Lake, sometime about the twenty-fourth or twenty-fifth of March.

CHAPTER 6

Discovery of the Massacre

The discovery of the massacre and the manner in which it was made public now deserve a passing notice. Reference has formerly been made to a trapper by the name of Markham who was boarding in the family of J. M. Thatcher. It seems that early in the winter some cattle belonging to Markham had strayed away and that he was unable to get any tidings of them until near spring, when he heard they were at Mud Lake (or Big Island Grove, as it was then called) in Emmet County. He went over there, found and identified the cattle, made arrangements for their care, spent some time in that locality, and finally started for home on the ninth of March. It will be remembered this was the day on which the Howe and Thatcher families were murdered and the day after the balance of the massacre. Shortly after he started for the lakes there came up one of the fearful storms so common that winter. The weather was intensely cold for the season of the year but there was no alternative but to press through if possible. He lost his course and struck farther south than he intended, and about eleven o'clock in the evening he reached the house of Mr. Gardner cold, hungry and nearly exhausted.

Upon his arrival he was not a little surprised to find the place apparently deserted and everything about the house in confusion, and although he did not encounter any dead bodies, he was pretty sure that there had been trouble with the Indians. He then started down through the grove for the Mattock place. The old foot path followed substantially the same track as is now the highway through the grove. The night was uncommonly dark and objects could not be distinguished at all any distance away. When he had nearly reached Mattock's cabin his attention was attracted by the barking of a dog and the voices of individuals. He stopped to listen, and after taking a careful survey of the situation he found that he had unconsciously walked into the centre of the Indian camp, they having pitched their *tepees* in a circle on both sides of the path.

To withdraw from the proximity of his unwelcome neighbours without attracting their attention was an exceedingly difficult job and required all of his tact and address. Aided by the darkness he finally succeeded. He now took his course up across East Okoboji Lake to the cabin of Mr. Howe, where he found everything destroyed and in confusion and the bodies of the murdered victims scattered around. From there he went to the cabin of Mr. Thatcher, where he had been boarding through the winter, but the condition of affairs was similar here to what he found it at the other places. Thinking it unsafe to stay in the house, he went into a deep ravine a short distance away, and spent the remainder of the night. In the morning he found that his feet were partially frozen, but he immediately started for the Des Moines River, which he succeeded in reaching at the George Granger place.

Here he fell in with some trappers, two of whom started immediately for Fort Dodge, where they gave the first account of the massacre. But having received the particulars at second hand, and being badly frightened at them, their story was so incoherent and their statements so contradictory, they were not believed and but very little notice was taken of them. Markham, in the meantime, went up the river to Springfield and carried the news of the massacre at the lakes to that settlement so that they had warning that trouble might be expected.

Mention has previously been made of the party from Jasper County, consisting of Howe, Wheelock and Parmenter, who were here in the fall and passed Inkpadutah's camp at Loon Lake at that time. Before leaving the lakes they had determined to make permanent settlement there in the spring. This party left Newton not far from the first of March. At Fort Dodge they crossed the river and came up all of the way on the west side. By so doing they missed the trappers who went down with the news of the massacre, as they went down on the east side, consequently they heard nothing of the troubles until their arrival there. They were travelling with ox teams through the deep snow, and of course their progress was necessarily slow. On the night of the fifteenth they camped in a small grove on the bank of Mud Creek, in Lloyd township.

The next morning they took an early start, thinking to reach the Gardner place before night, but a storm came up and they lost their course. Having their spring and summer supplies, of course they were heavily loaded. They abandoned their load in a slough some two or three miles east of Gar Lake and struck for the settlement, which they reached about midnight. They first went to Thatcher's, where they found everything in confusion, but did not happen on any dead bodies. Then they went to Howe's, where they camped for the night. In the morning they made such investigation of matters as they were able, and then for the first time the fact became apparent that the settlement had been wiped out by a bloody massacre. The party started immediately for Fort Dodge, arriving there on the twenty-second of March. They were so well known there that their statements were taken without question.

A public meeting was immediately called, at which it was decided to send an expedition to the lakes to bury the dead, relieve the living, if any were found, and if possible to overtake and execute summary vengeance upon the savage marauders who had thus destroyed the settlement. The difficulties in the way of such an enterprise were numerous. The snow, which lay on the ground to an unprecedented depth, was just beginning to soften, and all were aware that just as soon as it commenced melting the streams would be swollen so as to be impassable. The settlers on the river above Fort Dodge became alarmed and most of them left their places and came into town, thus leaving the country through which the expedition must necessarily pass practically uninhabited, and those who remained were so destitute that they could furnish nothing for the expedition. The meeting at Fort Dodge was held on the twenty-third of March. Major Williams being present read a commission he held from Governor Grimes authorising him in cases of emergency to take the proper measures for the defence of the frontier.

Volunteers were called for and it soon became evident that there would be no delay in getting the men. In a few minutes a force of about seventy men was raised. This force was organised in two companies. A and B, Company A under the command of C. B. Richards, and Company B under the command of J. F. Duncombe. Another, Company C, Captain J. C. Johnson, was raised at Webster City, which brought the force up to about a hundred men. The whole force was under the command of Major William Williams, of Fort Dodge, while George B, Sherman, of the same place, acted as quartermaster and commissary. The expedition was without tents and was but partially supplied with blankets, the men being limited to one apiece.

CAPTAIN COMPANY A.

The means of transportation were very imperfect. There was no grain in the country above Fort Dodge, and it was impossible to take any along as it was necessary to take provisions for the round trip. The snow was nearly four feet on the level and all of the ravines and low places were completely filled, and when the snow commenced melting it was one continued reach of water and slush. The enlisted men were no tenderfeet. They comprehended to its fullest extent the perils and privations they would necessarily have to overcome before completing the task they had undertaken, and while they went at the work of preparation with that careless gayety and nonchalance which usually characterize the representative frontiersman, they well knew that it was more than probable that some of their number would be left on that wild and desolate prairie, their flesh to be torn and devoured by the beasts and birds of prey and their bones to bleach in sun and storm until they turned again to dust. Looking back and recalling the events of that memorable expedition the only wonder is that the number of victims was not materially larger.

The expedition left Fort Dodge on the twenty-fourth of March. Some accounts say the twenty-fifth, but this is a mistake. They started on the twenty-fourth, and were nine days in reaching what was then known as the Granger place, in Emmet County, the point where the command divided and the main body turned back. Nine days of rougher campaigning it would be difficult to imagine. The snow had so filled in around the groves and along the streams that at times it was impossible to reach them. It was no uncommon experience to wade through snow and water waist deep during the day, and at night to lie down in their wet clothing, without fire and without tents, and on short rations of food. The only way the men could keep from freezing was by lying so close together that they could only turn over by platoons. The ravines were all filled level full of snow and it was often necessary to detach the teams and rigging a cable to the wagons for the whole party to take hold and make their way through. As the expedition neared the state line, and settlements became sparser and smaller, it was deemed prudent to send a force of scouts out in advance of the main body.

Accordingly, on the morning of the thirtieth of March, Manor Williams made a detail of ten men to act as scouts, under the command of William L. Church, who, by the way, was a veteran of the Mexican War. Mr. Church with his family, consisting of his wife, his wife's sister and two small children, had settled at Springfield the fall before, and in

CAPTAIN OF COMPANY B.

February Church had made a trip to Webster City for supplies, leaving his family in the settlement at Springfield during his absence. He had reached McKnight's Point, on the west fork of the Des Moines in Humboldt County on his return when he heard of the massacre at the lakes, and also that a relief party was being organised at Fort Dodge and would be up in a few days. He accordingly waited for their arrival, when he enrolled himself as a member of Company C. He had heard nothing of his family since he left home nearly a month before, and was continually in a state of feverish anxiety. Some of the accounts say that Lieutenant Maxwell had command of the scouting party, but this is a mistake. Church had charge of the scouts up to the time they fell in with the Springfield refugees, when he went down the river with them and the scouts were then turned over to Maxwell.

On the morning in question, as soon as the detail was completed, he started with his scouts some distance in advance of the main party. As they were crossing over the divide near the south line of Emmet County, they saw, a long distance ahead of them, a party of pedestrians, but whether they were whites or Indians could not then be determined, as the party when first sighted must have been nearly two miles away. Church brought his men together, had them examine their arms to see that they were in readiness, and gave the word for a cautious advance, he taking the lead. As the distance between the two parties was gradually diminished, it was evident that the strangers were approaching with fully as much caution as Church's party. It was now discovered that they had an ox team with them. This settled the question that they were not Indians.

About this time they commenced making signals, which the scouts answered, and throwing away their caution, started on the run to meet them, Church taking the lead. His eagerness was soon explained, as his wife, wife's sister and two children were members of the party, and this was the first intimation he had received since he heard of the massacre as to whether his family were dead or alive. It was a glad, yet a sorrowful meeting. Glad that their circle was yet complete; that none of their number had fallen victims to the savage foe. Sorrowful that so much of danger and suffering had been endured and that so much more of sorrow and privation must come to them before their comfort and safety could be assured.

It was now ascertained that they were a party of refugees fleeing from Indian depredations in the neighbourhood of Springfield (now Jackson), Minnesota. The party consisted of about twenty men, wom-

FIRST LIEUTENANT OF COMPANY C.

en and children, among whom were Mrs. Church, her two children, and her sister Miss Swanger; Mr. Thomas, his wife and several children; David Carver, John Bradshaw, Morris Markham, Jareb Palmer, Miss Eliza Gardner, Doctor Strong and wife, Doctor Skinner and several others. From them it was ascertained that the Indians had made a raid on the settlements along the Des Moines River three days before, an account of which will be given later on. They had with them three persons who had been severely wounded in that attack; namely, Mr. Thomas, Mr. Carver and Miss Swanger. They had been three days upon the road, during which time they had been without provisions, except a kind of lunch they took along with them, and in that time they had suffered incredible hardships. The women and children had waded through snow and water waist deep and at night had lain down in their wet clothes completely exhausted.

It was decided by the scouts and refugees to go into camp in the nearest grove and to send back messengers to the main body to hurry up supplies and to inform the surgeon that his services would probably be needed. The messengers detailed for this service were Frank Mason of Company C and the writer. The balance of the scouts, together with the refugees, started for the nearest grove, which was on the river directly west from where the two parties met. The place has since been known as "Camp Grove," and is situated on the line between Palo Alto and Emmet Counties. When the messengers reached the main body and delivered their message, excitement ran high. The troops hurried forward as rapidly as possible, and when they reached the grove the boys had campfires already started and everyone set to work immediately to alleviate the sufferings of the exhausted refugees. They gave up for their use the only tent in the command and furnished them with such provisions as they had, while the surgeon. Doctor Bissell, dressed their wounds and made them as comfortable as possible under the circumstances. The next day they started on their way down the river, while the volunteers continued their march toward the lakes.

Governor Carpenter in his account refers to this incident as follows:

> If the expedition had accomplished nothing more, every man would have felt himself repaid for his share in its toil and suffering by the relief it was able to afford to these suffering refugees. In the haste of their departure from Springfield they had taken

but little provisions and scanty clothing. The women in wading through the drifted snow had worn out their shoes, their gowns were worn to fringes at the bottom, and all in all, a more forlorn and needy company of men and women were never succoured by the hands of friends. They cried and laughed, and laughed and cried, alternately. A part of one squad then returned to the main command with the information of our discovery and the residue conducted the worn and weary party to the nearest grove on the Des Moines River, where the main body joined them later in the afternoon and where we spent the night. The next morning we divided our scanty rations and blankets with them and they went forward toward safety and friends, whilst we pushed towards the scene of the massacre.

On the afternoon of the first day of April the command reached Granger's place, when it was ascertained that a party of United States troops had come down from Fort Ridgley and were then at Springfield; that a detachment under Lieutenant Murray had been over to Spirit Lake and buried Marble, but did not go down to Okoboji Lake at all. They also reported that the Indians had made good their escape across the Big Sioux River. By the way, this company of United States troops was under command of Captain Barnard E. Bee, who, at the breaking out of the civil war, joined the Confederates and was made a brigadier general, and was killed at the first Battle of Bull Run. When it was learned that the Indians had made their escape, it was not deemed necessary that the whole force should go over to the lakes. Indeed, tliat would have been almost impossible, anyway. The supplies were nearly exhausted and the water was at its highest.

After consultation with his subordinates, Major Williams decided to turn back with the main body, while a party of twenty-three were detailed under the command of Captain Johnson and Lieutenant Maxwell to proceed to the lakes for the purpose of burying the dead and gaining what information they could.

Some accounts place the strength of this party at twenty-five or twenty-six, but twenty-three was the actual number. Their names were as follows:

Captain J. C. Johnson, Lieutenant John N. Maxwell.

Privates—Henry Carse, William E. Burkholder, William Ford, H. E. Dalley, O. C. Howe, George P. Smith, O. S. Spencer, C. Stebbins, S. Van Cleve, R. U. Wheelock, R. A. Smith, William A. De Foe, B. F. Parmenter, Jesse Addington, R. McCormick, J. M. Thatcher, William R. Wilson, Jonas Murray, A. Burtch, William K. Laughlin, E. D. Kellogg.

In the list given to the public by Captain Richards, the name of William De Foe does not appear, but it is pretty certain that he was a member of the party. Captain Richards himself volunteered to go and started with the rest, but upon reaching the river found that he could not cross his pony over, and so he and one other mounted man turned back. It was in this way that the number was reduced to twenty-three, while the original order was for twenty-five. This party took up their line of March towards the lakes on the morning of the second day of April, carrying with them two days' rations, and it was then very uncertain when they would get any more. They arrived at the Thatcher cabin about three o'clock p. m. and immediately entered upon the work they had to do. The bodies of Noble and Ryan were found back of the cabin and were the first ones buried. It will be remembered that Mr. Ryan was one of the men who came through from Hampton with Luce and Thatcher, and that he got through on the evening of the seventh, just in time to be killed, while Thatcher, by reason of his cattle giving out, was obliged to lay over and rest them a short time. This delay saved his life.

Chapter 7

Adventures of the Party That Remained Behind

The party camped that night at the Thatcher cabin. The old cook stove had been left standing in place undisturbed. This the boys utilised at once and fell to work cooking their supper. After going into camp, a small detachment of the party, including Thatcher, started out on a stroll and went as far as the Howe cabin, where in addition to the members of the Howe family, they found the bodies of the two children, Thatcher's and Noble's. They had probably been taken that far with their mothers, who, it will be remembered, the Indians had with them as prisoners. The boys brought the body of Thatcher's child back to the cabin and buried it that night near the head of the ravine, west of the cabin. The Noble child was left where it was found and buried next day with the Howe family. The night was passed in the Thatcher cabin. It could not have been over fourteen by twenty feet in size and no loft, and yet the twenty-three men managed to dispose of themselves so as to pass the night in comparative comfort.

They were on the move early the next morning and, after dispatching their scanty breakfast, started for the Howe cabin, about a mile and a quarter west. Upon arriving there Captain Johnson divided his command into three parties. One was to remain and bury the bodies found there. This party was under the immediate command of Captain Johnson himself. The second, under command of Lieutenant Maxwell, was to proceed to the Mattock place and bury those found there, while the third, under the direction of R. U. Wheelock, was detailed to find, if possible, the wagon with supplies that Howe and Wheelock had abandoned on the prairie the night they reached there and discovered the massacre, on their former trip. The captain's force commenced work at once. One spade and one shovel to each party were all the working tools that could be found. With these they dug a grave about six or seven feet square and about thirty inches deep.

In this grave were buried the bodies of nine persons, as follows: Mrs. Millie Howe; Jonathan Howe, a grown-up son, and Sardis Howe, a grown-up daughter; five younger children of Mr. Howe, and the child of Mr. and Mrs. Noble, which, as has been before stated, had probably been brought that far with its mother before being killed by the Indians. There is a discrepancy between the actual facts and all accounts so far published relative to the number massacred at the Howe cabin. The number given by Mrs. Sharp in her book, as well as other published accounts, give it as "Mrs. Howe, a grown-up son, a grown-up daughter and four younger children." When the bodies were disinterred for reburial at the time of the erection of the monument, there were certainly nine bodies found in that grave, and they can only be accounted for as above stated. There were no children found at the Thatcher cabin, and Thatcher himself identified his child found at the Howe cabin, and the men with him assisted him in carrying it back to his own place, where it was buried as before stated, near the head of the ravine west of the house.

It was well towards noon when this work was completed. In the meantime the other burial party, under Maxwell, proceeded at once to the Mattock place. A short time before their arrival there they found the headless body of Joel Howe on the ice. Here is another discrepancy in which ascertained facts differ from the usually accepted accounts. Henry Dalley, of Webster City, who is the only member of that party whose whereabouts is now known, insists that when they found the body of Mr. Howe they carried it to the Mattock place and buried it in the same grave with the Mattock family and the others that were found there. He says the recollection of that circumstance is the most, vivid and distinct of anything that transpired on the trip and that he cannot be mistaken about it. The usually accepted account is that Mr. Howe's body was taken to the shore by those who found it and buried on a bluff some distance southwest of his house.

It will be remembered the party had no provisions except the lunch they brought with them from their camp the morning before, and that was now exhausted. The party under Wheelock, consisting of five men, started at once in search of the abandoned wagon, which they found without difficulty among the sloughs that form the source of Spring Run, together with the supplies, all safe as they had left them three weeks before. They took what they could conveniently carry of flour, pork, coffee and sugar, and started back, joining the other parties at the Mattock place, reaching there just as they had finished digging the grave and were gathering up the bodies for burial. As has been stated, here was the only place that showed signs of any resistance having been made, and that has already been described. There were eleven bodies found here and buried. As identified by Thatcher and Wilson at the time, they were as follows: James Mattock, his wife and the three oldest children, Robert Madison, Doctor Harriott, Bert Snyder and Joseph Harshman. Right here comes in a discrepancy that has never been explained and probably never will.

Mrs. Sharp maintains that the bodies of Luce and Clark were found later and buried near the outlet of East Okoboji, they having been waylaid in their attempt to warn the other settlers. All accounts agree that eleven bodies were buried here. The writer found one body, that of a twelve-year-old boy, about a month later and assisted in burying it, and if one perished in the flames this makes thirteen to be accounted for. Who were they? Seven of the Mattock family, Madison, Harriott, Snyder, Harshman and two others. Even on the theory that none perished in the burning cabin, there is one more than can be accounted for. Was there one or two strangers stopping at either the Mattock or Granger cabin of whom no account was ever given? It is not strange that an occasional discrepancy is found. The only wonder is that they are not far more numerous.

From here the party went to the Granger cabin and found the dead body of Carl Granger, which was buried east of the cabin, near the bank of the lake. From there the whole force went to Gardner's, where were found six bodies, as follows: Mr. and Mrs. Gardner, Mrs. Luce, the young son of Mr. Gardner and the two children of Mr. and Mrs. Luce. These were buried in one grave a short distance southeast of the house. This finished the work of burial. There was no lumber here with which to make coffins, and no time to do it if there had been, and all that could be done was to dig at each place one grave wide enough to contain the bodies found there, put them in as they were found, cover them with prairie hay and then with dirt. One singular fact which was particularly noted at the time was that no scalps had been taken. Many of the accounts that have been published state that a part of the victims were scalped. This is a mistake. The matter was thoroughly investigated and fully talked over that night in camp, and Messrs. Howe, Wheelock and Maxwell and others unite in the statement that no scalps were taken.

After finishing their work the tired and hungry men camped for the night. Some of the party had seen Mr. Gardner bury a few potatoes in a box under the stove the fall before. These were found and roasted by a campfire. These, with the small amount of provisions which had been brought from the wagon on the prairie, constituted their stock of supplies. The next morning, which was the fourth of April, was foggy and misty, and the indications portended a coming storm. While the boys were preparing breakfast, the question of the return trip was discussed. A majority were in favour of striking right out in a southeasterly direction, in as straight a line as possible, for the Irish Colony, while the others argued that the distance was too great and the route too uncertain to do it with safety, and insisted on going back by the same route they came, which was by Estherville and Emmet. And more, they argued the weather was so threatening that if a storm came up the party was liable to be divided and possibly some might be lost on the prairie.

After breakfast the two parties were as far apart as ever, when Captain Johnson, seeing no prospect of coming to an agreement, gave the word to form a line. After the men had fallen in he gave the further order, "All who favour starting at once across the prairie, step three paces to the front; the rest stand fast." Sixteen advanced to the front, including Captain Johnson, Lieutenant Maxwell, Mr. Burkholder and thirteen others. Seven remained in their places. The names of these seven were: O. C. Howe, R. U. Wheelock, B. F. Parmenter, William R. Wilson, Joseph M. Thatcher, Asa Burtch and R. A. Smith. What little provision was left in camp was speedily packed and the party made ready to depart at once. Just as the main party were starting away, Captain Johnson and Mr. Burkholder turned back to where Messrs. Howe, Wheelock and R. A. Smith were standing and urged that they change their minds and go with them. They insisted that there was no evidence that the Indians had left the vicinity of the lakes, and that so small a party were taking their lives in their hands by staying there alone.

On the other hand, Howe and Wheelock endeavoured to convince Captain Johnson that the danger in going was far greater than in staying; that there was more to be feared from the coming storm than from the Indians. The seven who remained behind offered to go with the others if they would change their route and go back by way of Estherville and the Des Moines River, but they absolutely refused to strike out across the prairie. Seeing that their arguments were of no avail and that the smaller party were determined to stay, they shook hands with them, bade them goodbye and started on the run to join their companions, who by this time were some distance away. It was their last goodbye.

For the particulars of that return trip the reader is referred to Lieutenant Maxwell's account, which will be found further on. The party that remained now turned their attention to their own comfort and safety. Their first requirement was provisions. As soon as the other detachment had left, they made their preparations to once more visit the wagon on the prairie, which they found without trouble, and after loading themselves with such supplies as they could carry, returned to camp. Before reaching camp they were overtaken by the blinding storm, which proved so disastrous to the other parties, but fortunately they were so far along on their return trip that they succeeded in reaching camp without accident, with three or four days' provisions. Up to this time the party had been (tamped out on the north side of the cabin. They now moved inside, and as the storm was increasing in violence, their next care was to lay in fuel enough to last until it was over.

This they had no trouble in doing, and now it will be readily seen that they were far more comfortably situated than the main body, who were having their terrible experience on the banks of the Cylinder, so vividly described by Governor Carpenter, or the party who had left that morning for the Irish Colony, and were having such a bitter experience, as told by Lieutenant Maxwell, There was nothing now for the party to do but to take care of themselves the best they could until the storm was over. They were in a comfortable cabin, with plenty of fuel and provisions for the present. Of course, they were at any moment liable to an attack by the Indians, provided the Indians had not all left. After securing their fuel, they barricaded the door and window as well as they could, and then, removing some of the chinking, they made portholes on each side of the cabin; being fairly well armed, they considered themselves comparatively safe.

Sunday night the storm abated and Monday morning it was clear and cold. That Sunday night was the coldest April night known in the history of Iowa. On Monday morning the party started for home. The ground was frozen where it was bare and where it was not the strong crust on the snow was capable of bearing up any ordinary load, so that the walking was good. On reaching the Des Moines, they found it frozen over so hard that they crossed it without difficulty and reached Granger's place, where they had left the main body five days before. It will be remembered that on coming up no teams could cross the river, consequently they all turned back with the main body of troops except the one owned by Howe and Wheelock. That was left here, and Markham and another person were left here to take care of it until they should return. The party decided to rest here another day. That night they were joined also by Jareb Palmer, who, instead of going down with the main body, had been up to Springfield again. Wednesday morning the whole party started down the river.

They now had a team to carry their baggage and the walking was comparatively good. The weather remaining cold all of this time, the water had run down so that the small streams were crossed without much difficulty, and it was only such streams as Jack Creek and the Cylinder that offered any serious obstacles. The party rested another day at the Irish Colony, where they had overtaken a portion of the Springfield refugees making their way down the river; also Henry Carse, one of Maxwell's men, who had frozen his feet the night they lay on the prairie after leaving the Gardner cabin.

Saturday morning they made another start and arrived at Cylinder Creek a little after noon. The creek had fallen some but was still out of its banks, being nearly a quarter of a mile wide. The water was from one to two feet deep over the bottom, which was very level. The crossing of this stream was the most serious problem that the party had to solve on their way down. One man went ahead on horseback to try the route, then followed the teams with the wounded men and the women and children. The ground was a little higher at the bank of the stream than it was farther back, and at one place it was bare. On this knoll they all gathered to contrive some way to cross the river. An old wooden sled was found and a few pieces of driftwood. These were fastened together and the box taken off from one of the wagons and fastened to the raft. Two long ropes were then rigged, one to each side of the raft.

The man on horseback then took one end of one of the ropes and swam his horse across the channel to the opposite bank, which was quite steep and comparatively high. (The course of the channel was distinguished by willows growing on its banks.) He then dismounted, holding fast to the rope. Three or four men now took their places on the raft and the man that had ridden over slowly and carefully pulled them across, the men on the other side holding the raft by the other rope to keep it from floating down stream. Communication now being established, and there being men enough on each side to handle the raft without delay, the women, children and wounded men were soon taken over. The teams were then swam over, ropes rigged to the ends of the wagon tongues and the wagons hauled over. Then came the baggage and last of all the balance of the men.

This crossing took the entire afternoon and the party reached Shippey's, two miles away, about sundown, wet, cold and almost exhausted. Here they learned for the first time the terrible experience their comrades had at the same place nearly a week before them. From here the party proceeded on their way to Fort Dodge, which they reached without further adventures than such as are incident to swimming swollen streams and living on short rations, which, in some instances, consisted of a handful of flour and a little salt, which they mixed up with water and baked over a campfire. A few of the party shot, dressed and broiled some muskrats and tried to make the rest believe they considered them good eating, but that diet did not become popular.

In the foregoing account the writer has been confined mostly to what passed under his own personal observation, for more extended particulars the reader is referred to the official report of Major Williams, and to the accounts written by Lieutenant Maxwell and Governor Carpenter. These two papers have been selected from others equally readable and reliable for the reason that Maxwell, being in charge and taking notes at the time, would be supposed to have a clearer recollection of events than would otherwise be possible, while Governor Carpenter's account of the return trip of the main body will be taken at its face value.

CHAPTER 8

Terrible Sufferings

Lieutenant Maxwell's account:
"We left Fort Dodge March twenty-fourth, but owing to our commissary being hindered in procuring transportation, we were obliged to camp at Badger Creek, not more than four or five miles north. We now began to realise that we were soldiers. Cold, wet and hungry, we built up large campfires, provided a hasty meal, dried our clothes as well as we could, and without tents lay down and slept soundly.

"On the morning of the twenty-fifth we resumed our march, crossing the east branch of the Des Moines without difficulty, and camped at Dakota City. The twenty-sixth the road became more and more difficult. In some places the snow was so deep that it was necessary to break a road before our teams could pass through. In other places it had drifted in the ravines to the depth of eight or ten feet. The only way to proceed was to wade through, stack arms, return and unhitch the teams, attach ropes to them and draw them through; then perform a similar operation with the wagons. This performance took place every mile or two, and by such progress we were two days in reaching McKnight's Point on the east bank of the west branch of the Des Moines River, twelve miles from Dakota City. On the twenty-seventh we camped at McKnight's Point.

"On the night of the twenty-sixth the command camped out on the prairie, but a detail under Captain Duncombe had gone ahead to look out the road to the Point. Duncombe had been ill during the day, and he became so exhausted that he had to be carried into camp, running a very close risk of losing his life.

"Resuming our march on the twenty-eighth, we camped that night at Shippey's, on Cylinder Creek. Sunday, the twenty-ninth, we reached the Irish Colony, Emmet County, and were all cared for by the inhabitants who had assembled for protection in case of an attack, but were greatly relieved when we came in sight. The morning of the thirtieth found the command greatly refreshed, having butchered a cow that had been wintered on prairie hay. The beef was not exactly porterhouse steak, but it was food for hungry men. We left our teams, which were nearly exhausted, and impressed fresh ones. We camped that night near Big Island Grove. At this place the Indians had kept a lookout in a big cedar tree that grew on an island in the middle of the lake, and their campfires were still burning. A platform had been built in this tree, forty feet from the ground, from which one could easily see twenty miles. The place had probably been deserted several days but the fire was still burning. One Indian doubtless kept watch here alone, leaving in a northwesterly direction when he abandoned the place.

"The morning of the thirty-first the command moved out early. Ten men were sent forward as scouts. When about eight miles out we met the Springfield refugees, the Churches, Thomases, Carver and others. We went into camp, and our surgeon dressed the wounds of the fleeing party. On the morning of April first Major Williams sent an escort with the Springfield people back to the Irish Colony, and proceeded northwest, with an advance guard ahead. We camped that night at Granger's Point, near the Minnesota line. Here we learned that the United States troops from Fort Ridgley were camped at the head of Spirit Lake and that the Indians had fled to Owl Lake, some eighteen miles away. As we were on foot and the Indians supposed to be mounted, there would not be any chance of overtaking them.

"A council was held and it was decided to return the main part of the command to the Irish Colony and wait for the rest to come in. Twenty-six men were selected, including those having friends at the lake, to cross the river, proceed to that point to bury the dead, reconnoitre, and see if there were any who had escaped the Indians. I was one of the party. On the morning of the second of April, under Capt. J. C. Johnson, we crossed the Des Moines River and took a south and west direction. The travelling was much better than it had been since we left Fort Dodge. It was warm and clear.

"About two o'clock we struck East Okoboji Lake on the southeast shore. The first cabin we came to was that of Mr. Thatcher. Here we found the yard and prairie covered with feathers. Two dead men were lying at the rear of the house, both bodies being numerously shot in the breast. They evidently had been unarmed and everything indicated that they had been surprised. The rest of the family had been killed in the house or taken prisoners, and everything indicated that there had been no defence. From here we went to Mr. Howe's, where we found seven dead bodies. There were one old and one middle aged woman, one man and four children—all brutally murdered. It seemed that the man had been killed by placing the muzzle of a gun against his nose and blowing his head to pieces. The other adult had been simply shot. The children had been knocked in the head.

"We divided into parties to bury the dead, camping for the night near the residence of the Howe family. Old Mr. Howe was found on the third of April, some distance from the house on the ice, shot through the head. We buried him on a bluff southwest of the place, some eighty rods from the house. The next place was Mr. Mattock's. Here we found eleven dead bodies and buried them all in one grave, men, women and children. The ground was frozen and we could only make the grave about eighteen inches deep. It was a ghastly sight. The adults had been shot, but the children's brains had been knocked out, apparently by striking them across their foreheads with heavy clubs or sticks of wood.

"The brains of one boy about ten years of age, had been completely let out of his head, and lay upon the ground. Everyone else shrank from touching them. I was in command and feeling that I would not ask another to do a thing from which myself revolted, I gathered up the poor scattered fragments upon the spade and placed them all together in the grave. About forty head of cattle had been shot at this place, the carcasses split open on the backs and tenderloins removed—all that the Indians cared to carry off. The house had been burned with one dead body in it at the time. At this place it seems to me that the only man who fought the Indians was Doctor Harriott, who had formerly lived at Waterloo. He made heroic defence, probably killing and wounding two or three Indians. He was falling back toward Granger's, evidently defending the women and children, when he was finally shot himself. He still grasped his Sharp's rifle, which was empty and broken off at the breech, showing that he had fallen in a hand to hand fight. I have little idea that any other man about the lakes fired a gun at the Indians. It was simply a surprise and butchery.

"From here we went to the Grangers' and found the dead body of one of the brothers of that name. He had been first shot and his head had been split open with a broad axe. He and his brother had kept a small store, and the Indians had taken everything away excepting some dozen bottles of strychnine. We buried him near his own house. The next house was Gardner's. Here were the bodies of Mr. and Mrs. Gardner, one grown-up daughter, and two small children in the yard, and a baby in the house. We buried this family all in one grave, about two rods from the house. Tired and hungry we went into camp in a small grove at the rear of the house, with nothing to eat but potatoes.

"Some of our party had visited the lake in the fall and had seen Mr. Gardner bury two bushels of potatoes in a box under his stove. These we found and roasted in the campfire. They lasted two days. On the morning of the fourth, we completed our sad task, and without any food, turned our faces homeward, taking a southeast course, hoping to reach the Irish Colony the same day. In the forenoon it was quite warm, melting the snow, and consequently travelling was very difficult. We were obliged to wade sloughs waist deep or go miles around and run the risk of losing the course. We were wet to the shoulders and while in this fearful condition the wind changed. About four o'clock a blizzard was upon us. In a short time our clothes were frozen stiff. Many of us cut holes in our boots to let the water out, and several pulled their boots off and were unable to get them on again. Up to this time the detachment had kept together. About sundown we came to a township corner placed there the year before. Laughlin and I wanted to be governed by the pit.

"While we were talking, part of the detachment came up and passed us some distance to the right. Those who happened to be with Laughlin and me stopped on a piece of dry ground close to township corner, determined to remain near it all night, lest in the night we should lose our course as shown by the corner. We marched back and forth all night long. When a comrade would fall others would help him to his feet, encourage and force him to keep moving as the only hope, for no living being could survive an hour in such a storm without hard exercise. Captain Johnson's party, led by a trapper, became a little separated from us by a slough, where they found a dry place and commenced pacing back and forth as we were doing. They were within speaking distance of us. They stayed there all night, but in the morning took a southeast direction, while we went east. They seemed to have perfect confidence in the old trapper's knowledge of the country.

"During the night some of our men begged to lie down, claiming that it was useless to try to keep up any longer as the ice on their clothes gave them fearful annoyance. But the more hopeful would not consent to anyone giving up. In this distressed condition we travelled up and down that path all night.

"One man by the name of Henry Carse from Princeton, Illinois, had taken his boots off in the evening and wrapped his feet in pieces of blanket. He succeeded in getting along as well as the rest during the night, but in the morning when we went on the ice to break a road, his feet got wet and the wraps wore out. I staid with him until within three or four miles of the Des Moines River, when I became satisfied he could not get there, as his mind had failed. Every time I would bring him up he would turn away in any direction. Finally, Henry Dalley came along and succeeded in getting him "to the river. The river was three miles from the Irish Colony. We had no matches, but some of the party knew how to strike a fire by saturating a damp wad with powder and shooting it into the weeds. In this way we succeeded in striking a fire. Henry Carse was now unconscious and the blood was running from his mouth! We cut the rags from his feet and the skin came off the soles of his feet with the rags.

"As soon as the fire was well going, Laughlin and I being the least frozen, determined to try and cross the river and reach the settlement for help. We walked to the middle of the river, laid poles over the weak ice and crawled over. We reached the Irish Colony and sent back help to the rest of the party. I went to sleep soon after entering a warm room and did not awaken until the next day, when I took some nourishment and started on to overtake the command under Major Williams which had been detained at Cylinder Creek. In the morning C. C. Carpenter tried to get a guide to go and help search for Johnson and his friend Burkholder, but failed. As we left the colony I looked back and saw Carpenter going down the river to see if they had struck the river below. At Cylinder Creek the party broke up into squads, each reaching his home as best he could, and all of us more or less demoralized.

"Laughlin and I came by the way of Fort Dodge, while Frank Mason and some of the others came across north of here. Most of us had our ears and feet frozen, but we only lamented the loss of the slain settlers, and our comrades Johnson and Burkholder, whose precious lives had been given for the relief of the helpless. But it was always a wonder to me that we did not leave the bones of more of our comrades to bleach with these on those wild and trackless prairies."

★★★★★★

Concluding portion of Governor C. C. Carpenter's address on the same occasion:

"The third day after commencing our return march, we left Medium Lake, in a hazy, cloudy atmosphere, and a drizzling rain. By the time we had reached Cylinder Creek, beneath the descending rain overhead and the melting snow beneath our feet, the prairies were a flood of water. On arriving at Cylinder Creek we found the channel not only full, but the water covering the entire bottom bordering the creek to a depth of from three to four feet. When we found that it would be impossible to cross at a point where the road intersected the creek, we resolved to send a party up the stream to see if a better crossing could not be found. But in less time than I have occupied in telling this story the wind began blowing from the north, the rain turned to snow and every thread of clothing on the entire command was saturated with water and our clothing began to freeze to our limbs. I had still not given up the hope of either crossing the stream or finding a more comfortable place to camp, and await the result of the now freezing and blinding storm.

"So with one or two others I followed down the creek a mile or more, until we came to the bluffs overlooking the bottoms bordering the Des Moines. I had hoped we might discover some elevated ridge through the bottom, over which we could pass and reach the timber that fringed the river. But on reaching the bluffs and looking out over the bottom land which fell back from the river from one to two miles on either side to their base, it was a wide waste of water. So we concluded our only hope was to remain right where we were until the storm abated.

"On getting back to the road we found our comrades improvising a cover by taking the wagon sheet and one or two tents which we had along, and stretching them over the wagon wheels and staking them down as best they could to the frozen ground, leaving a small opening on the south side for a doorway. This done, we moved the animals to the south side of our tent, on ground sloping to the south, in order to afford them all the protection possible. Then we put all our blankets together, made a common bed upon the ground, and all crawled into it without removing our clothes, every thread of which was wet, and most of which was frozen as stiff as boards. There we lay through that long Saturday night. The air outside was full of fine snow. At different times during the night three or four of us crept out of our nests and went around our tents, banking it with snow on the north, east and west sides. And when the fierce winds would blow the banking away so as to open a new air hole we would repeat the operation. To add to the horrors of the situation during this more than thirty-six hours of absolute imprisonment, we were without food.

"By daylight, on Monday morning, we were on the move, and to our joy found the ice, which had formed on Cylinder Creek the day before, would bear us up. The severity of the weather cannot be better attested than by stating the fact that all the men, our wagon, loaded with the little baggage of the camp, and the few horses belonging to the command, were crossed upon this bridge of ice with perfect ease and safety. Since that experience upon Cylinder Creek, I have marched with armies engaged in actual war. During three and a half years' service, the army with which I was connected marched from Cairo to Chattanooga, from Chattanooga to Atlanta, from Atlanta to the sea, from the sea through the Carolinas to Richmond. These campaigns were made under southern suns and in the cold rains and not infrequent snow storms of southern winters. They were sometimes continued without intermission three or four days and nights in succession, with only an occasional halt to give weary, foot-sore soldiers a chance to boil a cup of coffee. But never in those weary years experienced a conflict with the elements that could be compared with the two nights and one day on the bank of Cylinder Creek.

"After crossing the creek on Monday morning we went to the Shippey house, some two miles south, where we cooked our breakfast. From this time forward no order of march was observed, but each man found his way home to suit himself. I followed down the river, in company with several comrades, to McKnight's Point, where we got our dinner. After dinner Lieutenant Stratton, Smith E. Stevens and myself determined we would go on to Dakota, in Humboldt County, that afternoon and evening, and accordingly started. We had gone but a short distance when George W. Brizee came on after us. We tried as delicately as possible to dissuade him from attempting to go further that evening. But go he would, and so we pushed on. Night found us on the wide prairie some eight or ten miles southeast of McKnight's Point and at least eight miles from Dakota.

"It became very dark, so that it was difficult to follow the track. Soon Brizee began to complain, declaring he could go no further and would have to take his chances on the prairie. As I had been over the road several times, Stratton and Stevens suggested that they would depend upon me to guide them through; so I kept ahead, looking and feeling out the path. I could hear them encouraging Brizee, while he persistently declared his inability to go any further. Stevens finally took his blanket and carried it for him, and soon after Stratton was carrying his gun. I now told them that Henry Cramer and Judge Hutchinson lived about a mile south of our road, and some three miles west of Dakota, and that we would go in there and spend the night. Brizee thought he could pull through that far. At last I thought we had arrived at a point nearly opposite of Cramer's, and we left the road and struck across the prairie.

"We had scarcely started before Brizee began to aver we were lost; that I, like a fool, was leading them a wild-goose chase, and that we would all have to lie on the prairie. I kept on, however, fixing my course as well as possible, and shouting back to 'come on, that we were all right.' Finally we were greeted by the barking of a dog, and in a few moments were in Mr. Cramer's house. After Cramer and his wife had gotten out of bed and made us a bunk on the floor, and Cramer had pulled off Brizee's boots, Brizee began to repeat in various forms the adventures of the evening, emphasizing the persistency and pluck it had required in us to pull through; and the hearty manner in which he commended my skill as a guide, over a trackless prairie, was hardly consistent with the upbraiding whilst we were plodding along in the darkness.

"The next morning Mrs. Cramer prepared the best breakfast I ever ate. My mouth waters today in memory of the biscuits which were piled up on that breakfast table. I have often thought since that there could have been but little left for the family dinner. That evening found us in Fort Dodge and our connection with the expedition had ended.

"I have frequently thought in later years of the good discipline preserved in a command where there was absolutely no legal power to enforce authority. This fact is really the highest compliment that could be paid the officers. Had they not possessed the characteristics which secured and maintained the respect of these men no shadow of discipline could have been enforced. On the contrary, during those trying days, on the march and in the bivouac, there was complete order. Of the three captains, two are living, (1902),—Messrs. Richards and Duncombe. Their subsequent careers in civil life have been but a fulfilment of the prophecy of the men who followed them through the snow banks of northwestern Iowa in 1857.

"With Captain Johnson I was but little acquainted, but I watched

WILLIAM E. BURKHOLDER.

him with interest and with admiration during the few days of our march. He was a man of fine physique, was deliberate, quiet almost to reticence, with a handsome face and manly eye. In short, from what I saw of him, I may say that the marble and brass, which we have come here today to unveil in commemoration of him and his company's virtues and heroism are not of a more solid and enduring character than were the noble and generous traits of his nature. His cruel death and that of his noble and promising comrade, William E. Burkholder was the one circumstance which veiled the results of the expedition in a lasting sorrow.

"The First Lieutenant of Company A, Franklin E. Stratton, was perhaps more fully endowed with all the qualities which constitute a soldier than any other man in the company, or perhaps of the command. He was quiet, prompt, uncomplaining, methodical, and in the line of his duty exacting. Remembering my comradeship with him on the Spirit Lake Expedition when he went in the War of the Rebellion, I prophesied for him a successful career. He rose to be the colonel of his regiment, and died a few years ago a captain of the regular army.

"But time fails me to name all who deserve honourable mention. I cannot close, however, without paying a few words of tribute to Major William Williams, who commanded the expedition. Having been the sutler of the battalion of regulars which was stationed at Fort Dodge, he knew something of the movements and sustenance of troops. He had the ability to make that knowledge available. There was a quiet, confident air in his deportment that commanded respect, and he moved those undisciplined men as quietly and as orderly as would have been possible by an experienced soldier. I have never thought that full justice had been done to the man who led this expedition, and who in many ways proved his interest and faith in the pioneers of northwestern Iowa.

" So I have turned aside, here and now, to speak a tardy word in recognition of his many noble qualities. He was born in Westmoreland County, Pennsylvania, December 5, 1796, and died at Fort Dodge, February 26, 1874, and at the date of these events was in the sixty-second year of his age. He was reared a banker, and for years was cashier of the branch of the Exchange Bank of Pittsburg, located at Holidaysburg. But he had been an open-handed, generous giver; had no innate love of gain; so he lost money instead of making accumulations, and sought the great West to rebuild his broken fortunes. Now he was a man well advanced in years. It was not easy for younger men to complain of hardships of the march when, day by day, they saw him resolutely pushing forward.

"The action of Hamilton County in thus inscribing his name upon an enduring tablet is a silent protest against the neglect and oversight of his own county, and the town which was the idol of his affection. Emerson has said that 'they who forget the battles of their country will have to fight them over again.' So they who forget the unselfish deeds of their countrymen will themselves be unworthy of a place in history. Next to a hero is the man who can appreciate a hero. All honour then to the citizens of a county that in these 'piping times of peace' can pause for a day and step out of the busy channel of commerce to gather some of the names of a generation of self-sacrificing pioneers into history's golden urn."

******

A few extracts from Mr. Laughlin's account written for the same occasion as the others will make some points a little plainer, especially as to how the party came to divide up and how they got together again after crossing the river.

The major's parting injunction was, "Boys, keep together, whatever happens." But this advice was easier given than followed. The first division was at the Gardner cabin when the party of seven refused to venture across the prairie over a route which none of the party knew anything about, and insisted on returning by the same route they went up, which was to strike the river at Emmet, cross there and go down on the east side.

******

The second division was when the party reached Mud Creek, and is told by Mr. Laughlin as follows:

"About noon we came to a large stream and had to follow up and down some time before finding a crossing. Two of our men, Robert McCormick and Owen Spencer, went far above and crossed and separated from us, but finally succeeded in getting through to the colony in safety. . . . .Late in the afternoon we came to some small lakes with some scattering trees on the opposite side. By this time the wind changed suddenly and it began to grow colder. . . . The lake was apparently between us and the course we ought to take and we followed close around the shore. Off to the west side lay a large marsh covered with tall grass. Those in advance passed between marsh and lake and succeeded in getting around, when we discovered that Captain Johnson, Burkholder, Addington, George Smith and one other

(Jonas Murray), five men in all, had dropped off in our rear and were going around the marsh.

"We expected they would return to us when they got around, but as it was growing dark and we could still see them on high ground beyond, we thought best to try and go to them, as Major Williams' parting advice was 'stick together, boys,' but they soon passed out of our sight into the darkness. We then retraced our steps, passed the south end of the lake, and travelled directly east..... We travelled until about nine o'clock, when we halted, finding we were making but little headway, having to meander ponds and wade streams that were fast freezing, and decided to go no further until morning. Soon the most of us were tumbled down in a promiscuous heap, lying close to keep one another warm, on the naked, burned prairie. Our pants were a sheet of ice. Some had blankets, but many only their wet clothes.

"Lieutenant Maxwell and myself did not lie down during that terrible night, but kept tramping around and occasionally rousing the sleepers and making them stir around to keep from freezing. I expected we would all be frozen before morning. I had taken my socks off the day before and wrung them out and carried them in my pocket and as soon as we halted I pulled off my boots, replaced my socks and put (in my boots again. I thus saved my feet and I got through without freezing any part. The following morning the sun was clear and we were in sight of timber directly east, eight or ten miles away. I was among the last to leave our camping ground. I remember picking up one empty provision sack and following on.

"I soon overtook Mr. Carse, the oldest and best clad man in our party, having double mackinaw blankets and a fur overcoat. He was on the sunny side of a gopher hill trying to put on his boots which he had pulled off at night. I passed him without a thought that they were frozen so that he could not get them on. The ponds and also the streams where there was not much current were frozen, so they bore our weight. Most of the men made a bee line, wading streams, running slush ice, but I was more fortunate, being long and light; by seeking places that were iced over and crawling at full length I got over without getting wet. Elias Kellogg and myself were first getting to the timber. I immediately went about starting a fire. I had no matches and neither had the others. My gun was empty and my powder dry, so I put a charge of powder in my gun and loaded with some cotton from out of my vest lining. I discharged it into some rotten wood, which caught, and by pouring on more powder and with vigorous blowing

I succeeded in starting a fire.

"Lieutenant Maxwell was among the first to get to the timber, and by the time we got our fire well to going most of the boys had straggled in. Mr. Carse came in last, led by Henry Dally, a mere boy poorly clad, whom Mr. Carse had befriended by taking him under his double blankets that night. Carse had his boots in his hands and was ill and delirious. The soles of his feet were worn out walking on the frozen ground. Kellogg was the next object of attention. He had seated himself by a tree and was almost helpless and unconscious of his misery. We had to arouse him and cut his frozen overalls away. Had he been left alone he would probably have never risen from his condition. With a good fire we were soon warmed.... The river had to be crossed. It was high and full of floating ice, but we got some long poles and with this help crossed from one cake of ice to another and reached the other side..... No sooner was the advance party over than the others all followed, and when we gained the open ground on the other side, we could see the colony as conjectured, and footsore and weary as we were, we soon made the distance.

"We found Major Williams and a part of the men there waiting for us, with much anxiety. Major Williams had made preparations for us. Fresh beef from the poor settlers' poorer oxen was cooked and ready..... The next morning Smith, Addington and Murray came. They had been to another cabin further on, and finding some provision, had stayed all night. They stated that they had separated from Captain Johnson and Burkholder early the previous morning; that they had taken their boots off at night and they were frozen so they could not get them on, and while they were cutting up their blankets and getting them on their feet they had disagreed as to the course to be taken. Pulling off their boots was a fatal mistake. To reach the place where their bones were found eleven years afterwards, they must have travelled all that day and part of the next night, and have lain down together in the sleep that knows no awakening."

******

From the foregoing extract it will be noticed that the way in which the party broke up and the members became separated was about as follows: First, Spencer and McCormick left the main body when they reached Mud Creek in Lloyd township, they going up the creek to find a better crossing. Where they crossed or how they crossed the Des Moines is not now known, but they were the first to reach the settlement. The next break was late in the afternoon, when on reaching a large marsh the main body passed it on the east, while Johnson, Burkholder, Smith, Addington and Murray passed to the west of it. They did not come together again that night, but were within hailing distance of each other. Murray was a trapper, had visited the lakes the year before and claimed to know something of the country, but proved a poor guide. Johnson and Burkholder separated from the other three sometime in the forenoon of the second day, going southeast, about parallel with the Des Moines River. How Smith, Addington and Murray got in has already been told, also the main body under Maxwell and Laughlin. The great wonder is that any of them lived through that terrible experience.

The October number of *Annals of Iowa* for 1898, contains several accounts of this trip written by different members of the expedition. Ex-Governor C. C. Carpenter, Hon. J. F. Buncombe, Captain C. B. Richards, Lieutenant J. N. Maxwell, W. K. Laughlin, Michael Sweeney and Frank Mason are each represented in that publication. Harris Hoover also wrote an account which appeared in the *Hamilton Freeman* during the summer of 1857. He afterwards revised it and it was published in *The Annals*. These several accounts agree in all of the main incidents, and yet each one notices something that is overlooked by the rest. Taking them collectively they give a full and intelligent summary of the facts of this the most remarkable expedition connected with the history of Iowa.

Chapter 9

The Attack and Defence

The last mention made of Inkpadutah's band was that they were camped at Heron Lake preparatory to their attack on Springfield. This is so closely connected with the massacre at the lakes that the story of one is incomplete without the other. According to Mrs. Sharp's account there were two other bands of Indians in addition to Inkpadutah's who were hovering along the western border of Iowa and Minnesota. She says:

> In the fall of 1856 a small party of Indians came and pitched their tents in the neighbourhood of Springfield. There was also a larger band, under the chieftainship of Ishtahaba, or Sleepy Eye, encamped at Big Island Grove on the same river.

The "Big Island Grove" here referred to is the same one mentioned by Major Williams in his official report, and also by Lieutenant Maxwell and Harris Hoover in their accounts of the expedition. It is none other than the grove on the north side of High Lake in Emmet County.

When Major Williams' force was on the march it was currently reported that Sleepy Eye was encamped with a large body of Indians at this grove, and as the expedition neared the place the scouts were doubled and extra precautions taken. Upon arriving there evidences were plenty of the recent occupation of the place by the Indians, but nothing to indicate the presence of a large party. The lookout and the abandoned campfire, mentioned by Lieutenant Maxwell, were there, also a canoe partly finished which the Indians were making from a black walnut log. Everything went to prove that Indians had been there but not in large numbers, and it is highly probable that the force under Sleepy Eye has been greatly exaggerated.

It is said that these Indians were on friendly terms with the whites during the winter. To how great an extent they were concerned in the troubles that afterward occurred is not fully known, but that they knew of the massacre at the lakes and participated in the attack on Springfield and shared in the plunder is pretty generally believed, Mrs. Sharp, in referring to events preceding the attack, says:

> On the twentieth of March two strange and suspicious looking Indians visited Wood's store and purchased a keg of powder, some shot, lead, baskets, beads and other trinkets. Each of them had a double barrelled gun, a tomahawk and a knife, and one, a very tall Indian, was painted black—so said one who saw them. . . . . Soon afterward Black Buffalo, one of the Springfield Indians, said to the whites that the Indians who were at the store told his squaw that they had killed all of the people at Spirit Lake.

Shortly after this the Springfield Indians left, but before going they told the whites that Inkpadutah's band had started for the Big Sioux and that there was no danger from them. During all of this time Inkpadutah was encamped at Heron Lake, preparatory to his attack on Springfield, which was made on Friday the twenty-seventh of March.

The settlement consisted of the Wood brothers, who were keeping a kind of general store and trading alike with the Indians and whites, and the families of Mr. Thomas, Stewart, Wheeler, Doctor Strong, Doctor Skinner, Smith, and one or two others. Mr. Markham, after making the discovery of the massacre at the lakes, made his way to Springfield and was at the house of Mr. Thomas at the time of the attack. It was he who carried the news of the massacre at the lakes and the people acted on his information in making preparations for defence and safety. On hearing of the trouble at the lakes, several families congregated at the house of Mr. Thomas for mutual protection, and several other persons assembled at the cabin of Mr. Wheeler for the same purpose.

Two trusty messengers, Charles Tretts and Henry Chiffen, were dispatched to Fort Ridgley, with a petition setting forth the massacre at the lakes, their defenceless condition and asking for aid. Fort Ridgley is located some seventy-five miles to the north of Jackson, and at that time there was no trail nor any settlement at any point on the route. They made the trip on snow shoes and it can easily be imagined that it was no picnic. They had not yet returned when the attack was made on the settlement, but were hourly expected. When the people on the Des Moines first heard of the massacre at the lakes they were filled with anxiety and apprehension, but as the time wore on and the attack failed to materialize they began to have some hopes that they would be spared, at least until they could receive government aid. Two weeks had now passed since they had heard of the trouble, and during this time they had kept continually on the alert, determined to make what resistance they were able in case of an attack.

Opinion seems to have been somewhat divided as to the probability of an attack. The Wood brothers, with whom the Springfield Indians had done considerable trading during the winter, would not believe the reports of the massacre. They had also traded with Inkpadutah's band when on their way down the Little Sioux the fall before, and scouted the idea of there being any danger. Indeed they carried this feeling to such an extent that some of the settlers accused them of being in league with the Indians. So positive were they that there was no danger that, against the remonstrance of the settlers, they sold the Indians ammunition only a few days before the outbreak, receiving in payment money that had doubtless been taken from the victims of the Spirit Lake Massacre.

As before noted, the attack was made on the afternoon of the twenty-seventh of March. It seems that the men of the party who were forted up at the Thomas cabin had been cutting and hauling wood during the day and had come in about three o'clock in the afternoon for their dinners, and after eating dinner were sitting around the fire talking and smoking when the attack occurred, the details of which are given in the graphic account written by Hon. Charles Aldrich, which is given in the following pages. Had the attack been made two hours earlier, while the men were in the timber at work, in all probability the entire settlement would have been wiped out.

The attack on Wood's place was doubtless made before that at Thomas'. Mrs. Sharp says:

> The confidence of William Wood in the friendship of the Indians proved altogether a delusion. He was one of the first who fell. It appears that after he was killed the Indians heaped brush upon his body and set fire to it. His brother, George, had evidently attempted to escape, but was overtaken by the Indians in the woods and shot down.

It will be remembered that the Wood brothers were the owners of the dry goods store robbed by the Indians. The Indians must have been divided into two parties, as Mr. Stewart's and Mr. Thomas' places were attacked about the same time. An Indian well known to the settlers, who had always professed to be friendly, went to the home of Mr. Stewart and wanted to buy a hog. Mr. Stewart started to go with him to the pen, when concealed Indians fired on him, killing him instantly. The balance of Mr. Stewart's family were then dispatched, with the exception of the oldest child, a boy about eight years old, who escaped by hiding behind a log, where he remained until after the savages left. He then made his way to the Thomas cabin, arriving shortly after the Indians had been repulsed at that point.

The following article on the defence at Springfield, and the heroic conduct of John Bradshaw, and the bravery of Mrs. Church, was written by the Hon. Charles Aldrich and read by him before the meeting for inauguration of Memorial Tablet at Webster City, in August, 1887:

> We have placed conspicuously on this beautiful tablet the names of Mrs. William L. Church and her sister, Miss Drusilla Swanger, with a high tribute to those heroines. Why we have done this I will briefly explain. Not many months before the massacre, the Churches had settled at Springfield, Minnesota, some fifteen miles from Spirit Lake, and about eight miles north of the Iowa line. They resided there when Inkpadutah's band so terribly raided the little settlement at Spirit Lake. Of this massacre Mrs. Abbie Gardner Sharp gives a full and most vivid narration in her book. At that time, in the absence of Mr. Church to this county (Hamilton), his wife was living in their log house with her two little boys and her sister.
>
> When the news came to this settlement of four or five families of the murders at Spirit Lake, the people assembled at the home of Mr. Thomas, one of the settlers, and prepared to defend themselves. This was what is called a double log house, quite a large building for that locality at that day, and standing in the margin of the oak grove, not far from the west branch of the Des Moines River. There were in the party Mr. Thomas, his wife and five children; Mrs. Church, her two children and sister; Mrs. Strong and two children. Miss Eliza Gardner, Jared Palmer, David Carver and John Bradshaw. . . . . Just after they had assembled, two young men, whose names I have forgotten, volunteered to go on foot to Fort Ridgley, seventy-five miles

away, and appeal for aid. Those who were left were well armed, reasonably provisioned, stout of heart and determined to make the best defence in their power if they should be assailed.

A week had nearly passed when little Willie Thomas, aged nine, came running in, exclaiming that the boys were coming who had gone for the soldiers. This was good news, and the people rushed to the door, forming a little group just outside. Sure enough two men were seen coming dressed like whites, but they were Indians in the clothing of men killed at Spirit Lake. Just then the main party of the Indians, who were approaching from another direction, fired a volley from a dozen pieces into the group of men, women and children near the door. Willie Thomas was shot through the head and fell to the ground; Miss Swanger was shot through the shoulder, inflicting a severe flesh wound; Thomas was shot through the left arm, which was broken and bled profusely; Carver was shot in the body, and for a time suffered the severest pain.

All except the wounded boy rushed into the house and speedily barricaded the doors and windows. In fact the poor boy seems to have been forgotten for the instant, but it mattered little in the result. The firing on both sides now became hot and frequent and continued so for two or three hours. Portholes were made on the four sides of the house by removing the chinking from between the logs. Through these the besieged could plainly see the Indians without exposing themselves. Whenever an Indian showed himself he was fired upon and so they were held at bay. Several times, however, the red devils made a rush toward the house, which they wished to set on fire, but each time discretion proved the better part of valour and they fell back. During this time the condition of things in this remote little fortress can scarcely be imagined or described.

Miss Swanger and Mr. Thomas were bleeding profusely from their wounds, while the little wounded boy lay shrieking and groaning outside. The little fellow lived about two hours, when death mercifully ended his sufferings. At one time the poor mother feared her husband would bleed to death in spite of everything she could do, while the shrieks and groans of the dying boy just outside the door could be distinctly heard. Miss Swanger at first bled very freely, but Mrs. Church stuffed her handkerchief under her sister's dress and so stopped the flow of blood, while Mrs. Thomas bound up her husband's arm and stopped the bleeding, which otherwise would have ended his life. Mrs. Church and Miss Gardner loaded the guns and kept watch at some of the portholes. At one time it was thought their bullets would be exhausted, and Misses Swanger and Gardner cast some from an old iron spoon.

The fight went on until the dusk of evening was beginning to come on. It then happened that Mrs. Church and Miss Gardner were in one of the rooms watching while the men were in the other. They now saw an Indian dodging behind a large oak tree. While here he kept peering out toward the house. No man was handy to 'draw a bead' upon him and Mrs. Church picked up a shotgun heavily charged with buckshot and levelled it in that direction. Presently he stuck his head out again farther than before. Mrs. Church says, 'I plainly saw a large dark object by the side of the tree, which I knew to be the head of an Indian, and at this I discharged the gun. I was terribly excited and fell back and cannot tell you whether I hit him or not. I certainly wanted to kill him.' Miss Gardner, who was watching the Indian, averred that she plainly saw him fall.

In the account written at my instance for the Hamilton Freeman, by Jareb Palmer, who was one of the besieged, he states it as at fact that Mrs. Church killed the Indian..... A year or more later the body of an Indian was found upon a rude platform in a tree top, tree burial being the custom of the tribe. The body was then wrapped in a buffalo robe and some white woman's feather pillow was under his head. What was left of this dusky brave was tumbled down upon the ground by the men of H. B. Martin's command, from our county. The skull was brought to me and I sent it to the Phrenological collection of Fowler and Wells, New York City.

I saw it there some time later with a notice which had appeared in the Freeman pasted across the forehead. Upon the return of some of the men to the locality a few months later the tree was examined and part of the charge of buckshot was still imbedded in it near the spot where Mrs. Church had aimed and the other part had plainly passed on. It would thus seem to be settled as nearly as such an event can be proven that she killed one of the assailants.

Immediately after this event the Indians ceased firing and left

Mrs. S. J. Church

the place.....

One of the settlers, a man named Stewart, with his wife and three children, had been stopping at the Thomas house. Fort Thomas it really deserves to be called henceforth, but the poor wife and mother became insane through her fears of the Indians, and being in such a crowd of people added to her discomfort and mental trouble. Her husband finally concluded to return to their own house a mile or so distant, believing the danger had passed away. But the same band which had invested the Thomas house came to Stewart's. They called him to the door and shot him the instant he appeared. The fiends then murdered the insane mother and the two little girls. The boy, Johnny, who was eight or nine years of age, managed to hide behind a log. The Indians plundered the cabin and soon left. The boy then fled to the double log house, where he was recognised and taken in at one of the windows.

The home of the Churches was also pillaged and everything movable carried away or destroyed. The other houses in the settlement shared the same fate. A span of horses was in the barn at the Thomas place, but the Indians took them away when they left. When darkness came at last, the besieged determined to start south toward the nearest settlement with an ox team and sled, which was the only means left them. The oxen were yoked, hitched to the sled upon which were placed the wounded, the little children and such provisions and clothing as could be carried. The forlorn little party, with this poor means of locomotion, probably started near the middle of the night, travelling very slowly, as the ground was covered with snow.

Mrs. Church and her sister each led or carried one of her little boys. The march was kept up until the oxen tired out, when there was a short rest. Progress was very slow and most wearisome for some two days. Finally on the third day they saw several men approaching from the south, whom they mistook for Indians.

This was a trying time for the poor refugees. The men, who were rapidly advancing upon them, wore shawls, which made them look like Indians with blankets. Then it was evident that they were well armed. Some of the women and children were wild with affright, and gave utterance to shrieks and lamentations. Two of the men were helpless from wounds, and another was not naturally an Indian fighter, though doubtless brave enough. John Bradshaw thought his time had come, but far from flinching, he took their eight loaded guns and stacked them some rods in advance. He asked the other well men to stay with the women and children and wounded and keep them from embarrassing him and he would sell his life as dearly as possible. Thus the dauntless hero stood until he saw a signal from the advancing party and knew they were friends.

When the latter came up his face was pale as ashes, but no one doubted that he would have fought while life lasted. We can well imagine that men can be brave when surrounded by other brave men, whatever the odds. But what a grand figure was that of our Hamilton County Bradshaw, going out alone to yield up his life, as he supposed, in so hopeless a fight with merciless savages. It seems to me that that was a scene for a painter or sculptor, and that some time it will be placed upon canvas or in imperishable marble for the adornment of our magnificent Capitol. Where did you ever read of anything more grandly heroic? The terrible alarm was turned in an instant into an abandonment of equally wild rejoicing, for the comers were a detachment from the expedition under Major Williams, and Mr. Church was with them. Mrs. Church and her young sister had worn their dresses off to the knees in walking through the crusted snow, and their shoes were nearly gone. They were almost exhausted from the toilsome march, lack of food, exposure to the inclement weather, and the terrible anxieties of the preceding week.

But I need take no more time with this narrative. The Churches returned to this county, where they resided until the spring of this year (1887), when they went to Washington Territory, whither two of their children and Miss Swanger (now Mrs. Gillispie) had preceded them. Mr. Church was also a soldier of the Union army as well as a veteran of the Mexican War. All who have known them will agree with me that the permanent record of their actions and sufferings, the heroism of these matchless women in our pioneer days, has been well deserved.

Chapter 10

The Pursuit

The next day after the attack on the settlement and the day before the Indians broke camp at Heron Lake, and while the refugees were slowly making their way through snow and slush into Iowa, the messengers, who had been sent to Fort Ridgley for aid, returned, accompanied by a company of regular troops under the command of Captain Bee and Lieutenant Murray. Could they have arrived thirty hours earlier the Springfield massacre would have been prevented, and possibly the savages brought to justice. But that was not to be. In point of suffering, hardships and privation the trip of this band of regulars from Fort Ridgley was the counterpart of that of Major Williams' volunteers from Fort Dodge, and on their arrival they were well nigh exhausted.

Judge Flandrau, in writing of this expedition, says:

> The people of Springfield sent two young men to my agency with the news of the massacre. They brought with them a statement of the facts as related by Mr, Markham, signed by some persons with whom I was acquainted. They came on foot and arrived at the agency on the eighteenth of March. The snow was very deep and was beginning to thaw, which made the travelling extremely difficult. When these young men arrived they were so badly attacked with snow blindness that they could scarcely see at all and were completely worn out. I was fully satisfied of the truth of the report that murders had been committed, although the details of course were very meagre. I at once held a consultation with Colonel Alexander, commanding the Tenth United States Infantry, five or six companies of which were at Fort Ridgley. The colonel, with commendable promptness, or-

dered Captain Barnard E. Bee with his company to proceed at once to the scene of the massacre and do all he could, either in the way of protecting the settlers or punishing the enemy.

The country between the Minnesota River at Ridgley and Spirit Lake was, at that day, an utter wilderness, without an inhabitant. In fact, none of us knew where Spirit Lake was, except that it lay about due south of the fort at a distance of from one hundred to one hundred and twenty-five miles. We procured two guides of experience among our Sioux half-breeds. . . . These men took a pony and a light train to carry the blankets and provisions, put on their snowshoes and were ready to go anywhere, while the poor troops, with their leather shoes and their backloads, accompanied by a ponderous army wagon on wheels, drawn by six mules, were about as fit for such a march as an elephant is for a ballroom. But it was the best the government had, and they entered upon the arduous duty bravely and cheerfully. . . . . We started on March nineteenth, at about one o'clock, p. m., at first intending to go straight across the country, but we soon decided that course to be utterly impossible, as the mules could not draw the wagon through the deep snow.

It became apparent that our only hope of reaching the lake was to follow the road down by the way of New Ulm to Mankato, and trust to luck for a road up the Watonwan in the direction of the lake, we having learned that some teams had recently started for that place with some supplies. The first days of the march were appalling. The men were wet nearly up to their waists with the deep and melting snow and utterly weary before they had gone ten miles.

Neither of the officers had ever made a snow camp before and when we had dug out a place for our first camp and were making futile efforts to dry our clothes before turning in for the night, I felt that the trip was hopeless. So much time had elapsed since the murders were committed, and so much more would necessarily be consumed before the troops could possibly reach the lake, that I felt assured that no good could result from going on. I told Captain Bee that if he wanted to return I would furnish him with a written opinion of two of the most experienced *voyageurs* on the frontier that the march was impossible of accomplishment with the inappropriate outfit with which the troops were furnished. . . . . The captain agreed with me that the chances of accomplishing any good by going on were very small, but he read his orders and in answer to my suggestion, 'My orders are to go to Spirit Lake and do what I can. It is not for me to interpret them but to obey them. I shall go on until it becomes physically impossible to proceed further. Then it will be time to turn back.' And go on he did. We followed the trail up the Watonwan until we found the teams that had made it stuck in a snow drift, and for the remaining forty or fifty miles the troops marched ahead of the mules and broke a road for them, relieving the front rank every fifteen or twenty minutes.

When the lake was reached the Indians were gone. A careful examination was made of their camp and fires by the guides, who pronounced them three or four days old. Their trail led to the west. A pursuit was made by a portion of the command, partly mounted on mules land partly on foot, but it was soon abandoned on the declaration of the guides that the Indians were by the signs several days in advance.

I learned afterwards by Mrs. Marble, one of the rescued women, that the troops in pursuit came so near that, the Indians saw them and made an ambush for them, and had they not turned back the prisoners would have all been murdered. The guides may have been mistaken or they may have deceived the troops. I knew the young men so well that I never have accused them of a betrayal of their trust, but it was probably best as it was in either case, because had the troops overtaken the Indians the women would have certainly been butchered and some of the soldiers killed. The satisfaction of having killed some of the Indians would not have compensated for this result.

The Indians were absent from their camp at Heron Lake in making their attack on Springfield two days, when they returned laden with plunder. Mrs. Sharp says:

> They had twelve horses heavily laden with dry goods, groceries, powder, lead, bed quilts, wearing apparel, provisions, etc. Among this plunder were several bolts of calico and red flannel. Of these, especially the flannel, they were exceedingly proud, decorating themselves with it in fantastic fashion. Red leggings, red shirts, red blankets and red in every conceivable way was the style there as long as it lasted.

The next morning after their return from the attack on Springfield, they broke camp at Heron Lake and started west with their prisoners and plunder.

The incidents of this weary march through the melting snows and across swollen streams are vividly portrayed by Mrs. Sharp in her thrilling narrative, but are too lengthy to be given here in detail. A few of the main events will be briefly noticed. The Indians must have been very deliberate in their movements from place to place after leaving their Heron Lake camp, or rather after the pursuit was abandoned. According to Mrs. Sharp's account they were six weeks in making the journey from Heron Lake to the place of crossing the Big Sioux, near the present town of Flandrau. Now, the distance from Heron Lake to Flandrau is not far from one hundred miles, so their progress could not have averaged more than twenty miles a week.

It has already been stated that Captain Bee's company of regulars arrived from Fort Ridgley the day before the Indians broke camp at Heron Lake. Their terrible hardships and sufferings on that trip have already been referred to. They were in no condition to pursue the savages, yet it seemed imperative they should make the attempt. Accordingly after one day's rest at Springfield they started on the trail. Heron Lake is between fifteen and twenty miles west of Springfield. By looking up and comparing dates it will be ascertained that the Indians left their camp at Heron Lake on the morning of the twenty-ninth. The soldiers arrived at Springfield on the evening of the twenty-eighth, resting over the twenty-ninth, and started west after the Indians the morning of the thirtieth. Thus it will be seen that the Indians had one day plus the distance between Springfield and Heron Lake the start of the troops.

These regulars were but little better prepared for such a campaign than were Major Williams' volunteers and were not nearly as much in earnest about it. They had two half-breed guides, Joe Gaboo and Joseph La Frombone. Gaboo had a full-blooded Indian wife. It was suspected at the time, and subsequent events seen to confirm the suspicion, that these guides were more interested in the escape of the Indians than in their capture or punishment.

The soldiers pressed on at a rapid rate, and at about three o'clock in the afternoon they reached the grove where the Indians with their prisoners had camped the preceding night and left that morning. This grove they surrounded, expecting to find the Indians there and intending to close in upon and capture them. In this they were disappointed. The Indians had left about nine hours before. The guides upon examining the campfires and the trails about the camp declared that they were two or three days old, and that the Indians had that much the start. If such was the case, it was evident that further pursuit would be useless. Accordingly the expedition was abandoned and they turned back to Springfield.

The actual facts were that the Indians kept scouts in the rear to cover their retreat, and these scouts saw the troops when they first made their appearance at their abandoned camp, and kept close watch of all of their movements. The main body of the Indians were hurried forward into a ravine or creek bottom, where they awaited results.

When the Indians were first aware that they were being pursued, the wildest excitement prevailed among them. They had just gone into camp when the troops were first discovered. The tents were immediately taken down, the campfires extinguished and the whole camp moved further down the ravine. A guard was set over the prisoners with orders to kill them in case of an attack. One Indian had climbed a tree, which stood on some high ground, where he could watch and report the movements of the soldiers. It seems that these events were taking place in the Indian camp just at the time that the soldiers were counselling whether they would continue the pursuit or turn back. In all probability the prisoners would all have been murdered there and then had the pursuit not been abandoned just as it was.

The details of this flight and pursuit are given at length by Mrs. Sharp, and form an interesting chapter, at the close of which she says:

> Whether the guides were true or false or whether or not the soldiers were justified in turning back it was life to us as captives.

After the Indians became satisfied that further pursuit was not probable, they moved forward with all the haste possible, encumbered as they were with their prisoners and their plunder. Mrs. Sharp further says:

> No time was given us to rest, much less to prepare any food, till some time next day, and we did not camp for two days and nights. . . . . Thus ended our flight from the United States soldiers, and their attempt to rescue us only made our situation more terrible.

As before stated, the Indians started westward the next morning after their pursuit was abandoned, going by way of the great Pipestone quarry, which is located in Pipestone County, Minnesota. Here they rested a short time and busied themselves in gathering pipestone 'and making pipes, after which they resumed their journey, arriving at the Big Sioux about the last of April or the first of May. Of this event Mrs. Sharp writes as follows:

> After six weeks of incessant marching over the trackless prairie and through the deep snow, across creeks, sloughs, rivers and lakes, we reached the Big Sioux at or about the point where now stands the town of Flandrau. Most of the journey had been performed in cold and inclement weather, but now spring seemed to have come. The vast amount of snow which covered the ground that memorable winter had nearly gone by reason of the rapid thawing during the last few weeks, causing the river to rise beyond all ordinary bounds and assume majestic proportions.

It was in crossing this stream that Mrs. Thatcher was murdered. Mrs. Sharp's account is too long to be reproduced in full here, but some extracts will be given. Mrs. Thatcher's health was more delicate and she had suffered more than the other prisoners during their long, tedious march, and during a portion of the time she had not been compelled to carry a pack as the other prisoners had. During the last few days she had partially recovered and was therefore compelled to carry her pack as before. It seems that at the point where the party reached the river a bridge of driftwood had formed across the stream over which a person with clear head and steady step could cross with tolerable safety.

> On such a bridge we were to cross the now swollen waters. As we were about to follow the Indians across one of these uncertain bridges where a single misstep might plunge us into the deep waters, an Indian, not more than sixteen years old who had always manifested a great degree of hatred and contempt for the whites, approached us and taking the pack from Mrs. Thatcher's shoulders and placing it on his own, ordered us forward. This seeming kindness at once aroused our suspicions. When we reached the centre of the swollen stream, as we anticipated, this insolent young savage pushed Mrs. Thatcher from the bridge into the ice cold water, but by what seemed supernatural strength, she breasted the dreadful torrent, and making a

last struggle for life, reached the shore which had just been left, and was clinging to the root of a tree at the bank. She was here met by some of the other Indians who were just coming upon the scene. They commenced throwing clubs at her and with long poles shoved her back into the angry stream.

As if nerved by dread of such a death she made another desperate effort for life, and doubtless would have gained the shore, but here again she was met by her merciless tormentors and was beaten off as before. She was then carried down by the furious, boiling current of the Sioux, while the Indians on either side of the stream were running along the banks, whooping and yelling, and throwing sticks and stones at her until she reached another bridge. Here she was finally shot by one of the Indians in another division of the band, who was crossing with another division of the captives some distance below.

Reviewing these events in the light of present conditions and surroundings, the strange thing about the whole matter is that any one of those four captives bore up for a single week under the extreme suffering and hardships to which they were exposed. Just think of it! Wet to the waist every day from walking through the snow and slush, indifferently clothed, nearly starved, often going two days without anything to eat, compelled to carry a pack, which would test the endurance of a strong man. All this they had now endured for over six weeks.

American history furnishes no parallel to their suffering and endurance; language fails to describe them; the intellect fails to grasp them,—and the end is not yet. True, spring had come, and the condition of the unfortunate captives was somewhat alleviated. But they still had a long, tedious road to travel, and many dangers and vicissitudes through which to pass.

After crossing the Big Sioux they continued their march westward into Dakota. In their wanderings they frequently met roving bands of Sioux with whom they always seemed to be on good terms. It has been claimed by the Indians and their apologists that Inkpadutah's band were not annuity Indians, but that they were regarded as outlaws, and were not fellowshipped by the agency Indians. This certainly could not have been true to any great extent. Mrs. Sharp saw nothing of the kind while she was with them. On the contrary, she says:

Whenever we met any of the other bands our captors would

go over the story of their achievements by word and gesture and the display of booty, giving a vivid description of the affair, reproducing in fullest detail even the groans and sighs of the victims. To all this the other Sioux listened not only without any signs of disapprobation, but with every indication of enjoyment and high appreciation.

On the sixth of May, when the Indians were camped at a small lake some thirty miles west of the Big Sioux, their camp was visited by two young Indians from the Yellow Medicine Agency, who, upon seeing the prisoners, took a fancy to them, and after a considerable bantering bought Mrs. Marble, trading guns, blankets, ammunition and such things as they had with them. After completing the trade they started immediately on their return, and after several days weary journeying arrived at the Yellow Medicine Agency. Through the instrumentality of missionaries, Messrs. Riggs and Williamson and Major Flandrau, the Indian Agent, a sum of money amounting to $1,000 was raised and paid to the Indians for her ransom.

It is the generally accepted belief that both of the prisoners, Mrs. Marble and Miss Gardner, were rescued by friendly Indians sent out from the agency for that purpose. But such, it seems, was not the case so far as Mrs. Marble was concerned. The facts connected with her release will be better understood from the following extract from Major Flandrau's report, accompanied by a statement written out for the two Indians by Mr. Riggs. Judge Flandrau says :

> I was engaged in devising plans for the rescue of the captives and the punishment of the Indians in connection with Colonel Alexander of the Tenth Infantry, but had found it very difficult to settle upon any course which would not endanger the safety of the prisoners. We knew that any hostile demonstration would be sure to result in the destruction of the women, and were without means to fit out an expedition for their ransom. While we were deliberating on the best course to pursue, *an accident* opened the way to success.
>
> A party of my Indians were hunting on the Big Sioux River, and having learned that Inkpadutah's band was at Lake Chauptayatonka, about thirty miles west of the river, and also knowing of the fact that they held some white women prisoners, two young men (brothers) visited the camp and after much talk they succeeded in purchasing Mrs. Marble. They paid for her all

they possessed and brought her into the agency and delivered her into the hands of the missionaries stationed at that point. She was at once turned over to me with a written statement from the two Indians who had brought her, which was prepared for them at their request by Mr. Riggs, who spoke their language fluently. I will allow them to tell their own story.

It was as follows: 'Hon. C. E. Flandrau: Father. In our spring hunt, when encamped at the north end of Big Wood on the Sioux River, we learned from some Indians who came to us, that we were not far from Red End's camp. *Of our own accord, and contrary to the advice of all about us,* we concluded to visit them, thinking that possibly we might be able to obtain one or more of the white women held by them as prisoners. We found them encamped at Chauptayatonka Lake, about thirty miles west of our own camp. We were met at some distance from their lodges by four men armed with revolvers, who demanded of us our business.

'After satisfying them that we were not spies and had no evil intentions in regard to them we were taken into Inkpadutah's Lodge. The night was spent in reciting their massacre, etc. It was not until the next morning that we ventured to ask for one of the women. Much time was spent in talking and it was not until the middle of the afternoon did we obtain their consent to our proposition. We paid for her all we had. We brought her to our mother's tent, clothed her as we were able, and fed her bountifully on the best we had—duck and corn. We brought her to Lac qui Parle, and now, father, after having her with us fifteen days, we place her in your hands. It was perilous business, for which we think we should be liberally rewarded. We claim for our services $500 each.'.... This communication was signed by the Indians and witnessed by the missionary, Mr. Riggs.

Judge Flandrau adds:

By the action of these Indians we not only got one of the captives but we learned for the first time definitely the whereabouts of the marauders and the assurance that the other women were still alive as these Indians had seen them in Red End's camp.

It will be seen from the foregoing extracts that the release of Mrs. Marble was not the result of any preconcerted plan worked out by the government officers, but was styled by Judge Flandrau himself a "lucky accident."

About four weeks after the release of Mrs. Marble, while Inkpadutah's band were roaming over the prairies, they fell in with a small party of Yanktons. Their leader, after some bantering, purchased both of the prisoners from Inkpadutah. His object was simply to make money by selling them to the whites, but he didn't seem to be in any particular hurry to realise on his investment. Instead of starting at once for the settlements, as the purchasers of Mrs. Marble had done, he continued to journey with Inkpadutah's party in their aimless wanderings. One evening, a few days after the purchase. Roaring Cloud, a son of Inkpadutah, came to the tent of the Yankton and in a fit of rage dragged Mrs. Noble from the tent and regardless of the protests of her Yankton owner, seized a club and murdered her on the spot. Of this event Mrs. Sharp writes as follows:

> The next morning the warriors gathered around the already mangled corpse and amused themselves by making it a target to shoot at. To this show of barbarism I was brought out and compelled to stand a silent witness. Faint and sick at heart, I at length turned away from the dreadful sight without their orders to do so, and started off on the day's march expecting they would riddle me with their bullets, but why should I escape more than others? But for some unaccountable reason I was spared. After going a short distance I looked back and they were still around her, using their knives cutting off her hair and mutilating her body. . . . . At last the bloody camp was deserted and the mangled body left lying on the ground unburied. Her hair, in two heavy braids, just as she had arranged it, was tied to the end of a stick, perhaps three feet long, and during the day as I wearily and sadly toiled on, one of the young Indians walked by my side and repeatedly slashed me in the face with it, thus adding insult to injury.

If Mrs. Noble could only have escaped the vengeance of Roaring Cloud a few days longer she doubtless would have been set at liberty and restored to civilized society and the companionship of her sister and brothers. . . . Could she only have known the efforts being made for her rescue and how near they already were to success, she would have had courage to endure insults a little longer and hope to bid her look forward. At the very moment when she was dragged from her tent and brutally murdered, rescuers under the direction of the United States Commissioner fully prepared for her ransom were pressing forward with all the dispatch possible.

Mrs. Marble's arrival at the settlement was the first intimation that had been received of the fate of any of the captives and created great excitement. A deep interest had been manifested in the fate of the prisoners from the first and now that it was definitely known that two of them were still living and in captivity there was a general demand that ample measures be immediately taken for their rescue. Major Flandrau immediately set to work to fit out an expedition for that purpose. He had no government funds at his command, but he and his friends used their own private credit in securing an outfit. Volunteers were not wanting and three trusty scouts were soon selected. In regard to further operations, he says:

> The question of outfit then presented itself and I ran my credit with the traders for the following articles at the prices stated:

	$
Wagon	110.00
4 Horses	600.00
12 3 Point Blankets (4 blue, 8 white)	56.00
32 Yards of Squaw Cloth	44.00
37½ Yards Calico	5.37
20 Lbs. Tobacco	10 00
1 Sack of Shot	4.00
15 lbs. Powder	25.00
Corn	4.00
Flour	10.00
Coffee	1.50
Sugar	1.50

With this outfit, and instructions to give as much of it as was necessary for the women, my expedition started on the twenty-third day of May from Yellow Medicine. I at once left for Fort Ridgley to consult Colonel Alexander as to the plan of operation for an attack upon the camp of Inkpadutah the instant we could get word as to the safety of the white women. The colonel entered into the spirit of the matter with zeal. He had four or five companies at the fort and proposed to put them into the field, so as to approach Skunk Lake, where Inkpadutah had his camp, from several different directions and insure his destruction. If an event which was wholly unforeseen had not occurred, the well laid plan of Colonel Alexander would undoubtedly have succeeded.

But unfortunately for the cause of justice, about the time we began to expect information from my expedition, which was to be the signal for moving on the enemy, an order arrived at the fort commanding the colonel with all his available force to start immediately and join the expedition against the Mormons, which was then moving to Utah, under the command of General Sidney Johnston. So peremptory was the command that the steamboat that brought the order carried off the entire garrison of the fort and put an end to all hopes of our being able to punish the enemy.

So it will be seen that the blame for not adopting more energetic measures to secure, capture and punish the Indians cannot be laid upon the commandant at Fort Ridgley, nor the agent at Yellow Medicine. Whatever induced the War Department to leave the northwestern frontier in this defenceless condition at a time of such imminent danger by withdrawing all the troops for a wild goose chase through Utah after the Mormons is something that cannot be satisfactorily explained. The fort was regarrisoned the latter part of July.

A few days after the murder of Mrs. Noble the Indians with their remaining captive reached the James River, where now is situated the town of Old Ashton in Spink County, South Dakota. Here, on the opposite side of the river, was a powerful Yankton camp of nearly two hundred lodges. These Yanktons had evidently never been in contact with civilization. They were armed with bows and arrows and clubs. Their tents and clothing were manufactured entirely from buffalo hides, and there was absolutely nothing in their appearance to indicate that they had ever had any intercourse with the whites. To them the "white squaw" was a source of much wonderment and they never tired of commenting on and examining her "flaxen hair, blue eyes and light complexion."

They had been in this camp but a few days, and the novelty and excitement of Inkpadutah's coming with a white captive had not yet subsided, when on the thirtieth of May three Indians dressed in white men's clothes came into camp. These Indians were the ones that had been sent out from the agency for the express purpose of securing the release of the remaining prisoners. The death of Mrs. Noble having

Indian Council Negotiating for the Surrender of Miss Gardner.

occurred in the meantime. Miss Gardner was the only one left. Some three or four days were spent in parleying and bantering, when an arrangement was finally reached and the captive was turned over to her new purchasers.

Mrs. Sharp says the price paid for her ransom was two horses, twelve blankets, two kegs of powder, twenty pounds of tobacco, thirty-two yards of squaw cloth, thirty-seven and a half yards of calico, and ribbon and other small articles with which these Indians had been provided by Major Flandrau. As soon as possible after the completion of the transfer the rescuing party crossed the James River and prepared to start at once on their return trip east. They had brought a team of horses and a wagon with them, which they had concealed among the brush and willows on the east side of the river, pending negotiations. In all probability had the Yanktons known they were there they would have insisted on their being added to the purchase price. The party consisted of the three agency Indians sent out by Major Flandrau and two Yanktons from the James River.

Mrs. Sharp's description of her rescue and the return trip are intensely interesting and at times highly dramatic. A few extracts are all that can be given. She says:

> Almost the first move was to cross the James River. I was put into a frail little boat made of buffalo skin stripped of hair and dressed so as to be impervious to water. The boat was not more than five feet long by four wide and incapable of carrying more than one person. When I found I was the only occupant I concluded that the story of the Indian who told me I was to be drowned was after all a true one. . . . . . I was, however, happily disappointed to see my new purchasers divest themselves of their fine clothes and swim across, holding the end of a cable made of buffalo hide which had previously been fastened to the boat. With this they drew the boat with me in it to the eastern shore. Thus, though I knew it not, I was being drawn towards home and friends, and the river was put between me and my cruel foes. . . . Hiding the team and wagon was not only a piece of sharp practice but a wise stroke of policy, and showed diplomacy.
>
> The names of the persons composing this rescue party should be put on record and held in remembrance not alone for this mission but for other humane deeds done by them. They were

Mazaintemani . . . .now familiarly known among the whites as John Other Day, Hotonhowashta or Beautiful Voice, and Chetanmaza or Iron Hawk.

These three Indians were prominent members of the church at the mission station at Yellow Medicine. Other Day was a prominent figure during the Sioux War five years later. Many were the times that he risked his own life in warning the settlers of impending trouble. His services will be referred to again. Chetanmaza or Iron Hawk visited Mrs. Sharp at her home during the summer of 1895 and was present at the dedication of the monument. Of the return trip Mrs. Sharp says:

> The Yankton chief having been placated and I safely towed across the river the team was brought out. The Yanktons filled the wagon with dried buffalo meat and buffalo robes. I was installed driver and the five Indians (three Yellow Medicine and two Yanktons) leading the way in single file we took up our march. . . . . After seven days of incessant travelling we came into a region thickly peopled with Indians.

Two days later they arrived at the home of a half-breed who could speak English. This was the first she knew of her whereabouts or what was to become of her. She here learned that these Indians had been sent out from the agency on purpose to secure her release "and that the long journey with its perils and sacrifices had been made for me." She further says:

> I also learned from this half-breed that Mrs. Marble had been there about a month before and had gone on to St. Paul. After a day and a half spent at the half-breed's trading post in which time I had tried to make myself as presentable as possible, we proceeded to the Yellow Medicine Agency and then to the mission station of Dr. Thomas Williamson.

A scare almost amounting to a panic occurred at the agency about the time of the arrival of Miss Gardner, but in no way connected with her. The trouble was over the delay in paying the Indians their annuities and came near being serious, but the money for the annuities came just in time to save further trouble. Further on Mrs. Sharp says:

> While this dun cloud of war hung over our heads, one of the Yanktons who had accompanied us as an escort from the James

Chetanmaza and his friend

River brought out a beautiful Indian war cap that had been carefully packed away in the wagon without my knowledge. I was seated on a stool in the centre of the room and with great display of Indian eloquence it was presented to me and placed upon my head in the name of the great chief Matowaken. The instructions of the chief were that I should be crowned with it on our first arrival at the abode of the whites and that it should be exhibited when we came into the presence of the Great Father, meaning the Governor of Minnesota. . . . . In the presentation speech it was stated that it was given as a token of respect for the fortitude and bravery I had manifested and it was because of this that Inkpadutah's Indians did not kill me. It was also stated that as long as I retained the cap I would be under the protection of all of the Dacotahs.

From the agency the party passed down the river to Fort Ridgley and thence across the country to Traverse, which was at the time the head of navigation on the Minnesota River, where they embarked on a steamer to St. Paul.

Several pages of Mrs. Sharp's book are devoted to an account of the journey to St. Paul, the audience with the governor, the address to Mazaintemani upon surrendering the captive, the governor's reply, and the address of Major Flandrau, making it one of the most interesting and attractive chapters in the whole volume. The amount paid the Indians was $1,200 or $400 each in addition to the amount paid the Yanktons at the time of her purchase. The leader of the rescuing party always remained the firm friend of the whites and during the terrible days following the massacre of 1862 exerted himself in every possible way to prevent the outrages and protect the settlers.

CHAPTER 11

Government Apathy

The apathy of the government in not attempting to devise some more effectual means for the detection and punishment of this marauding band of savages was much criticised. It was known all summer that the headquarters of the band were at Skunk Lake, in Dakota. What was asked was that another fort be established at some place, say Sioux Falls, and then that troops enough be sent to the frontier to not only secure protection, but to make an aggressive movement practicable. It will be seen that the moves made against these Indians were made by wholly inadequate forces. Could a strong column have been sent out simultaneously from Fort Ridgley, Fort Randall and Sioux Falls, the band could have been captured or destroyed. The feeble attempts that were made by the Indian agent and the commander of the fort were not sanctioned by the Federal authority.

Judge Flandrau and the commandant at the fort did everything they could do with the means at their command, but the War Department seemed to be perfectly indifferent and the only measure proposed by them to accomplish the object was to withhold the annuities from the agency Indians until the outlaws were surrendered. Of course, the agency Indians regarded this as a great wrong. How much it may have had to do with intensifying the hostile feeling existing at the time we don't know; also whether it may be reckoned as one of the factors in precipitating the Minnesota outbreak in 1862, we don't know, but, view it as we may, the stubbornness and stupidity of the War Department at this time are wholly incomprehensible.

Some time in July word was received by Major Flandrau that a portion of Inkpadutah's band were in camp on the Yellow Medicine not far from the agency. Upon holding a consultation with the commandant of the fort it was decided that an effort must be made to capture or destroy them if possible. Accordingly Lieutenant Murray, with a small force of about twenty regulars and as many or more volunteers, was detailed for that service. John Other Day, the same Indian who led the rescuing party that rescued Mrs. Sharp from the Indians, was sent forward as a scout to reconnoitre and ascertain the facts.

This force left Fort Ridgley about dark. They moved forward as fast as possible, and when a few miles from the Upper Agency were met by their guide, and were informed by him that the report was true that a part of Inkpadutah's band were in camp not a great distance from the agency. How many, he did not know. They consisted of six *tepees* and were out at one side by themselves about five miles up the river. The party again moved forward, piloted by their Indian guide, and reached the river where they intended to cross just after daylight. The hostile camp was in full view on the high ground on the opposite side of the river.

As the soldiers were nearing the spot an Indian holding a squaw by the hand sprang from one of the *tepees* and started rapidly for the river. Other Day, the guide, recognised him as Roaring Cloud, the son of Inkpadutah. The soldiers opened fire on him at long range with their rifles, but with what effect they did not know, as the Indian did not halt until he reached cover. From there he returned the fire of the soldiers three or four times. Every time he shot the soldiers would fire a return volley at the spot from which the smoke arose and he was soon riddled with bullets, and as the firing ceased a soldier rushed forward and finished the work with a thrust of his bayonet. It will be remembered that this was the same Indian that murdered Mrs. Noble after she had been purchased by the Yankton. The squaw was taken prisoner. The other Indians escaped.

It seems that the wife of Roaring Cloud was one of the agency Indians, and this accounts for the risks he ran in coming so near to the agency at a time when he was sure to be killed if recognised. The taking this squaw prisoner came very near causing serious trouble with the agency Indians. In going down to the agency, the expedition passed through a camp of several thousand Indians. These Indians were nominally friendly to the whites but the sight of one of their tribe being held a prisoner aroused their indignation to an alarming degree. The surprise of the troops in making this squaw a prisoner was to get such information as they could regarding the Indian that was killed, also the balance of the party. The troops realised that they had got themselves into trouble.

The excitement was intense. The angry warriors crowded around them on every side, making all kinds of hostile demonstrations. A shot from either side would have doubtless precipitated a collision, and in all probability, the force would have been annihilated on the spot. Fortunately no collision occurred and they reached the agency in safety. Here they took possession of a log house and awaited results, determined in case of an attack to defend themselves the best they were able. After a few days anxious suspense and sleepless anxiety they were relieved from their perilous situation by the arrival of Major Sherman with a force of regulars and a battery of artillery, having been ordered there from Fort Snelling to attend the payment of the annuities. Thus strengthened the troops were powerful enough to defend themselves in case of an attack. But with the release of the prisoner the affair blew over and matters quieted down to their normal condition.

The only other attempt made by the government to capture the renegade chief was later in the season. The garrison at Fort Ridgley had been materially strengthened and as the time approached when the annuities were to be paid the Indians were informed that they would be required by the government to deliver Inkpadutah and his band to the authorities as a condition on which they would receive their annuities. To this the Indians strenuously objected. They regarded it as a great wrong, punishing the innocent for the crimes of the guilty. However, they succeeded in organising a force made up of squads from the different bands, numbering in the neighbourhood of a hundred warriors. This force, under the leadership of Little Crow, made a campaign into the Indian country and were gone about two weeks. Upon their return they claimed that they had killed three of his band, wounded one and taken one squaw and one *papoose* prisoner. The Indians now claimed that they had done all that they could do and all that they ought to be required to do to entitle them to their annuities.

The agents of the government on the other hand insisted that it was the duty of annuity Indians to pursue and either capture or exterminate the outlaws. The time for paying the annuities had now arrived and matters began to look serious. After discussing the question in all its bearings the government authorities decided that it would be better to yield the point and pay the annuities than to run the risk of precipitating hostilities with the entire Sioux nation by withholding them longer. This opinion was largely held by the settlers along the border and by the population of Minnesota generally. Accordingly, on the eighteenth of August, Major Cullen sent the following dispatch to the Department:

> If the department concur, I am of the opinion that the Sioux of the Mississippi have done all in their power to punish or surrender Inkpadutah's band, and their annuities may with propriety be paid them..... The special agent awaits answer to this dispatch at Dunleith and for instructions in the premises.

The annuities were accordingly paid and the government made no further effort to capture or punish this little band of marauders, who had wrought such destruction and spread such consternation along the entire northwestern frontier. Nothing definite is known of the remainder of Inkpadutah's band subsequent to this time, but it is supposed that they scattered, the different members uniting with other bands, thus destroying their identity and making their pursuit or capture as a distinct band impossible.

So far as can be ascertained there is absolutely no tradition claiming to give the final fate of Inkpadutah. Several times during the summer of 1857 rumours were circulated telling of his death, and these were as often denied. Had he remained among the Indians along the frontier, he must at some time have been seen and recognised by some of the traders, trappers, half-breeds or friendly Indians of that region, but so far as known, nothing of the kind ever occurred. He dropped out of sight completely, and there is no authentic account of his ever having been seen or heard of since.

Mrs. Sharp, in speaking of his family, says:

"His family consisted of himself and squaw, four sons and one daughter."

As has been related, the eldest son, Roaring Cloud, the murderer of Mrs. Noble, was killed some time in July by a party of soldiers and volunteers near the Yellow Medicine Agency. There is a theory, and it is a plausible one, entertained by many that the three sons hovered around the frontier for some years; that they were leaders in many of the petty difficulties along the border, and that they were active in inciting the annuity Indians to deeds of violence and insubordination. When the outbreak at the agency came, in August, 1862, they were among the foremost in their deeds of violence and bloodshed, and later that they participated in the many sanguinary conflicts on the upper Missouri, and the great western plains, and that they were known to have been present at and participators in the Custer Massacre on the Little Big Horn in 1876.

A little book, entitled *Twenty Years on the Trap Line*, by Joseph Henry Taylor, insists there is abundant proof of this fact. The author claims to have been a member of Captain White's company of the Northern Border Brigade, stationed at Correctionville, and other points along the frontier, and that after receiving his discharge he spent the next twenty years trapping on the Missouri River and its tributaries. In his reminiscences he mentions several instances of coming into close proximity with these Indians and had several narrow escapes from them. "Mill Creek," in Cherokee County, seems to have been one of his favourite trapping grounds. In writing of his experiences there, he says:

> As the rapidly changing season commenced to spot the furs, I made ready to pull up traps and move down to the settlements. On the morning of my final departure I noticed a man passing along the edge of the bluffs without seeming to see the camp. With gun in hand, and with a brace of pistols in my 'war' belt, I intercepted him with a 'Hello!' On approaching, I discovered him to be a half-breed, and seemed to be trailing something. 'Did you see anybody pass here?' he said in good English. 'No,' I answered. 'You were in luck they didn't see you.' 'Why so?' 'Because Inkpadutah's boys don't often let a chance slip.' 'Inkpadutah's boys,' I repeated mechanically. 'Yes, Inkpadutah's sons. Inkpadutah's sons—I well remember the cold chill that crept over my nerves at the half-breed's mention of the dreaded name.
>
> As soon as he had disappeared down the winding valley I critically examined the trail he was following and found the *moccasin* tracks of six different Indians all pointing down the valley. After having taken up the traps, I moved up on the high divide and took a bee line for Correctionville. . . . .Striking the valley of the Little Sioux at least once a year on a hostile raid seemed to be a fanatical observance of Inkpadutah's band that they could not abandon. Whether fishing for pickerel around the shores of Lake Winnipeg, or hunting antelope on the plains of the upper James River, or buffalo in the Judith Basin or along the Muscleshell River, time and opportunity were found to start out hundreds of miles on a dreary foot journey to count a *coup* on their aggressive conquerors.

The battle on the Little Big Horn is still rated the most important engagement between the whites and Indians since that day on the banks of the turgid Tippecanoe, when the sycamore forests hid the broken columns of Tecumseh and the prophet from Harrison's victorious army. Various writers have ascribed Custer's death as the culminating episode in this latter day fight and to heighten the colour of the picture have laid his death to the personal prowess of Rain in the Face or on the field altar of Chief Priest Sitting Bull. It has long since been proven that Rain in the Face was not on the field of battle that day, but was miles away in charge of the pony herd.

About Sitting Bull's hand in the affair, he has expressed himself again and again by saying in about these words to the charge, 'They tell you I murdered Custer. It is a lie. I am not a war chief. I was not in the battle that day. His eyes were blinded that he could not see. He was a fool and rode to his death. He made the fight, not I. Whoever tells you I killed Custer is a liar.' . . . Any intelligent Yankton, Santee, Unepapa Blackfoot or other Sioux, who participated in the fight against Custer's battalions on that twenty-fifth day of June, 1876, will tell you it was difficult to tell just who killed Custer. They believed he was the last to fall in the group where he was found. That the last leaden messengers of swift death hurled amongst this same group of falling and dying soldiers were belched forth from Winchesters held in the hands of Inkpadutah's sons.

CHAPTER 12

Effect of the Massacre Elsewhere

The massacre at Spirit Lake created great excitement and consternation along the entire frontier. Nearly the whole line of frontier settlements were abandoned and in some instances the excitement and alarm extended far into the interior. Indeed, in many cases where there was no possibility of danger the alarm was wildest. Military companies were formed, home guards were organised and other measures taken for defence hundreds of miles from where any Indians had been seen for years. The alarm spread to adjoining states. The wildest accounts of the number and force of the savages was given currency and credence. Had all of the Indians of the Northwest been united in one band they would not have formed a force so formidable as was supposed to exist at that time along the western border of Iowa and Minnesota. Doubtless there are at this time many who were then residing in the central portion of this state, and some even in some parts of Wisconsin, who remember the wild excitement and the needless and unreasonable alarm following these events as above related.

One of the results of the Spirit Lake Massacre and the excitement following it was to attract the attention of settlers, emigrants and adventurers in that direction. The party from Jasper County, to which allusion has formerly been m.ade, consisting of O. C. Howe, R. U. Wheelock and B. F. Parmenter still persisted in their determination of making a permanent settlement at the lakes. It will be remembered that this was the party that explored the lake region the fall before and passed Inkpadutah's camp near Loon Lake. They were also the first to discover and give an intelligent account of the massacre and it was on the strength of their representations that the relief force under Major Williams was raised. They returned to Fort Dodge with Major Williams' command, after which Mr. Howe went on to Newton, while Parmenter and Wheelock remained in Fort Dodge to procure a new lot of supplies and await his return.

Just previous to this time a party, consisting of J. S. Prescott, W. B. Brown and a man whom they employed as guide by the name of Overacker, started on an exploring trip to the lakes, passing up the Des Moines on the west side, while Major Williams' command on their return trip were coming down on the east side and thus avoiding them. Prescott and Brown reached the lakes about the fifteenth of April, and after spending a few days in exploring the country they returned again to Fort Dodge, where they purchased supplies and made other necessary preparations for their return to the lakes for permanent settlement.

Mr. Howe upon his arrival at Newton succeeded in raising a party to accompany him on his return trip to the lakes. This party consisted of Hon. George E. Spencer, since United States Senator from Alabama; his brother, Gustave Spencer, M. A. Blanchard, S. W. Foreman, Thomas Arthur, Doctor Hunter and Samuel Thornton, all of Newton, Jasper County. Mr. Howe was detained at home by sickness in his family and could not accompany the balance of the party at the time. They came on to Fort Dodge, where they found Wheelock and Parmenter, who were waiting for them. There were some others who had decided upon making a trip to the lakes, some from a desire for adventure and others for the purpose of settlement.

Perhaps a short notice of some of the more prominent characters that took part in making the first settlement of the county, subsequent to the massacre, would not be wholly devoid of interest. J. S. Prescott, one of the most active of the early settlers here, was one of the original projectors and founders of the college at Appleton, Wisconsin. He had also been partially successful in starting an institution at Point Bluff, Wisconsin. He, having heard of the romantic beauty of the lake region, made his first trip to this locality with the idea of establishing here some time in the future an institution of learning similar in its provisions to that at Appleton. Visionary, as such a scheme must seem at this time in the light of subsequent events, it was not at that time regarded as an impossible undertaking.

For this project he had associated with him several gentlemen in Ohio and Wisconsin who had advanced him considerable sums of money for that purpose. Prescott was a man of great energy and ability, a college graduate and a fine scholar, but he was a poor judge of human nature. He lacked discretion, was impatient, impetuous and excitable, and while he was very enthusiastic in everything he undertook, he was, at the same time, visionary and often unpractical and impracticable.

He was educated by his parents for a physician, but disliking the profession went into the practice of law in Ohio, in which he was very successful. After following that for a while he joined the Methodist Church and commenced preaching. As a speaker he possessed extraordinary ability and power. It is no disparagement to the ministers who have represented the different denominations here since that time to say that his pulpit oratory has seldom if ever been equalled by any other man in northwestern Iowa. His sermons were of that rare character which church members and men of the world alike regard as moral and intellectual treats. At the same time, his visionary and impractical ideas rendered his selection for the position, to which he was assigned and for the work laid out for him to do, a most unfortunate one. As might be expected his scheme was a failure.

Prominent among the others who assisted in making the first settlement subsequent to the massacre were O. C. Howe, B. F. Parmenter, R. U. Wheelock, W. B. Brown, C. F. Hill, R. A. Smith and Henry Backman. Messrs. Howe and Parmenter were attorneys, formerly from Erie County, New York, but had been stopping for a short time at Newton, in this state. Their object in coming here at that time was to select a location for a town site, secure the location of the county seat, and secure claims on the adjoining land for themselves. Their scheme was a feasible one, and had times remained as they had been for a few years previous, would doubtless have been successful. They succeeded in securing the county seat all right but after the financial crash of 1857 values became so unsettled that the whole scheme was worthless. Mr. Howe was chosen district attorney at the general election in the fall of 1858 for the Fourth Judicial District, which then comprised nearly one-fourth of the state. This office he held four years after which he enlisted in the Ninth Iowa Cavalry and was promoted to the rank of captain, which position he held at the close of the war.

One of the most unique and remarkable characters that came into prominence in the settlement of northwestern Iowa was George E. Spencer, for whom the town of Spencer, Clay County, was named. It was a part of the original arrangement that he should be associated with Messrs. Howe, Wheelock and Parmenter in the town of Spirit Lake, while in his operations in Clay County he was associated with other parties. For two or three years he divided his time between the two counties. In one of his trips to Sioux City he succeeded in trading for a tract of land some four or five miles southeast of the present town of Spencer. This he had surveyed and had an elaborate plat made, naming the town after himself.

He succeeded in getting commissioners appointed and having the county seat located there, while the county records were kept at Peterson. He had a post-office established there which was also kept at Peterson. Indeed, the two post-offices, Peterson and Spencer, were for a time kept in the same house. All of this when there was not a house within fifteen miles of Spencer, Then he issued circulars and commenced selling lots, representing that they had an eighty thousand dollar courthouse, a fine public schoolhouse, stores, hotels, mills and all of the material advantages of a prosperous western town. This was probably the most conspicuous instance of working a paper town that ever occurred in northwestern Iowa.

Spencer was chosen Chief Clerk of the Senate for the Eighth General Assembly, which position he filled with ability. But inasmuch as his operations were carried on far more extensively in Clay County than in Dickinson it is hardly profitable to follow his career farther. After two or three years he abandoned his. schemes in Dickinson County and his interests fell into other hands.

The balance of the party whose names have been given were younger men, most of them well educated and just starting out in the world, and were ready to engage in anything that might afford a chance for speculation or a spice of adventure or excitement.

CHAPTER 13

The Trip to the Lakes

It may be well to remember at this time that during the winter of 1856 and 1857 Congress passed the Minnesota Railroad Bill or an act granting subsidies of land to all of the then projected railroads in Minnesota. Prominent among these was the St. Paul and Sioux City, or, as it was then called, the Minnesota Valley Railroad, which provided for the building of a railroad up the Minnesota Valley to the south line of the state in the direction of the mouth of the Big Sioux River. A direct line from the south bend of the Minnesota River to the mouth of the Big Sioux would run a little to the east and south of the centre of our lakes. The idea that that road would be located and built as it was, over thirty miles west of here, was not thought of at that time.

It will be well to remember here also that this was during the fast times preceding the crash of 1857. During the preceding five years railroads had been built throughout the West at a rate and upon a scale unprecedented in the history of the world. The states of Illinois and (Wisconsin were virtually covered with a network of railroads, all of them constructed within the brief period of six years. If Illinois could be covered with a network of railroads in six years, why not Iowa? As yet the only road built in Iowa was from Davenport to Iowa City, with a branch to Muscatine.

Innumerable towns had sprung up in every locality on these new roads and many men had made respectable fortunes in selling town lots, some of them in towns where improvements were actually being made, and many in towns that had no existence except on paper. Iowa lands were held at figures that would have delighted the real estate owners of twenty years later.

Taking the past as a criterion, however, men were not at that time to be considered as extravagant or unreasonable, who expected that the system of railroads for Iowa and Minnesota would have been completed in the next five years as those of Illinois and Wisconsin had been within the preceding five years.

Taking into consideration the natural advantages and the unequalled beauty of the lake region, and, as was then supposed, the almost positive certainty that they would soon have railroad communication with the rest of the world, it is not strange that a different class of men were attracted here than the representative pioneers who had subdued the older portions of the country. People who leave the older states with the last magazine in their pockets and the last daily paper in their hands are very much the same people after landing in Iowa or Minnesota that they were before leaving New York or New England. The term "The Wild and Woolly West," with its peculiar significance, never was applicable to the pioneers of northwestern Iowa and more particularly to the first settlers of Dickinson County.

The several parties of which mention has heretofore been made, completed their arrangements at Fort Dodge and started for the lakes again on Wednesday, the 30th day of April, 1857. The different parties were made up as follows: First, Doctor J. S. Prescott, W. B. Brown, Charles F. Hill, Moses Miller, Lawrence Furber and George Brockway; second, the Newton party, consisting of the Spencers and others whose names have been heretofore given; third, a party consisting of B. F. Parmenter, R. U. Wheelock, William Lamont, Morris Markham, Alexander Irving, Lewis Hart and R. A. Smith.

These parties were mostly independent of each other but proposed keeping together as much as possible for the purposes of company and protection. It would require too much space to give the details and incidents of travel along the road. Most persons can imagine what a trip of that kind would be in times of high water across an unsettled country without bridges, and without so much as a footpath for a guide. Add to this the ever-present danger that roving bands of Indians were hovering along the border liable at any time to put in an appearance when least expected. From this combination of circumstances it will be readily seen that it was no May day picnic these hardy adventurers were planning for themselves.

After leaving Fort Dodge, which they did on the thirtieth of April, they followed up on the west side of the Des Moines River to a point about ten miles below where Emmetsburg now stands. At this point the Newton party parted company with the others and struck across the prairie to Olay County for the purpose of examining the land there and making arrangements for carrying out the scheme they had in contemplation relative to laying out the town of Spencer.

The main body followed up the river a short distance farther and then struck across to Lost Island where they camped on the night of the sixth of May on the north east shore of Lost Island Lake. They arrived at Okoboji on the eighth, about noon. The Newton party which had been prospecting about Spencer and Gillett's Grove, arrived the same evening, the entire party going into camp at the Gardner place.

Naturally the first business to be disposed of after arriving there was the taking of claims and adjusting their boundaries. One word in reference to the claims of those who had settled here previous to the massacre is in place now. It will be remembered that the land was unsurveyed and all that anyone could do was to "squat" on a piece of land and defend possession of it under the laws of the state. Measures were taken as far as possible to settle with the heirs of those holding *bona fide* claims, and in every instance they were paid a valuable consideration therefore. There was no instance of any person settling upon any *bona fide* claim that had been improved previous to the massacre without an equitable settlement having been made with those entitled to receive it.

The impression has gone abroad and is pretty generally believed that Doctor Prescott took possession of the Gardner place without making any settlement therefore. This is a mistake. It will be remembered that Eliza Gardner was at Springfield at the time of the massacre, and, that in company with the other refugees there, went down to Fort Dodge with the return to that place of Major Williams' command, and was in Fort Dodge when Doctor Prescott came back from his first trip to the lakes. William Wilson, who had spent a portion of the winter at the lakes and who afterwards married Miss Eliza Gardner, was with the burial party acting as guide. It was through him and Thatcher that the victims of the massacre were identified. The burial party, which was the last of Major Williams' command to report at Fort Dodge, arrived a few days before Prescott and his party.

Wilson and Eliza Gardner were married the day following their arrival in Fort Dodge. Immediately upon Prescott's return, they sought him out and proposed selling out their claims to him, as they had no intention of returning to the lakes. The land being as yet unsurveyed, the boundaries were indefinite. Gardner's claim was along the shore of West Okoboji Lake, to the south and west of the Gardner cabin. Next came his son-in-law, Harvey Luce, whose claim adjoined Gardner's on the east. Luce had rolled up the body of a log-house but had not finished it. East of that was Wilson's claim, which embraced the site of Arnold Park and the land east of it. These were the claims that Wilson and his wife proposed to sell to Prescott. They made a proposition to him which he accepted, paying them down in gold the amount of eleven hundred ($1,100) dollars. In the arrangement they were to settle with Abbie (Mrs. Sharp) if she ever returned. She was then a prisoner with the Indians. When she was there the following season, he made another settlement with her, though not so liberal a one as he had formerly made with the Wilsons, upon her representation that she had received no part of the money paid to Wilson and his wife for the claim.

Some of Joel Howe's heirs came as far as Fort Dodge on their way to the lakes to look up Mr. Howe's matters, but upon meeting Prescott proposed to sell to him. He accepted their terms, paying them down a good round sum. He also purchased Thatcher's claim of him, paying liberally for it. In every instance the parties expressed themselves as well pleased with the amounts they received and with the manner in which they were treated.

So far as the Harriott claim is concerned, Harriott had made no improvement whatever. He had not resided on the claim at all, neither had he done any of the acts which were even then considered necessary to give validity to a claim on the public land. He simply expressed his intention of doing so at some future period, yet his claim was respected for a year. His father was here the summer following the massacre, but made no attempt to either secure or dispose of it, and it lay vacant until the following year. The Granger place was also unoccupied for about a year. The impression that the early settlers took possession of the homes of the victims of the massacre, without compensation to those rightfully entitled to receive it, is an erroneous one, and it is only justice to them that it be corrected. So far as Prescott's operations were concerned, his wrong consisted not in wrongfully getting possession of the claims, but in attempting to hold four or five when the law allowed him to defend his possession to but one.

Mention has heretofore been made of a party from Red Wing, Minnesota, consisting of the Granger brothers, Harriott and Snyder, who occupied a cabin on a point a little northeast of the Okoboji bridge. All of this party were killed by the Indians excepting William Granger, or "Bill" Granger, as he was for years known along the border. For some time previous to the massacre it was more than intimated that a band of horse thieves and counterfeiters had their headquarters somewhere in the northwest and the Grangers were to some extent connected with it. It was reported that counterfeit money had been put into circulation at different times which had been traced back to them and other little irregularities and crookednesses were attributed to them. Whatever proof there ever was in existence to substantiate these charges is not now known, but it is true that such charges were outspoken among the settlers all along the Des Moines River.

Granger made up a small party at Red Wing and started from there about the same time that the others started from Fort Dodge, and arrived at the lakes about two days later. He assumed to represent the heirs of the different parties who had been killed by the Indians, and with great flourish and bravado he forbade the settling upon or occupying any parcel or tract of land that had been settled upon previous to the massacre, and even went so far as to make his boast of the number of blankets he had put under the sod, and to intimate that unless those who were there left at once, they would be disposed of in the same summary manner. But he soon found out that he had misjudged his men, and that while they made no exhibitions of bravado or *braggadocio*, they were not at all inclined to pay any attention to his absurd pretensions.

It will be noticed that Granger's claim, which is now known as Smith's Point, and Harriott's, which is now known as Dixon's Beach, were respected and were not disturbed until a year after this time, which was after Granger had abandoned all attempts to maintain his footing there.

It has been before stated that Prescott's project was the establishment of an institution of learning. His plan was to secure as desirable a location as possible, lay out a town, and then secure the most desirable tracts of land adjoining and hold them as a permanent endowment for the institution. For that purpose he selected as a site for his town the tract upon the east side of East Okoboji Lake, now known as Tusculum Grove. As before stated, he bought the claim of Mr. Thatcher and settled with the heirs of Mr. Howe in order that there might be no conflicting claims. He then proceeded to lay out his town, which he named Tusculum, after the country residence of the great Roman orator. That he had undertaken more than he could accomplish soon became evident, but the failure of his scheme will be noted further on.

The plan of Howe, Wheelock and Parmenter was to hit upon

some locality most likely to become the county seat and centre of business for the county, and lay out a town which was to be owned in common, and then take the land adjoining as their individual claims. For this purpose they made the selection of the site where the town of Spirit Lake now stands, and took their claims adjoining. The parties known as the original proprietors of Spirit Lake City, as it was then called were O, C. Howe, B. F. Parmenter, R. U. Wheelock and George E. Spencer. Dr. J. S. Prescott afterwards bought an undivided one-fifth interest in it, giving one thousand dollars for it. The county seat was located there in 1858, James Hickey of Palo Alto County, C. C. Smeltzer of Clay County and S. W. Foreman of O'Brien County acting as commissioners. It is understood that the proceedings of that commission are lost and that no minutes of their action have been preserved.

The others who came in at the same time scattered around upon their claims in different localities about the groves and lakes. It is impossible here to give anything like a connected account of all of the different transactions that transpired at the time, but simply to give a passing notice of the most important incidents and those that had the most to do in shaping the course of future events. Other persons came in at different times during the spring and summer of 1857. Henry Barkman with a small party from Newton came in some time in June. A party from Sparta, Wisconsin, consisting of Rosalvo Kingman, William Carsley, J. D. Hawkins and G. W. Rogers, put in an appearance on the fourth of July. Jareb Palmer was another of the settlers of that summer. He had previously determined to settle on the Des Moines, but for some reason changed his mind. He was at the house of Mr. Thomas at the time of the attack on Springfield, and rendered valuable assistance in the defence of that place. He was with the refugees when they started down the river, but on meeting Major Williams' forces joined them for the balance of the expedition. From this time on different parties continued to arrive, most of whom were on exploring expeditions, with occasionally one for settlement, but they cannot be noticed in detail.

The fact of the land being unsurveyed and the boundaries of the different claims being but imperfectly defined, there was at different times considerable trouble in regard to conflicting claims. It has been the lot of all new countries to have more or less claim quarrels, and while those of this locality were not as sanguinary as many that have transpired in other places, it was by no means free from them, but they were not carried to the extent this season that they were afterwards.

They were confined mostly to Granger's attempt to enforce respect for his bogus pretensions that he was acting as agent or representative of the heirs of the victims of the massacre. Finding his authority disregarded and his pretensions unheeded, he, as a last resort, endeavoured to frighten the inhabitants away by reporting that the Indians were about to make another raid on the settlement. Failing in this, he and his party gathered up their effects and left. While the settlers were somewhat apprehensive of danger from the Indians and were on the alert as much as possible to guard against surprise, yet they were too much in earnest to be frightened away without good cause. Reports of Indians hovering along the border were occasionally put into circulation, but there were no depredations or outbreaks during the summer.

One of the results of these periodical Indian scares was the building of the old fort at Spirit Lake, which, as one of the oldest landmarks, deserves a passing notice. The town site as selected before the United States survey was made, was nearly half a mile north of its present location. After the site had been decided upon, a building was erected which was intended to be a kind of general headquarters, all contributing towards its erection. It was a log building about 24 x 30 feet with a shake roof and puncheon floor and doors. Not a foot of lumber was used in its construction. Around the outside of the building, at a distance of from six to ten feet, a stockade was erected, which was formed of logs cut ten feet long and about eight inches in thickness. These were set on end in a trench from two and a half to three feet deep. A well was dug inside of the stockade. This building was erected in June and July, 1857, and stood there about two years, when it was torn down and the hotel then known as the Lake View House was erected on or near the same spot. During its short existence it had rather an eventful history and will be referred to again.

As would be natural under the circumstances, the settlers scattered around the lakes in different localities and had two or three places as their general rendezvous, or headquarters. The largest number gathered at Spirit Lake, and several small cabins were built in the immediate vicinity of the old fort. It was the intention, in case of an outbreak or attack by the Indians, for all parties to gather at the fort and make such defence as they were able. A second party, including W. B. Brown, C. F. Hill, William Lament and one or two others, had their headquarters in Center Grove. A third, consisting of Prescott and his hired men, was at Okoboji, at the old "Gardner Place."

The first religious services in the county were held at the Gardner place, on Sunday, May 11, 1857, and conducted by Rev. J. S. Prescott, and deserve more than a passing mention. As has been heretofore mentioned, Prescott was a speaker of extraordinary ability and one to whom it was a pleasure to listen, no matter what a person's particular religious ideas might be. But that fact was not known then. It became patent later on. On the evening preceding that Sunday morning, word was sent around to the different cabins that there would be religious services at the Gardner place, the following day. Accordingly at the appointed hour the crowd assembled to the number of from fifteen to twenty. It was a unique sight, especially to those who had just come from the East, to see those rough looking, hardy pioneers on their way to church, come filing along, either singly or in parties of two or three, dressed in their red shirts, without coats or vests and with their rifles in their hands, their ammunition slung from their shoulders, and leather belts about their waists, from most of which dangled revolvers.

Singular as such a spectacle would be at the present time, it was strictly in keeping with the surroundings of that occasion. As the parties arrived they disposed of their arms by standing them in the most convenient corner and then arranged themselves about the room on stools and benches or any thing else that would do duty as a seat. The parties were mostly strangers to each other at that time, and whether they were about to listen to the wild harangues of a professional "Bible whanger," as a certain type of frontier preachers were then designated, or to be treated to an interesting and intelligent discourse on some live topic, they did not know, nor did they much care. It was a change, and the novelty was enough to bring them out. Promptly at the appointed hour the exercises were opened by Prescott reading the hymn;

A charge to keep I have,
A God to glorify
A never dying soul to save
And fit it for the sky.

Wheelock led the singing, assisted by C. F. Hill and Lawrence Furber. Next was prayer by Doctor Prescott. And such a prayer. After the dangers, hardships and privations that little party had endured for the last month, it certainly was a spiritual and intellectual treat not soon to be forgotten. He made a fervent appeal that the divine blessing be vouchsafed there and then on this first attempt to establish and foster the growth of a true and genuine religious sentiment, that should broaden and deepen as the settlement that was then being founded should grow older and stronger.

After prayer a second hymn was sung, and then the text announced, *"Be strong and show thyself a man."* The sermon was one long to be remembered by everyone who heard it. It was a plain, simple and direct appeal to every one present to realise the position which he at that moment occupied. They were reminded of the importance of asserting there and then the principles and practices which should govern them in the future. They were reminded that *"like seeks like"* in emigration as in other things, and that in the moral, intellectual and religious tone of the society which they then inaugurated they would see the counterpart of the emigration they would attract. If the first settlers adopted a high plane of moral and intellectual development, the emigration that would follow would be of the same high character.

On the other hand, if the standard were made low, it would be the low and depraved class that would be attracted by it. In conclusion he appealed to all present to use their best endeavours to build up in this frontier country such moral and social conditions as they would wish to have their names associated with by future generations. The entire discourse was delivered in that plain, simple, and yet dignified and scholarly manner that always commands respect and admiration. After the close of the services the parties all filed out as they came, and it is not recorded whether any luckless ducks or chickens fell victims to their marksmanship on their return to their cabins, but considering the scarcity of provisions at that time, such a violation of the Sabbath would have been deemed excusable if not justifiable.

The manner and style of living in those early days was decidedly primitive. If a person now wishes to ascertain how few of the comforts of life are really necessary and how many of them can be dispensed with, he can gain a vast amount of such instruction by a few years of pioneering. Perhaps it would not be out of place to give in this connection some kind of an idea of the manner of living here in those early times. "Keeping bach," as it was termed by the boys, is particularly and peculiarly a pioneer institution. Men don't know what they can do until they are tested. They don't know their own capacities or capabilities until circumstances bring them out.

Now it will be remembered that there were no women in the settlement, and most of the men were of that class who give the least attention to household affairs, many of them hailing direct from stores and offices, and of the class usually designated by the phrase "fine haired," and while possessed of a goodly share of intelligence and general information, were wholly ignorant of the mysteries connected with the art of keeping shirts and pants in repair and converting bacon and flour into edibles. Could all of the ludicrous incidents and ridiculous experiences of those times be properly written up they would, by no means, form an uninteresting chapter.

The settlers, a majority of whom were young men, were scattered in their little cabins in the neighbourhood of the several groves where they commenced, for the first time, the solution of the great problem of what it takes to make up the measure of human happiness. There was nothing very peculiar about the cabins themselves. In short they could not very well have been much different from what they were without being peculiar. They were usually small and low and covered with either shakes or sods. A board and shingle roof was an extravagance not to be thought of. The door and window, or more commonly a half window, were set in one side, while a large stone fireplace was at the end, with a chimney made of clay and sticks up the outside. But it is in the internal arrangement and fixtures that the greater peculiarities are noticeable.

In one corner stands the bunk, which is one, two or three tiers high, according to the number that are expected to occupy it. These bunks, which were filled with prairie hay and covered with a few blankets thrown over them, composed the sleeping accommodations. A shelf running along the back wall of the cabin and resting upon several huge pins is indispensable in every well regulated establishment. Its contents are worthy a moment's notice. First, and in the most convenient place, is a pipe and tobacco, next a copy of Shakespeare, then a Bible and a pack of cards lie as peacefully together as members of Barnum's *Happy Family*, while Scott's poems, Waverly novels, *Pilgrim's Progress* and *Davies' Mathematics* swell the list.

Mixed up among the literary treasures are boxes of ammunition, fishing tackle and, as the Yankee peddlers say, "other articles too numerous to mention," while scattered about in curious confusion are various articles of household use, which usually consisted of a sheet iron coffee pot, a frying pan, or skillet, as the boys usually called it, a few in tin plates and cups, and possibly the luxury of knives and forks.

The mystery of bread-making was usually a stumper, or, as Barnum, in his molasses candy experience, expresses it, the rock on which they split, and many and varied were the ridiculous experiences of the pioneer's first bread making. Washing was another obstacle that required all of their patience and philosophy to overcome.

Chapter 14

The First Family After the Massacre

Important among the first acts of the settlers was the naming of the different lakes, or rather familiarising themselves with the names they had already received. Spirit Lake had been known by the Indians as Minnie Waukon, and by the French as *Lac d'Esprit*. Professor McBride, in his report of the geological survey of the county, unearths a somewhat amusing instance of the comical results of attempting to apply English orthography to French words, he says:

> The redoubtable Clarke in his notes relates how 'The Ceuoux River passes through Lake Despree.' If this matter had not been corrected by the French interpreter, in all probability Spirit Lake would have gone on to the maps as Lake Depree, and by this time local archaeologists would have been puzzling their brains in a vain attempt to ascertain and explain its origin and meaning. Granger and his party made an attempt to have it called Green Lake, but it did not succeed.

East Okoboji Lake was called by the Dacotahs "Okoboozhy," and West Okoboji "Minnietonka," signifying Big Water. Minnietonka was and is the name of a somewhat celebrated lake in Minnesota, and to avoid confusion the Iowa Minnietonka was abandoned and West Okoboji adopted instead. Granger made an attempt to name West Okoboji "Lake Harriott," in honour of Doctor Harriott and East Okoboji, "Rice Lake," in honour of Senator Henry M. Rice, then United States senator from Minnesota, but the inhabitants finally settled down upon the present names, East and West Okoboji.

The origin and meaning of the word Okoboji is a little uncertain. Professor MacBride says, "place of rest." The preponderance of testimony, however, seems to be that Okoboji simply means "rushes." Mrs.

Wood, who was for years a successful teacher among the Dacotahs, gave that as the meaning, "And there are others."

The impression exists in some quarters that Okoboji was a powerful Sioux chief, who formerly had his headquarters in Okoboji Grove, and that the lake was named for him. The question is often asked where Okoboji was buried, but as has been before explained, such belief is wholly unfounded.

The Indian name of Center Lake is unknown. Previous to the massacre it was called by the first settlers Snyder's Lake, for Bert Snyder, who had a claim on the east side of it. After that for a year or two it was called Sylvan Lake, but finally that name was dropped and the present name. Center Lake, substituted, which has come into general use.

Gar Lake was at first designated by Granger as Carl Lake in honour of Carl Granger. Whether the name Gar Lake is a corruption of that cannot be positively stated, but the presumption is that it is not, as the outlet was known by the name of Gar Outlet long before anyone knew anything about Granger's name for the lake. It had its origin in a little incident which, though not important, may be worth telling.

On the evening of the day of the arrival of the first party of settlers subsequent to the massacre, as a small party of the boys were cruising around on a voyage of discovery, they brought up at the outlet in which were a school of gars working their way upstream. The boys had never heard of such a fish and thought them pickerel and became much excited. One of them ran to the cabin where he procured a spear which they had brought along, and for two hours they waded up and down the outlet spearing and throwing out the worthless gars. When they tired of that they strung what they could carry on some poles and started for the cabin with their wonderful catch.

Upon arriving there a young fellow from Illinois saw what they were and exclaimed: "Boys, those are gars and are no earthly good." When the boys became convinced that they had had all their work and wetting for nothing, and that their fish were indeed worthless, they were somewhat crestfallen. They took the guying they received from the others in good part, but it was some time before they heard the last of their wonderful exploits. And this is how Gar Outlet first received its name, and Gar Lake soon followed.

Recently the name of Middle Gar has been changed to "Minnie Washta." *Washta* is the Dacotah synonym for good or nice. Originally there were three lakes known as the Gar Lakes, forming a chain about two miles in length, and were called Upper, Middle and Lower Gar Lakes. The outlet for the Okobojis is through this chain. Middle Gar, or Minnie Washta, as it is now called, is the finest of the three. The other two retain their old names of Upper and Lower Gar Lakes. Various considerations seemed to emphasize the fact that it would be desirable to organise the county at as early a date as possible. While nominally attached to Woodbury County for judicial and financial purposes, it was practically outside of any civil jurisdiction whatever.

It was early foreseen that it would be a great advantage to be able to settle all questions liable to arise in the future under the forms and provisions of the statutes. It was therefore determined to organise at the earliest practical period, which would be at the August election. That election was held on the first Tuesday in August, 1857, at the house of J. S. Prescott. Under the law as it then stood it was necessary to send in a petition signed by two-thirds of the voters of the new county to the county judge of the county to which it was attached and if in his judgment the interests of the county demanded it, he issued an order for the organisation of the new county.

The petition for organisation had twenty names attached, and was taken to Sioux City by C. F. Hill some time in June. John K. Cook was at that time county judge of Woodbury County. He issued an order for holding the election, which was held accordingly. The first officers elected were as follows: O. C. Howe, County Judge; B. F. Parmenter, Prosecuting Attorney; M. A. Blanchard. Treasurer and Recorder; R. A. Smith, Clerk of the District Court; C. F. Hill, Sheriff; Alfred Wilkins, County Surveyor; W. B. Brown, Coroner. R. U. Wheelock and R. A. Smith were elected Justices of the Peace. After the election it was necessary that the returns he sent to Sioux City, and that either the county judge, district attorney or clerk of the district court elect go before the judge of Woodbury County and give bonds for his approval and be sworn in in due form. This journey fell to the lot of the clerk of the district court.

These trips to Sioux City were no holiday affairs. The route by which they were made was to strike out in a westerly direction to the head of the Floyd and follow that stream to Sioux City. There were no settlements on the route until within eight miles of the city. The time required for making the trip was seven days; the distance one hundred and twenty miles each way, or two hundred and forty miles in all. Let a person imagine himself taking a trip that distance alone on horse back, drinking from the streams he might chance to cross, eating a dry

BRIDGE BETWEEN MINNIE WASHTA AND GAR LAKE.

NATURAL TERRACE ON WEST OKOBOJI.

lunch from his portmanteau, at night rolling up in a saddle blanket with the saddle under his head as a pillow, his horse picketed by his side, and with no probability of seeing human being for the next three days, and he can form some idea of what those trips were. Add to this the ever-present danger that roving bands of Indians were continually hovering along the border ready at any moment to waylay any luckless adventurer who may have ventured beyond the line of the settlements, and it will be understood that no slight amount of courage and hardihood were exhibited in their successful accomplishment.

The following letter, written by C. F. Hill and published in the *Sioux City Journal*, June 10, 1900, conveys a pretty vivid idea of what these early trips were. In his letter Mr. Hill says:

Hazleton, Pa., June 4, 1900.

Neil Bonner, Sioux City. Iowa.

Dear Sir: Yours of May 30, referring to my early visit to Sioux City, is received. In the spring of 1857 I located at Spirit Lake, shortly after the massacre took place under Inkpadutah, and I helped bury some of the dead that had been overlooked by the soldiers sent down from Fort Ridgley. About the month of May, 1857, the settlers at Spirit Lake decided to organise Dickinson County, which before that had been attached with all northwestern Iowa to Woodbury County, and I was designated to go to Sioux City and get an order from the court there to hold an election and organise Dickinson County.

I started out on my mission mounted on an Indian pony which had both ears badly burned in a prairie fire, and accompanied by a young man by the name of Barnum, a relative of P. T. Barnum, the great showman. Barnum was on foot, and as he was a good fellow, I shared my pony with him and allowed him to ride half of the time. After we left Spirit Lake we did not reach a white man until we reached the Floyd River in Plymouth County, where we met a party of surveyors, who were staking out Plymouth City. Barnum and I were glad to meet these men, and we begged the privilege of camping near them, which they reluctantly granted. The next day we reached Sioux City, and put up at the Sioux City House, a storey and a half building, and to my great surprise I found it kept by the Trescott Brothers, Wesley and Milo, who were from near Shickshinny, Pa. I knew them well, but I had some little trouble in making myself known to them, as my camp life, my leggings, Indian pony and other Indian fixings led them to believe that I was a half-breed, which amused my companion very much.

Next day I looked up his honour, the Judge of Woodbury County, and in a day or two had matters all arranged to start the wheels of government for Dickinson County. While I remained at Sioux City I heard much talk that the remains of Sergeant Floyd were exposed by the action of the Missouri River. and the citizens were about to remove the remains to another bluff, where the aggressive Missouri River could not reach them. A man by the name of Brughier, a Frenchman, lived at the mouth of the Big Sioux River, and he had two squaw wives.

Sioux City at that time was an unpretentious village of one story and story and a half frame houses. The town was hemmed in closely by bluffs, which were so numerous and so close together as in some cases to admit only of a wagon road between them. I remember many interesting incidents while in the city, regarding the Indians who came there. I remember a one storey clothing store on the wharf which had a large picture on canvas of an elephant, which the boys called the 'land elephant.' The land elephant was the great animal of those days, and woe to the poor fellow who indulged in too much land and allowed the elephant to lie down on him.

An Indian Carousal.

Having completed the object of my mission, I made my arrangements to return to Spirit Lake, and was directed to a saloon, restaurant and grocery store, where I could purchase a supply of provisions for my return. While selecting my outfit a band of Indians and half-breeds entered. They seemed to have plenty of money and one of the braves called up the drinks for all hands. They were all well armed and in a state of carousal that would have laid 'Pat in a Grog Shop' in his palmiest days in the shade, the brave who was treating stepped up to me and in an animated tone asked:

'Are you my fren?'

I replied: 'Oh, yes, I am your friend.'

'Then come and take a drink wi' me.'

I declined with many apologies.

'Then you no my fren.'

I thought I saw trouble ahead and I quickly changed my mind, as I had just discovered that I did want a drink, and I stepped up to the bar and took a ration of Missouri corn whisky. I proceeded with preparing my outfit, when a second brave asked me to take a drink with him. This invitation followed the first in such quick succession that I was forced to decline, when he sang out:

'You drink wi' him—you no drink wi' me—eh?'

So I was in for a second ration, and so it went on, growing more lively. At no time was it long between drinks, and I devoted the brief time between drinks to collecting my purchases and completing my outfit, and at the first opportunity that offered I made a straight coat-tail out of the door. And as I walked up the street I wondered how that poor bartender expected to get out of that green corn whisky dance alive. He, however, had a six inch Colt's revolver lying on the bar behind him in easy reach. It was wonderful what a inspect a Colt's revolver inspired for its owner in that day.

Well, I was happy. I escaped that drunken, carousing band of Indians and was pleased with my little outfit, which contained a bottle of raspberry syrup, one can of peaches and a box of good cigars. Mr. Trescott was very kind to me and asked for my pocket compass which he compared with a surveyor's instrument and it was pronounced correct. This was the last thing done. I was now ready to start for Spirit Lake alone, as Barnum did not return with me.

Lost on the Prairie.

Sherman's battery had passed through the country a few days before, *en route* from Fort Scott to Fort Ridgley, in Minnesota, and it had left a well beaten trail along the Floyd River. This battery suffered severely in the first Battle of Bull Run, July 22, 1861. On my way back I decided to follow this trail as far as I could north and then I left it in a right line for Spirit Lake. I left this trail either in Buncombe (now Lyon) or Osceola County. In the following day, while riding under a hot noon-day sun, I became very somnolent and slept while riding. In fact, I fell off my pony, and then I tied my pony to my foot with my lariat and lay down and slept it out. When I awoke, to my great surprise, the sun was in the north. I now had to resort to my pocket compass to discover, if I could what had gone wrong with the sun. Imagine my surprise when I discovered that the compass was just as erratic as the sun. It now began to dawn upon me that my idea of direction was muddled and I was lost. The question now arose, Where am I? Which way have I been travelling? Which way shall I go?

I, however, took a course and while riding along I suddenly came upon what seemed to me to be a camp of Indian *tepees* on the prairie. My first thought was to turn back, and then I was afraid if I should be discovered the Indians would give chase, so I decided the best thing I could do was to move right on, which I did, and when I neared the supposed camp of *tepees*, to my great surprise up jumped a herd of elk and ran away over a divide. The elk horns which I saw were so magnified by the clear atmosphere that I mistook them for *tepees*.

After the herd ran over the divide I heard several shots fired, and as there were no white men in that country, as I believed, I made up my mind that the shots had been fired by Indians. I did not want to meet any Indians, yet I was curious to know from whence the shots came, so I dismounted and crept cautiously to the top of the divide; the elk had disappeared, but I saw a man going in the opposite direction to which I was going, and I, for the time, was greatly relieved. After going a few miles I was hailed by two men coming towards me, whom I took for Indians, and I tried hard to avoid them, and they tried as hard to intercept me.

They finally waved their hats, and then I knew they were white men and turned to meet them. When we met these two men simply exhausted their vocabulary of profanity on me. They were members of a party of government surveyors and said they had not seen a white man for so long that they almost had a mind to shoot me for trying to evade them. They soon informed me that their chief surveyor, Alfred Wilkins, was lost and they were trying to find him. I then related the incident of the elks and how I saw a man going in the opposite direction that I came. They then put one of their party on a horse and started him after him with a very large tin horn. He returned to camp during the night with the lost surveyor all right.

I camped with the party and at our mess I shared with them some of the delicacies I had brought with me from Sioux City, which they enjoyed, especially the cigars. They now informed me that I was in Osceola County, and in the morning gave me the direction to take to reach Spirit Lake. I was glad that I had not wandered away farther than I did, for had they told me that I had wandered into the then unceded territory of Dakota I would have scarcely been prepared to dispute it. However, I consoled myself with the thought that if I was lost the government surveyor had undergone a similar experience. '*Misery loves company.*'

DICKINSON COUNTY ORGANISED

I reached Spirit Lake the next day, and soon posted the notices for the election in Dickinson County. The election came and Ave elected a full line of county and township officers. I had the honour of being elected the first sheriff. The election over, we held a jollification, made speeches, etc. O. C. Howe in a speech said we had the most independent set of officers he ever knew, that each man in the county had an office of some kind, and we owed no thanks to anyone, as we had elected ourselves. The election passed off very quietly. There were no charges of ballot box stuffing and no contests.

It certainly was an honest election, and I know of no election since that I have had the same good opinion of. Every man had an office and the harmony that followed was great. The secret of good government and honest election lies in the plan of giving every man an office. If the administration at Washington will act on the line of this theory there will be no reason why turbulent Kentucky in time should not become as peaceable and order loving as Ohio. I make no charge for this tip.

C. F. Hill.

Mr. Hill in his letter mentions the fact that "a few days before Sherman's battery had passed from Fort Scott to Fort Ridgley in Minnesota, and that in doing so they left a well beaten trail along the Floyd River to the state line, which they crossed near the northwest corner of Osceola County." This trail was visible for years and served as a road through that country when going to Sioux City from here. The practice was to go west until that trail was struck and then follow it. Later the usual route to Sioux City was by way of Peterson and Cherokee, then across the prairie to Melbourne. By this route a fifty mile prairie had to be crossed without a house. "Twelve mile slough" and "twenty mile slough" were as well known by the early traveller as stopping places as the leading hotels now are.

It is well known as a historical fact that during the years of 1855 and 1850, there had been a rush of emigration to the West, such as had hitherto been unknown. People neglected their legitimate business and many run wild in town lot and real estate speculations. Emigration had been booming and all kinds of property throughout the West advanced in value at fabulous rates. Vast amounts of money were loaned at as high rates as five *per cent* a month for the purpose of investing in western lands. Everybody was dealing in real estate. Towns were laid out and railroads projected in every possible direction. The wildest extravagance took the place of judicious economy and business sense. This state of affairs could not last, but finally culminated in the financial crash of 1857, which everyone admits was induced by over speculation.

The revulsion was instantaneous and complete, and nowhere were the consequences more severely felt than on the frontier. Emigration immediately came to a standstill, real estate became valueless and town property a byword. The gold was soon swept out of the country and the currency was worthless. Perhaps there are some at this time who don't understand what was implied in a bank failure previous to the time of the national banks. Not only did the depositors suffer, but the bill holders as well. Many banks were based on the fictitious and inflated values prevalent at that time, and when the bottom fell out, depositor and bill holder went to ruin together. All projected enterprises and improvements were for the time abandoned.

The effect of this state of affairs upon the frontier settlements was disastrous in the extreme, and in no place was the depressing effects felt more keenly than in this county. To remain here seemed to court a life of hardship and privation, while to return to the older settled portions of the country offered nothing that was much better. It was the old orthodox dilemma, "*You are lost if you do, and you are lost if you don't.*" Of course the conditions of the settlers became much changed. Frontier life, instead of being a short period of adventure which in a few years would be rewarded by positions of influence and affluence, became a desperate struggle with adverse circumstances for existence.

Some emigration came in in the fall of 1857, but in most cases it was made up of persons who had been stripped of their property by the panic and struck for the frontier to try their luck anew. In the fall of 1857 a couple of men named Isaac Jones and William Miller, from Story County, brought in a small steam sawmill, which they set up on the bank of East Okoboji Lake, at a point a little southwest of the Stevens' boat-landing. It was a small affair, but it supplied a want that had been severely felt. Previous to this time no lumber had been used in the construction of the cabins. Doors, window frames, door frames, stools and benches had been constructed by splitting out puncheons from the bodies of trees and then dressing them down to the desired thickness with a hand axe and jack plane. Heretofore the nearest mill was at Algona.

The first man to bring his family into the county subsequent to the massacre was Hon. O. C. Howe, who arrived here with his wife and one child on the sixth of August. Mrs. Howe was the first woman to set foot in the county after the massacre, and her coming was counted as an event of considerable interest, if not importance. Their daughter, a bright girl of three or four years of age, was the first child in the settlement. It had been from two to four months since any of the boys had seen either woman or child, and it was wonderful what a transformation the contact wrought in their habits and deportment.

Not much was done at farming during the summer. Some few had breaking done on their claims, but as a rule, farming was neglected. In fact, but few had come here to farm anyway. They had come to secure government land, which they imagined would soon appreciate in value, thereby making them forehanded. They were wiser after two or three years' experience. Had they gone into stock-raising for all there was in it, and kept at it during all those years when the vacant prairies stretching indefinitely in every direction furnished unlimited range for stock, they might have made a good thing of it, provided the straggling parties of marauding Indians that infested the frontier up to 1863 did not come in and compel them to divide profits. But then they were like the proverbial Dutchman, their foresight was not near so good as their back sight.

The second man to bring his family was Rosalvo Kingman, who came from Sparta, Wisconsin. Mr. Kingman was first here early in July, then went back for his family and returned sometime in September. About the same time a roving character by the name of Thurston came along with his family and spent the winter, but left early in the spring. These three, with a Mrs. Peters, who lived upon the isthmus between East Okoboji and Spirit Lake, constituted the sum total of female society in Dickinson County during the winter of 1857 and

1858.

The mention of the name of Peters brings to mind the old red mill which may as well be noticed here as anywhere. In the fall of 1857 a man by the name of James S. Peters, from Bureau County, Illinois, conceived the project of building a mill on the isthmus between Spirit and East Okoboji Lakes, and for that purpose cut a race across from one lake to the other. There was at that time nearly eight feet difference in the level of the two lakes, so that had the water supply been sufficient the mill could eventually have been made a success.

In the summer of 1858, with the assistance of such of the inhabitants as had faith enough in the project to lend a helping hand, Peters succeeded in getting up the frame and putting in the machinery, which was of a very rude and primitive character, having made the most of it himself. He finally got the mill in operation in 1859, but his work was so unsatisfactory and defective that it was a failure. The supply of water was also insufficient, as was afterwards proven. Peters was a half crazy fanatic and a believer in witchcraft, and when by reason of low water or the imperfections of his machinery his mill refused to work, he invariably ascribed it to some person having bewitched his machinery.

Having decided in his own mind who the guilty person was, he would draw an outline of their profile with a piece of chalk on an oak tree that stood near the mill, and then would sometime spend a half day at a time shooting the figure with silver bullets. He seems to have imagined that if he could only hit upon the right person and then shoot his figure with a silver bullet, that the spell would be broken and his power over him and his operations would cease. He was always very careful to cut the bullets out again after he had exhausted his supply. After trying in vain to do something with his mill for a year or two, dividing his time about especially between witches and work, he sold it to Stimpson and Davis, of Emmet County, who overhauled it, but failed to achieve any great success.

The story is told that one day a half-witted chap from the head of Spirit Lake was down to the mill waiting for his grist, and getting impatient, remarked that he could eat the grain faster than that mill could grind it.

"Well, but," said Stimpson, "how long could you do it?"

"Until I starved to death," replied the boy.

Stimpson kept the mill until 1869, when he disposed of it to Oliver Compton, who overhauled it again thoroughly, putting in an entire new set of first-class machinery. But it was of no use, the water power was a failure. The drawing of the water out of Spirit Lake had lowered that lake and raised Okoboji accordingly, and the project, after sinking several thousand dollars in it, had to be abandoned. The old frame was torn down afterwards and the timbers used for bridge timbers.

Among those who were here previous to the massacre were Philip Risling and Robert Madison, from Delaware County, both of whom were stopping temporarily with the Mattock family. Along about the holidays Risling went back to his home, but Madison remained here, and as a consequence fell a victim to the massacre. In the summer of 1857, Mr. Risling, with a party of neighbours, consisting of William Oldman, George Deitrick, Levi Daugherty and William Wisegarver, came out, bringing with them coffins for the interment of their friends, the Mattocks and Madison. They brought seven coffins in all. They disinterred the bodies of their friends and took them out southwest on the prairie and buried them on Mr. Oldham's claim. The place has since become the property of Wood Allen.

Instead of taking his claim about the lakes, Mr. Risling took his claim down on the Little Sioux. Shortly after that some half dozen claims were taken over on the Little Sioux, the earlier ones by Moses Miller, Andrew Oleson, Gunder and Omen Mattheson. A little later H. Meeker and Mr. Close commenced their enterprise of building a mill on the outlet which they abandoned a couple of years later. Before the close of the war this settlement was reinforced by R. R. Wilcox and Hiram Davis, who also took claims on the Sioux. This little settlement, although insignificant in numbers, was important from the fact that it was the first point reached after crossing a forty mile prairie, in coming from Sioux City by way of Peterson and Cherokee. Mose Miller's shack was small and dirty and inconvenient but the light from his window looked mighty cheerful and encouraging to a person who had been toiling all day through the snow across that inhospitable prairie without meeting a human being or seeing a vestige of anything indicating the existence of civilized life.

We will now resume the current of events which we have been considering as having occurred in the fall of 1857 and the winter of 1857 and 1858. Under the old constitution, we had two fall elections, one in August when the county officers were chosen, and one in October when state and legislative officers were elected. The August election has already been noticed. This county at that time was embraced in the Fort Dodge representative district. C. C. Carpenter and

John F. Duncombe, both of Fort Dodge, were the opposing candidates. The vote of this county was almost unanimous for Carpenter.

After the vote had been duly canvassed and certified to, then the question arose how were the returns to be sent in in time to be counted. There was no post-office and no mails, and it was not known that any person was going out by whom the returns could be sent in time. In this dilemma it became necessary for some one to volunteer to carry in the returns. It was finally arranged that R. A. Smith should take them to Fort Dodge, but fortunately, on reaching the Des Moines River, on the evening of the first day out he fell in with R. E. Carpenter, a brother of C. C, who was on his way to the lakes for the purpose of getting them. The election was very close, the returns from this county deciding it in favour of Carpenter, and the county has stood by him loyally ever since.

The winter of 1857 and 1858 was a remarkably mild one and in marked contrast with the one previous. There was no difficulty in getting in a sufficient supply of provisions. The hard times did not affect the people here, so seriously then as later. The total number wintering at the lakes that winter was not far from forty. At this time there had been erected about a half dozen cabins in the immediate region of the old fort, and they made up in high sounding names what they lacked in pretentious appearance. The "St. Charles" was a one room log cabin, with a large stone fireplace in one end, while a short distance from it was the "St. Cloud," a cabin about twelve by fourteen feet and about seven feet high with a half window and a dirt roof. Still further on was the "St. Bernard," where three or four of the boys divided their time that winter between reading Shakespeare and playing seven-up.

Although no outbreak had occurred, many entertained serious apprehensions of danger from the Indians. While there was no serious alarm felt, all acknowledged the necessity of being on the alert and keeping a sharp lookout for danger. At one time, in order to allay the fears of the women and children, a system of standing sentry was adopted, whereby two men were selected each night to do duty as a kind of picket guard by patrolling the immediate neighbourhood of the fort and cabins. After a while this became monotonous and was finally abandoned.

A small party of Indians representing themselves as belonging to Little Crow's band from the Yellow Medicine Agency, put in an appearance here some time in January. they claimed to belong to the same party that had rendered such signal service in rescuing Mrs.

Marble and Abigail Gardner from the Indians the previous year. They camped in Center Grove, and remained there about six weeks, when they returned to Minnesota. The leader of this band called himself Little John, and claimed to be a son of Little Crow, which claim was afterwards known to be false. Little Crow was not so well known then as he was later. Later in the winter a party near Peterson, in Clay County, had a brush with a small party of Indians. Mr. Jareb Palmer, of Spirit Lake, who was then carrying the mail from there to Sioux City, was a member of the party. After a running fight for about an hour, in which one or two were slightly wounded, but no one seriously, the settlers drew off, leaving the Indians in possession of the field.

This affair created a considerable alarm, and it was decided to apply to the state for protection. A meeting was called at the "old fort" to consider the situation, and a committee appointed to draw up a petition and present the matter to the state authorities. The legislature was in session. A statement of the affair and a petition to the legislature asking immedi.ate assistance was drawn up. Mr. Jareb Palmer was selected to take the petition to Des Moines and lay it before the authorities.

C. C. Carpenter represented this district. He took hold of the matter in earnest, and in the shortest time possible, a bill was passed providing for the raising of a company of volunteers for the defence of the northwestern frontier. The company was raised principally in Hamilton and Webster Counties, though not entirely. Upon arriving at the lakes, the captain was authorised to enlist ten additional men from the settlers here. The names of these additional enlistments were as follows: A. Kingman, J. Palmer, E. Palmer, W. Donnelson, J. D. Hawkins, George W. Rogers, Charles Clark, William Carsley, William Allen and one other whose name is unknown. It was organised by the election of Henry Martin of Webster City, captain; William Church of Homer, first lieutenant; and a Mr. Jewett of Border Plains, second lieutenant. It was the wife of Lieutenant Church who acted so heroic a part in the defence of the cabin of Mr. Thomas at Springfield against the attack of the Indians the spring before.

This company arrived upon the frontier about the last of February or first of March, and was divided into three squads; Captain Martin, with the main squad, making his headquarters at the old fort at Spirit Lake; Lieutenant Church with one squad at Peterson, and Lieutenant Jewett with the remaining one at Emmet. This company had nothing to do with the force known as the Northern Border Brigade, which was not organised until some three years later.

This force was kept on duty until about the first of July, when they were ordered off, but not disbanded. In the fall of 1858, upon the earnest representations of a large majority of the inhabitants, they were again ordered into service and kept on duty along the frontier until the following spring, when they were discharged. This was the last of any military operations until the breaking out of the war in 1861.

CHAPTER 15

The Spirit Lake Claim Club

Among the incidents of the winter of 1857 and 1858 may be mentioned the formation of a claim club. It will be remembered that the government surveys were not yet made, and that claims were held under the laws of the state, giving each person the right to defend his possession to three hundred and twenty acres. Of course, it gave him no title to the land, but simply the right to defend his possession against everything but an adverse title. Under the provisions of the Dickinson County Claim Club, each inhabitant was entitled to two claims, one in his own name and the other in the name of some other party who was to settle upon and improve it within one year from the time it was taken. According to the articles of association adopted, the club was to be under the command of a captain and two lieutenants, who were to call out the club when the assumed rights of any of the claimants were trespassed upon. The captain of the club at the time of its organisation was William Carsley. The lieutenants were Charles F. Hill and J. D. Hawkins. The organisation was short-lived and was never called into service.

The first post-office in the county, and, in fact, the first one in all northwestern Iowa, was established at Spirit Lake in February, 1858, by the appointment of R. U. Wheelock as postmaster. Previous to this time most of the settlers had their mail addressed either to Fort Dodge or Sioux City and forwarded from there as opportunities presented themselves. There had been a semi-monthly mail route from Mankato to Sioux City, established as early as 1856, but it was not regularly carried until the winter of 1857. The contract was in the hands of a Mr. Babcock, of Kasota, Minnesota, for which he received the sum of $4,000 a year, besides a government subsidy of one section of government land for each twenty miles of route in Minnesota.

A Mr. Pease, of Jackson County, Minnesota, had taken the contract of Babcock as sub-contractor. He carried the north part himself, and sublet the south part from Spirit Lake to Sioux City to Jareb Palmer, as has been before stated. During the summer of 1858 this mail contract fell into the hands of two young men residing at Kasota, Minnesota, Orin Nason and Cephas Bedow, who run it until 1802. In addition to carrying the mail, which they did promptly and faithfully, they did numberless errands for people along the route. There was no store between Mankato and Sioux City, consequently there was no end to the little purchases they were required to make, and upon their weekly arrival their vehicle had much the appearance of a Yankee peddler's outfit—loaded down with articles "too numerous to mention."

When they commenced running the route there was no trail whatever between here and Peterson, so on one trip they took along a lot of bushes and set them along their route at such distances apart that they could easily see from one to the other. In this way they soon had a trail they could follow without difficulty. At one time while they had the route there came a heavy snowstorm which rendered crossing the wide prairies with a light rig like theirs impossible. Bedow started with the mail as usual and got as far as the Norwegian settlement at the head of the south branch of the Watonwan when he found it would be impossible to get through. Accordingly he engaged a Norwegian by the name of Torson to make the trip. A person who has never seen a Norwegian on his snowshoes can have no idea of the rapidity with which they get over the road. All of the ravines and low places were filled with snow which had been packed hard by the strong wind, making the finest kind of a track for the long, slender "skees."

On this occasion Torson made the trip from Spirit Lake to Sioux City and return in five days, with the heavy mail sack strapped to his shoulders. The distance as then travelled was over one hundred and twenty miles, or for the entire trip near two hundred and fifty miles, or an average of fifty miles a day. Some days he must have made considerably more than this. He made a few more trips until the snow went down so they could put their teams on again.

R. U. Wheelock continued in this position as postmaster at Spirit Lake until he left the county in 1861, when it was turned over to B. F. Parmenter, his brother-in-law, who performed the duties of the office until he left the county, a year or two later.

The Okoboji post-office was established about a year after the one at Spirit Lake. G. H Bush was the first postmaster, but as he left after a few months the office was transferred to M. J. Smith, who, after a few years, turned it over to J. W. O'Farrell. These were the only two post-offices in the county up to the time of the establishment of the Milford office about 1869.

The semi-monthly mail from Mankato to Sioux City was kept up until 1862, although other mail facilities were provided before that time. In 1859 a weekly mail was put on between Algona and Spirit Lake. Judge Asa C. Call, of Algona, had the contract, which he sublet to a Mr. Henderson, of the same place. Bob Henderson is well and kindly remembered by all the old settlers of that day. These routes were both discontinued in 1862, and a weekly route from Spirit Lake to Fort Dodge substituted in their place. This route was carried by John Gilbert and may be referred to again.

It will be difficult to give the minor events of the period now under consideration in anything like the order in which they occurred, and, indeed, except for the fact that they are the first, the commencement, of anything like civilized life in this new country, would be considered decidedly commonplace and not worth relating at all.

The first funeral services held in the county were at Okoboji in the spring of 1858. Daniel Poorman, a blacksmith from Newton, had commenced the erection of a shop at Okoboji, and had it partly completed when one Sunday several of the boys were in bathing, he among the rest. He struck out some distance where he was seized with a cramp, and before they were aware of any trouble, he was past resuscitation. They recovered the body and did what they could to bring him to, but without success. The boys made a rude coffin out of such materials as could be found, and he was buried the next evening near the south end of the east shore of West Okoboji Lake.

Later on, during the same summer, a child of William Barkman was drowned while playing on the dock to which a boat was fastened. This was on the isthmus, near the old red mill. Mr. Barkman lived on the isthmus at that time, and was helping Peters get the old mill into operation. It was a singular circumstance, and one that occasioned a considerable remark at the time, that for three or four years after the first settlement of the county there were no deaths except by accident. But such was the case.

The first white child born in the county was Robert Wheelock Howe, son of Mr. and Mrs. O. C. Howe, born in February, 1858. The first girl, and second child born in the county was Dena Barkman, daughter of Mr. and Mrs. Henry Barkman, born in the summer of

1858.

In the spring of 1858 there was a reasonable amount of emigration. Many of those who had been here the previous year on prospecting tours, returned in the spring for permanent settlement, bringing their families with them. Other families also came on the representations of their friends. Prominent among those who brought their families here that spring were J. D. Howe, R. U. Wheelock, B. F. Parmenter, J. S. Prescott, Henry Schuneman, Henry Barkman, James Ball, Leonidas Congleton, Alvarado Kingman, William Barkman, George Ring, Philip Risling and several others. M. J. Smith and his sister, Myra Smith, came that spring. These, with those who wintered here, constituted quite a company and was the commencement of the formation of society in northwestern Iowa.

The young ladies belonging to the several families at that time were as follows: Misses Sarah and Mary Howe, Miss Belle Wheelock, Miss Myra Smith, Misses Mary and Emma Congleton, Miss Sarah McMillen and Miss Dema Adams. The number of young men here at the time was about thirty.

As has been before stated, the places claimed by Granger and his men remained vacant until this spring, when M. J. Smith made a claim on what is now known as Smith's Point, a couple of young men by the names of Dan Calwell and T. S. Ruff on what is known as Dixon's Beach, and Jareb Palmer on upper Maple Grove, now known as Omaha Beach. Cabins were built on most of the claims, and some farming was done this season. It seems like a wild statement now, but it is a fact nevertheless, that the greatest hindrance to successful farming at that time was the ravages of the blackbirds. No person who was not a witness to it can form any conception of the extent of the destruction possible to be wrought by a flock of healthy blackbirds.

Corn was the principal crop, as no machinery for handling small grain had been introduced into the country. The time when the blackbirds were the most destructive was when the grain was just coming out of the ground, or about the last week in May and the first two weeks in June. They would come in such clouds as to almost darken the sun, and lighting down on the mellow fields where the corn was just coming up, would destroy a large area in an incredibly short space of time. They have been known to destroy for one man an entire forty acre field in one day. And one great difficulty about it was that there was no way of keeping them off. Scare them up in one place and they would immediately light down in another and keep right on with their work of destruction. Shooting among them had no appreciable effect, but it was lots of fun for the boys and gave them good practice. Fred Gilbert, who has so long held the world's championship trophy, first acquired his wonderful skill as a wing shot by shooting blackbirds in his father's cornfield with an old muzzle-loader.

Effigies and scarecrows placed in the field had no effect whatever. Various schemes and devices were tried to circumvent them, but with indifferent success. Some claimed that soaking the seed in copperas water or in tar so as to give it a bitter taste kept them off, but about the only remedy that had any appreciable effect, and one by which many farmers saved a portion of their crops, was to scatter corn on their fields every day for the birds to pick up. By this means, and a continuous working of the corn until it was too large for them, a portion of the crop was saved for the time. But the farmer's tribulations were not by any means over when his corn was too large for them to pull or scratch up. Just when the kernel was forming, or when it was in "roasting ears," the birds were very destructive; nearly or quite as much so as in the spring. They would light on the ears, and stripping down the silks and the husks, would destroy the grain on the ear in a very short time.

Many a man who had neglected to watch his field for a few days was surprised on going to it to find only a few dried cobs. Some farmers saved a portion of their crops by erecting several high platforms in their fields and keeping their children on them yelling, screaming, ringing cowbells and drumming on tin pans until they were completely worn out. This plan had one advantage, if no other; the children made all the noise they wanted to and nobody scolded them for it. The pest became so general that in the Eighth General Assembly Mr. Blackford of Algona, succeeded in getting a bill through providing for paying a bounty on blackbirds, which remained in force about four years, when it was repealed. The pest died out gradually as the country settled. As the area of tillable land was gradually increased, the birds scattered until their depredations were no longer noticeable.

The emigration during the summer of 1858 was not quite up to the expectations of the settlers, but was all that could have been reasonably expected under the circumstances. The summer was a remarkably wet one. Continuous rains had swollen the streams so as to render them almost impassable. The larger streams were out of their banks for weeks at a time, while the smaller ones, which were ordinarily nothing but little rivulets that one could step across, were now spread out to a width of several yards and swimming deep. As a matter of course, such a season was very unfavourable to emigration and settlement. To a person having had no experience in matters of this kind and unacquainted with the various devices and contrivances which were resorted to for crossing swollen streams and bottomless sloughs, it would seem to be an utter impossibility to make any progress whatever in the face of such formidable obstacles.

And yet the emigration of the summer of 1858 was made in the face of just such difficulties. Most of the travel was with ox teams, but very few horses being used at that time. Oxen were preferred on account of requiring so much less grain, and from the fact that all the care they needed was to be turned loose on the prairie at night, and they were all ready to start again in the morning. It was customary to travel in small parties consisting of three or four or half a dozen teams, each team consisting of two to four yoke of oxen hitched to the proverbial covered wagon, or "prairie schooner," as it was then best known.

Each wagon was or should have been provided with a cable rope from seventy-five to one hundred feet long. In travelling, whenever a party reached a slough or marsh, or other place difficult to cross, it was customary to "double up" and help each other over. This was done by driving up as near to the slough as could be done without miring down, and then one or more of the boys would take two or three yoke of cattle, or as many as were needed, and cable enough to reach to solid ground on the other side and cross over. The cables were then rigged from the team and wagon on the one side to the teams that had crossed over, and as soon as everything was in readiness the signal was given to start, when by dint of much yelling and whipping, and some swearing, which, under the mitigating circumstances, wasn't usually considered a very serious offense, the other side was usually reached without any mishap other than a general bespattering of everything with mud and water. It was absolutely necessary after once starting in to keep going until solid ground was reached on the other side, since if by any unforeseen accident, a wagon should "mire down," it would keep settling and the black, sticky mud would settle in around the wheels until it would be impossible to extricate it in any other manner than by unloading and prying out, and this in two or three feet of mud and water was no picnic. This process had to be repeated with variations until every wagon was over.

In crossing streams that were too deep for fording, the method of procedure was somewhat different. It was customary to take the best wagon box in the outfit and caulk it, making it as nearly watertight as possible. Cattle are natural swimmers, and they seem to like it when they get used to it. They soon learn, upon arriving at a stream, to strike straight across and make a landing upon the further side without any delay whatever. Upon arriving at a stream too deep for fording the wagon box that had been fitted up for that purpose would be taken off and transformed into a ferry boat. A cable would be rigged to each end of it, when a boy would mount one of the oxen that had been trained for that kind of work, and swim the stream, holding the rope in his hand.

Arriving at the opposite side, he would make fast his rope, turn his cattle loose and proceed at once to business, which was to ferry the balance of the party across. The first load to go over would of course be men enough to manage the ferry and take care of the goods as they were sent over. The wagons would now be drawn up to the bank of the stream, where they would be unloaded and their contents placed aboard the improvised ferry boat, and drawn over to the further side by the men who had previously crossed over, and there unloaded again. The wagon box would then be drawn back and loaded and again sent over. This operation would be repeated and re-repeated until the contents of all the wagons were over. Then the wagon boxes would be lashed down to the running gear and the wagons floated over. The cattle would then swim across, the balance of the party be ferried over and the labour of crossing the stream finished.

The next job was reloading and repacking the wagons and getting ready for another start. It was no uncommon experience for a party, on arriving at the banks of a stream, to go into camp for the night and then spend the whole of the next day in crossing over and getting reloaded, and camp the second night on the opposite side of the stream. The experience described above was the rule and not the exception in the summer of 1858.

But this was not all. The financial crash of the previous year, which, by the way, was the most disastrous the country had ever known, was now being felt through the West with terrible severity. It became necessary to adopt a system of economy and self-denial, such as had not been experienced for many years previous and has not been known since. There was absolutely no money in the country. People residing in the older portions of the state well remember how utterly impossible it was at that time to raise money by any ordinary means. Nearly all of the banks in the country had failed, and as there was then no provision for securing and redeeming the circulation, the bills became worthless. From the crash of 1857 to the breaking out of the war business was at a perfect standstill.

It was with the utmost difficulty that the commonest necessities of life could be secured, and all luxuries, and much of what is now deemed necessary to support existence, had to be wholly dispensed with. Such necessaries as tea, coffee and sugar, and, indeed, groceries of all kinds, were indulged in by but very few, and by them but sparingly. Corn, wheat or barley was made to answer as a substitute for coffee, while "prairie tea" was a very common beverage. This "prairie tea" was nothing more nor less than the leaves of the "redroot," that grew so plentifully on the wild prairie, treated or drawn in the same manner as ordinary tea. It was an astringent, and was said to have much the same effect on the human system as the tea in ordinary use.

In the matter of clothing the same rigid economy had to be observed. Many were the men who wore moccasins made of rawhide, and pants made of grain bags, because they could get nothing better,— not worthless tramps, either, but men of education, energy and intelligence. It was no uncommon experience for families to live for weeks with no breadstuffs, except such as they could grind in a coffee mill, which, together with a little meat, milk, and game or fish, furnished their entire supply of provisions.

CHAPTER 16

The Troops Ordered Back to the Lakes

When we now look back and consider the obstacles that met the early settler at every stage of his progress at this time, the only wonder is that any exhibited the energy, hardihood and pluck necessary to overcome them and gain a foothold under such adverse conditions. As might be expected, jealousies and differences of opinion began to manifest themselves as different and apparently conflicting interests began to develop.

One question on which the sentiment was divided was the policy of applying for troops as a protection against the Indians. One portion insisted that, from the exposed position of the settlement on the frontier, we were liable at any moment to be attacked by the Indians and swept out of existence before any aid could be obtained or resistance made. On the other hand, it was argued by those who were opposed to applying for troops, that inasmuch as the large bodies of savages had left the country, there was really no danger, and that the act of asking for troops for the purpose of protection had the appearance and effect of advertising to the world that there was danger and that this was dangerous ground to occupy, thus preventing emigration. The consequence was petitions and remonstrances went in from both sides, each side representing the condition of affairs as viewed from its own standpoint.

It will be remembered that the troops stationed here the previous winter had been called in in the spring, but not discharged, the organisation having been kept intact, and the proposition was to have this body of troops ordered into service again. This plan finally prevailed. The troops were ordered back here in the fall of 1858, and kept here until their discharge in the spring of 1859.

In the fall of 1858 the first election was held under the new constitution. In the Fourth Judicial District, Hon. A. W. Hubbard, of Sioux City, was elected District Judge and Hon. O. C. Howe, of Spirit Lake, District Attorney.

The winter of 1858 and 1859 was not marked by any event out of the ordinary other than has been related. The more timid suffered from continued apprehensions of Indian troubles. There apprehensions were somewhat intensified by the arrival at the lakes, some time in January, of a party of Indians in charge of a half-breed by the name of John Campbell, who acted as chief and interpreter. These Indians claimed to be friendly, but a couple of trappers from the Des Moines River, by the names of John Dodson and Henry Chiffen, who were trapping at the lakes at the time, claimed to recognise two of them as having belonged to Inkpadutah's band. They had been trapping along the Des Moines River for a year or two and had frequently come in contact with the Indians. It will be remembered that Mr. Chiffen was one of the messengers who went from Springfield to Fort Ridgley for help after learning of the massacre at the lakes and before the attack on Springfield. Dodson and Chiffen both claimed to identify two of Campbell's men as belonging to Inkpadutah's band and presumably as participating in the massacre at the lakes.

Acting upon this information, Captain Martin determined to arrest them and send them to Des Moines, that their case might be investigated. A detail of soldiers was made for that purpose, and the party started, arriving at Mahan's place on the Des Moines River the first day. During the evening the Indians were very uneasy and kept going in and out of doors, and kept their guards busy looking after them. Finally about nine o'clock in the evening they both went out at the same time, the guards accompanying them. When a short distance from the house they commenced talking to each other by the usual Indian grunts, when all at once they both dropped their blankets to the ground and sprinting away from their guards, started on the run and were soon lost in the darkness.

The surprised guards returned next day to headquarters, where they were most unmercifully nagged by their comrades for allowing their prisoners to escape them so easily. The balance of the band were kept prisoners at Spirit Lake for nearly three weeks, when Captain Martin decided that he had cared for them long enough and the best thing to do would be to send them back to the agency at once. Accordingly he dispatched a squad of eight or ten men in charge of A. Kingman to escort them out of the state. Kingman and his men accompanied them as far as they could and be sure of getting back to the fort the same day. Then they left them with orders to get back to the agency as soon as possible and not try to visit the lakes again.

Upon arriving at Marble Grove on his return, Kingman fell in with a squad of four or five soldiers and as many Indians who had been sent out by the commandant at Fort Ridgley to look after Campbell and his party. Kingman and his men followed a different route on their return than they did on going out. This accounts for their not falling in with the other party earlier in the day. The sergeant in charge at once enquired for news of Campbell's party, when Kingman proceeded to tell them the whole story. This the sergeant and his men accepted as true, but the Indians were suspicious, and one of them, a strapping big fellow who could talk English stepped before him and looking him square in the face, exclaimed: "You lie! God damn you. You have killed those Indians." Except for the presence of the soldiers there might have been serious trouble then and there, but they soon had the Indians cooled down and started at once for Fort Ridgley, and as was afterwards learned, overtook Campbell's party when about halfway there.

As before stated, Campbell was a half-breed, and at the breaking out of the War of the Rebellion, in company with several half-breeds and Indians, enlisted and went south, but were soon after discharged for disability. It was a curious fact that came to the surface during the war that the Indians and half-breeds enlisted from Minnesota could not withstand the hardships and vicissitudes of camp life at all in comparison with the volunteers. After his discharge, Campbell returned to Minnesota, where he lived a kind of roving life along the Minnesota River in the vicinity of Mankato and New Ulm. Later on he was accused of the murder of the Jewett family, on Elm Creek in Minnesota. He was taken to Mankato, tried, found guilty and hanged.

Another party of Indians visited the lakes that winter that may as well be noticed here as anywhere, inasmuch as the date of their coming cannot be definitely determined, although the incident is vouched for by several credible witnesses. They were in charge of a chief by the name of "Bad Hail," a very old man. They came down from the Northwest, and went into camp in the bend of the Little, Sioux west of Milford, in what was then known as the Risling Grove. The first seen of them, two of their number came to the settlement begging for provisions and stated that one of the squaws was very sick. Captain Martin immediately dispatched a squad of troops to the place with orders to bring the Indians to headquarters at once. This order was obeyed. Upon their arrival at the fort the squaw proved to be really quite sick, whereupon the medicine man of the party proceeded to treat the case in accordance with the most approved methods of Indian practice. They laid her down at full length upon the floor and then proceeded to deposit gunpowder in small quantities at different places in a circle entirely around her. Then they formed in Indian file and commenced marching around her, chanting their monotonous "*Hi Yi, Hi Yi*," and every little while touching off one of the deposits of the powder.

These incantations were kept up for some time, and the curious thing about the whole matter was that the squaw was soon visibly better and by the next morning was able to resume the journey. The captain sent a squad of men to escort them beyond the state line, giving them strict orders to go back to the agency as soon as possible and stay there. The discouraging circumstances under which the settlers laboured and the difficulties they encountered were much intensified by the bitter quarrel which about this time broke out among the leading men of the settlement. A steam mill had been purchased the previous year by Howe, Wheelock and Parmenter and shipped to Iowa City, which was at that time the terminus of the railroad. There was no advance payment made, but one was due before it could be moved from Iowa City. The financial panic coming on at the time it did, the purchasers found themselves without the money necessary to meet the payment they had promised, or even to pay the freight. In this emergency they turned the contract over to Prescott, who paid the freight and assumed the entire obligation for the mill.

At the same time he entered into a kind of written agreement with Howe and Wheelock whereby they were to retain a kind of partnership in running the mill. The language of this agreement was somewhat vague, and afterward gave rise to no end of trouble. In the spring of 1858 this mill was lying in the Rock Island depot at Iowa City. The distance to Spirit Lake by the then travelled route was but little short of three hundred miles. For the last two hundred miles of the route the streams were not bridged, the low prairie was under water, the streams were bank full and some of them overflowing. The boiler weighed about four tons; the balance of the machine was in such shape that it could be (distributed in such a way as not to overload the wagons.

An old government wagon was procured for hauling the boiler. Something like twenty yoke of oxen were required to haul the entire outfit. The train was placed in charge of Mr. Wheelock. The time occupied in bringing it through was something over six weeks, which, considering the obstacles and drawbacks in the way, was a remarkably quick trip.

The mill was located in the grove south of the Okoboji bridge. It was not got into running order until some time in the winter following. Through some misunderstanding or misconstruction of the terms of the contract, a bitter quarrel arose between Doctor Prescott on one side and Howe, Wheelock and Parmenter on the other in regard to the control of the mill. The merits and demerits of that controversy are too voluminous and are not of sufficient importance to be given in detail. The contest was a long and bitter one, and before it was ended most of the people in the county had been drawn into taking sides with one party or the other.

While it would be both impossible and undesirable to give a detailed account of the events entering into this unfortunate controversy, one or two incidents will give some insight into the nature and intensity of it. Prescott, in addition to the Tusculum claims, endeavoured to hold the Okoboji Grove and the Gardner place. the Okoboji Grove he had staked off as a town site and was endeavouring to hold it as such under the town site law, although he didn't comply with its provisions very well. The Gardner place he was trying to hold under the pre-emption law. The mill was located in the northeast part of the Okoboji Grove. A log boarding house about sixteen by thirty feet in size had been built near it, also a blacksmith shop.

During the early part of the winter Prescott's men had cut and hauled into the yard where the mill was then being set up, about twelve hundred saw-logs, with the intention of cutting them into lumber as soon as the mill could be started. Howe and Wheelock and their party had thrown all the obstacles they could in the way of starting the mill, they claiming that Prescott was going ahead in violation of their contract.

Among other things they contended he was not complying with the law in relation to his town site claim, and, therefore, that it could be taken by any one who saw fit to file a contest on it. Consequently John Gilbert filed a claim on it under the provisions of the pre-emption law, and by virtue of so doing claimed ownership of the saw-logs that had been cut and hauled together, and commenced proceedings in the district court to take them out of Prescott's hands by a writ of replevin. C. F. Hill, the sheriff, refused to serve the writ, but they made a short job of removing him by requiring additional bonds and then refusing to accept any he could obtain, and appointing another. Matters came to a crisis on the twenty-second of February, 1859, when the newly appointed sheriff, with a posse of eight or ten men with six or eight teams, came to take possession of the logs and deliver them to Mr. Gilbert, whose plan was to remove a portion of the best ones to Spirit Lake to be used in making shingle.

In the meantime Prescott's men had kept pretty well posted on what was going on, and they made up their minds the logs should not go without a fight. Prescott himself was away. He went East some time in December, and his affairs were left in charge of G. H. Bush. the boys made it in their way to be in the mill-yard when they knew the sheriff was coming. The sheriff's party drove into the yard, where he read his writ to Mr. Bush and gave him a copy. They then commenced the operation of loading the logs, but when one was fairly loaded Prescott's men would grab it and roll it off on the other side. These proceedings were kept up for some little time, the sheriff's men loading a log when Prescott's men would tip it over, some of the time sled and all. In the meantime the conversation between the two parties was more remarkable for strength than for its beauty. In other words, the air was blue with profanity. But there weren't any logs taken away that day.

After two or three hours' wrangling, the sheriff and his party left, and in the evening came back with a warrant for the arrest of all those who had been engaged in resisting the service of the writ of replevin. This time he was accompanied by a small squad of soldiers, Captain Martin with his company of state troops being stationed at Spirit Lake at this time. The excitement now ran higher than ever. A majority were in favour of resisting, and it is more than probable that such would have been the outcome except for a very unexpected occurrence. Just as the excitement was at its height and the prospect seemed good for a general scrimmage, a messenger out of breath came running with all his might, stating that Indians were in the grove at the head of Spirit Lake.

The soldiers started for headquarters at once and a majority of the sheriff's posse started for home, regardless of prisoners or saw-logs. The sheriff insisted on taking with him two or three of the leaders and the balance were let off on their promise to appear and answer at the proper time, which they did. As soon as possible, Bush, Mr. Prescott's manager, consulted a lawyer. Judge Meservey of Fort Dodge, and by his advice obtained a counter replevin, which, together with an injunction obtained later on, put a stop to further proceedings, and the matter quietly died down. Gilbert never made any further attempt to get possession.

In the meantime Howe and Wheelock were determined the mill should not run without their claims to a part ownership were recognised, consequently when the mill was about ready to be started up they went down with quite a party of men and took away the valves from the pump and some of the minor pieces of machinery, thinking the mill could not be started without sending to the works where it was made and getting duplicates of the parts taken. But Mr. Mastellar, Prescott's engineer, being a very ingenious man, went to work and made new valves and supplied the missing parts. Prescott now obtained an injunction against all of the parties concerned, restraining them from interfering with his work and then started up the mill. In a few days, however, Howe and Wheelock with their men came down again and this time they took parts of the machinery that could not be replaced without sending to the works where the mill was made.

Prescott on his return from the East obtained the requisite papers for arresting the other parties for violating the injunction, he was accompanied by an officer and a posse of men from Webster County, but upon arriving here his men were missing, having skipped to Minnesota to avoid arrest. It seems that one of Captain Martin's men was in Fort Dodge at the time, and on learning what was up rode all night to get ahead of Prescott's party and warn the men. They remained in camp just over the state line for a few days, when that becoming irksome they boldly came back to town, submitted to an arrest and then went before Judge Congleton, who was in sympathy with them, and procured a writ of *habeas corpus* and were discharged. The first term of the district court for this county, which is mentioned in another place, coming on soon after this, the injunction was dissolved.

This was but one of the many episodes of this unfortunate quarrel, which was kept up with more or less bitterness until both sides were practically exhausted, but it will be neither interesting nor profitable to follow the details of it further. Taking a retrospective view of the matter it must be admitted that the blame should be about evenly divided.

It is now necessary to go back to where we left the inhabitants in a state of wild excitement over the appearance of a party of Indians in the grove at the head of Spirit Lake.

As soon as possible after the alarm was given, Captain Martin dispatched a small force to the head of the lake to investigate the Indian scare. Upon their arrival there they found old Chief Umpashota with his family and a few followers in camp, who upon seeing the troops were worse scared then they were. The soldiers took the Indians to headquarters as prisoners, where Captain Martin found himself in about the same predicament as the man who drew the white elephant in the lottery. He couldn't keep him, he couldn't sell him, he couldn't give him away, he hated to kill him and what to do with him he didn't know. In this case Captain Martin finally decided to send his prisoners to Fort Dodge and turn them over to the authorities there.

In pursuance of this plan he dispatched Lieutenant Church with a small detachment of men to carry it out. Church really understood the situation better than Martin himself, and knew that upon arriving at Fort Dodge he would be no better off than he was then; consequently, upon reaching Gillett's Grove he released the Indians upon their promise to stay away from the lakes in the future. This was without doubt the old chief's last visit to Spirit Lake.

No public schools had been established in the county up to this time, and were not until sometime Later. A private school was established by Doctor Prescott soon after the arrival of his family in the fall of 1858. Prescott had erected a comparatively convenient and comfortable house during the summer, one room of which was set aside for a schoolroom. The teacher employed was Miss Amanda L. Smith, Prescott's family, with a few outsiders, furnishing the pupils. The expense of this arrangement was borne by Doctor Prescott. It was kept up about a year and a half, or until the spring of 1860. A private school had also been started at Spirit Lake about the same time with Miss Mary Howe as teacher.

The first public school in the county was taught at Okoboji during the winter of 1862 and 1863, Miss Myra Smith, teacher, and will be noticed further.

The first term of the district court in the county was held at Spirit Lake in June, 1850. Judge Hubbard presided, with O. C. Howe, district attorney; Jareb Palmer, clerk of the district court, and Alfred Arthur, sheriff. Attorneys in attendance were B. F. Parmenter, Dickinson County; C. C. Smeltzer. Clay County, and Patt Robb, Woodbury County.

Nearly, if not quite all, of the business of this term grew out of the quarrel heretofore mentioned between Prescott on one side, and Howe, Wheelock and Parmenter on the other. If this quarrel was not the means of breaking up the enterprise of establishing the institution at Tusculum by Doctor Prescott, it certainly hurried up the event, for it demonstrated the fact that it would be utterly impossible for him to hold or maintain his claim to the land he had selected for that purpose, as there was no law under which he could do it. His enemies questioned his honesty and sincerity of motive and claimed that he was holding, or rather endeavouring to hold, all of these choice places simply as a matter of speculation; that he had no expectation of establishing an institution of learning hero, such as he had been describing, and that all of his talk in that direction was cheap bluff just for the purpose of keeping other people from claiming the land.

Add to this the fact that his friends were getting heartily sick and tired of being dragged into quarrels, in which they had no individual concern. Some of the more prominent of these became so thoroughly disgusted with the way things were being managed that they unceremoniously pulled up and left. Among this number were C. F. Hill and G. H. Bush, both of whom had ably and earnestly seconded Doctor Prescott's efforts to gain a foothold, but they could see nothing but contention ahead with no chance for advantage to themselves. Many others felt the same way. Prescott, seeing that he had lost the support, sympathy and confidence of a majority of the inhabitants, decided to abandon the whole project, so far as trying to found the institution was concerned, and sold off his Tusculum claims for what he could get, which was but a nominal sum and a mere fraction of what they cost him.

Looking at the project in the light of subsequent events, it is hardly possible that it could have succeeded even without those early troubles. The claims to the land were bought by Alfred Arthur and disposed of by him to parties who settled upon them at once. These parties were H. D. Arthur, John Francis, John P. Gilbert, Crosby Warner, Peter Ladu and Charles Carpenter, who came from Wisconsin, part of them in 1859 and the balance in 1860. Prescott still retained his claim to Okoboji Grove.

CHAPTER 17

Emigration in 1859

In the spring of 1859, a company, consisting of A. D. Arthur, John P. Gilbert and Spencer Humphrey, erected a shingle mill at Spirit Lake. It was kept there about a year and a half, when it was removed to some other locality.

The government surveys were completed in 1859, and the settlers were enabled to establish the boundaries to their claims, and take the necessary steps toward eventually securing the title. The first government survey was made in 1857 by a surveyor from Van Buren County by the name of Wilkins, but was rejected by the government inspector as defective, when a second survey was made by C. L. Estes, which was commenced in 1858 and finished in 1859. In the light of subsequent developments it is more than probable that the first survey was the more accurate of the two. It certainly was made with far more care than the second.

It will be remembered as a historical fact that Congress in the spring of 1860 passed the first bill granting homesteads to actual settlers, but that the bill was vetoed by President Buchanan. This created much disappointment, and not a little indignation, among the frontier settlers, as every one then imagined that the passage of the homestead law would give a new impetus to emigration and impart new life and energy to the frontier settlements. The bill was again introduced in the succeeding session of Congress and passed, and was approved by President Lincoln, and became the law of the land in 1862. Whatever stimulating effect this law might have had it passed at an earlier date, it was of but little advantage now.

At this time the Civil War had assumed such gigantic proportions that every man that could be spared was required by the army. The soldier and the pioneer are both made of the same material, and that element all through the country which usually strikes for the frontier for change, adventure or excitement, went into the army. These facts will be noticed more in detail in their proper place.

The first physician in this county was Dr. James Ball, from Newton, Jasper County, who settled here in 1858, and remained here until after the breaking out of the war, when he went into government employ as a surgeon, first at Sioux City, and from there he was transferred to some of the upriver posts.

The first marriage solemnized in Dickinson County was in the spring of 1859, the contracting parties being William E. Root and Addie Ring, both of Okoboji. Doctor Prescott performed the ceremony. The second was in the summer of 1860, at the residence of W. B. Brown, when Abel Keene of Mankato was married to Miss Carrie Doughty of Center Grove, R. Kingman, Esq., officiating.

The first regularly established religious services in northwestern Iowa were under the auspices of the Methodist Episcopal Church, which established a circuit here in 1859. This circuit was put in charge of Rev. Cornelius McLean with headquarters at Okoboji. While there had been no regular appointments up to that time, services had been held by Doctor Prescott and such other ministers as had happened to be travelling through the country. Among the first settlers of those who professed any particular religious belief, a decided majority were Congregationalists, but of those who came later more were Methodists.

It was through the efforts of Doctor Prescott that the Methodist Conference of 1859 decided to send a minister to the frontier. This circuit at that time comprised Emmet, Dickinson, Clay and O'Brien Counties. Services were held once in three weeks as follows : In Emmet County, at Estherville in the morning, and at Emmet in the afternoon; in Dickinson County the next Sunday, at Spirit Lake in the morning, and at Okoboji in the afternoon; and on the Sunday following that at Peterson in the morning, and at Waterman, in O'Brien County, in the afternoon. This round had to be made every three weeks,

Mr. McLean was among the best educated and most talented men sent into this county by the Methodist Church, and far superior to many who were afterwards sent in that early day. Up to 1876 the ministers who were sent to this circuit by the Methodist Episcopal Church since Mr. McLean's time, were as follows: J. A. Van Andor, J. W. Jones, W. Hyde, Seymour Snyder, W. A. Richards, W. W, Mallory, G.' Brown, William Preston and J. E. Cohenone, While preachers of other denominations occasionally held services in the county, there was no other society organised than the Methodists until 1870, when a society was organised by the Congregationalists which will be noticed in its proper place.

In February of 1859 the question of disposing of the swamp lands for public improvements was submitted to a vote of the electors and carried almost unanimously. It would have been far better for the county had the project been defeated. Those residing in the central and southern portions of the county were at first inclined to oppose the scheme, but after a little campaigning they ascertained that they would probably be in the minority any way and so concluded that they had had quarrelling and trouble enough where there was nothing to be gained by it, and stayed away from the polls altogether. Consequently the vote on the question was very light and all one way.

The parties to the contract as originally made were Hon. Leonidas Congleton, county judge, on the part of the county, and J. D. Howe, A. D. Arthur and B. F. Parmenter, as contractors. According to the terms of that agreement the contractors were to take the swamp lands of the county (which, by the way, were not then selected), be the same more or less, and pay all of the expenses for selecting them, and in consideration for them erect a courthouse upon a site, and according to plans and specifications furnished by the county; and three bridges, one across East Okoboji Lake east of the town of Spirit Lake, one across the straits between East and West Okoboji Lakes, and one across the Little Sioux. The original contractors disposed of their interest in the contract to J. S. Prescott and Henry Barkman, receiving as a consideration therefore several thousand acres of the swamp land.

At the present time, (as at time of first publication), this swamp land question is not understood by most people, and as it has occupied so prominent a place in our county history a short explanation and review of the question is in order here. It is a historical fact that the states along the Mississippi River had long been importuning Congress for the passage of a law making an appropriation for the purpose of reclaiming the swamp and overflowed lands along that river and its tributaries, and urging various reasons for the necessity of such action. This Congress persistently refused to do. Finally, however, a law was passed turning the whole matter over to the states in which these lands were located, and granting the swamp and overflowed lands to them, and making it incumbent on them to have the lands reclaimed as far as possible.

The state of Iowa, instead of doing anything towards reclaiming these lands, granted them in turn to the several counties in which they were situated upon the same terms she received them from the general government, at the same time authorising the county authorities to apply the proceeds arising from the sale of any such lands as could not be drained or otherwise reclaimed by ordinary methods, to be used for the purposes of education or applied to the building of county buildings and roads and bridges. There is no question that Congress in passing such an act never intended it to apply to the uplands, or the small sloughs and marshes which are common in this section of the country, and it is only by a forced construction of the law that any of these northwestern counties secured a title to any swamp land whatever.

Again, the laws of the state and the general government were somewhat conflicting as to the manner of making the selections and obtaining the title to the lands. All of the laws relating to the subject were carelessly drawn and were differently construed by the officers whose duty it was to execute them and carry their provisions into effect. The commissioners for selecting the swamp lands in this county were Andy Hood and B. F. Parmenter, and the amount selected and returned by them aggregated nearly sixty thousand acres. This amount was ridiculously large and was branded as fraudulent at once. Had a smaller amount been selected and returned, it is possible the title would have been confirmed without delay. Had matters remained as they were in the good old days of Buchanan's administration, doubtless the entire selection would have been approved and no questions asked, but a change of administration occurring about the time of the selection, the entire business of the Interior Department received an overhauling, the swamp land business among the rest, and the consequence was a halt was ordered and the burden of proof thrown upon the claimants of the lands to show that they were in truth swamp and overflowed lands as contemplated by the act granting them. With this explanation the reader will be better able to understand the swamp land question and the difficulties growing out of it.

The contractors, acting on the supposition that the title to the land would be perfected in the same manner that it had been done in the older counties, obtained quit-claim deeds from the county and then sold it for the purpose of raising means to go on with their improvements, giving warranty deeds for the same. It was not until about a year and a half that they began to have any fears that their title would not be good. As soon as it became evident that the title to the swamp land was likely to fail, Mr. Barkman set to work to compromise and settle with those to whom he had sold this land, and in many cases succeeded in doing so, but Prescott had carried it on on so large a scale that any attempt to compromise was hopeless. In most instances he had sold the land in large quantities to parties who understood the question of the title as well as he did himself, and at prices varying from twenty-five to fifty cents per acre, thus proving conclusively that they were perfectly aware of the defect in the title.

As before stated, the amount selected in this county and returned as swamp land aggregated nearly sixty thousand acres. These were quit-claimed by the county to the contractors and in turn sold by them for a mere nominal sum, they giving warranty deeds therefore. Many of these lands have changed hands repeatedly, and the matters growing out of these bogus titles and conflicting claims have been a source of great annoyance to the county authorities since that time. The amount of land that was finally certified to the county was something over three thousand acres. This had been quit-claimed with the rest to the original contractors, but afterwards it was understood that the manner in which the question was submitted to the vote of the electors and the transfer made was not strictly in accordance with the provisions of the statute. Suit was brought in equity on behalf of the county against the original contractors and their assignees for the abrogation of the contract.

Messrs. Wilson and Dye, a law firm in Sioux City, were retained by the county authorities to manage this suit on behalf of the county. The contractors made no defence. In fact, they had all left the county except Mr. Barkman, and he was interested in having the old transfers set aside, consequently the conveyances were declared void.

In the meantime another contract had been entered into by the county authorities with Mr. Barkman alone by which he was to receive the entire amount of the swamp land certified to the county; hence his interest in having the old deeds cancelled. It was the understanding when Wilson and Dye were employed to bring this suit, that it was to be without expense to the county, or rather, that as the lands were really bargained away at that time that those interested in getting the old transfers cancelled should stand the expense of the suit. Be this as it may, no sooner was the decree rendered abrogating the old contract than Wilson and Dye filed their claim against the county for attorney fees to the amount of four thousand dollars. They emphatically denied ever having agreed to accept anybody else as responsible for the pay for their services but the county, and there was no evidence to the contrary. The minutes showed that they had been regularly employed, and there was no way out of it, but to settle. The amount was finally compromised and they were allowed twenty-five hundred dollars.

Mr. Barkman had been a heavy loser in the original contract, and the county now entered into a new agreement with him whereby they transferred to him all of the land they had received or might receive in the future. Taking all things into consideration this whole swamp land question and the manner in which it was managed has been a most intolerable nuisance. In the first place, the expense to the county has been heavy. They made repeated endeavours to get the question settled, each of which was attended with great expense, but without success, the general government steadily refusing to take any action whatever upon the question, either to approve or reject the selection, and it was not until after a delay of nearly twenty years that the matter was closed up by the county getting the amount heretofore mentioned.

On the part of the contractors the matter was still worse. They had sold the lands in good faith and given warranty deeds for them. It is true they had sold them cheaply. The amount they realised from the proceeds was small and they could ill afford to subject themselves to the outlay necessary for the perfection of the title. They put forth every effort to have the matter disposed of, keeping agents in Washington at a heavy expense, but finally were obliged to give it up as a hopeless job.

Nor are these the only ones who have been injuriously affected by this vexed question. Many of these defective titles were finally purchased by parties who thought they an opportunity to secure homes for themselves upon uncommonly easy terms. These were mostly poor men and they expended what little property they had in trading for these bogus titles, and then removing from their eastern homes came here with the intention of settling, when they found the title to their land not worth the paper it was written upon.

These matters have also been a source of great vexation to our county officers. The difficulty of nudging abstracts and giving satisfactory information in regard to lands affected by these conflicting claims has been great indeed. Even at this time our county officers are repeatedly importuned by parties holding these defective titles, wanting

OKOBOJI BRIDGE IN 1874.
From an oil painting by Mrs. A. L. Buckland.

to know the reason why their titles are not good and will he satisfied with nothing less than full explanation of the whole matter.

In giving this review of the swamp land question, the details of the building of the courthouse and bridges have been overlooked. Of the work to be done by the contractors, the two bridges across the lake were finished in 1800. The one at Spirit Lake, east of town, was three hundred feet long, and the one at Okoboji was two hundred and ten feet long. They were built on bents, or trestles, set sixteen feet apart, with a main span over the principal channel thirty feet in the clear. This span was strongly trussed with heavy braces, king-posts and needle beams. The bridge at Spirit Lake was built by the contractors themselves, employing and paying their help by the day. Harvey Abbott, a brother-in-law of Howe and Wheelock, furnished the plan and acted as foreman. The bridge at Okoboji was built by John Loomis, he having a contracted for it from Howe and Arthur before the main contract was turned over to Barkman and Prescott.

Since they were first erected these bridges have been rebuilt four times. The first time was in 1874 or 1875. At this time the trestles were all taken out and at each side of the main channel were erected log cribs and these cribs filled with rock to hold them to their places. Grades were put in in lieu of the portions of the bridge taken out. These bridges were built by contract and were to be at least four feet above the water level. After being completed the distance was carefully measured and it was found to be Tour feet and two inches to the top of the planking, and yet, such was the rise of the lakes that spring that on the first of July the planking was under water. As the bridges rested on piers it was an easy matter to raise them and block them at any point desired. They were strongly built and would have answered all purposes for many years, but for the fact that the question of the navigation of the lakes began to be agitated about this time and the necessity for swing bridges discussed.

Mr. L. W. Waugh, then a member of the Board of Supervisors, claimed that a light, strong bridge could be so constructed that it could be raised by tackle and blocks to an upright position, so that boats might pass through. His scheme looked so plausible that the board adopted it and he went to work and built new bridges on the old piers, erected derricks and procured ropes and pulleys and rigged everything to his. satisfaction. But his plan was defective. It didn't work. He raised the bridges once or twice, but it took so much time and required so much power that the attempt to raise them was abandoned. The bridges were used in the shape they were until about 1883, when they were taken out and swing bridges erected instead. The first swing bridges were set on piles, but when they were rebuilt in the winter of 1897 and 1898, the piles were taken out and solid stone piers laid in cement were substituted in their place.

At the time the bridges were first built, the sand bars reaching to them from the further side were well out of water and from three to four rods wide. They were covered with vegetation, the one at the south end of the Okoboji bridge being covered with a growth of trees and bushes, some of which showed evidences of being forty or fifty years old. The idea that the approaches over those sand bars would eventually have to be graded up at a heavy expense to the county was not then thought of. But the heavy rains of the next two decades raised the water to such a height that it became necessary to build a grade four or five feet high over the sand bars at the end of each bridge. At the Okoboji bridge the sides of the embankment were ripraped with boulders floated in front along the lake shore on flat boats. This work was done piecemeal, but was finally finished in 1882.

The brick for the courthouse were burned on the isthmus in the fall of 1859 by William Barkman, a brother of Henry Barkman, the contractor. Mr. Barkman had formerly helped Peters on the old mill. While digging the race across the isthmus, the peculiar adhesive quality of the clay attracted his attention. He was a brickmaker by trade, and he soon became convinced that the material they were working in was the best brick clay he had ever seen.

After the contract for the courthouse was let he took the job of furnishing the brick. He burned two kilns. They were located on the ground afterward occupied by the Orleans Hotel. His experiment was a complete success. He succeeded in producing a brick that has never been equalled in quality by any other, either shipped in or produced here. They were hard as flint and absolutely fireproof.

Since that time other parties have tried their hand at making brick on the same ground but none succeeded in producing an article that at all compared with those made by Mr. Barkman for the old courthouse. What the reason is, or what the secret of Mr. Barkman's success was is not known. Whether or not the industry can be revived on the old ground and made remunerative remains to be demonstrated.

The lime was burned from limestone boulders bricked up on the bank of the lakes and boated to the kiln on flatboats.

Prescott being one of the contractors furnished the lumber from

Steamer passing the Okoboji Bridge.

his mill in Okoboji Grove. The lumber was principally oak. The building was also covered with oak shingles sawed in the Okoboji Grove. What little pine lumber was used had to be hauled across the country by teams from Mankato, having been previously brought up the Minnesota River from St. Paul on flatboats.

The foundation for the courthouse was laid in 1850, and the walls put up and the roof put on in 1860. Harvey Abbott furnished the plan and superintended the carpenter work, while William Lamont, one of the party who originally came up with Wheelock and Parmenter, did the mason work. The house was in this partly finished condition when it was taken possession of for military headquarters in August, 1862, and used as barracks and headquarters until 1865. The details connected with its occupancy as such will be given in another place. Of course, the building was subject to very hard usage during the time it was occupied as a military post, and it was impossible for the contractors to complete their contract while thus occupied.

During that time the fact became apparent that the title to the swamp land, which had been voted by the county as a consideration for public improvements, would prove worthless, thus entailing great loss to the contractors. In consideration of this state of affairs, the Board of Supervisors passed a vote releasing the contractors from any liability for the non-completion of the work and authorised the cancellation of the agreement under which the work had been carried forward thus far.

This action of the board was sharply criticised. It was considered on the one hand that the contractors understood upon the start what they were going into, that they had no reason to expect that all of the selections would be approved, and that had they been, the value of the land would have been very much in excess of a reasonable compensation for the amount of work contemplated in the contract, far more than the loss to the contractors would be if the work was completed and then the title to the land should fail. It was like a ticket in a lottery. If they succeeded in getting the title perfected, they had a "big thing," but on the contrary, if they failed, they would lose the amount expended in making the improvements. They, therefore, advocated the policy of holding the contractors to the strict letter of their agreement.

On the other hand, it was urged by the contractors that their losses had already been very heavy, the cost of doing that kind of work being many times as great as it would be now. They contended that they had spent more than the entire value of the land which would probably be certified to them in endeavouring to get the swampland question settled, and that it was as much to the interest of the county as themselves to have the matter closed up and that they had already lost more than the entire value of the work they had done. This was undoubtedly true, and the board took the responsibility of cancelling the contract and releasing the contractors and their sureties upon their turning over to them the bridges and courthouse in the condition they then were.

After it was vacated by the United States troops, and at the time it was turned over to the county in 1865, it was totally unfit for use as a public building, and inasmuch as the contractors had been released from any further work upon it, it became necessary for the county authorities to make some provisions for a county building. So it was finally decided to go on and complete the courthouse according to the original plan. This was accordingly done. County warrants were so depreciated at that time that they were worth but about twenty cents on the dollar, consequently this work proved expensive to the county. The work was done in detached portions, but was finally completed in 1868.

The offices in the lower storey were occupied by the county officers in their several capacities. An arrangement had been made with the officers of the school district whereby the district bought seats and seated the court room in consideration of having it to use for school purposes, and as there was but two terms of court a year, they did not conflict much. The old courthouse was used for almost every imaginable purpose. Revival meetings, dances, travelling shows, political gatherings, in short, anything that would bring a crowd met there on equal terms. These conditions continued to the time of the burning of the courthouse in February, 1872.

ALSO FROM LEONAUR
AVAILABLE IN SOFTCOVER OR HARDCOVER WITH DUST JACKET

LIFE IN THE ARMY OF NORTHERN VIRGINIA by *Carlton McCarthy*—The Observations of a Confederate Artilleryman of Cutshaw's Battalion During the American Civil War 1861-1865.

HISTORY OF THE CAVALRY OF THE ARMY OF THE POTOMAC by *Charles D. Rhodes*—Including Pope's Army of Virginia and the Cavalry Operations in West Virginia During the American Civil War.

CAMP-FIRE AND COTTON-FIELD by *Thomas W. Knox*—A New York Herald Correspondent's View of the American Civil War.

SERGEANT STILLWELL by *Leander Stillwell*—The Experiences of a Union Army Soldier of the 61st Illinois Infantry During the American Civil War.

STONEWALL'S CANNONEER by *Edward A. Moore*—Experiences with the Rockbridge Artillery, Confederate Army of Northern Virginia, During the American Civil War.

THE SIXTH CORPS by *George Stevens*—The Army of the Potomac, Union Army, During the American Civil War.

THE RAILROAD RAIDERS by *William Pittenger*—An Ohio Volunteers Recollections of the Andrews Raid to Disrupt the Confederate Railroad in Georgia During the American Civil War.

CITIZEN SOLDIER by *John Beatty*—An Account of the American Civil War by a Union Infantry Officer of Ohio Volunteers Who Became a Brigadier General.

COX: PERSONAL RECOLLECTIONS OF THE CIVIL WAR--VOLUME 1 by *Jacob Dolson Cox*—West Virginia, Kanawha Valley, Gauley Bridge, Cotton Mountain, South Mountain, Antietam, the Morgan Raid & the East Tennessee Campaign.

COX: PERSONAL RECOLLECTIONS OF THE CIVIL WAR--VOLUME 2 by *Jacob Dolson Cox*—Siege of Knoxville, East Tennessee, Atlanta Campaign, the Nashville Campaign & the North Carolina Campaign.

KERSHAW'S BRIGADE VOLUME 1 by *D. Augustus Dickert*—Manassas, Seven Pines, Sharpsburg (Antietam), Fredricksburg, Chancellorsville, Gettysburg, Chickamauga, Chattanooga, Fort Sanders & Bean Station.

KERSHAW'S BRIGADE VOLUME 2 by *D. Augustus Dickert*—At the wilderness, Cold Harbour, Petersburg, The Shenandoah Valley and Cedar Creek..

AVAILABLE ONLINE AT **www.leonaur.com**
AND FROM ALL GOOD BOOK STORES

ALSO FROM LEONAUR
AVAILABLE IN SOFTCOVER OR HARDCOVER WITH DUST JACKET

THE RELUCTANT REBEL by *William G. Stevenson*—A young Kentuckian's experiences in the Confederate Infantry & Cavalry during the American Civil War..

BOOTS AND SADDLES by *Elizabeth B. Custer*—The experiences of General Custer's Wife on the Western Plains.

FANNIE BEERS' CIVIL WAR by *Fannie A. Beers*—A Confederate Lady's Experiences of Nursing During the Campaigns & Battles of the American Civil War.

LADY SALE'S AFGHANISTAN by *Florentia Sale*—An Indomitable Victorian Lady's Account of the Retreat from Kabul During the First Afghan War.

THE TWO WARS OF MRS DUBERLY by *Frances Isabella Duberly*—An Intrepid Victorian Lady's Experience of the Crimea and Indian Mutiny.

THE REBELLIOUS DUCHESS by *Paul F. S. Dermoncourt*—The Adventures of the Duchess of Berri and Her Attempt to Overthrow French Monarchy.

LADIES OF WATERLOO by *Charlotte A. Eaton, Magdalene de Lancey & Juana Smith*—The Experiences of Three Women During the Campaign of 1815: Waterloo Days by Charlotte A. Eaton, A Week at Waterloo by Magdalene de Lancey & Juana's Story by Juana Smith.

TWO YEARS BEFORE THE MAST by *Richard Henry Dana. Jr.*—The account of one young man's experiences serving on board a sailing brig—the Penelope—bound for California, between the years 1834-36.

A SAILOR OF KING GEORGE by *Frederick Hoffman*—From Midshipman to Captain—Recollections of War at Sea in the Napoleonic Age 1793-1815.

LORDS OF THE SEA by *A. T. Mahan*—Great Captains of the Royal Navy During the Age of Sail.

COGGESHALL'S VOYAGES: VOLUME 1 by *George Coggeshall*—The Recollections of an American Schooner Captain.

COGGESHALL'S VOYAGES: VOLUME 2 by *George Coggeshall*—The Recollections of an American Schooner Captain.

TWILIGHT OF EMPIRE by *Sir Thomas Ussher & Sir George Cockburn*—Two accounts of Napoleon's Journeys in Exile to Elba and St. Helena: Narrative of Events by Sir Thomas Ussher & Napoleon's Last Voyage: Extract of a diary by Sir George Cockburn.

AVAILABLE ONLINE AT **www.leonaur.com**
AND FROM ALL GOOD BOOK STORES

www.ingramcontent.com/pod-product-compliance
Lightning Source LLC
Chambersburg PA
CBHW021958160426
43197CB00007B/168